Praise for *Balancing Act*

"This book has certainly stood the test of time. Its teachings can help any woman who applies them to achieve her financial dreams. Outstanding!"
—David Chilton, author of *The Wealthy Barber*

"Joanne has a wonderful way of telling a story. Her sense of humour flows through every page, which makes *Balancing Act* a fast-moving, informative, and fun read. She doesn't spend a lot of time looking through the rear-view mirror—she's a lady that focuses forward. Listen to the advice she gives her readers: her message is critical in helping leaders understand this emerging and dynamic market. This is the tenth anniversary edition of *Balancing Act,* and it keeps getting better. Wow, that's performance."
—Annette Verschuren, president, The Home Depot Canada

"Reading her book is like chatting with a good friend over your kitchen table—a practical, realistic, no-baloney kind of friend."
—Margaret Wente, *Globe and Mail* columnist

"Information equals independence, and *Balancing Act* travels the full distance in helping Canadian women to that end. Joanne has the superb knack of making you belly laugh while shocking, cajoling, and guiding you to making smart choices about your financial future."
—Pamela Wallin, Canadian Consul General to New York
and author of *Speaking of Success*

"WOW! I defy any woman not to identify with this book. I loved it … I can say without reservation that this is the most entertaining personal finance book I've ever read."
—Sherry Cooper, global economic strategist and executive
vice-president of Bank of Montreal (Toronto) and
Harris Bank (Chicago), and author of *Ride the Wave*

"Joanne Thomas Yaccato has done it again! *Balancing Act* is as relevant today as it was 10 years ago. As more and more boomer women enter mid-life, issues of retirement, being on one's own financially, and staving off 'old-age bag-lady' fears loom large. This is a hopeful, reassuring, and reader-friendly resource."

—Judy Turner, Ph.D., co-author of *The Healthy Boomer Guide for Women and Men* and *The Juggling Act: The Healthy Boomer's Guide to Achieving Balance in Midlife*

"I wish *Balancing Act* was around when I signed my first credit card agreement and took out my first RRSP (with its next-to-nothing interest). My financial profile would have been far brighter. This is a must-read book for women who understand the connection between financial security and independence."

—Laura Robinson, sports journalist, former national team athlete, and author of *Black Tights: Women, Sport and Sexuality* and *Great Girls: Seventeen Profiles of Extraordinary Canadian Athletes*

"Joanne Thomas Yaccato shines a light on what really matters to working women: managing our money so one day we can retire in style!"

—Pamela P. Jeffery, president and founder, The Jeffery Group Ltd. and WXN

"Joanne *gets* it! In this book she combines a pool of superb research from financial experts with her own in-depth knowledge of women consumers and the women's market, and adds a liberal sprinkling of her zesty storytelling ability."

—Mirabel Palmer-Elliott, general manager, Todaysparent.com, Rogers Publishing

"I've watched her go from footloose to financially secure, and I know you'll enjoy taking the journey with her."

—Ellen Roseman, *Toronto Star* columnist

PENGUIN CANADA

BALANCING ACT

Joanne Thomas Yaccato is the president and founder of the Toronto-based consulting firm The Thomas Yaccato Group, known as *Corporate Canada's Gender Lens*™.

One of Canada's most popular business writers, Joanne uses her personal experience and hilarious misadventures as the backdrop to all her books. Her bestselling books *Balancing Act: A Canadian Woman's Financial Success Guide* and *Raising Your Business: A Canadian Woman's Guide to Entrepreneurship* continue to sell to new generations of women.

Joanne is a regular contributor to Canada's media, including CBC, CTV, and the country's top financial presses and national newspapers. She has been nominated for the Governor General's Award and has received two nominations each for Ernst & Young's Entrepreneur of the Year Award and the YWCA's National Women of Distinction Award.

She is married to aerospace engineer Michael McNeill and is mother to an eight-year-old dynamo named Kate.

Also by Joanne Thomas Yaccato

The 80% Minority:
Reaching the Real World of Women Consumers

Raising Your Business:
A Canadian Woman's Guide to Entrepreneurship

10TH ANNIVERSARY EDITION

balancing act

A CANADIAN WOMAN'S

FINANCIAL SUCCESS GUIDE

JOANNE THOMAS YACCATO

PENGUIN
CANADA

PENGUIN CANADA

Published by the Penguin Group

Penguin Group (Canada), 10 Alcorn Avenue, Toronto, Ontario, Canada M4V 3B2
    (a division of Pearson Penguin Canada Inc.)

Penguin Group (USA) Inc., 375 Hudson Street, New York, New York 10014, U.S.A.
Penguin Books Ltd, 80 Strand, London WC2R 0RL, England
Penguin Ireland, 25 St Stephen's Green, Dublin 2, Ireland (a division of Penguin Books Ltd)
Penguin Group (Australia), 250 Camberwell Road, Camberwell, Victoria 3124, Australia
    (a division of Pearson Australia Group Pty Ltd)
Penguin Books India Pvt Ltd, 11 Community Centre, Panchsheel Park, New Delhi – 110 017, India
Penguin Group (NZ), Cnr Airborne and Rosedale Roads, Albany, Auckland, New Zealand
    (a division of Pearson New Zealand Ltd)
Penguin Books (South Africa) (Pty) Ltd, 24 Sturdee Avenue, Rosebank, Johannesburg 2196, South Africa

Penguin Books Ltd, Registered Offices: 80 Strand, London WC2R 0RL, England

First published 2004

(WEB) 10 9 8 7 6 5 4 3 2 1

This publication contains the opinions and ideas of its author and is designed to provide useful
advice in regard to the subject matter covered. The author and publisher are not engaged in render-
ing legal, accounting, or other professional services in this publication. This publication is not
intended to provide a basis for action in particular circumstances without consideration by a
competent professional. The author, publisher, and source providers expressly disclaim any responsibility for any liability, loss, or risk, personal or otherwise, which is incurred as a consequence,
directly or indirectly, of the use and application of any of the contents of this book.

Manufactured in Canada.

LIBRARY AND ARCHIVES CANADA CATALOGUING IN PUBLICATION

Thomas Yaccato, Joanne, 1957–
    Balancing act : a Canadian woman's financial success
guide / Joanne Thomas Yaccato. — 10th anniversary ed.

First ed. published 1994 under title: Balancing act : a Canadian woman's financial survival guide.
Includes bibliographical references and index.
ISBN 0-14-301748-9

1. Women—Canada—Finance, Personal. I. Title.

HG179.T56   2004   332.024'0082'0973   C2004-903538-X

Visit the Penguin Group (Canada) website at **www.penguin.ca**

To David Chilton …

Eleven years ago you said I could.

I didn't really believe you.

Who'd have thought it?

Contents

three

Building your financial base: tackling some fundamentals 67

four

Admitting mortality 94

five

The golden years 150

six

seven

eight

nine

Acknowledgments

The fact that *Balancing Act* has not only survived, but thrived through three editions is a testament to the good sense and intuitive wisdom of Canadian women who know they need to take on financial responsibility in their own lives. This book exists only because of David Chilton's unfailing instincts, a knowledge-starved audience, and a courageous publisher who was willing to take chances on an unknown entity—in both subject matter and author.

I am also blessed with a tight circle of support. Thank you, Michael and Kate. You are my muses and inspiration for every book I write. Mom, your spirit infuses every page. Rosa, I do what I do only because you stand beside me every step of the way. Peter Volpe, you've never failed me on anything I've ever asked of you in these book projects. You, sir, are a saint.

A group of technical advisors gave up non-existent spare time to help with this project. Two people in particular went beyond the call of duty with time and brainpower: Joe Chisholm and Bev Evans. Alberta Cefis, Leslie Slater, Laurie Campbell, Janet Freedman, Sharon Cohen, Al Hansen, Dianna Flannery, Michelle Lennox, Jeff Greenberg, James Craig, Kit Bennett, Uncle Al Hardy and his offspring, Alex, and the folks at CMHC also contributed significant insight and expertise.

To all my readers over the years, I can only say that I keep on keeping on because of you. Your support of my work grounds me and makes me grateful every single day that I draw breath.

It's true. Canadian women rock ...

Introduction

I can hardly believe that this is the 10th anniversary of the first edition of *Balancing Act*. Eleven years ago, I had effectively completed a stunning metamorphosis from a single, fast-living financial reprobate making every conceivable financial mistake known to womankind to a single 30-something enjoying a thriving career as a financial advisor with a corner office in Toronto's financial district. Then, with the enthusiastic urging of many friends (most notably Dave Chilton, author of the bestseller *The Wealthy Barber*—his foot was on my backside as I sailed off the cliff of this particular adventure) and a publishing contract, I dumped everything in storage—my furniture and my life—and went to live on a friend's farm for a year to write *Balancing Act*. Today, a husband, a daughter, my own company, an almost paid-off mortgage, a pretty decent investment portfolio, and three books later …

I must admit, though, it's been a bit unusual to have grown up and "matured" so publicly over the years. Recently, I cracked up when I read in a book review that *Balancing Act* is "the grandmother of its genre." I can't believe I'm saying this, but it felt quite right.

I have the four *Balancing Act* book covers in their various incarnations, spanning the last ten years, hanging on my home office wall. Oh lordy, would you look at that first one? Just who is that fresh-faced idealist with the world by the tail? Then there's my personal favourite, the cover that came five years later proudly boasting a mother-to-be, fully seven months pregnant, in awe of what life was about to bring. The third edition reveals a no-nonsense, competent 40-something who, in reality, was frantically trying to figure out how the hell to balance family and career demands. Then, finally, the cover for this edition, which I think reveals a more serene and complete person (albeit always the rabble-rouser). With 50 peeking over the horizon, I can honestly say I've finally connected all of the dots—financial, physical, emotional, and spiritual. There exists now the beginnings of an inner peace and sage wisdom that comes from having lived all of the experiences I'm about to share with you.

It's a profound experience to know that thousands of Canadian women can lay claim to having lived a variation of a personal metamorphosis in their own lives and that this book has in some small way played a part. This is a personal finance book to be sure, but at its heart it is one woman's journey, a woman who both won and lost some pretty big battles. When you read this, all I ask is that you to use your head to learn the facts, but, as I did, use your heart to choose your path.

The road may be a little longer … but the scenery is infinitely more interesting.

one

My story

Money will buy a bed but not sleep; books but not brains; food but not appetite; finery but not beauty; a house but not a home; medicine but not health; luxuries but not culture; amusements but not happiness; religion but not salvation.

SOURCE UNKNOWN (BUT I'D GUESS IT WAS A WOMAN)

The image is still vivid, even though this happened over 40 years ago. I can close my eyes and see myself, a five-year-old red-headed moppet, sitting on the corner of my bed. I'm anxiously picking away at the frayed edge of my much-loved yellow teddy bear bedspread. It's the earliest memory I have of my mother talking to me like a grownup. Now, I was one of the first of 29 grandchildren in a large Irish Italian family. For four years my status remained unchallenged and I gloried in the enviable spot of being an "only." Queen of the castle, as it were. But then something happened that knocked me out of top spot.

It was the arrival of a soggy, remarkably loud lump named "Your New Brother Jeff." It was also the impetus behind my mother's motivation in introducing me to my first adult concept: allowance. It was Saturday morning. Mom had just finished helping me bathe and change Your New Brother Jeff, and had invited me to sit with her on my bed for a talk. I remember that as I followed her into my room a stab of fear went through me. (I had a finely tuned sense of guilt even at four.) "Joanne," she began, "you've been such a big help to Mommy with Your New Brother Jeff, I think it's time to start giving you an allowance."

Looking at my blank face, she continued, "Honey, do you understand what I'm saying?" This was a poignant moment between mother and daughter. I sensed that she was talking about something very important. I nodded my head gravely in spite of the fact I had no idea what an allowance was.

"Daddy and I think you're big enough to have your own money. You can do whatever you want with it."

The implication of what she was saying began to resonate in my tiny brain. My eyes widened with visions of licorice, ice cream, and sour balls.

My mother went on. "An allowance is money you earn by doing extra things around the house. We're going to give you 10 cents a week." With that she pressed a shiny, thin dime into my palm and gently closed my fingers around it. Her tone grew serious. "We trust you with this responsibility, sweetheart. If you spend it all at once, you'll have to wait until next Saturday before you get any more money. Try to budget and spend one or two cents each day for your special treats."

I looked up at my mother's face and saw it glowing with a special pride. Her little girl was growing up. I smiled. Then I did what any self-respecting, budding contrarian would do.

I promptly went out and blew the whole bundle.

That behaviour pattern repeated itself in varying degrees for the better part of 25 years. There isn't a financial mistake that I, or a member of my family, hasn't made. I used to describe myself as being one of the "financially challenged." When they pick up this book and see my name on the cover, people who knew me years ago will react in one of two ways: they'll either gasp in total disbelief or laugh uproariously.

Laugh on, McDuff! I'm what you call a born-again, a recovering spender. I've put away childish notions that money woes eventually take care of themselves, or that "he" will come and relieve me of this tiresome burden of money. I discovered that when it came to money, I needed to become the man I wanted to marry. I've buried the knight in shining armour. I went from being diagnosed as hopeless and thrown out of grade 11 algebra to doing tax and estate planning for a living for several years. Before I "crossed over from the dark side" my eyes would glaze over at any talk of money or investing; now I endeavour to keep thousands of people awake each year while giving speeches on this very same topic. In my early 20s I'd managed to get in trouble with credit cards, so much so that I needed the services of the Credit Counselling Service of Toronto. Today I sit on their Board of Governors. How did this amazing transformation take place? What deep, profound experience provoked such a change?

I turned 30.

Alas, my misspent youth

There's nothing like changing a decade in age to get your attention. On the morning of my 30th birthday I woke up and mentally looked about. The scenery wasn't anything like what I'd envisioned for myself growing up. I had a rented apartment with a leased car in the driveway. My closet boasted the finest quality clothing money could buy, but a family of moths had taken up permanent residence in my bank account. If an emergency happened that cost more than $24, I was in deep trouble. I used to joke that I had all the money I needed—if I died by four o'clock. It was a "live for the moment" type of existence.

It was the booming '80s and the computer industry was exploding. I had a very successful career as a senior account executive for a major computer company selling technology to the Canadian Business Top 100. There was a certain irony in the fact that I was responsible for selling to banks, brokerage firms, and insurance companies. There was a group of us in our late 20s earning absurd amounts of money in the six-digit range. Like that five-year-old with her allowance, I was spending it as fast as I made it. Bills eventually got paid, but way too many didn't until the hammer came down, usually in the form of a collection agency. Credit card bills often waited months before I'd take care of them. Rent and car payments were always on time, but only because of post-dated cheques. Savings consisted of the odd Canada Savings Bond deducted at source from work, but invariably it would be cashed before the year was out, usually to pay a bill. If the bond made it to maturity, I'd use it to buy my family or that special someone a ridiculously expensive Christmas gift. My money disappeared like a snowflake on a hot stove.

I assumed that one day I might own my own home. But the reality was that, unless I could find one in the $40 price range, it wasn't going to happen. Subconsciously I believed it to be completely out of my financial reach. (Remember, dear readers: I was earning a six-digit income.) The truth was that I had no desire to alter my high-spending, single (read: partying) lifestyle to try to save for curtains, let alone a down payment. Underneath this carefree lifestyle, however, cracks were beginning to appear. I was living with that low-level anxiety that creeps into the base of your neck and shoulders and takes up permanent residence there. I went to bed with it and I woke up with it. It was taking tremendous energy to ignore it. I'd think about money only when absolutely necessary, like when the phone company called and threatened disconnection. I lurched from one financial crisis to another.

As I write this, I'm struck by the absurdity of it all. I was privileged and gifted enough to have a good income-earning ability. Yet I abused it terribly, treating it with extraordinary disregard. The '80s were a tumultuous time for me. I became part of a fast-living culture that put more emphasis on drinks after work and expensive cars than Registered Retirement Savings Plans (RRSPs) and responsibly paying credit card bills. Although many of my saner peers got married, bought homes, and began families, I continued on like a teenager, partying and spending into oblivion. The sad thing was that I wanted that settled life more than anything. I'd wanted a family since I was that impetuous five-year-old, but for reasons so complex that I can barely understand them, I continued to live this unfulfilling existence.

Ironically, a huge part of the problem *was* my sales skills, which became a double-edged sword. Income did not determine my lifestyle—on the contrary, lifestyle determined my income. Because I was a very good salesperson and was paid commission, I could essentially write my own paycheque. If I needed more money, I reasoned, I could simply go out and earn more. I thought I was impervious to economic climate, quota increases, bad products, changes in customer demands, and the eroding effect of too many late nights. I believed the gravy train would last forever. And although I made a lot of money, my attitude toward it was the same as when I was an impoverished university student. The concepts of budgeting, saving, and self-restraint were as foreign to me as cuneiform. I came to depend on my earning power for financial stability. In short, it was a harrowing way to live.

Well, the gravy train did indeed derail. I should have been aware of a burgeoning budgeting problem when I found myself giving the woman in charge of our payroll an expensive bottle of wine and a thank you card for Christmas. She and I had gotten to know each other as a result of my frequent visits requesting advances until payday. Sales has a way of being cyclical, even at the best of times. At the worst of times, there were months when the money simply wasn't there.

What began to push the train off the tracks was the seductive power of credit cards. I was in my 20s when I passed through the portals of adulthood and became the proud owner of my first Visa card. I wasn't educated to the dark side of credit, which quickly reared its head. It began when I broke my ankle in three places and subsequently lost my job. I was a commissioned salesperson. If you can't walk, you can't sell. If you can't sell, you can't work. If you can't work, you can't keep your job. No job, no income. Enter Vera Visa and her trusty sidekick, Mary Mastercard. These proved to be a very expensive source of emergency funds. They were also the beginning of an insidious downward spiral into debt. For me, using credit cards wasn't like spending real money. They were natural extensions of my paycheque, pieces of plastic that allowed my indulgent personality to flourish. I was able to continue my lifestyle uninterrupted, especially during those lean periods commonplace in sales. At the time I believed credit cards saved my life.

I only ever paid the minimum balance each month. There would be months when I paid nothing at all, not at all aware of what was happening to my long-suffering credit rating. And there were other minor annoyances, such as rent, car payments, student loan, and so on.

Another irony was that I hated debt. As a teenager I'd witnessed first-hand the destructive power of unmanaged debt. The recession of the '70s saw my father get caught in the dying economy. That, with his own penchant for spending money, forced him to file for personal bankruptcy. I was 18 when we lost everything. The memory of this experience did much to intensify the fear I had deep inside that I'd end up a bag lady—old, alone, and broke. It was a terrifying image to break from.

I lived in the dark shadow of that oppressive credit card debt for five years before I finally cried uncle. I decided that, if nothing else, I had to get out of debt. I was beginning to see how easily one could lose control. So by the age of 28, with the help of the credit counselling agency, I'd managed to wrestle the debt monster to the ground. But even though I actually became debt free, I had unknowingly destroyed my credit rating. I couldn't even get a Zellers credit card.

RRSPs? Mutual funds? Emergency fund? Insurance? Not entirely too likely. Money was something you spent. Invest? The thought never occurred to me. On the odd occasion when one of my more responsible colleagues suggested that a portion of my commission cheque would do well in some kind of savings mechanism, I always responded with a light-hearted "Thanks anyway. There's a stereo out there with my name on it."

Taking stock

So, on that wintry, grey March morning that I turned 30, I had an epiphany. Well, more like a bash on the head with a large, blunt object. I did the prover-bial mental "life checklist" and became concerned not so much by what was there, but by what wasn't. Where was that house with the white picket fence? The 2.5 children? The golden Lab? What about Mr. Right? To date, they had all turned into Mr. Left. (Be it far from me, though, to create the impression that the "all" part of this equation was any great number. There were only two.) My previously mute biological clock began to tick. It came down to this: all there was, quite simply, was me—and that was a very sobering thought indeed. The seed of my epiphany began to germinate. I needed to start living my life as a grownup, not some arrested adolescent with a magic bank account that never went dry. I had to start creating the life I wanted and always thought I'd have, since it wasn't even on the radar screen. I needed to feel secure about my present life and my future one.

"At least," I thought, "I'm still on the youthful side of adult. There's some-thing to be said about having only myself to worry about." I looked at myself in the mirror with a very critical eye, squirming with discomfort as I tried to examine my inside. But my outside kept getting in the way.

My outside. That was something else again.

I'd quit smoking five years earlier. I turned around slowly, looking in the mirror and gasping in amazement. The 115-pound body I'd always taken for granted had gone into hiding. Deep hiding. For some bizarre reason, the blinders from my eyes fell away and I *really* saw myself for the first time in years. I could no longer ignore the fact that 30 pounds had, under the clandestine cover of night, found its way to my hips. "Fat and broke," I thought miserably. The urge to go back to bed with a lifetime supply of M&Ms was overwhelming. I had hit rock bottom. I was frankly quite confused. Why, since I had discipline in other areas of my life, wasn't I able to tackle these two thorns in my side? "That's it," I announced to that stranger in the mirror. "I need to connect the dots here. I need to integrate all the pieces of my life—physical, emotional, financial, and spiritual. I need to introduce my head to my heart and my soul to my body. It's time to get serious. It's time to take emotional and financial control." A swell of elation swept through me. And then, quick on its heels, came pure, unadulterated fear.

The task seemed huge. Even though I'd managed to pay off the equivalent of the national debt, credit was an integral part of life and I was unable to get it. There was advanced mathematics to learn, the Income Tax Act to master, banks to rob to acquire enough money to invest, and the care and feeding of the stock market. Not surprisingly, by my second cup of coffee I'd convinced myself that I was still much too young to be concerned about financial security. My life's mantra—"Live for today! Tomorrow will take care of itself!"—reverberated again through my ever-so-thick head.

I stood up fast enough to knock my chair over, shaking my head to clear it of these demoralizing messages. Pacing back and forth across my kitchen, feeling exasperated, I began to wonder how I'd gotten to this place. What do I do now? How does one get good with money? Is it something you're born with? The conventional wisdom I grew up with suggested that men came out of the womb with inherent knowledge about finances and how to fix cars. Women, on the other hand, knew all about babies and how to cook. "Good news!" I thought dismally. "I'm 0 for 2." But it was like coming out of a long coma—as much as I might have wanted to, I couldn't go back to blissful oblivion. Through the simple act of waking up, I'd put an end to my old financial habits. There was no turning back.

I realized that it would be virtually impossible to change my behaviour around money until I knew why I behaved the way I did. Believe me, I'd tried many times before to get my money life on track, only to have it derailed after a credit-card-paid-for impulse purchase. I'd spent years trying to will myself to change and develop this elusive discipline. All it did was reinforce my belief that I wasn't any good in this area. I slowly began to see that beliefs about money can be based on emotional responses to certain life experiences. Part of my cavalier approach to money stemmed from the devastating experience of losing everything near and dear to me at the tender age of 18—house, furniture, bike, record collection—in my father's bankruptcy. I also needed to acknowledge that even *I* had beliefs about money, and to stop caring whether they made sense or were true. They were there and had to be recognized. I was getting pretty tired of the huge gap between what was supposed to happen in my money life and what really went on.

I also needed to stop the perpetual questioning: "Why can't I control my spending? Why can't I be more disciplined? Why can't I get rid of this stupid fear around money? Why can't I get this math thing? Why can't I ... Why can't I ..." I had to change my language. Instead of "why can't I?" the drill needed to be "why not?" I decided to delete the phrases "I shouldn't have to," "I don't want to," and "I can't" from my vocabulary. I found myself beginning to question all the conventions I had accepted at face value. I was struck by how little I was taught and how little I was expected to know about looking after myself financially. And I don't mean just my parents. Everyone had a hand in it: school, religion, media, government. But criticizing myself and the world around me was a waste of valuable energy. There was absolutely no risk here for me. It's hard to fall off the bottom.

And so that morning was my first baby step in a long, often arduous journey to physical and financial fitness. I had to find a way to ease my fears around money. Admitting that I needed to do something was a good first step. I found myself talking with others who had surprisingly similar experiences, which helped to rid me of the shame of my youthful indulgences. There were few resources readily available. In those days personal finance sections in bookstores didn't exist. Bankers, investment advisors, and insurance agents didn't fall over themselves to knock on your door if you were a woman. Their advice wouldn't have meant much to me anyway until I understood what the crux of my financial problem was. I demonstrated discipline and skill in many areas of my life, so I couldn't understand why I had none (or so I thought) with money. Well, I finally figured it out.

I had no training about money, didn't know the language of money, and had no personal expectations except, certainly subconsciously, those of the man I was going to marry. My mother married her financial plan, and although she was an astute money manager, in this area she deferred as women often did in her time to the man of the house, much to our family's peril. With so little understanding of the symptoms around my behaviour with money, it was no small wonder that my attempts at budgeting and planning had failed so miserably in the past. It was a huge relief to realize there was really nothing wrong with me. Nothing that a little *unlearning* wouldn't fix. I just had to concern myself with the minor business of completely unlearning what I had been taught or subconsciously believed to be true and of learning what I hadn't been taught, which was workable money behaviour. A crucial element in the success of my financial recovery was recognizing that the solution to becoming financially secure was not to be found outside of myself. I had to unlearn that I didn't need to worry about paying my bills or that being late a month or 10 wasn't a big deal. I had to unlearn that I didn't need to know the rules of the credit game. I had to unlearn that someone else was going to come along with a house or at least the money to buy one. Unlearning that putting off paying taxes for three or four years isn't really prudent and unlearning that someone else will be there to look after me in old age was a particularly wise move. The most important unlearning meant dismissing the messages everywhere that I didn't need to worry about being successful, financially or otherwise, as long as the man I married was.

I still feared that learning new behaviour around money was going to be unbelievably hard, until I realized it was going to be a cakewalk compared to the way I was living. So it was first things first. I grappled with my weight by eliminating red meat, sugar, and alcohol. I began to exercise in earnest. One year later, I was 30 pounds and almost three sizes smaller. As easy as it was to get caught in the downward spiral, I discovered the reverse was also true. I joyfully embarked on a positive spiral. Bolstered by my recent successes, I was committed to getting on my way to financial health.

Although my debt was under control, I still had no savings or investments of any sort. I didn't understand what an RRSP was. I was still caught in the old paycheque-to-paycheque regime. In short, I had no long-term financial goals. Long term to me meant figuring out what I was doing on the weekend. As fate would have it, the solution fell right into my lap.

A year after my financial epiphany I closed a deal to provide laptop computers to a major insurance company for their agents in the field. This same company had developed a marketing concept of selling financial services to women. When I heard about this centre I became intrigued. One of my biggest goals was to find a place that could give me what I needed: education. I wanted a place that would treat me seriously and take the time to teach me the most basic elements of financial planning. I wanted to talk with someone to whom I wouldn't be embarrassed to admit that the only thing I knew about an RRSP was how to spell it.

I understood instinctively that if women were to achieve real freedom, it had to start with financial independence. So I gritted my teeth and plunged headlong into the world of financial planning. Talking to an advisor was the beginning of a journey that would become one of financial and personal self-discovery. And it was an evolving process, with stumbles along the way. The hardest part of getting my financial house in order was developing realistic expectations. I was 20 miles into the woods, and I wasn't going to get out in 2.

Me? A financial advisor?

As I was slowly getting my financial act together, there were several attempts to recruit me at this centre. My reaction was always a light-hearted and jokingly pompous "You couldn't afford me." But this jocularity hid the real issue. I would have felt like an impostor. I knew how to make money. But although I was slowly learning, I still didn't know what to do with it or how to keep it. I became friends with Elaine, the manager of the centre and my financial advisor. One day over lunch she pinned me down with a formal job offer. She started by saying that she thought I'd be a tremendous asset in helping educate women to become financially knowledgeable. I was a successful business person, so I'd be a terrific role model. Since I was committed to helping women achieve gender equality, why not give them the greatest gift they could have—financial literacy? The idea of being of service by helping women learn and make money was almost too good to be true. Elaine had struck a chord.

Sure, I'd have to go back to school to learn everything I needed. Elaine threw around terms like mutual funds licence, life and disability insurance licence, chartered financial consultant, certified financial planner, registered financial planner, and chartered life underwriter. I felt considerable skepticism. One thing in particular kept echoing in my mind: "This is absurd, you can't do this! You're lousy in math." There'd been little encouragement for young women to go into math or science in my day (am I actually old enough to say that?), and there were significantly fewer females than males in these areas of study. The girls who did go into them were in the "brainer" league and proclaimed by some as decidedly uncool. Most of us followed the more traditional female route of social sciences, languages, or the humanities. In grade 11 I'd found myself face to face with a formidable challenge—algebra. To say I hated it would be a grave understatement. I stood firm in my refusal to remain conscious during class. I was convinced that in real life there was no such thing as algebra. I remember my algebra teacher calling my mother to the school for a meeting to discuss my difficulties. He informed us that since it wasn't unusual for girls to struggle with math, it would likely be in my best interest to concentrate on what I'd shown an aptitude for—English. We all agreed, I most enthusiastically. This incident changed the course of my life. Instead of being encouraged in an area where I experienced a certain conceptual difficulty, I was pulled out of it completely. At that moment, I came to believe what so many young girls are often socialized to believe—that I wasn't any good with numbers.

I went on to get my Arts degree in psychology, which I chose specifically for its alleged lack of math. But as it's known to do, life threw me another curveball. I discovered too late that quantitative statistics was a compulsory course. One of my professors told me this in passing and nothing could have prepared him for my reaction. We were sitting in the cafeteria at lunch time. The silence hung heavily between us for about 10 seconds as I processed this news. I was now in the unenviable position of having to draw on grade 11 math to help me master the elements of university-level statistics. I blinked once and began to laugh. Not a casual titter or giggle, but an actual howl, with a notable edge of hysteria.

Interestingly enough, as a result of countless sleepless nights and fierce, stubborn determination, I passed (barely) that demonic statistics course. I often wonder if my high school disdain for anything mathematical might not have been so pronounced with a little encouragement and a lot of tutoring. At the very least, I would have had far fewer "Algebra Teacher Dies Under Mysterious Circumstances" fantasies throughout that statistics course.

As Elaine continued to talk about the rewards of this new career she was offering me, my thoughts wandered to the strangeness of it all. It was evident that my image was pretty convincing. The outside package reflected a highly competent woman. I was, in fact, very competent. I made my living at managing national accounts and conducted and negotiated financial transactions in the hundreds of thousands of dollars as a matter of course. Yet my own finances had been a shambles. So, if I were to seriously consider this career change, I'd have to deal with the impostor syndrome. Money was about power and I certainly didn't feel powerful in that area. And what about the math? If the word "financial" is in a job description, then, I reasoned, you'd damned well better know math. All those designations required courses in accounting. Hadn't I already been told I couldn't do this? And hadn't I wanted to believe it because it was the softer, easier way?

And there was another matter: surely someone with my financial past couldn't possibly begin to advise others on financial matters. Or could they? It's always been my experience that the best teachers are the ones who "walk the walk." Anyone could "talk the talk." Maybe I was as good a candidate as anyone. Maybe better. I began to wonder why I was being asked to consider doing something for a living that involved the number one nemesis in my life.

The possibility of helping women become financially literate would force me to turn and look full in the face my fear about money and everything it stood for. I decided to come clean and tell Elaine my story. All of it.

After listening to me for over an hour, this wonderful woman looked at me evenly and said, "You're hired." At that moment, I ended a lucrative career in the computer industry, took the next six months off, and studied to become a licensed financial advisor. It was over the course of my time with Elaine that I became financially literate. Each session offered new insights and information that proved invaluable. I was astounded to learn that fear disappears proportionally with education—the more you know, the less you fear. I ended up demystifying the process by becoming part of it.

Financial planning is a gender issue

Over the next five years I counselled thousands of women and men on the importance of financial planning. I often shared my own experiences, which broke the ice and eased people's angst around this topic. I became fascinated by women's wide-ranging attitudes toward money and what it represents. Men's attitudes toward women's attitudes on money were even more compelling. As part of my ongoing research I conducted regular focus groups, each one concentrating on a different aspect of the subject. The men's groups were of particular interest. I discovered that, in spite of appearances, little has changed.

The focus groups clearly illustrated that, as girls grew up, the family of many of them hadn't taken their financial goals and dreams as seriously as those of the boys in the family. I had my own experience of having my career and financial contribution disregarded. I can remember on several occasions trying to discuss money matters with one particular partner. As we attempted to plan financially for a house and children, I noticed that he never factored in or even acknowledged my income. Everything was based entirely on his. It was my intention to continue my career, which would have been possible if he were willing to assume 50 percent of the work at home. I often brought this to his attention, but he'd always fall silent. It was as if I didn't exist financially. I finally figured it out: aside from his own prehistoric beliefs, it was probably tough to take seriously someone who continually blew money the way I did. I was fiercely independent in all spheres of my life, but had done nothing to financially ensure this independence. Even though it was clear I was trying to mend my ways, my history spoke for itself.

If I, and thousands of women like me, were to move forward, we'd need to put to rest the proverbial knight in shining armour. In my capacity as a financial advisor for women, I take great pride in the fact that I've been instrumental in the assassination of countless knight-in-shining-armour syndromes. There are now many more women who are comfortable with having themselves to count on financially. It's easier to deal with life on life's terms when you finally realize that Prince Charming doesn't come on a white horse anymore. He comes in a Ford and needs help with the payments.

Although a stock is oblivious to the chromosomes of its owner, financial planning is a gender issue. There are differences in what motivates each sex on the topic of money, which are the direct result of how women and men are socialized. Having said that, I must also say that trying to put a segment of the population as large and as diverse as women into one special interest group is not only inaccurate, it's downright idiotic. Women are not a homogeneous group that thinks, feels, acts, and dreams the same way. Economic class, race, sexual orientation, age, geographic location, and a host of other characteristics all help to diversify women's identities. To try to make general statements about all women and their financial practices is irresponsible. To categorize women as spendthrifts, conservative investors, or—my personal favourite—being afraid of risk is so absurd it's insulting. One recent Canadian book on financial planning for women went so far as to say that women are biologically predisposed to fear risk because we never had to hunt. I wonder what that author was smoking.

The world is brilliant in its diversity and Canada is a microcosm of that world, perhaps one of the most successful on the entire planet. Look at the following to put it in perspective.

The village of 100—the world in perspective

If we could shrink the earth's population to a village of precisely 100 people, with all the existing human ratios remaining the same, it would look something like the following:

57 would be Asians
21 would be Europeans
14 would be from the Western Hemisphere, both north and south
 8 would be Africans

52 would be female, 48 would be male
70 would be non-white, 30 would be white
70 would be non-Christian, 30 would be Christian
89 would be heterosexual, 11 would be homosexual

6 would possess 59 percent of the entire world's wealth and all 6 would
  be from the United States
80 would live in substandard housing
70 would be unable to read
50 would suffer from malnutrition
 1 would be near death; 1 would be near birth

 1 (yes, only 1) would have a college education
 1 would own a computer

When one considers our world from such a compressed perspective, the need for acceptance, understanding, and education becomes glaringly apparent.

A financial plan needs to be as individual as the person who has it. Women in their 20s have different financial goals than women in their 50s and 60s. This is the result not only of age, but of differing experiences and expectations. There are, however, some noteworthy similarities in women's attitudes about money that derive from our socialized role. There's also the matter of biology. Outliving men and being the childbearers of the species create financial realities that contribute to women's "financial alikeness." I'll return to this a little later in the chapter.

In my research I discovered that many women don't use the male standard to measure success. Women are often motivated by variables that include but go beyond money and power. This is certainly the case for me. I was more interested in independence, being of service to others, liking my work, and receiving recognition from my peers. Pursuing these goals subsequently brought money and then power. This is not to suggest that men aren't also motivated by such things as a desire for independence and being of service. If you ask a man and a woman (as I often do) to compile a list of what motivates them and what constitutes success, both lists most often include the same things. Money, power, adequate family time, financial freedom to travel or stay at home, secure retirement, material possessions, and peace of mind are just a few of the items frequently mentioned. It's the order of importance in which they're listed that separates the sexes. To prove the point, I conducted an experiment with several women who were ardently against the notion that there were any differences between men and women on the issue of money. Along with their mates they did this simple exercise of listing their priorities. Most of them were astonished by the results. What headed many of their lists often sat at the bottom of their partners' lists. Certainly not in all cases, but the trend was sure there.

Frankly, there are still way too many people who aren't used to the idea of women having money and power. There are pervasive attitudes that women have no place in or no head for business and finance, and that these are still a man's domain. In most cases these are unconscious, deeply inbred expectations that have been passed on through generations.

I remember an incident that happened in my health club one morning. It was customary for me as a Stairmaster enthusiast to climb those stairs to nowhere while reading the newspaper. As a financial advisor, naturally the first thing I turned to was the business section. As I finished each section I'd put it in a pile beside me. A gentleman in his early 50s approached me politely and asked if he might read some of my paper. Before I could answer affirmatively, he picked up the just-discarded business section and said, "Oh terrific, I'll read this. It's business, you won't want it." I was dumbfounded. "Why might that be?" I quietly inquired. He stood there for a moment, then started to stutter and stammer some kind of reply. I was then witness to his dawning realization that he'd made this assumption because I was a woman. He looked horrified as he fell over his feet apologizing, trying to offer some kind of explanation. He couldn't get away from me fast enough. What was interesting wasn't so much my reaction, but his own reaction to what he'd said. It shocked him that he'd made such a remark, but even more so that he'd thought it. Attitudes can be so deeply ingrained that much of the time we don't even know we hold them.

Every year I'd been in the financial planning business I'd qualified for the insurance industry's Million Dollar Round Table. Based on service and sales performance, this designation is attained by less than 2 percent of the industry worldwide. Even though I'd earned the right to be part of this so-called elite, predominantly male club, I still had to deal with being called "babe" and "honey" by a few of my older male colleagues.

One year, I qualified to attend my company's U.K. division's conference in Paris as one of Canada's top representatives. Once there I had the most eye-opening experience. Out of over 300 delegates I was one of only three women attending who wasn't married to a qualifier. My then partner, whom I'd invited along, was totally amused by the fact that everyone who approached went to shake his hand and congratulate him. He'd smile and quickly retort, "Wrong person, chap! Joanne's the one you should be congratulating." This was invariably met with surprise and the look of wide-eyed curiosity one generally experiences when seeing snow for the first time. Over dinner one night, even the company president's wife had the audacity to ask what my position was with the human resources department. The comment prompted the president to make an announcement the next day that it was I, not my partner, who had qualified to be in Paris. This experience drove home something that I didn't really want to ever acknowledge:

neither women nor men are used to seeing women in positions of power and prestige yet.

Thankfully, these definitions, roles, and labels are starting to break down and men and women are crossing over into each other's traditional territories. But it's impossible to change overnight something so fundamentally ingrained, which may explain why many of these traditional attitudes persist even with today's generation. I call it a generational hangover. The experiences I'd had did little to help combat the impostor syndrome I fought with. They reinforced the "you don't belong here" feeling. No matter what job I was in, as I reached a higher echelon I'd think how "lucky" I was. Seldom did I think "you deserve this because you worked your tail off!" At the same time, I was anxious at the prospect of being successful. My mind would race at a dizzying pace: "What happens if I can't continue at this level of success? What do I do for my next trick? Do I really belong here or is this a weird accident or twist of fate?" It was only after realizing and admitting that this was a self-esteem issue and not a capability issue that I started to feel less and less the impostor. The words of Eleanor Roosevelt rang very true for me: "No one can make you feel inferior without your consent."

The more I learned, the more I realized how little the financial services industry knew about women and their money behaviour and potential. I knew because I worked at the grassroots level teaching women and men proper financial planning based on the realities of women's lives. The demand for information was growing at a monumental rate. I started to preach the edict, "Never confuse lack of education with lack of ability." Women and men both in the financial services area and outside of it needed to be educated about women and money and women's enormous consumer power. This was to be my calling. I eventually decided to stretch my wings and start my own company, The Thomas Yaccato Group, which specializes in helping companies connect with the country's most powerful economic force—women.

And that economic power? It's huge.

Where women are now[1]

Women wield considerable consumer clout, making and influencing an average of 80 percent of all consumer decisions. We know that the number of wealthy women around the world is growing faster than the number of wealthy men, and that women control most of the consumer spending. We know that single women are buying more homes than single men and that in families women do most of the househunting, along with making most of the decisions about what household goods to buy, where to go on holiday, which cable and telephone services to choose, and what Internet service provider to go with—not to mention which vehicle is best for the family. We know that women buy most of the over-the-counter drugs and herbal remedies and vitamins, and they buy half the computers and sports equipment sold.

Lordy, have we come a long way. In reality however, these changes have been relatively recent in the general scale of time. The law permitting women to be considered "persons" in the eyes of the law came into being a mere three years before my mother was born. She's in her early 60s. My Aunt Margaret, a Quebec resident, wasn't allowed to vote in provincial elections until the mid-1940s. Birth control was in the Canadian Criminal Code up until 1969. That was in my lifetime. So it's not surprising that there's still some serious catch-up to do. During the course of my research I uncovered several things to which women need to pay attention.

The *UN Human Development Report* says that in every region of the world, women placed a distant second to men in terms of wages, leisure time, political power, legal rights, and business opportunities. John Stackhouse of *The Globe and Mail* reported, "In no society do women enjoy the same opportunities as men."[2]

The United Nations survey ranks Canada first among nations in terms of overall human development such as literacy and life expectancy; however, the country drops to fourth when the gap between men and women is considered. That's an improvement from 1995, when Canada ranked ninth in gender-related development. Since 1970, Canada's ranking on gender equality—once second to the United States'—has fallen, mainly because Canada has made less progress than other industrial nations in closing the wage gap between women and men. The 1995 report stated that in non-agricultural sectors Canadian women earned only 63 percent of what men earned, as compared to the global average of 74.9 percent. This puts Canada in 47th place out of 55 countries and last among members of the Organisation for Economic Co-operation and Development (OECD).[3]

Globally, there is some light at the end of the tunnel. A 2002 report by OECD on the employment outlook showed that, on average, hourly rates of pay for women are 84 percent of men's wages. It went on to say that over the 15- to 20-year periods analyzed, the wage gap fell between 14 percent and 38 percent, indicating substantial progress. However, the wage gap decreased most in the United States and France, whereas the figures for Sweden and Canada displayed less rapid movement in closing the gender wage gap.

As reported in *The Globe and Mail,* the findings are "a major indictment of the continuing discrimination against women in most societies," said James Gustave Speth, administrator of the UN development program.[4] The report goes on to say that on every continent women work longer hours, earn less money, and are more likely to live in poverty than are men. There are 1.3 billion people who live on less than a dollar a day, and 1 billion can't meet their basic consumption requirements. The share in global income of the richest fifth of the world's people is 74 times that of the poorest fifth. Here's the kicker—the UN report estimates that a full 70 percent of the world's 1.3 billion poor are women. The report also says that the formal economy fails to account for $11 trillion a year of economic goods and services—from home care in Canada to firewood collection in Kenya—produced by women.

The news isn't all bad, however. Between 1990 and 1997 the net secondary school enrollment for girls increased globally from 36 percent to 61 percent. Women's economic activity rose from 34 percent to 40 percent.[5]

Incidentally, women don't fare much better in the UN itself—only 30 percent of all professional jobs and 11.3 percent of senior management jobs in its various agencies are held by women.[6] Statistics Canada (StatsCan) supports these findings with its own research.

Single mothers make up a disproportionate number of Canada's poor. Single mothers under the age of 65 with children under the age of 18 make up 61.4 percent of Canada's poor. In 1997, families headed by single females under age 65 had an average income of $25,400, only 39 percent of the average income of non-elderly two-spouse families with children, and just 65 percent of that of single-parent families headed by men. This means that over half the single-parent households in Canada have incomes below the poverty line. Living longer on less money makes women financially vulnerable. In the same year, 49 percent of senior women who lived alone had low incomes, compared with 33 percent of unattached senior men. StatsCan indicates that a baby girl born today is expected to live 81 years and a baby boy 76. What's more significant is that women aged 65 today can expect to live on average another 20 years, and a man that age 16.2 years.

Statistics Canada reports that in 2001 single women employed full-time for a full year earned 91.3 percent of what men earned. Earnings of married women were 67.2 percent of men's, and that nebulous category "other" earned 77.9 percent of men's earnings.

The average annual pre-tax income of women aged 15 and over from all sources was $35,258, just 71.6 percent the average income of men at $49,250.

Women represent 45 percent of the Canadian paid labour force, yet 56 percent of them work in jobs that don't provide pensions. Part of this is the recent trend of women going into business for themselves. Women make up almost two-thirds of the part-time workforce, which has no benefits of any sort. One-third of this part-time labour force are women who can't find full-time work. As childbearers, women lose the ability, or have that ability seriously diminished, to make RRSP, Canada Pension Plan (CPP), and private pension plan contributions while on maternity leave. And what about women who choose to work full-time unpaid in the home? They can't benefit from any of the above.

The professional world is another telling story. According to Statistics Canada, women represent close to 50 percent of the students graduating from the legal and medical faculties at universities. Yet they leave these professions in disproportionately higher numbers than men, largely because of the stress of having to handle two jobs—the one at the office and the unpaid one at home. The corporate world offers its own set of challenges, with its glass ceiling and often inflexible attitudes toward women and men juggling career and childcare. StatsCan states that even when employed, women are still largely responsible for looking after their homes and families. Employed women with a spouse and at least one child under the age of five spent 4.9 hours a day on household activities, including domestic work, primary childcare, and shopping. This was about 1.5 hours more per day than their male counterparts spent on unpaid housework. Broken down, it looks like this: women in Canada prepare 76 percent of the meals, are responsible for 71 percent of the child-care, and perform 59 percent of the shopping and other housework.

StatsCan[7] also reveals that women's standard of living dropped anywhere from 16 percent to 23 percent in adjusted family income after divorce and separation, while men's standard increased anywhere from 2 percent to 10 percent. There's a 34.8 percent chance within 30 years of marriage that divorce will occur for each marriage in Canada. It's actually at the point now that when a women meets the man of her dreams, the first question she asks herself is, "Is this the man I want my children to spend every second weekend with?"

Clearly, there's no doubt that women face greater financial challenges than most men do. But we must never lose heart. We've seen the economic clout that women are now beginning to exercise. For example, in 2000, 16.9 percent of women aged 55 to 64 were below StatsCan's low-income cutoff (LICO), which isn't necessarily the poverty line, and is in fact considered by most experts as considerably higher than a level of poverty. Twenty-three percent of women 70 and over were below the LICO for their geographic locations. This is an improving situation. I do want to make the point, however, that we shouldn't buy into the message that women have arrived and are finally equal to men in Canadian society. In fact, there's a backlash occurring as women begin to make significant inroads into positions of power. This is evidenced everywhere. Take Ontario, for example. The former Conservative government eliminated employment equity programs and drastically reduced funding for pay equity programs and daycare in the name of balancing the budget. Programs affecting women and children are often the first on governments' chopping blocks. As the studies suggest, there's much work left to do, so we can't afford to be complacent. Never before has it been so essential for women to have their wits about them. This means taking financial control of their lives.

Now, you need to know that I hate quizzes. Especially the kind that set you up to find out how much of a man magnet you are or whether or not you're adept at pleasing him. But after reviewing the 1997 American Express Financial Responsibility Survey, I began to rethink these kinds of quizzes and their place in our lives. This particular survey asked people if they knew the difference between a charge card and a credit card. Half the survey respondents said they did, but when given a short quiz less than 2 percent got it right. People's lack of knowledge presents me, a financial educator, with an undeniable conundrum. How do you teach people about personal finance if they think they already know about it? So I've devised a light-hearted quiz that you can quickly take to determine whether or not you need to read the rest of this book for reasons other than how my love life fares. It's designed to test your financial literacy on a variety of issues that affect the building of a strong financial foundation. The questions cover everything from credit to estate planning, life and disability insurance, and mutual funds and RRSPs. The answers are buried throughout the book.

Financial literacy quiz

1. You have an R9 rating. This means:
   a) you can drive without wearing glasses
   b) credit card companies are filling your mailbox with unsolicited, preapproved credit cards with high spending limits
   c) every time someone knocks on your door, you dive for cover out of fear of bill collectors

2. A grace period:
   a) allows you to pay your credit card bills whenever you have the money
   b) is the period of time just before your diet is scheduled to start when you can eat anything you want
   c) is the time between when your credit card bill is sent and the due date

3. A personal line of credit:
   a) is designed specifically for the mathematically challenged who bounce cheques

b) must be paid back in monthly installments within a certain time period

c) allows you to choose how much money to borrow within a preapproved limit

4. The quickest way to establish a credit rating is to:
a) beg for money
b) borrow money
c) steal money

5. If you die without a will:
a) your life partner gets nothing, except maybe your glass armadillo collection
b) the government steps in and writes one for you
c) the Office of the Public Trustee swoops in and takes everything

6. Probate fees are:
a) the tuition costs of becoming a probation officer
b) what you pay to have your estate looked after if you die without a will
c) what you pay to have your estate looked after if you die with a will

7. Power of attorney for personal care:
a) designates someone to be your head, your heart, and your hands should you die
b) organizes your hair stylist and esthetician appointments
c) makes health care decisions for you when you can't

8. The way to avoid someone having too much power over your affairs is to:
a) appoint your unemployed brother
b) appoint two attorneys to act jointly
c) don't do anything

9. The primary purpose of term life insurance is to:
a) make sure your insurance lasts as long as you do
b) pay off your term loan from the bank when you die
c) provide insurance coverage until your obligations end or leave home

10. The best part of the death benefit from your life insurance policy is that it:
a) goes directly to Canada Revenue Agency to pay your terminal or final tax return after you die

b) allows your survivors to grieve in Tahiti
c) enjoys tax-free status

11. Company or employer-provided disability insurance:
   a) is good for only as long as you work there
   b) has the most generous definition of what constitutes a "disability"
   c) has tax-free benefits

12. You're a brain surgeon who becomes disabled. You can't perform surgery but you can sell pencils. You want to be sure your disability policy:
   a) has an "own occupation" clause
   b) is held by a company that owns stock in EB Eddy
   c) covers you for 100 percent of your previous earnings

13. A tax shelter is:
   a) the same as a homeless shelter, but this one gets really crowded every April 30th
   b) a place to invest your money tax free until it comes time to cash it out
   c) a tax benefit that allows you to claim certain costs of your home, like your mortgage

14. The amount of money Revenue Canada holds back when you cash out your RRSP before its time is called:
   a) withholding tax
   b) shock therapy
   c) early-withdrawal penalty

15. The type of investments that can qualify for an RRSP are:
   a) stocks, bonds, guaranteed investment certificates (GICs), Canada Savings Bonds, mutual funds, savings accounts
   b) your priceless glass armadillo collection
   c) stocks, bonds, GICs, Canada Savings Bonds, mutual funds, savings accounts, unemployment benefits, Canada Pension Plan payments

16. The most effective way to double your money is to:
   a) fold it over and put it in your pocket
   b) invest in an RRSP
   c) buy art

17. One of the best ways for people, especially investing novices, to get the most foreign content allowable in their RRSPs is to:
   a) put their money in an envelope and mail it overseas
   b) choose individual stocks from foreign companies
   c) invest in a mutual fund that maximizes foreign content capability

18. Mutual fund management fees are:
    a) much lower in Canada than they are in the United States
    b) the costs of administering the fund, including the money
       manager's salary and sales reps' commission charges
    c) incredibly annoying

19. If you're retiring in 35 years, one of the best types of investment to
    use in saving for it is:
    a) a GIC
    b) a high-quality mattress
    c) an international equity mutual fund

20. A front-end load is:
    a) what my Uncle Leigh drives on his farm in Prince Edward Island
    b) sales charges that you pay up front when you buy a mutual fund
    c) sales charges you pay when you cash out of the fund. This means
       that all your money goes directly into the investment up front
       instead of to sales commissions.

First things first

Needless to say, before I began the process of getting my own financial
house in order I would have bombed seriously on this quiz. If you didn't
do as well as you would have liked, buck up. I'm going to teach you the
language of money and, with the help of a fabulous tool, help you find a
concrete direction. When I first went to the centre to get a grip on the money
scene, Elaine showed me a picture that simplified and took the mystery and
confusion out of where to start. The priority pyramid is used in some form
by most financial advisors, and provides an easy-to-understand road map to
successful financial planning. One of the main reasons I'd waited so long to get
started was that I didn't have a clue what, how, and in what order things
needed to get done. This concept saw that I stuck to first things first.

I have a standard procedure at my seminars. I stand inconspicuously off to
one side as the crowd files in. I listen carefully (okay, so I eavesdrop) as the
women chat among themselves. I'm never disappointed. Invariably there are
one or two who comment: "I don't know what I'm doing here. I don't have
any money to financially plan with!" I smile at the irony of this. You'll never
have any money unless you financially plan. It seems to me that most of the
world has this backwards. There's a common misconception that you need to
be wealthy or a reasonable facsimile thereof in order to get involved in financial planning. Absolutely not so. For people just getting started, financial planning can mean something as simple as getting organized. That's financial

planning. Paying your bills on time or taking your receipts out of the shoe box and putting them into a proper filing system is financial planning. Reading books like this one or attending a free seminar, that's financial planning. Any step you take toward financial literacy is part of the process. And it doesn't have to cost you a cent. Eventually, however, you're going to have to start organizing the actual dollars you spend and siphon some off to build your financial base. I had to reorient my thinking to realize that the money I was putting into retirement savings and mutual funds wasn't money "spent"—it was money that would eventually come back to me, in larger quantities. I had to let go of the idea that this money was "gone."

The first thing to do is to build a financial base. There's no sense in having Jacuzzis and fancy chandeliers in your house if the foundation is cracked and leaking water. I was told that my foundation was in grave disrepair. I needed to fix it so that I could have a safe and secure base to work from. Then, and only then, would I be allowed to wander off and play in the big sandbox.

The Priority Pyramid

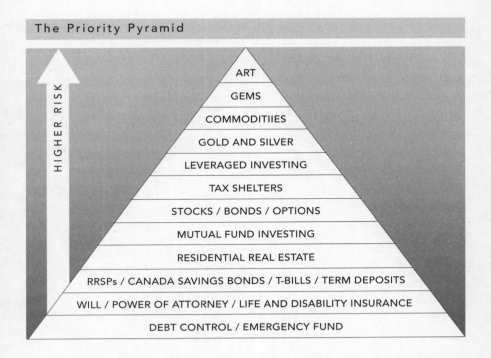

The pyramid is built up according to risk, with the base being safe and virtually risk free and the top being the riskiest investment. This pyramid isn't suggesting that the first thing to do is pay off your debts and then, just before you die, run out and buy a painting. It simply allows you to choose the type of investments that are in your particular comfort zone while minimizing the risk to your complete portfolio. You may never invest in gold or art. But if you choose to, at least you'll have the security of your financial base to fall back on should your brilliant investment scheme turn into a turkey. The base of your pyramid should provide adequate money in the event of emergency, disability, or death. This is after your non-deductible debt load is paid off or at least manageable.

Although I hadn't had any debt for several years when I went to the centre, there was still the mangled credit rating to fix. In fact, I was completely in the dark about the inner workings of the world of credit. My experience with it hadn't been a warm one, so I made it my business to understand it. Understanding how credit works and the different forms available to use and abuse is a wonderful place to start your financial journey.

two

Getting started

*The surest way to establish your credit is to work
yourself into the position of not needing any.*

MAURICE SWITZER

Getting savvy about credit

It was one of thousands of business lunches I'd endured while in the computer
industry, but this one was to be the most memorable. The deal had taken over
two years of intense negotiating and hand-holding. A major financial institution
had finally agreed to go with my company for their national software and hard-
ware requirements. This deal was very big. It was May, and thanks to the signed
piece of paper safely tucked into my briefcase, I had just made my year's quota.
I'd whisked away the three executives, including the company president, to an
elegant restaurant in Toronto's King and Bay district for a celebratory lunch.

It was a festive occasion, with wine flowing and food in abundance. This
was a stellar moment for me. I'd faced fierce competition from the best in the
business. The deal was almost lost a couple of times. One of the men casually
commented, now that the t's were crossed and the i's dotted, that his wife was
thrilled that I, the only woman out of seven vendors in the game, had won the
business. As I basked in the glow of this significant achievement the bill
arrived, which I promptly scooped up, not even giving it a token glance. The
waitress took away one of the many credit cards I owned, all of which were
suffering from varying degrees of chronic fatigue syndrome. At the precise
moment the three executives congratulated me on a job well done, the waitress approached the table. Now, I could have endured, "I'm sorry, your card is
over its limit." I would have been embarrassed, but it does happen. Instead, the
waitress, in a brusque tone and with a complete absence of tact announced,

"Madame, not only has your card been refused, but the credit card company has asked me to confiscate it. How do you propose to pay this bill?"

Stunned silence hung in the air for what seemed like an eternity. Where was that massive tidal wave when you needed it?

I knew these men quite well as a result of our frequent meetings over the course of two years. They completely fell apart. As the room filled with peals of laughter, I, red-faced, spoke with the owner of the restaurant and finally persuaded him to take a personal cheque. Apparently this is what happens if you constantly park at your credit limit and have only a semi-consistent payment pattern. I'd receive a bill, throw it on the pile, and promptly forget it until a month or six later. My debt had been slowly accumulating over the years and was now reaching critical proportions.

Evidently.

There was one other event that had to happen before I finally admitted defeat. A word of advice to all of you who take the repayment of your student loan lightly: don't.

I'd moved to Vancouver a few years after graduating from university and the student loan people and I kind of lost track of each other. After I had destroyed my ankle and lost my job, there was little money for items such as student loans. So I stopped paying it. Mind you, my intention was that this was only until I started to work again. But since I hadn't heard a word or received a single notice, I easily (read: conveniently) dismissed the loan from my memory. Around the same time as the business luncheon fiasco, the government and I had a reunion. It came in the guise of a collection agency. Collection agents, I'm convinced, are graduates of the Mike Tyson School of Charm. They're the pit bulls of the financial world. People come to me in a state of panic and anxiety after receiving threatening and abusive phone calls from a collector. Provincial law prohibits collectors from harassing or making unreasonable threats. But many cross over the line and use humiliation tactics. Now, in the collection agencies' defence, they save companies millions of dollars each year by collecting money from so-called deadbeats. But, I can tell you, not everyone who has a tough time paying bills is a deadbeat. Far from it. Yet many bill collectors are remarkably adept at making you feel like one.

When I received that brutish phone call from the agency, I didn't get scared. I got angry. I agreed that I had to begin paying the student loan back, but wanted to do it on a reasonable payment plan. The collector's version of reasonable was that the balance (several thousand dollars) was due in full within 48 hours or they were going to take me to court and garnish my wages. I think what angered me the most was that the guy seemed to really enjoy his job. I could virtually hear him smiling over the phone. I was curious as to why there hadn't been any warning before such drastic action was taken. Apparently, once the computer sends you a certain number of notices, you automatically get to enjoy deadbeat status whether you received them or not. Although I had to take full responsibility for not instituting a payment plan when I started work again, I've since come to realize that debtors have rights. The right not to be threatened, distressed, and humiliated is one of them. Collectors are supposed to be businesslike and polite. If you're being harassed, be sure to contact the appropriate provincial government agency.

Had I contacted the bank and told them of my financial difficulty when it occurred instead of suffering a peculiar memory loss that affected only financial matters, the chances are reasonably good that it would never have come to this. One of the many lessons I learned during this period was to be honest with your creditors when you're in trouble. This is especially true in this day and age when so many people are finding it tough to manage. The traditional intimidating attitude among financial institutions toward bad debt has evolved. Many major banks are taking a total customer relationship approach. In the realm of credit, some banks approve credit, manage the risk, and view collections at a total customer level, rather than account by account. At the end of the day, they want you to be able to make your payments; banks can work with you to find a solution if you're having difficulty.

It's a piece of cake to call up your banker when you're only five days late with a payment. I can personally vouch for how much more difficult it becomes after that. If I'd called the bank when I was in trouble, I may have been able to take advantage of a variety of options, from a no-payment period to a renegotiation of the loan. Hindsight is 20/20.

Let it be known that humiliation can be a powerful motivator. After that disastrous lunch, I humbly took myself off to the bank to try to get a bill consolidation loan. It made sense to me that my first step to sleeping more soundly at night might be to find a way to manage this debt albatross around my neck. I was paying over 22 percent on my credit cards at the time. It seemed to me that interest rates on bank loans were a darned sight lower. In fact, I discovered that I could cut the interest rate by almost two-thirds. The necessary paperwork was done and I assumed, because of my income, all would be rosy. I couldn't have been more wrong. I was about to discover how up to my neck in it I really was.

As I sat in her office, the loans officer did a quick scan of my credit history. Her response to my loan application was a decided "not on your life." She asked me if I was aware that I had an R9 rating on one of my credit cards. I queried if that was good, knowing full well what the answer would be. She informed me in a grave tone that this meant repossession. I smiled and quietly responded that I was only too keenly aware of that fact. She mentioned the Credit Counselling Service of Toronto and strongly suggested I pay them a visit. She told me they would organize my debt and work out a palatable agreement with my creditors. "They're tough," she warned. "No tougher than Attila the Hun from the collection agency," I thought to myself. I was surprised to learn there was such a service. I immediately began to feel better knowing there were other people out there as bad or, gasp, worse than me. Credit Counselling Service of Toronto is one of 27 such agencies in Ontario. Many credit counselling organizations are nonprofit and have a charitable licence. Their services are mostly free, but some may charge a nominal fee. Women seek credit counselling more than men—57 percent of women and 43 percent of men, according to Laurie Campbell, program manager at Credit Counselling Service of Toronto. In couples, it's usually the women who call to make the appointment. Laurie says this is indicative of the fact that women are much more willing to resolve their issues. Women don't feel the same kind of intense shame that men do around financial problems. I've often said publicly that I couldn't balance my chequebook on top of my purse. You'd be hard-pressed to hear a man laugh about money troubles. Laurie says the debt levels that people have when they get there are significant. The average debt load is $23,000, usually on credit cards. That extends over an average of seven creditors. I felt right at home.

Through credit counselling I learned many things, but the first lesson was the importance of a good two-way relationship with your counsellor. After sitting down with my first counsellor and going over the grisly details, I was astonished when this gentleman suggested, albeit in jest, that I marry a wealthy man as a solution to my problem. I retorted that a wedding would take 20 minutes. What would he suggest I do next? He looked at me blankly. It was evident he had missed my point. I excused myself and asked to see another counsellor. With my new counsellor, I devised a workable payment structure based on a realistic budget (shudder) that I religiously adhered to. The service contacted Canadian Imperial Bank of Commerce (CIBC) and the Bank of Montreal, the two holders of my cards, and my personal favourite, Mr. Attila of the collection agency, to inform them of our intentions. Once credit counselling came on the scene, all harassment from the collection agency and the nasty "pay or die" letters from the bank ceased. And although I felt immeasurably relieved, I had to learn patience. I had several thousand dollars in credit card bills to pay off, which wouldn't happen overnight. I also had to park the notion that "all is well now." While significantly better than my previous "hide and seek" credit management program, the fact that I was working with a credit counselling agency did appear on my credit record. It's noteworthy that financial institutions donate to these nonprofit organizations in an effort to help reclaim some of their bad debt. Banks and major department stores will stop charging interest once you begin a debt management program.

Most provinces have nonprofit credit counselling agencies. Some provinces offer a scaled-down version through the government, generally the Ministry of Consumer Relations (or Consumer Affairs). They don't have the resources to offer financial counselling, and a default judgment will be granted to the creditor if you fail to meet any of the terms of the program.

My best friend Cheryl's story

Cheryl Chafe has been my best friend since we were 13 years old. We did everything together. We experienced much of life's "firsts" together. And in that same spirit, as we progressed into adulthood we experienced credit hell together. Cheryl, her husband, Dave, and two unbelievably busy boys live in Dartmouth, Nova Scotia. This is one of the provinces that provide scaled-down counselling through the Department of Consumer Relations. I'll let her tell her own story:

"We bought our first house and soon found our credit cards parked at the maximum. So we consolidated the debts. We maxed our cards again. Now we had the credit card payments and the consolidation loan payment. So we consolidated again. At this point our banker suggested we put our cards in a safety deposit box, which we did. Then we bought a bigger house. We beat a hasty path to the safety deposit box and maxed our cards again. We consolidated again. The only reason I can think of that the bank was so cavalier with us in terms of letting us keep the cards was because Dave's parents were life-long bankers. The woman we dealt with knew them well, so she made things very easy for us. In retrospect, much too easy.

"However, the gravy train had to end. On our fourth trip to our banker's office we were roundly denied. Our debt now equalled $30,000, all from credit card misuse. She cut up our Visa card right in her office. She recommended a visit to the Department of Consumer Relations. We were actually desperate enough to look into bankruptcy, but that wasn't an option because we had too much equity in our house. We also felt that bankruptcy was a complete abdication of our responsibilities.

"So we contacted the Nova Scotia Department of Consumer Affairs OPD (Orderly Payment of Debt) department. Our application was accepted, we were counselled, put on a budget, and our creditors were contacted by OPD. The interest rate was around 5 percent and the term was five years with an affordable monthly payment. Our payments were made to OPD and they disbursed the money to the creditors, and creditors weren't allowed to contact us, which was a relief. It was explained to us that our credit record would remain at an R7 for three years instead of seven years with bankruptcy after repayment of debt. After so many years of trying to make our consolidated payments and payments of new credit card debt, and years of arguing about money (which put a great strain on our marriage), the anxiety and pressure were gone, plus we were paying our debt. After three years with OPD we were able to make a lump sum proposal to our creditors. This was a new agreement with OPD. We made a proposal of approximately $10,000, which was accepted, and re-mortgaged our house. This basically paid our creditors their principal only and saved us money.

"We now had to wait three years for our credit rating to improve. After three years we applied for a credit card with our bank with $1,000 in a GIC and were denied. We assumed that after three years we'd automatically have good credit, but this wasn't so. Equifax hadn't removed our old debt, which we assumed was already done. After repeated attempts to get our record straight, it wasn't until I contacted Consumer Affairs and had them call Equifax themselves that it was finally removed. So instead of three years for a clean record, we ended up having to wait five years because of the difficulty getting this black mark removed.

"Having a card was very scary but liberating. We hadn't been able to rent a car, hotel, or even our son's trumpet for school band because we didn't have a credit card and needed to rely on family members. We paid a heavy price for credit card abuse. Our mortgage and our amortization increased, we experienced many difficulties by not having a credit card number and, not the least of which, our marriage was terribly strained. The upside is that we now have a credit card and we use it only as a deposit number or for an amount we know will be paid at the end of the month. Our top priority today is to teach the boys real-life lessons about money. They won't make the same mistakes we did."

For people caught in the trap of overextended credit, Consumer Affairs or credit counselling organizations can be a welcome second chance. Cheryl and I are living examples of how they can work.

It's very clear to me now that one's credit rating is a privilege, not a right. Once the dust settled and we had effectively implemented damage control, I made a sobering discovery. I had unknowingly obliterated my credit rating. Here I was in full swing specializing in financial planning for women. I had cast off the old ways with a vengeance by performing "plastic surgery" and transforming myself into a financially literate person. I couldn't help but smile at the irony that I was teaching people about good financial management and I couldn't get credit. It had been five years since my last bout of trouble and my nose had been clean the whole time. But when I applied again for a card, I was turned down.

When my credit cards were finally paid off (a feat more easily accomplished when I stopped using them), it was my honest intention not to use them again. Ever. But this was proving to be more difficult than I had imagined. Have you ever tried ordering flowers or writing a cheque without one? Taking clients out for lunch became a problem. It was hard to impress the senior partners of a prestigious law firm when you try to pay for lunch discreetly with a pile of bills that would rival the height of the CN Tower. The change in my attitude toward money was so pronounced, and at such a deep, fundamental level, that it now seemed absurd not to have a credit card. I couldn't even get overdraft protection with the damage I'd done. So I took the bull by the horns, and contacted the credit bureau to find out the exact status of my rating. I was fascinated by how the whole process worked. It was frightening to discover how much in the dark I'd been about something that had such an impact on my life. I firmly believe that information on how to make and break your credit rating should be in the school curriculum. I often wonder—if I'd known how the system worked, would it have changed my cavalier attitude toward credit? This is what I learned …

How credit ratings and the credit bureaus work

Credit lenders decide on your credit worthiness based on three principles, known as the three C's of credit:

Your character Are you dependable? Do you pay your bills on time? Does your past show you to be a financially responsible person?

Your capacity Do you have a steady means to pay back what you're borrowing? Do you own a home or rent? Have you lived at your current address for long? Credit lenders like to see your name on one mailbox for at least a year.

Your collateral When everything is added up, is what you're worth more than what you owe? Do you own something that's worth at least as much as your credit limit or the amount you want to borrow? This might include the equity in your house, household goods, a car, savings, investments, and life insurance.

If yes figures prominently in your answers, then you're a good candidate for credit.

What's a credit rating?

Your credit rating is a scorecard of your credit behaviour. Everything you do with credit is tracked and rated according to how responsible you've been in paying it back. Most of your credit transactions are kept on file at an independent credit bureau. These transactions include things like loans and credit cards, but not rent or utility bills. The greatest misconception about credit bureaus is that they determine your credit rating. In fact, they're simply the clearing house for information that credit grantors may want access to in order to figure out your credit worthiness. They're not interested in any personal data. The reason it's important to make timely monthly payments is that your records are updated every 30 days by information provided by your creditors on what balances remain and what payments have been made or missed.

Financial institutions, retailers, and other lenders who have an interest in your financial status check your rating before deciding whether to grant you credit. To be sure your record is accurate, write or phone the bureau for a free copy of your history. You need to include two pieces of ID, and be sure to check *both* of the country's two largest bureaus—Trans Union of Canada Inc. and Equifax.

Establishing your credit rating

The merits of having your own driver's licence and social insurance number are obvious. It's equally important to have your own credit rating. If you've lived under the umbrella of your partner's credit, for example, by using a supplementary card instead of one in your own name, you may be surprised to learn that the credit bureau doesn't even know you exist. This becomes dangerous should you wake up one morning to find yourself on your own and handling money for the first time. Something you always took for granted—credit—is gone. To be sure that you're establishing a credit history of your own, apply for credit in your own name, using your partner's name as a co-signer or guarantor if necessary.

The first step in establishing credit is to get something on your record to rate. Your credit record begins once any kind of application for credit is filled out. Notice that I say filled out, not approved. This is something to be very aware of. If you have a lot of inquiries on record, it could work against you. Credit granters are suspicious of people who are chronic credit appliers. Only apply if you seriously need that particular form of credit.

People looking to establish credit include women who've recently survived the death or divorce of a partner and who now need their own credit identity. They could also be graduating students or empty-nester Moms earning their first full-time paycheques. Other people may have a poor credit rating due to bankruptcy or delinquent repayment of debt.

No matter which group you belong to, the best way to create a credit rating that will allow you to borrow money is to borrow money. Confusing? Yes, but it's easier than you think. Credit lenders often like to see a good repayment history before lending money or offering credit. You can begin to develop this history by trying any of the following:

• Make regular deposits to a savings account.
• Pay all your bills, such as rent and utilities, on time.

- Get a credit or charge card at a department store with a $500 limit and repay on time.
- Get a joint card with your partner so that the credit reporting is done in your name.
- Take out a car loan and pay it back promptly.
- Take out an RRSP loan and repay it within one year.
- Apply for a secured credit card.

This is how you establish a good credit rating. Keeping it is equally as important.

Keeping a good credit rating

As soon as you've been approved for any type of credit, you're rated from 1 to 9 based on your performance as a debtor. R0 means you have a credit card but have not yet used it. R1 means you're glowingly perfect, and the ratings continue all the way to R9, which signifies a very delinquent and essentially deadbeat status. This is when they call in our friend, the bill collector, and the debt becomes classified as a bad debt.

Making the Credit Grade

There are three types of ratings: R for revolving, O for open credit, and I for installment loans.

Rating	#
Account is too new to rate: approved but not yet used	0
Pays within 30 days and all payments are up to date	1
Pays within 30 days to 60 days and is not more than 1 payment behind	2
Pays within 60 days to 90 days or is 2 payments behind	3
Pays within 90 days to 120 days or 3 or more payments behind	4
Account at least 120 days overdue but not in collection	5*
Is making regular payments under a consolidation order or similar arrangement	7
Is in voluntary repossession	8
Account is in collection or debtor can't be found	9

* THERE IS NO 6 RATING.

My R9 rating became an R7 as soon as I completed my debt with credit counselling. If I could have mustered a logical explanation for the R9 rating, the bank might have given me a bill consolidation loan. Unfortunately, financial stupidity doesn't qualify as a logical explanation. The first time I went just one day over the allotted 30 days for a credit card payment, my rating changed from R1 to R2. It was as simple as that. When I was off work with my injury and consistently owing two months' payments, as well as being 60 days in arrears, I was silently downgraded to an R3 rating, and so it went. When the loans officer did my credit check she saw a series of R3 ratings, most of them from several years back. While I was out of work I'd been ashamed and fearful that they might take away my only source of credit if I told them I wasn't able to work and therefore make regular payments. In the eyes of the creditors, based on the little they know of your situation, an R3 rating tends to show that you're "light" in the financial discipline department. It's not likely they'll extend you more credit. Once the payments are made, however, the ratings don't change. The file of late or missed payments becomes a permanent part of your record for six years. The good news is that derogatory information, such as collections, has to be removed by law from your credit file after six years. Judgments will remain on your file for 20 years.

You don't actually receive an overall rating. Each of your creditors or lenders has different credit requirements. Harry's Discount Furniture Emporium will have different credit standards than American Express. Your rating for each form of credit you have is matched with the lender's own specific requirements for granting credit. These ratings are part of what's evaluated when an institution decides whether or not it's going to give you credit. Current income and ability to pay are, of course, major factors as well. There's a point system. Being the president of a corporation for 20 years, and living at the same address in the exclusive Montreal neighbourhood of Westmount for 30 years, will rate you pretty high. If, like myself, you've been mobile and have missed a few credit card payments, you'll likely be rejected and feel the humiliation that comes with a "Sorry, but we aren't going to let you have any" letter.

The best way to keep a good rating is to make all your payments on time and to take on only as much debt as you can handle. Don't put anything on a credit card unless you know you can pay for it in full by the time the bill comes in, or at the very most, within a couple of months. It's to your advantage to keep your credit performance clean because a bad record can affect your ability to borrow money for a car or your home; it can also inhibit your ability to get insurance and maybe even a job.

It's very important that you keep on top of what's in your file. Mistakes do, in fact, happen. Credit can be denied based on inaccurate or insufficient information. The CBC program *Marketplace* asked Canadians to visit their credit bureaus and check the status of their files. A staggering 47 percent of the files had varying levels of inaccuracy, and 13 percent had mistakes serious enough to lead to possibly being refused credit.[1] Although this survey was done in the early '90s, it still holds true. Laurie Campbell of Credit Counselling Service of Toronto states that everyone should check their credit file before applying for further credit to ensure that his or her file contains no mistakes. "Unfortunately mistakes do happen and better you find out about them before a potential lender," she says.

Denise Araiche, who worked in a bank for many years, has an interesting take on credit bureaus. She says, "Getting my own personal credit file to ensure everything was correct was a daunting experience. I ended up with a list as long as my arm. Listed were all kinds of credit cards under D. Araiche. The only problem was that some of them were my sister Danielle's cards and some of them were mine. I spent a couple of months getting this cleared up with the credit bureau and ensuring that they didn't overlap. Had I gone for a loan when my credit file looked like that, I may have been declined due to the fact that it looked like I had a lot of outstanding debt.

"From my point of view as a banker, we would get a credit bureau file for clients and there would be all kinds of credit cards that had been cancelled (by letter or through the institution) or amounts that had been paid long ago. There were even debts that didn't belong to the clients. One woman I dealt with had four write-offs on her credit bureau file that had been paid—she even had the letters from the institutions to prove it—she just couldn't get them off the credit bureau file.

"In 1997, another client had a $13 write-off from *our* institution because *we* made a mistake with one of his investments. We knew it was our error and we had asked the credit bureau to remove it by calling and sending letters saying that it was a bank error. But we couldn't get it removed. To this day, the client still takes that letter with him everywhere he goes. And he needs to. That silly write-off still shows up and he still automatically gets declined for loans, even by our institution, the one who made the mistake in the first place."

Denise advises, "Even though your credit bureau file is essential to financial institutions and other companies, it's so easy to have problems with it. For example, many people cut up their credit cards but forget to ask the companies to close their account. It will still show up on a credit bureau, even if the balance is zero. The financial institution still assumes you can borrow on that account up to its limit. We therefore add it into the calculation we make when deciding if we should lend you money (debt servicing ratio). You should get a copy of your credit bureau report every single year to ensure that the information is correct."

The credit bureaus are under provincial jurisdiction and have to do what they can to ensure that their files are accurate. But their information is only as good as the information that they receive. They guard carefully against unlawful use, but at the same time have to make sure that the information is easily available to the customer. If you have a difference of opinion about the information found in your file, you have every right to dispute it.

Equifax, one of the country's largest credit agencies, will look into any formal complaint that has been filed. For information on how to do this by fax or mail, call Equifax at 1-800-465-7166. The process usually takes a couple of weeks. The other credit reporting agency in Canada is Trans Union, which can be reached at 1-800-663-9980. These companies handle over a million requests for reports each year.

And mine was one of them. It seemed that the only thing standing in the way of my securing credit was an old R7 rating from the Bank of Montreal for my Mastercard. But this debt had been paid off in full over five years ago. Time to give them a call. I had a lengthy discussion with a woman in their credit department who chuckled when I told her what I now did for a living. It seemed she also had a finely tuned sense of the absurd. She understood completely my dilemma and suggested I write a letter to the bank asking them to remove the bad rating. I did and they did. Today, information is removed from the credit bureau file two years after a person completes a debt management program.

I've come a long way in terms of saving and investments from that day, but little has given me as much satisfaction as that did. For the first time I was beginning to feel like an adult, and surprisingly it really wasn't so bad. To this day I use only two credit cards. The balances are paid off in full faithfully every month on pain of death, no exceptions.

Types of credit

You can get credit in many ways. To reiterate this chapter's opening quotation, the surest is to work yourself into the position where you don't need any. But that doesn't apply to most of us. I needed to learn more.

There's an abundance of different types of credit or loans. They range from term loans that we use to buy cars to investment loans that we use to get rich. But like so many people, I found that the variety of loans, overdraft protection, and personal lines of credit was confusing. Each type of credit serves a particular purpose. I wanted to be sure I wasn't putting a square peg in a round hole.

Installment credit (personal loans)

This type of credit is most often used to acquire those big-ticket necessities that life can be so bleak without, like cars, computers, or furniture. My bill consolidation loan was this kind of loan. Its principal characteristic is a specific repayment schedule—that is, equal monthly amounts for a set time period such as 48 months. You can pay it off at any time with no penalty. You generally have a couple of options as to which type of interest rate you choose, variable or fixed. If it's a fixed rate, the payment amount is the same each month for the term of the loan. A variable rate is tied to the bank's prime lending rate. This means that the amount going to principal and interest on a monthly basis could fluctuate with the changes in the prime rate. This is ideal if you believe interest rates are heading downward in the future. (As if anyone really knows …) A term or installment loan has a term that usually ranges from one to five years.

Depending on what you're purchasing, your loan may be secured or unsecured. My bill consolidation loan, for example, was unsecured because I didn't have to offer up any collateral. This type is generally for things like an orthodontist's bill or a computer purchase.

My first car, however, was bought with a loan that used the car as security. This means that if I failed to make the payments the lender could come stealthily in the dead of night and whisk the car away. (They don't really do this anymore. They call first.) That's why a car loan is a good way to establish a credit rating. What you're actually purchasing becomes the collateral, therefore giving the bank some measure of security. This item is called a chattel. When I bought my car the bank had me sign a chattel mortgage—an intimidating term that simply means that my car secured the loan. Chattel also means asset. For example, let's say you wanted to renovate the old homestead (jokingly referred to by those who've survived the experience as the second leading cause of divorce). You could secure a personal loan with the equity that's been built up in your home up to a maximum of 75 percent of the appraised value. The difference between what the property is worth and what's owed is your equity. In this case, a legal document called a collateral mortgage is required. This way you're not locked into a conventional mortgage and you have the freedom to pay it off anytime without penalty. You also don't have to renew an existing mortgage. Secured personal loans will generally receive lower interest rates than unsecured loans. Residential mortgage loans are actually a form of installment credit. They'll be dealt with in detail in a later chapter.

Overdraft protection

Many people confuse overdraft protection with a personal line of credit, but they're completely different animals. Overdraft protection is for those of us who are mathematically challenged and bounce cheques, which is a godsend to many when you consider that a bounced cheque these days can cost you anywhere from $20 and up. And there's nothing quite like that sinking feeling and rising embarrassment that comes from those three terrible letters of the alphabet: NSF. Overdraft protection is a way to avoid this. It simply means that you've arranged to have your bank automatically cover you up to an agreed amount above what you have in your account, usually up to a maximum of $5,000. Say you've got a balance of $1,000 and a $1,500 overdraft protection in place. Let's assume for demonstration purposes that you temporarily take complete leave of your senses and mistakenly (?!) write a cheque for $2,200. The bank will pay out your $1,000 and make up the remaining $1,200 from its own funds so that your cheque clears. Most overdraft protection plans will also cover you if you exceed your balance when making withdrawals through banking machines or when using a debit card.

There are two costs to watch for with overdraft protection. Many financial institutions levy a fixed monthly fee, sort of like an insurance premium. You'll be charged a dollar or two each and every month, regardless of whether or not your financial institution ever has to cover you. If it has to put up some money to cover a withdrawal that's larger than your balance, you'll have to pay interest on that amount as well. The rate charged when your bank or trust company has to cover you is usually steep—often above the rate charged on credit card balances. You're likely looking at somewhere around 20 percent to 22 percent. Not all banks, however, apply a huge levy to the service: Scotiabank has no monthly fee and charges interest at prime plus 5 percent. The bank's minimum charge is five dollars for any month in which you use the service (if interest is less than five dollars). Generally, you have to replace the overdraft amount within a few months. Technically, you don't have to make regular payments, but the banks do want to see a positive balance in your account at least once a month. Any deposits you make will automatically go toward reducing your debt to zero. Only when the debt is gone can you start building up a positive balance.

Overdraft protection is a useful tool when it comes to keeping your dignity if you bounce a cheque once in a while, but it's strictly a short-term solution. If you find yourself using it constantly, or find that you never hit a positive balance, it's time to do some soul searching. You may be standing precariously on the edge of a credit cliff.

After my credit was re-established my next step was getting overdraft protection. Although I had many financial faults, bouncing cheques wasn't one of them. Even so, this type of protection can give you a certain peace of mind in the event that the uncertain becomes certain. You apply for this as you would any form of credit.

Personal line of credit (PLC)

I believe this to be a wonderful invention, provided it's managed properly. It's not for those who can be enticed by easy access to ready cash. PLCs had traditionally been reserved for the wealthy, but in the '80s the banks began to market them aggressively. This form of credit can be the best financial friend you've ever had. Without mine I'd never have been able to take a year off to write the first edition of this book, and my company would still be a mere gleam in my eye. But, as some people do discover, PLCs will talk about you behind your back.

First, a primer. A PLC is a pot of money that sits at permanent attention, patiently waiting for you to tap into it. You can scoop out any amount you want, up to the maximum that you've negotiated with your financial institution. Let's say you have a $5,000 credit line. Once it's set up, the $5,000 is always there for you to use—if and when you need it. It's there when daughter number one backs into the garage door and you need to come up with $1,000 to repair it. You then repay the money when your paycheque comes in. Later you can borrow, say, $2,000 to upgrade the bathroom, which became necessary after son number two stuffed eight action figures into the toilet. Most financial institutions give you access through a chequebook or through their automated tellers and online banking. When you need to borrow money, it's as simple as writing a cheque or punching a few buttons.

If you never touch your PLC, you won't pay a dime of interest. But if you do, the interest rate you pay is variable, which means it will follow whatever the general interest rates are doing. PLC interest rates can fall way below credit card rates, depending on the variety of PLC you use. PLCs are both secured and unsecured. If you have assets like stocks, bonds, or GICs, you can put them up as security and get a better interest rate, usually around the lender's prime rate. You can also use some of the paid-off portion of your home as security to get what's called a home equity line of credit. You'll usually pay two or three percentage points above the prime rate if you go the unsecured route.

The big advantage of a PLC is that it's credit for life. Once you have it you don't have to go back and renegotiate and reapply every time you need something, whether it be an RRSP, your child's education, a car, or home renovations. As you go through the cycle of life, a PLC can grow to accommodate your borrowing requirements. (However, they may be reviewed every one or two years and you must provide up-to-date information. If the bank sees that you're having difficulty making payments or getting the balance down, it can convert your PLC to a term loan.)

That's why PLCs are for grownups only. There are as many uses for a PLC as there are people who use them. For example, technically you should have an emergency fund equivalent to three to six months' salary set aside in something liquid and accessible. This means that you have to use savings accounts and money market funds, and unfortunately they're at the lowest end of the interest rate scale. That's a tidy sum of cash to have tied up in something that earns next to nothing. Having a PLC can free up that money to be invested in something else that gives you a decent return. But here's a red flag: if you have children, own a home, and work in a volatile industry, using a PLC as an emergency fund could be dangerous. Having three to six months' salary put aside is essential. Not easy, but essential.

The financially sophisticated often use PLCs to invest. If you know what you're doing, having money to buy different investments when market conditions are ripe can be smart. The interest is even tax deductible when you borrow to invest. But all experts agree that this can seriously backfire and is absolutely *not* for the weak of heart.

Though still considered an "upmarket" product, PLCs are becoming more popular. But is that because banks push PLCs? Only to the right customer. The bank saves money as well because, compared to other loans, a PLC is set up only once and pretty much services the customer for life.

Strangely enough, income isn't the critical factor in determining whether or not you can get a PLC. It's your total debt service ratio—how much you owe in relation to what you make—that's key. PLCs are riskier because it's you, not the financial institution, who decides how much money to borrow and when it gets paid back. Run-of-the-mill loans have a fixed payment schedule, but PLCs don't, though in some cases banks can establish a payment schedule to suit your needs.

Sound perfect? Possibly. But remember that debt is the only thing that we can accumulate without money. Before you read another word, stop and ask yourself, "Am I credit-savvy?" If there's even the slightest hesitation in your answer, forget about this option. If you're peering over the precipice of credit hell, a PLC will get you there by jet, assuming that you can even get one. Duke Stregger, president of my old alma mater the Credit Counselling Service of Toronto, says, "PLCs are a great invention, but you need to have a plan when using them. PLCs are excellent for monthly shortfalls, as long as you can pay it back immediately. But using them to continually subsidize income can be a sign of serious trouble. It starts with running out of money on the 20th of the month and needing money just to pay rent. You have the intention to pay it all back next payday. But something else always comes up. And it begins to snowball. Know exactly how and how long it will take to pay it back."

This has a familiar ring to it. Although my PLC was an incredible tool at my disposal, it still took me five years to bring the balance back down to zero. That something-always-crops-up syndrome is particularly prevalent in a small business.

But people who qualify for PLCs tend to be responsible. Royal Bank research shows that Canadians are very conservative when it comes to borrowing. Abusing credit isn't part of the archetype of the Canadian customer, and in fact very few Canadians take advantage of home equity PLCs because they don't want to run any risk of losing their homes. But while this may be true on a macro level, North Americans are carrying more debt than we ever have in recorded history.

To figure out whether or not you're headed for trouble, Mr. Stregger offers this advice: the first time you find yourself using your PLC, ask yourself, "Why did I use it? Was it a planned purchase or was it a reaction to a situation?" The answer will tip you off to your tendencies. So the question isn't whether a PLC is a good or bad idea, but rather whether you personally can handle the financial freedom it gives you. As Woodrow Wilson once said, the way to stop financial joyriding is to arrest the chauffeur, not the automobile.

At the end of the day, when you balance the pros and cons PLCs are a pretty good bet. But it doesn't hurt to remember that credit is like a mirror. Once sullied by a breath, it may be wiped clear again but once cracked can never be repaired.

Putting you in charge with credit cards

Thinking about replacing that cool white suit you bought while Trudeau was prime minister? If you're anything like I was, that three-by-two-inch piece of plastic makes updating and expanding your wardrobe fast and easy. In the late '90s, Decima Research did a survey that showed that convenience is the number one reason Canadians use credit cards. It's also ironic to note that, according to Laurie Campbell of Credit Counselling Service of Toronto, 90 percent of purchases made on credit cards are impulse purchases, which is probably why you own that frightening white suit in the first place. But, as I and thousands of others have had to learn, plastic must be treated as respectfully as you would a thousand-dollar bill. Credit cards are a financial tool that puts tremendous buying power into your hands.

The kind of power we'd like from credit cards comes from knowing how to use them properly. Of course, the wise and responsible use of credit cards should be as commonplace as brushing our teeth twice a day. When we neglect either, the consequences aren't pleasant. Despite this, and even though credit affects every aspect of our lives, we don't know nearly enough about it. Decima's study showed a wide discrepancy between what consumers think they know and what they actually know.

Using credit is borrowing money and it's a privilege you earn, not a consumer right. Credit and charge cards are the most popular, most convenient, most abused, and least understood form of credit. According to both the Ministry of Corporate Affairs and Industry Canada, there are an estimated 54 million credit cards in circulation in Canada, which works out to 2.3 cards for everyone over 18 in this country. Of these, 49.4 million cards are from Visa or Mastercard, and 19 million are from department stores, gas companies, and other issuers like American Express and Diners Club/enRoute. In 2002, the accumulated outstanding balance on Mastercard and Visa was a staggering $43.99 billion, up from $23.9 billion in 1998. The average size of transaction went up to $100.51 from $90.00 in 1998. The Canadian Bankers Association says that only 58 percent of cardholders pay off their Visa and Mastercard balances each month. Sixty percent pay off their retail cards in full monthly.

This is a very big business. I used to contribute significantly by not paying off my balances in full every month. Banks have received enough interest from me to build my own gold-plated automated teller in my front hall that passes me a martini as I come home from a long day at work. Today, exactly on the due date, I pay the bill through Internet banking. (Be careful, though. Interbank and some internal bank payments are not received on the same day, so you risk being "late" if you input the transaction on exactly the due date.) This way I earn interest on my money right up to the last minute, and avoid paying any interest costs. I've saved hundreds of dollars each year by managing my cards properly. I discovered through my own painful experience that you never put anything on a credit card that you don't have the money for in the bank or expect to have by the end of the month.

Credit and charge cards are for convenience. Period. Full stop. They're a way to get free money for 21 days. They are, however, the most expensive way to finance purchases if you don't pay off the balance each month. If you find that you're consistently carrying balances from month to month, explore a less expensive form of credit, like a personal bank loan or line of credit. I didn't bother because I assumed that the interest rate was no big deal. I didn't do the math until it was too late. The average interest rate on charge cards is in the stratosphere of 24 percent. Credit card rates vary, but average around 17 percent. PLCs are somewhere between prime to prime plus 3 percent. In today's numbers that looks like 7 to 10 percent. Retail cards charge 28.8 percent interest.

Important vocabulary

It's a little known fact that there's actually a difference between credit cards and charge cards.

Charge cards American Express, gas, and retail cards are examples of charge cards. Because they offer no preset spending limits, they must be paid in full every month. They don't charge interest per se, but they do levy delinquency fees. Charge cards are really designed for short-term credit needs, usually 30 days or less.

Credit cards Credit cards like Visa and Mastercard represent revolving credit and require minimum monthly payments. They're like expensive lines of credit extended to you through a bank or trust company. They allow you to carry a balance as long as a minimum portion of the bill is paid each month. You're charged interest for this benefit, unless, of course, you pay off your balances in full each month.

You can choose from two categories of credit cards. The first is offered by banks, trust companies, credit unions, and other financial institutions. The second is offered by retailers and the oil companies which don't fall into the charge card category. The major difference is that store and gas cards have higher interest rates and fewer features.

Supplementary cards These cards are generally issued to the partner of the principal cardholder. Even though there may be two different names on the card, the responsibility for paying the bill is with the principal cardholder. However, as many women have discovered, the supplementary partner can get dinged for the debt if the cardholder skips out and if the creditor can prove the supplementary cardholder used the card. This kind of card doesn't establish a credit record, since all credit reporting is done in the main cardholder's name; however, it may be done in the name of both parties if they fail to pay the debt.

What are my choices?

It used to be that a credit card was a credit card was a credit card. Choosing the right credit card has become almost as mind-boggling as choosing running shoes these days. In response to the demand for options and added value, companies are introducing a large variety of products to address different consumer needs. But it still comes down to three main categories:

Low-rate cards Some banks now offer low-rate credit cards, but Industry Canada warns consumers to beware because they often have higher annual fees. It's necessary therefore to determine the break-even outstanding balance that makes the higher fee on the low-rate option worthwhile. If your annual balance is low, you're not paying a lot in interest, so interest rates shouldn't matter. Minimizing the annual fee should be your priority. These cards are generally stripped-down versions of standard cards without the added benefit of points programs, and can offer interest rates up to six points below conventional cards.

Have you noticed a lot more direct mail credit card offers these days? Most of them seem to be these low-rate cards. Typically, the cards have special introductory interest rates and spending limits in the tens of thousands of dollars. The offers are generally quite appealing and there's no reason why you shouldn't consider them, but only if you know what you're doing. As always, you've got to do your homework. Make sure the company is legitimate. As soon as you sign on the dotted line, the company becomes a creditor of yours. If you do decide one of these cards is for you, be aware of the fine print. Introductory rates are temporary—they usually shoot up after about six months. Find out what the rates are once that term is over and if there are annual fees or charges for late payments.

But if you have the slightest doubt about controlling your credit cards, forget it. There's no quicker way to descend into credit hell. And if you're considering getting more than one card, think again. Applying for these credit cards, just for the sake of having them, could do more harm than good as far as your credit integrity is concerned. It doesn't matter if you have five credit cards and only use two of them. Remember, every card you get will be etched on your credit history for six years from the date of the last transaction.

Standard cards These cards are offered by financial institutions, carry interest rates in the 16 percent to 18 percent range, and some offer various incentives like points toward travel, entertainment, and merchandise. Cards offered by retailers charge interest rates as high as 28.8 percent.

Premium cards Otherwise known as gold cards, premium cards are enhanced products with a generally higher annual fee and a range of benefits. Features may include higher credit limits, cash back, travel insurance, purchase protection plans, guaranteed hotel reservations, collision insurance on rental cars, health insurance, credit card registry services, and itemized annual spending records. The same incentive programs that are attached to standard cards apply to premium cards as well. Premium cards usually charge from $50 to $150 in annual fees, though if you look, you can find no-fee gold card options available today.

If you travel out of the country, some gold cards provide travel health insurance. It's mandatory that you read the fine print on these benefit plans. On some cards travel insurance is available that will pay a death benefit in the event of an accident. There's also trip cancellation and interruption coverage if someone becomes sick or injured or there's an emergency back home.

On merchandise that you buy, most gold cards offer a 90-day warranty for loss or breakage over and above the regular warranty. I love the commercial one company uses to sell this benefit: a little boy emulates his father as he cheerfully feeds his oatmeal to Daddy's brand-new VCR. The credit card company ensures its replacement.

The premium cards can be an asset if you can justify them because of your business, lifestyle, or income. If you're a heavy but responsible spender (say, $10,000 a year) or a frequent traveller, such a card would likely be worth it for you. Don't fall into the trap of seeing prestige and status as reasons for carrying one of these cards. Everyone eventually will figure out that you are an important person. Because merchants often complain about the cost of honouring American Express, not everyone accepts it. It's wise to carry another card for those circumstances. Also note that if you use credit cards for business, you can write off credit card fees on your income tax. This applies to all fee-based credit cards. Be sure you do this if you qualify.

Secured credit cards There's another little-known, unadvertised option banks offer that's ideal for someone digging out from under a financial mess or who has no credit history. Some banks will allow you to secure your credit card request with a deposit equal to your credit limit. A typical example would be using a $500 Canada Savings Bond, which is left in the hands of the bank, to secure a $500 credit limit. GICs and term deposits are other examples of security. While secured cards are very big in the United States (over 700,000 Americans have one), in Canada they're more of a customer service than a promotable item. Your bank manager is the best person to talk to about this type of credit card. It works like a regular card, and is subject to the same interest charges and potential abuses. If you miss too many payments, wave goodbye to your deposit. But if you're on the road to financial recovery, this is a wonderful way to earn a better credit history. You can negotiate with your bank manager the length of time before the black mark on your credit history is washed away. If the black mark is a bankruptcy, erasing it could take years; most derogatory information will stay in your file at the credit bureau for six years from the date of the last transaction.

The real costs of credit and charge cards

Let's look at the anatomy of a credit card.

How is interest calculated?

It's pretty simple. Cards from financial institutions charge interest on daily outstanding balances. No interest is charged on new purchases if you pay the entire balance by the due date. In most cases, if the balance isn't paid by the due date, interest is charged from the date you made your purchase until the balance is paid in full. In this case, you lose any grace period.

Retailers, on the other hand, tend to charge interest on monthly as opposed to daily balances. In most cases you'll pay less interest if you pay at least half the balance each month.

Let's assume that you don't pay your credit card bill off entirely the first month and the second bill comes in stating that it must be paid by November 15. Interest is still accumulating from the month the bill is issued until the bill is paid, and that interest will show up on the third month's bill even though the balance has been paid off in its entirety. Interest is compounded, so if you miss a payment, the next month you'll pay interest on the balance plus interest. For example, at the current rate of 2.4 percent per month, one month's interest on $100.00 is $2.40. If no payment is made on this at all, the next month's interest will be charged on $102.40 and will amount to $2.47. And so on. Make it your business to know exactly how interest is calculated on the type of card you've chosen.

The other sobering point I learned about credit card interest is how it relates to the power of compounding. Our parents told us about the value of letting money sit and letting compound interest do the work. The rule of 72 states that if you find an investment that will net you a 10 percent rate of return, your money will double every seven years. (According to this rule, you simply divide the number 72 by the annual rate of return, and the result will be the number of years it will take for your money to double.) Compound interest can be your best friend, but watch it. It will turn on you very quickly when it comes to credit cards, since the power of compound interest can work in reverse. To illustrate the point: before most financial institutions decided to waive credit card interest, I paid almost $500 in interest on an outstanding $1,100 Visa bill while I was receiving credit counselling. This is because it took me a period of time to pay the bill off and the interest continued to compound. At 28.8 percent, the interest rate on retail cards means that the store will double *its* money in two and a half years.

If you make only minimum payments each month, you'll be mostly covering the interest, with very little going to the principal. Count on grey hair, stiff joints, and collecting Canada Pension before it actually gets paid off.

Grace periods

The number of days you have on a card before a company starts charging you interest is called a grace period. Usually that period is the number of days between the statement date and the payment due date.

Credit cards from banks, trust companies, and credit unions offer a grace period, which can range from 21 to 26 days. This means that you have three weeks, or a little more, from the statement date (the date when the monthly statement is issued) to pay your balance before you start paying interest. Retail stores and gas companies allow anywhere from 25 days to 30 days to pay. American Express gives you a 30-day grace period. This being said, however, American Express also demands full payment upon receipt of the statement. You can pay up to 30 percent per year on unpaid balances. If the balance remains unpaid, American Express sends the charge card police after you and cancels your privileges. This company needs to be strict because there's no spending limit on this card. It's only for the financially mature.

Be very aware, though, that there are some low-interest cards that have no grace period at all. When you carry balances from month to month, there's likely no grace period for balances carried forward from previous months.

Fees

Watch for annual and administrative fees. Depending on your balance, the fee may end up costing you more than a card with a higher interest rate but no fee. For instance, on an average yearly outstanding balance of $1,500, a card with an interest rate of 13.5 percent with a $60 annual fee ends up costing you the same as a no-fee card at 17.5 percent.

In the recent credit card war some banks have eliminated their annual fee, which actually has the same effect as lowering interest rates. Industry Canada in a recent report shows that dropping a $12 fee is equivalent to a 0.8 percent reduction in interest rate on an outstanding balance of $1,500.

When choosing which type of card you should have, interest rate will be the least of your concerns if you pay in full each due date. If you don't, consider the one with the lowest rate. There are a few new low-interest cards that offer limited services. I do, however, adamantly maintain that this is the worst way of financing your purchases. Most cards have annual fees for the privilege of using them, but there are a few that offer a no-fee setup. These fees are generally to cover administration and transaction costs and can range from $8 to $150 for a platinum American Express card. At the time of writing, Bank of Montreal and National Bank of Canada offer a no-fee basic Mastercard. Some Visa cards now offer this feature as well, including the Scotiabank no-fee Value Visa.

Premium or status cards like gold cards offer an abundance of features, but you pay for them. Some of these features may be worth the expense, however. A particular feature offered on the American Express gold card significantly enhanced my quality of life. Or, I should say, my accountant's. It's work to be financially organized. I've always held that if you can get someone else to do it for you better and more easily than you can do it yourself, then go for it. I detest going through receipts at tax time, trying to figure out how much I spent where and how often with whom. The gold American Express card offers a once-a-year summary that beautifully organizes your annual spending into different categories like education, health care, gas, airline travel, professional services, and so on. It even details the charges for your account. It will also break down the information further and provide a month-by-month analysis of your spending. This service alone justifies the annual $130 in my particular circumstances. I use my credit card for everything and this summary provides an accurate snapshot of the kind of year I've had and of my spending patterns. My accountant was jubilant when I moved to this system. It sure beats the shoe boxes stuffed with tiny folded pieces of paper.

Debit cards: cash or swipe?

Yikes—as Canadians, we sure like our debit cards, to the tune of a mere $104.9 billion in 2002.[2] Whether we use them to pay for a hamburger or an airline ticket, we're the most frequent users of the debit card payment system in the world. When you lump in credit cards, plastic seems to be our preferred method of purchasing. With numbers like these, it's a safe bet that you already know what they are and how they work. But for those of you who've just moved out of your cave, electronic point-of-sale systems allow you to pay for purchases at a store by swiping a card through a handheld device that scoops the money directly out of your bank account. Instantly.

One of the benefits of these cards is that you can walk around relatively cashless. Interac says that cash is predominant in purchases under $25, debit cards for expenditures between $25 and $100, and credit cards reign in the over-$100 range. Having a debit card reduces trips to bank machines, which often have limits as to how much you can take out. And if you use a machine that isn't in your bank network, you're zinged with a larger fee.

But for those who struggle with managing credit cards, a debit card still isn't a foolproof escape into the world of plastic. Technically, you can't spend more than you have, no matter how hard you try. But what you can spend is the money you put aside for rent. You might want to try putting essential funds, like money for rent and utilities, into an account that you can't access with a card.

As for those who pay off their credit card balances every month, the debit card has less appeal. It doesn't offer the "21 days of free money" on the financial institution's dime and it also doesn't help you collect points.

Merchants like the debit card system because there are fewer chances of robberies, less cash handling, and fewer bounced cheques, all of which are very costly. Banks like the Interac system because it reduces the expensive costs of handling paper, i.e., cheques.

Regardless of where you are on the evolutionary scale of credit, the debit card is here to stay and, like any financial tool, works great if one learns how to use it properly.

Managing your cards

I remember doing some Christmas shopping the year I finally got my credit cards back. I discovered a whole new meaning of the term "holiday card," and I don't mean picturesque winter landscapes, Santa, Chanukah candles, and cavorting children. I was standing at a cash register after having just bought a department store's entire toy inventory for my twin nieces. The sales clerk asked me how I'd be paying—a seemingly innocent question, now fraught with previously unimagined possibilities. I became overwhelmed when I innocently asked, "What do you take?" She went on autopilot, rhyming off, "Our store card, American Express, Visa, Mastercard, debit card, cheque, but not without a cheque cashing card." That oddity called cash was conspicuously absent from her litany. It got me to thinking how wild the world of financial convenience has become.

However, as Laurie Campbell of Credit Counselling Service of Toronto pointed out earlier, impulsive spending is a chronic problem. So what's a person to do now that there are 62,000 options? Frankly, exercising self-discipline is the only way to save face in your budget. Gimmicky ideas like freezing your cards in blocks of ice (ever hear of a microwave?) are so lame I won't even consider giving them airtime here. Self-discipline and understanding exactly what each of these cards is designed to do are essential so that you can match them with your spending (and paying-back) behaviour.

Find yourself in one of the following loosely defined categories. It may help you decide which card is best for you.

The chronic "Whoops my credit is maxed on Visa so on to Mastercard" card user Every emotional spike you experience is reason to dust off the cards and go shopping. You buy an alternative rock CD on your credit card because it's on sale. You hate alternative rock. In other words, you're buying stuff on credit you wouldn't go near with cash. You spend more time juggling accounts and bills to accommodate your spending. With any luck, your plastic will melt from overuse.

These card users are still paying for December holiday gifts while sunbathing in August. They use credit cards to support a lifestyle they otherwise couldn't have.

If the above behaviour sounds like you, if you carry a balance or pay only the minimum requirement, rethink using plastic. If you find you still buy CDs with your Visa but then struggle to make your rent, put this book down and cut up your credit cards. Now. If you consistently miss payments without a single pang of guilt, then you're unaware of the damage being done to your credit rating.

These card users should be banished to credit card jail since they're missing the point behind credit cards in the first place. Credit cards provide nothing more than convenience. Credit and charge cards are the most expensive form of borrowing out there. A better option is to pay off your cards with your line of credit if you have one because the interest rates on PLCs are still generally lower than those on low-rate cards. Better yet, borrow from Aunt Ernestine if you're comfortable with love money.

Tucking the cards under the mattress, freezing them in a block of ice, or giving them to a friend isn't an option for this kind of user. Easy accessibility, whether through a microwave or a half nelson, will always waylay the best-made intentions. Credit cards are not an option for you at this point in your life.

Though responsible credit behaviour still needs to be learned, debit cards can be an option. Unfortunately they can still accommodate impulse buyers, but at least you're dealing in no-interest cash. You'll know you're in trouble again when you're spending rent money to buy Uncle Gus a high-tech juicer for Christmas.

The "It's only a little bitty balance, it can't hurt that much" card user If you consistently take a couple of months to pay off balances and carry a balance of $400 a month, low-rate cards are a better bet. The best bet is to get rid of the card completely until you're in a position to get and keep your balance down to zero. Also, if you carry a monthly balance, *do not* use your card more in order to accumulate points.

The "I need to buy this gold-plated weed-wacker to get enough points to fly/buy free" card user I can't believe how many people actually get in over their heads with debt in order to get something "free." To buy something that you don't really need in order to accumulate points to buy more things that you don't really need is grounds for a psychiatric assessment. This "points" thing has become an immense business. Some keen young assistant vice president of marketing must have got her creative juices flowing one morning after her fourth cup of high-test coffee and second chocolate doughnut and decided that the financial institutions needed to expand their horizons. I don't think she realized what a monster she'd created. Look at who the credit card companies have been getting into bed with lately.

The first were the airlines, which allowed customers to earn air mileage points with credit card purchases. Hence the CIBC Aerogold (Air Canada) card. American Express will allow you to choose between airline miles or merchandise. Zellers has the cutest teddy bear that offers points that can be redeemed toward purchases in its store. The Bay does the same thing. The car companies must have felt slighted, so now you can have a GM Visa. Your points go toward up to 5 to 7 percent on the purchase of a new car. If that wasn't enough, a Bank of Montreal Mastercard will help you save up to $3,500 toward a mortgage. (Certain restrictions apply.) What next? I envision a card with a "Moriarty's Funeral Home" logo on the corner that's designed to ensure you're laid to rest in that finely crafted mahogany coffin you so richly deserve.

Consciously accumulating points through credit cards offers the most value to those who pay off balances each month and would be purchasing the goods anyway. But flat out forget it if your cards are gasping for breath. You don't need more incentive to use your already overused cards. Move away from credit cards entirely and tame that impulse monster by going the debit card route.

The "I hate carrying cash and going to the bank 18 times a week" card user The debit card saves you from beating a well-worn path to the bank machines. It's great for those who don't have credit cards and don't like carrying lots of cash around. It's treated the same as your chequing account by your bank. Transaction fees range from 20 to 50 cents but can be waived depending on your balance condition and the type of account you have. If you use a bank machine of a financial institution at which you do not have an account, be prepared to pay up to $1.50 for the privilege.

The "Yikes, I'm short this month but I'll pay it off next month" occasional but responsible credit user If you generally pay off balances in full each month but have been known to occasionally take a couple of months, you can feel comfortable choosing just about any of the card options available. You're in the responsible range.

The "I pay off credit cards on pain of death every month because the interest rates are so obnoxious" card user This is the credit puritan category. You pay off your cards each month, no exceptions. Your best option: any card at all, but in particular the value-added ones. Your financial discipline means you're getting the financial institution to finance your purchases for 21 days. And with a value-added card, you'll also be earning points for trips and gifts. This is a great bonus, especially if you were planning to purchase the goods and services anyway.

To choose the right rewards program, consider the following:

- Evaluate your lifestyle and figure out what you're after. A free trip to Istanbul, a dinner out, or a toaster oven?
- Compare program fees and value. You don't get anything for free. To be sure the incentive program works for you, do the math. Consider the annual fee against the reward you might qualify for.
- Evaluate what type of spender you are. Reward or incentive programs only work if you spend money. If you spend more than $250 a month, they're a good bet.
- Whatever program you choose, stick with it so that you can rack up the points faster.

Once you figure out what category you're in, take immediate action if required. If you're in the first three categories, here are some tips on managing your impulse buying:

- (I really like this one.) Subtract credit card purchases from your chequing account balance when you make them rather than when the bill comes in. You'll be less apt to overspend that way.
- I have a friend who curbs his impulse spending by writing down the five last completely useless purchases he made with his card and wrapping the list around it. Instant reminder.

- If the situation is really bad, get help. Go to a credit counselling service or even a therapist. This kind of complex behaviour has its roots in so many different places, it may take years to get to the crux of the real problem.

Bad debt and good debt

Encouraged by interest rates that are near historic lows, Canadians have taken on record amounts of debt in credit card purchases and the refinancing of real estate. The debt-to-income ratio of Canadians hit a record high of almost 103 percent in the year ended April 2003. A report from CIBC World Markets said Canadians are borrowing more than they earn. They increased the amount owed on credit cards by 14 percent in that year, to a total of $43.8 billion. If each of Canada's 31.9 million residents carried a credit card, that debt would amount to $1,373 per person, but the actual figure per person is much higher.

But borrowing isn't necessarily a financial sin. Ignoring the 52 gazillion that went bust, consider that software developer who got his friends and family to lend him money so that he could bring his latest program to market. Ten years later, he's a billionaire. The point is that there are both good and bad kinds of debts. Do you know when it's financially wise to take out a loan, and when you should "just say no" to an offer of credit?

One easy way to recognize good debt is to apply this basic principle: borrow money if it's going to be used to buy things that go up in value. One of the most common uses of good debt is to buy a home. As well as a place to live, housing values have traditionally risen over time. Very few people can afford to pay cash for their home, so this form of debt is quite acceptable, although the interest isn't tax deductible. Using borrowed funds to start or buy a business is another example of a good debt. Just ask Bill Gates.

Student loans can also be a financially responsible move because they advance your station in life. By going to university or college, you not only become a more interesting person to talk to at dinner parties, but your value in the job market goes up.

There are RRSP loans that should be used if you find yourself short and can't make your contribution. The interest on these isn't tax deductible, but they're often available at prime. The math shows that you're further ahead having a loan (which should be paid off in 12 months) and an RRSP than no loan and no RRSP. I'll discuss this in more detail in a later chapter.

There's also investment debt which, if used carefully, can be advantageous. Let's say I borrow $10,000 (like from my PLC as described earlier) to buy a mutual fund. The interest on this loan is tax deductible. Our government likes it when we invest in ourselves, so it gives us a bit of a break. This type of investment debt is also called leveraging. One must be very cautious in using it. Leveraging was responsible for wiping out many people in the '80s; they borrowed and used other people's money to invest in everything from investment real estate to the stock market. When everything crashed, these people not only lost their own money, but were still responsible for the money they had borrowed.

Make sure the investment you choose will earn higher interest than the interest you're paying on the loan. It doesn't make sense to be earning 5 percent on a GIC when you're paying 8 percent on the loan to buy it, even with the deductible interest.

Something to keep in mind about investment debt is that if owing money keeps you awake at night, forget it. Save this method of investing until after you've built your financial base and have successfully accumulated your first million. The most important thing is securing your financial foundation, and leveraging is not foundation material.

Borrowing money to buy things that depreciate is bad debt (like, unfortunately, borrowing to buy a car). Now, a car loan is often the only way people can buy a vehicle, and unfortunately for our pocketbooks as well as the environment, having a vehicle is often a necessity. But that still doesn't make it good. Things like credit card interest, loans for other consumer items like furniture and vacations, and, frankly, anything that's consumable are all bad debt.

That's why you should pay off your non-deductible debt before investing your money. Or at least make sure your debt is manageable before you start. A good way to do that is what I ended up eventually doing: consolidating your debts with an appropriate loan from your bank that has a significantly lower interest rate than credit cards and other forms of credit. What you save in interest payments alone could be enough to start a savings program. All you need is $25 a month in a preauthorized contribution program to start most types of investments.

If you want some motivation to minimize bad debt, think of it this way. If you cut down on your bad debt, you'll actually be able to make many more enjoyable purchases over your lifetime. The money you'll save on financing charges can easily add up to several thousand dollars in a few years. That may mean postponing purchases until you actually have the money. It's an awesome concept, isn't it? Like my mother says though, running into debt isn't so bad. It's running into creditors that hurts.

But the reality for many of us is that if we wait until we pay off our debts before we start to save, we'll be buying our first mutual fund out of the death benefit of our life insurance policy. Use common sense when determining your ratio of debt versus savings. Much will depend on your lifestyle and weekly paycheque.

Every financial advisor on the planet will tell you to avoid consumer debt at all costs. It's solid advice. However, I'd like you to do an informal survey of people you know and tabulate all who are completely free of consumer debt. Out of a hundred, there may be three. This is a very "I want and deserve it now" society, with little encouragement for waiting until you have the cash to do "it," whatever "it" might be. I think back to my grandmother's and mother's generations. Life was radically different. What did these people do without credit cards, lines of credit, overdraft protection, and "Don't Pay a Cent" events? They saved their money until they had enough to pay cash for what they wanted. My mother recalls the story of her grandfather pinning a huge wad of cash to his flannel shirt pocket when he went into town to buy a new tractor. A little hint: save for your purchase until you have enough to buy it outright. Then buy it with your credit card and pay the card off in full on the due date. That way you earn interest for an extra 21 to 30 days and you don't have to pay any credit card interest, providing your full payment is made by the due date.

Women and credit

Up until the mid '70s women were often turned down for credit simply because they were women. It was assumed that women earned so little of their own money that it was commonplace for banks to require that they have a male co-signer. Nowadays it's illegal to discriminate on the basis of gender, marital status, race, religion, or age. There have been general improvements in financial institutions, especially in their awareness levels, but women feel they are still fighting for fair and equitable treatment. Blatant sexual discrimination against women has stopped, but as I personally discovered, more subtle bias still occurs. In other words, it's gone underground.

The following is a story that acutely illustrates this bias.

I went to my bank, armed with a comprehensive business plan, to ask for a business line of credit. I assumed it wasn't going to be easy because, like most women, I had no hard assets except for the one between my ears. Because my ideas were good and my business plan was solid, the bank approved my request in no time. I was greatly heartened. A couple of days later I was in my account manager's office to clean up the paperwork. While my banker, Kathrine, and I were going over the papers, the credit risk manager who actually approved our request walked by. Kathrine called him over so he could put a face to a name. I'll call him Chester to protect the guilty. The exchange went like this:

"Chester," Kathrine began. "This is Joanne Thomas Yaccato, one of the bank's newest customers."

Chester stuck out his hand and said, "Terrific to meet you, Joanne."

I said, "Chester, I'd like to thank you for your vote of confidence in our endeavour. I realize you had to go out on a limb to approve us and I'd like you to know I really appreciate that."

Chester didn't miss a beat. "No problem. You know, that's quite a nice little hobby you got going for yourself there."

I heard a small gasp escape from Kathrine.

Hobby?!

This was one of the few times in my life I've been rendered speechless. Chester left and Kathrine began a litany of apologies on his behalf. You've heard it before, the "white, middle-aged man who doesn't know better" argument. What this incident proved to me was that discrimination wasn't the problem. What does exist, and does so in spades, is gender bias. My request for credit was approved—no discrimination—but the comment referring to my business as a "hobby" clearly showed a powerful gender bias. You can rest assured that if it were a man with the same business, he never would have heard a demeaning comment like that one.

Everything crystallized for me at that moment. I decided to talk to Chester and discuss what had happened. I wanted him to understand how patronized I felt. Certainly Chester hadn't *intended* to insult me. He didn't have a clue that he had. Gender bias isn't some nasty overt prejudice, because in the vast majority of cases, it's unconscious. A couple of weeks later, when I had suitably recovered from the shock of Chester's comment, we met. He was the most pleasant person. I got quickly to the point. I repeated the conversation verbatim and watched the look of horror spread across his face. "I actually said hobby?!" he asked incredulously. Kathrine was there to verify it. I nodded my head. As he had daughters of his own, Chester was appalled and suitably regretful.

I told him that I wanted to educate bankers that this stuff goes on all the time and in 99 percent of the cases it's done unconsciously. To illustrate the point that people don't understand each other's reality, I gave Chester a little quiz.

I asked him, "Chester, tell me who said this, a man or a woman: I was wondering if I could possibly get a loan for new computers?"

With no hesitation, he said "A woman."

"Why?" I queried.

"I was wondering, if I could possibly—those are things a woman would say."

I continued, "What about this: I need an operating line for $50,000."

He started to laugh as he said, "Definitely a man."

"Why?" I asked.

Chester said, "He's direct and assumes he's going to get the money."

I probed a little further. "So the first style is indirect?" I asked him.

"Absolutely," he said.

Pushing him a little further, I said, "How does that style sound to you?"

He thought briefly, then replied, "To be honest, it sounds hesitant, tentative, not very confident. Actually, it sounds pretty weak."

Bingo. I had him. "Would you agree that many women speak in that style?" I asked.

"For sure," he said. "My wife and daughters, to name a few."

This was going exactly where I knew it would go. "Okay, Chester, what percentage of the credit granting process is based on gut feel or subjective evaluation of the person asking for money?"

He was surprised by my question. "A lot," he exclaimed. "For a business loan, anywhere from 30 to 50 percent of an account manager's decision is based on gut feel. Maybe a little less for personal loans."

Feeling a home run just around the corner, I asked him, "Do you think tentative, hesitant, and lacking in confidence are character traits that bankers look for when deciding to lend someone money, especially to an entrepreneur?"

The light went on. Chester smiled. He knew he'd been had. "Absolutely not."

I said, "Do you think you can put lacking in confidence and entrepreneur in the same sentence?"

He said, good-naturedly, "I'm seeing your point."

I went in for the kill. "Is it possible, Chester, that bankers confuse a conversation style with a character trait?"

Rather sheepishly, he said yes.

I went on to say, "I invite you to consider that most women do not lack confidence and are in no way tentative. Many have a communication style that is based on *politeness,* not weakness. Chester, did you know that women entrepreneurs report being taken seriously as their greatest challenge as business owners? Would you consider this an unconscious bias and could it have an effect on granting credit if the banker wasn't aware of it?"

"Quite possibly, Joanne," Chester said, resigned.

Maybe Chester fell into that category of truly not knowing better. In fact, I wouldn't be surprised if there was a large percentage of men who are exactly like Chester and only need to be told what the boundaries are. People are confused as to what the rules are today. Perhaps, if they're addressed with tact and a touch of humour, many of the biases will disappear gradually if the offending person knows they're out of bounds. If they aren't told, how can their behaviour change? Chester's eyes are so wide open now, I can guarantee you his daughters will benefit greatly from his new insight. Since then, Chester and I have grown to respect each other immensely. He even sends me cartoons from the paper that are relevant to gender difference.

I've read the literature from all the chartered banks in Canada, and they all make it very clear that they don't discriminate on the basis of gender. I absolutely believe they believe this. In fact, for the most part it's probably true. It's actually in writing that they treat everyone the same. But there's failed logic here. The ability to access credit is generally based on "who earns the most wins," meaning the more income and assets, the better the chance of getting credit. This policy doesn't help women who've worked unpaid in the home raising families and who have no money of their own. It doesn't help women whose credit history has always been attached to their partners'. It doesn't allow for the sociological realities that still create a gender wage gap. Women still earn on average two-thirds of what men earn. It ignores women's severe time poverty. Women entrepreneurs earn 70 percent of what male entrepreneurs earn because they (as most women) are responsible for the lion's share of child and home care. It doesn't acknowledge that women make up the vast majority of the part-time labour force, and that the majority of those women want full-time work but can't find any. It doesn't acknowledge that women entrepreneurs can't obtain any maternity benefits because self-employed people can't contribute to Employment Insurance, which happens to be where maternity benefits come from. This policy doesn't deal with the glass ceiling, which means that women have a harder time getting to the big bucks. It doesn't acknowledge the effect of women's different communication styles, as illustrated in the Chester example, or even their different attitudes toward money. Most women hate debt. There's plenty of research to show that women are an excellent risk for banks because *they pay the money back*. Take a look at third world micro-lending projects specifically in place to help women. Seventy percent of those women are still in business and 95 percent of the money has been paid back.

In other words, historically, and still to some extent today, credit-lending policies are based on a traditional male model that assumes there is a level playing field and that everyone is a mawg (middle-aged white guy) or married to one.

Bankers' views

We spoke with some bankers to get their views on how the world of banking has changed. How come women still feel discriminated against?

Jennifer Tory, senior vice president at Royal Bank, says that women resent banks in large part because they were always asked to have a co-signer when they came to borrow money. "The reasons bankers did this was due to the Family Law Act of Ontario; specifically, that the assets in a marriage would be divided 50/50 in the event of a marriage breakdown. This was the reason banks looked for co-signers from spouses. Unfortunately, some bankers thought this was a 'black and white' issue and didn't look at the business first. More often than not, women were not being looked at on their own merits but strictly as a 'spouse of ...' On the small-business side, people's perceptions of a woman's business was as more of a hobby. More credibility was needed to attach to women's businesses by the bank.

"To address these erroneous perceptions, Royal Bank has been delivering training courses to small-business account managers. The training was key, not only to show statistics about the women's market, but also to show that perceptions are wrong and needed to change. Employees went through awareness training to show that how they communicate can affect women's perceptions. The change has been dramatic, but there's still a long way to go. We need to have focus groups with clients to ensure they were treated the way they should be to eliminate any negative perceptions."

Alberta G. Cefis, executive vice president, Retail Lending Services at Scotiabank, offered this point of view: "When I think back at how things were done some 24 years ago, there was a disconnect between women and financial services ... for example, in terms of what security documents were required, in how processes and forms were designed ... there was little understanding or targeting of the women's market. Financial institutions were run by men, and their views shaped the culture and the customer offerings. The men had the power ... in the branches, in credit, in management, and the executive ranks ... and, their customers were other men. At the time, about 75 percent of the banks' staff consisted of women, but most were concentrated in the ranks of tellers and secretaries ... the pink ghetto. With the forceful advancement of the women's movement, which revolutionized the economy and spilled over into the business world, fundamental changes to the social fabric evolved. For example, there were now independent single working women, and divorced women; women were setting up their own bank accounts; women had cash to invest; women were applying for loans on their own without a spouse; women were buying homes; women were both suppliers and users of capital. They forced the transformation of many businesses, including the financial services sector. With women's increasing participation in the workforce and their growing economic independence, they became increasingly important customers for a broad array of financial services. Their level of sophistication in financial decision-making has continued to grow. The banks had to adjust to the changes in the marketplace in order to take advantage of the many opportunities these changes provided. While gender bias might not be completely rooted out, it's more the exception than the rule. Women are now well represented in the managerial and senior banking ranks; there are now as many or more female personal bankers in branches as there are men; similarly, the ranks of female small business account managers have continued to swell, reflecting the growing female entrepreneurial population of the clients they serve. The women's market is powerful because women have financial prowess and are typically the key decision makers in most purchasing decisions, for example, for durables, cars, vacations, homes, and education."

I wanted a man's perspective as well, so I went to Charlie Coffey, executive vice president at Royal Bank. I was blunt. I asked him, "How come women still feel discriminated against? What can women do about this?" This is what he had to say:

"Discrimination is an age-old issue that exists in every woman's life. How many times have we heard the story about the woman stymied in her career—trying to break through the glass ceiling—compared to her male counterpart? What about the corporation that has yet to appoint women to its board of directors? Or the banker who believes a woman's home-based business is a diversion rather than an export hub?

"Although much progress has been made over the years, the attitude, the behaviour, the approach—the discrimination—still surfaces from time to time. Is the solution to hire more women as managers, headhunters, or executive bankers? Not entirely. The solution lies in choosing the balance of power. Grab the power at home, in the workplace, in the community, and yes, at the bank. Grab the power through credibility, creativity, and confidence. When you visit your bank to discuss starting a new venture or to get a mortgage, use the three C's to strike the power balance:

- *Credibility* (credit-ability) differentiates your business or credit plan from others.
- *Creativity* fosters relationship-building—cooperative communication (words/body language) helps you to understand and educate.
- *Confidence* in yourself reflects everything that's not in the business plan. It's your style, presentation, approach, attitude—your predisposition to persevere and succeed.

"No matter what you're negotiating, whether it be a mortgage or a car loan, the same principles apply. If you're treated unfairly or are uncomfortable with a situation/individual, use the power of the three C's: speak up, write a letter, send an e-mail … or walk across the street to another financial institution with your business, product/service, or idea.

"It's a man's world. There are gender-specific barriers for women. So strike the balance, as the power of credibility, creativity, confidence … and the power of women, is here to stay." Charlie concludes, "Just ask Chester."

Both Charlie and Alberta were in total agreement and went further to say, "The next market that needs to be understood and supported is the gay and lesbian market."

Good point. What about same-sex couples? I asked Denise Araiche, our banker friend, to talk about her experience in this area.

"Today, when we ask a woman her marital status, bankers need to be prepared for anything. As soon as we ask, 'Are you married?' we can get a simple 'yes,' or 'yes, in a common-law relationship,' or 'yes, I have a wife,' which renders most bankers completely silent. Bankers are often conservative and mainstream. They get embarrassed over sexual terminology or drawn-out detail, let alone flagrant sexuality. Don't even go there if it's the same sex. But as bankers we need to know marital status for loan guarantor or net worth purposes. If only one person comes in, often you have to guess. If two people come in who are the same sex and they're around the same age, we get it. If one is older and one much younger, we get into the 'is it Mom and daughter?' If they call ahead and say they're bringing in their partner, it's easy.

"Another tough question is asking where your spouse is employed. Karen went in for a car loan. The banker smiled and started to fill out the form. 'Okay, Karen—are you married?' Karen says yes. 'Where is your husband employed?' Karen hesitates, because she thinks, 'Oh great, here I go again.' Karen states, 'My partner is employed at Home Depot as manager.' The banker writes it down, totally missing the fact that Karen was trying to tell her something, and plods on. 'Okay, what's your husband's name?' Karen stares at the banker and feels so uncomfortable and indignant that she wants to leave. But she thinks there's someone who needs to be hit with the facts of life. She calmly says, 'Melanie Smith.' The banker looks up and says, 'Your husband is named Melanie???? Is it like that football player Lynn Swann?' Karen just stares. The banker knows she's made a mistake and has no idea how to correct it. She knows she's too late. Karen stands up because she's leaving. 'No, I'm a lesbian, my partner is another woman. I'll go get a loan from somewhere where they make me feel like a part of society.'"

It's a different world out there.

The importance of a credit rating

It's essential that women have their own credit rating. As the experts warn, 90 percent will be on their own and looking after their own affairs, frequently through divorce or death of a partner. Women live longer than men, so they will most assuredly be looking after their money at some point. Also, more and more women are staying single. The message here is, why wait until catastrophe hits? Become proactive instead of reactive.

Women who become divorced or widowed often find themselves in a terrible bind when they realize they can't get credit. I've seen too many women destroyed emotionally and financially because they left the financial matters to their spouse. A friend of mine suddenly became a widow at 49. She had worked in the home raising the family for over 20 years and was totally dependent on her spouse for everything. When he was killed in an accident this woman didn't know how much money they had, had never opened a bank account, and didn't even have a driver's licence. Her husband had set up charge accounts for her at a taxi company, drugstore, and the local grocer. Though she paid these bills out of her housekeeping allowance, her money management skills never progressed beyond that point. She was denied credit because everything had been in her husband's name. She went by Mrs. John Doe, not even Mrs. Jane Doe. As a credit entity, she didn't exist. It was only after repeatedly imploring the bank to give her a credit card because of the gravity of her situation that they finally relented. But they did so only because there was money coming in from the sale of the house. It was her first credit card. She was given a $500 limit. It was under these circumstances that she was forced to learn about financial planning.

You may think this is an extreme case, and it is. But it's not unique. I know this only too well because I lived it. More specifically, my mother did. Before I leave the subject of credit, you need to hear my mother's story. Hopefully you'll be left with the sense that "there but for the grace of God go I."

My mother's story

My mother hails from an era when women married their financial plans. Mom worked in the home and was dependent on my father for her money. When we were young she did work on occasion, selling Beauty Counsellor cosmetics and Sarah Coventry jewellery through home parties. But this was only when Dad could babysit. These occasions were always squeezed in around her primary job, which was raising us kids and maintaining the household. Like any woman who chose to work at home, my mother received no pay, benefits, security, or pension. Dad represented all those things for her. This was the accepted norm for that generation. Dad was busy climbing the corporate ladder to success, hypertension, and ulcers. He also had the responsibility of providing financially for a wife and three children. He left the running of the home and the childcare completely to my mother, as his father had done, and his grandfather, and so on in perpetuity. My mother wouldn't have had it any other way, even if there were other options.

I consider my mother to be the eighth wonder of the world. She managed the household finances and could turn a loonie into a $10 bill. My dad, on the other hand, was remarkably adept at turning a $10 bill into a loonie. He always said that anything we had was a direct result of my mother's financial acumen. My father has always been a wonderfully generous man and loves to spend money. That is, after all, what it was invented for. Mom, on the other hand, was more frugal in order to balance her partner. It's evident who my role model was in the early years. If it were a choice between Mom's "bring a lunch and save a little over time" or Dad's "put that stereo on credit and worry about paying for it when the bill comes in," Dad's way won hands down.

Like myself, my father always managed to make a very good living, but never kept any of the money. In 1976, while living on the East Coast, my father received an excellent job offer with a significant salary increase that he couldn't turn down. Around the same time my parents bought a new home and completely decorated it with new furniture. My mother co-signed the loan for a part of the down payment. The house was in my father's name only, which was not unusual at that time. It never occurred to my mother that it should be any other way. This turned out to be a blessing. Dad's salary had increased, but the debt load was increasing disproportionately. Credit cards were my father's nemesis. Again, it seems I came by my affliction honestly. Then the worst happened. The '70s recession was especially pronounced in the Maritimes. Shortly after we moved into our new house, my father was laid off from his new job.

Lay-offs were happening at a fearful rate and the financial institutions were experiencing critically high loan default rates. The bank turned on my mother with a vengeance that can only be described as brutal. It was simple. She'd co-signed; she was now liable for the debt. She received threatening phone calls at all hours. She was terrified. It was a horrible experience for someone who took debt very seriously and managed what money she did have brilliantly. Like most women of her generation, my mother was raised to "listen to your husband because he'll take care of you." Her wedding vows included "love, honour, and obey." She let Dad manage the money even though he was terrible at it.

To keep the bank at bay, my mother worked double shifts at a department store cosmetic counter to try to keep up with the payments. She was paid minimum wage. When I think back to this time, I remember her always rushing and being chronically exhausted. I don't think I ever saw her taking time to read a book or sit still for more than a moment. There was still the laundry to do, meals to plan and prepare, the house to clean and so on. I pitched in as much as any teenager would. Ashamedly, that wasn't too much. But I was going to school and worked part-time at the mall so I wasn't around a lot. When my mother took on those double shifts, her responsibilities at home didn't change. That's when I remember her beginning to age.

It wasn't long before my parents realized they couldn't keep up the payments on everything. Dad had found a job that paid commission, but with the recession there was no income to speak of coming in. My mother carried the debt for a few months, until the end of the school year, but my father was finally forced to file for personal bankruptcy. My family then moved to begin a new life in Ontario. But even then the bank harassed my mother long distance. It finally ended when my mother lost her legendary Thomas temper with an unsuspecting representative from the bank who had just taken over my parents' case. They never called back.

The ramifications of this experience were tremendous. Children are resilient, but I didn't escape unscathed. One afternoon my boyfriend and I were walking home from high school. As we rounded the corner, we saw strange men loading my bedroom furniture into a truck. Everything had been repossessed. I stood there in complete shock, the tears streaming helplessly down my face. I was shaking in disbelief. My parents had told us this was going to happen, but actually seeing it was too painful to bear. Chris put his arm around my shoulders, wheeled me around and started walking quickly in the opposite direction. At that moment I felt a physical sensation that can only be described as "shutting down." My cavalier "here today, gone tomorrow" attitude toward money solidified.

But our possessions were just things. The real losses were far more dramatic. My father had destroyed his credit rating and my mother had lost her innocence. My father had to deal with the devastating feeling of letting his family down. He'd been taught it was a man's responsibility to bring home the bacon. My mother lived through the death of the dreams and ideals she had held since childhood. Her whole thought process had to be realigned. Everything she'd been taught about life had to be unlearned and relearned. It was a terribly painful time for her. This was how my mother buried her knight-in-shining-armour syndrome.

My mother began to rebuild her life, as did my father, on a much more realistic emotional and financial foundation. She had received a college diploma in business administration many years previously and snagged her first full-time job at the tender age of 40. Though she had many years of earnings and pension to make up, she remained undaunted. She started to build her own financial base, much the same way I would. Her first step was to get a credit card in her own name. She then started her own savings account and got her own life insurance. She has since paid cash for every car she's owned or trip she's taken. She maximized her RRSPs every year and began to invest what little extra she could pull together into mutual funds. My mother stopped depending on others and took control of her own financial affairs. In her own words, "I stopped being a passive little twit and started to develop some backbone." Today she's a supervisor for a company that provides home care services to the terminally ill and the elderly. Like most women in this industry, she's paid well below her worth. However, she has a quiet dignity and confidence that come from surviving a trip to hell and back. I can only pray to have half this woman's strength.

Precautions to take

Keeping my mother and Mrs. John Doe in mind, here are a few precautions you can take to ensure you don't end up in the same place.

1. Make it your business to know what's going on with the family finances. Just ask my mother about this one. By marrying her financial plan, she got a trip much rougher than she ever dreamed. As for Mrs. John Doe, I had to go through boxes filled with cancelled cheques to see if there were any payments being made to an insurance company. It was the only way to tell if there was an insurance policy, since we couldn't find one in the husband's office or at home. I did find a couple of entries in his records, but upon calling the insurance companies I discovered the policies had lapsed a few months earlier. It was well over two years before we determined all of the husband's debts and assets; the process was an inordinate amount of work.
2. Always have your own account. This sure would have helped out my mother, who ended up with nothing. As is the case with way too many people, joint accounts have been emptied by whoever gets there first in a nasty divorce, and the remaining partner is left with no cash resources. If your partner dies, often all the assets, including credit cards in your partner's name, are frozen until the will is probated. It's not inappropriate but profoundly smart to have your own money stashed away somewhere in case a crisis occurs.
3. Get your own credit rating. Open up your own line of credit and have your own credit card in your own name. Become an individual, an

identifiable person in the eyes of the financial institutions. At your request, the credit bureau will open a file in your name and will list the accounts that you use in your partner's name and the accounts in your partner's name for which you are contractually liable for payment. But you must contact all your creditors directly and tell them to report the credit history of both you and your partner.

4. Even though the Family Law Act of Ontario and other similar provincial legislation offers some protection upon divorce, be sure to list everything that was yours and his before the nuptials.

Incidentally, there's a series of books written by Michael Cochrane that is a must for anyone going through a divorce. *Surviving Your Divorce* is an important and readable guide that will give you all the tools you need to get through this devastating time. He's even written one for kids called *Surviving Your Parents' Divorce*. They're published by Wiley and are available at bookstores everywhere. The next one he needs to do is *Surviving Your Husband's Financial Shortcomings*. Maybe I should get my mom to write that one ...

So. Your debts are now paid off and you've gained a working knowledge of credit that ensures you'll stay out of trouble, inadvertent or otherwise. I've got to tell you, when I reached that point, it was a powerful feeling. But I was eager to do something sexier. I wanted to embark on a whole new experience: amassing unimaginable wealth or at least opening a savings account.

three

Building your financial base: tackling some fundamentals

"The most powerful force in the universe, you ask?
The power of compound interest."

ALBERT EINSTEIN

With the worst behind me, I found myself actually looking forward to learning more about this mysterious world of money. That, and bantering with Elaine, my new sparring partner. In our next session she dropped the bombshell.

"You mean I have to give you money?" I feigned incredulity. I was ready to commit to financial security, but I'd hoped I wouldn't have to give up money to do it. Elaine looked at me with ill-disguised exasperation. She waved that annoying pyramid in my face. My chest heaved with a resigned sigh.

"Joanne," she began, "tell me what happens when you receive your paycheque each month."

"I pay my butler, Steed, then Lance, the chauffeur, and last but not least, I send my pool boy Fabio a retainer fee to be on call when I need him." I wasn't going down easy.

"Girl, you need to get a life." She pressed on. "Now again, what's the first thing you do when you get paid?"

"I, uh, pay my bills, I guess. It's much more relaxing now that I've banished Attila to greener pastures. Let's see. I pay my rent, utilities, food, credit card bills, that kind of stuff first. I might buy a suit or dress if I see one I like."

"So whatever is left over, you save?" she asked. Judging by her expression, I could only guess Elaine was dead serious.

I snickered. "Yeah, Elaine. That's how I got to buy the 40-room mansion I live in. Ah … no. Whatever's left over I spend, woman!"

"Aren't you tired of doing everything backwards?" (The problem with becoming friends with your advisor is that they take certain liberties with you.) "Joanne, have you heard the famous story, 'The Richest Man in Babylon?' In 1926 a gentleman named George S. Clason wrote this story that helped millions of people get on the right financial track. The plot is simple. Paraphrased, Clason said the first bill you should pay every month, before your rent or mortgage payment, kid's orthodontist bill, or the pool boy's, is the bill to yourself. And I don't mean pay yourself with that new digital camera or Group of Seven painting that your life is worthless without. I mean savings—treat your savings as a bill. These savings can be for a wonderful business opportunity that comes up, or maybe a cottage. It's entirely up to you how you use the money. You work hard for your money, and you deserve to have it when you want it. First, though, we must protect you against yourself and the demands of day-to-day living."

"Pay myself first?" I repeated softly. I could do this. Since I had a long history of self-indulgence, the idea of paying myself first fit right in. "I'll become the Richest Woman in Toronto!"

"Before we decide where your millions are going to go, you need to understand a few basic investing principles," Elaine informed me. She went on to explain a number of things that became the premise on which my own financial base was built. I share them with you here as a simple, easy-to-understand primer on the basics you need to help with your financial planning and investment decisions. It's always good to know why you're doing something. Develop the habit of a three-year-old and always ask why.

Inflation

I've seen women who had anywhere from $5,000 to $60,000 sitting in a bank account earning 0.25 percent interest and who believed they were taking care of business. I saw to it that it did not remain there long. This is not investing; this is resting. And it's not enough. Investing doesn't mean dumping money into a low-interest-bearing account. I was perplexed to discover that there was work to do in order to have my money work in the best way for me. An emergency fund, although essential, isn't nearly enough. There are hundreds of financial products out there designed to do very specific jobs. They're also taxed differently. There are RRSPs for retirement. There are stock-market-based mutual funds best suited for long-term goals that may include retirement. There are money market mutual funds or general-purpose savings accounts for short-term goals like an emergency fund or the mandatory week away at a cottage. There's life and health insurance and investment real estate. One paltry savings account will do nothing for you in the long term. In fact, it can be a guaranteed route to the poor house.

We've been accustomed for so long to think in terms of "interest rate," but that thinking will get us nowhere fast. During the '80s I was delighted to be earning at least 10 percent (sometimes even 15 percent) interest on Canada Savings Bonds. I took them out for forced savings (read: spending) purposes. Around the same time the newspapers and TV were filled with talk of "runaway inflation." It had no impact on me whatsoever. I thought inflation was some techno-economic term eggheads used to describe a phenomenon that only affected corporations and big business.

As it happened, I was wrong again. I thought I was in line telling Elaine I wanted 10 percent for my guaranteed investments. (Remember, this was the early '90s.) After all, that's what I got during the '80s. In Elaine's eminently tactful style, she suggested that, once more, I was seriously deluded. She said 10 percent may have been the interest rate but it was not the "real" rate of return. The real rate of return, she explained, is actually a reflection of "purchasing power" or the ability to purchase goods and services. If the real rate of return is negative, then you as an investor have less purchasing power than the year before.

"Real, schmeal," I retorted. "I have a little piece of paper from the bank in one of my shoe boxes showing that at one point I was earning 19 percent on my Canada Savings Bonds."

It seems that didn't matter much. I discovered that the rate of return the banks say you're earning on your money isn't the final story. You must subtract the rate of inflation and account for the effect of taxes to get your real rate of return. Canada Savings Bonds peaked at 19.5 percent in 1981 while inflation hit 12.5 percent the same year. All of a sudden I became curious about these concepts of inflation and taxes.

Uninformed conventional wisdom suggests that it's great to have high interest rates so that we can earn more interest on our money. But when we have high interest rates, high inflation generally lurks close behind. Said another way, it ain't good news. Inflation is another way of saying cost of living. It used to be $500 bought you a car. Now it's the sales tax. When you clutch your heart from shock as the real estate agent tells you the price of that one-bedroom, 900-square-foot house located just next to runway two, when the same amount of money that filled your grocery cart last year now buys you a head of wilted romaine and one-day-old bread, when you put a $25 steak on your Visa card and it fits, you know inflation is running amok.

Now, you may have seen them in Canadian Tire or in your dentist's office. They wander about with hand-held computers, madly inputting the prices on everything they see. These people are a band of 80 shoppers that descend on any place Canadians spend money. The purpose of their work is to collect the cost of goods and services from 182 categories, like health, food, shelter, recreation, and education. The numbers are then lumped together and sent to Ottawa to create an all-items index called the consumer price index (CPI).

The consumer price index is used to measure inflation. The result gives us a sense of how inflated or deflated our economy has become. In 1971 if the consumer price index was set at $100, that suggests $100 of cash bought $100 of goods and services. If you fast forward 30-odd years to now, the same stuff would cost you around $450. Allowing for 2 percent inflation, a 30-year-old earning $40,000 a year will, at 55, need $65,624. She will need it. This is inflation.

In January of 2004 the CPI-all-items index was 122.90. This means that compared to 1992, when the number was set at 100, prices have gone up 22.90 percent. So the CPI gives us a general picture of how quickly prices are rising or falling and whether or not we need to worry. It plays a crucial role in establishing interest rate policy. Social and welfare payments are adjusted every so often to reflect any changes in the CPI.

As an investor, it can help you figure out how much you're *really* making on your investments. There's often a huge difference between the posted rate of return on that GIC and what you actually put in your pocket. If the financial institution shows your rate of return to be 5 percent, in reality you need to subtract the inflation or CPI rate. If the inflation rate is 1 percent, then you're really only getting 4 percent as a rate of return. Where you really see a difference is in inflationary times, like we had back in the '80s. My Canada Savings Bond was getting 10 percent and higher. I was happy. However, let's say the CPI rate was 6 percent. Do the math. I would have earned the same rate of return as you do on today's GIC at 5 percent.

Consider someone like my grandfather, who retired at 65 on a fixed pension. He died when he was 79. He had 14 years to struggle through on the same amount of money each month. His Canada Pension was indexed to keep up with inflation, but CPP represents on average only 39 percent of your total retirement picture. For women, the picture can be very grim. The latest Statistics Canada figures show women live on average to age 81. That's, on average, five years longer than men. Because of their lengthened life span, women's retirement can last longer than their careers. I always start the retirement segment of my seminars with the question "How many of you can afford to be unemployed for 20 or 30 years?" Oddly, no one raises their hand. These are retirement years when you're not working, but they must still be paid for. If you don't factor in the impact of inflation in your financial planning, your golden retirement will be tarnished.

The average rate of inflation in Canada has been about 3 percent per year over the last 20 years and about 4 percent for the last 50 years. That means it costs, on average, that much more each year for essentials like food, shelter, and clothing. The key word here, however, is average. The early '80s saw what economists call double-digit inflation, when inflation hits 10 percent or more. That's when interest rates jump up. High interest rates encourage people (including foreign investors) to invest in our economy. It was during that decade that I purchased Canada Savings Bonds at 10 percent. Since inflation was running at 6.5 percent, after I took into consideration the increase in my cost of living what I was left with was a sobering 3.5 percent as a real rate of return.

When you see interest rates as low as they are now, that usually means inflation is under control. Even though my guaranteed investments are only earning around 1.5 to 4 percent, I'm still in the same position I was in the '80s. Inflation today is around 2 percent. Therefore my real rate of return is in the same realm.

The bottom line is to be sure to factor in inflation in any long-term planning. Given women's life span, the risk of living longer than your money is high. People in general are living longer, so inflation is a serious concern for everyone. Inflation does fluctuate, so a good rule is to look for a minimum growth in your net worth of 6 to 8 percent each year to keep you swimming. Many advisors will tell you to make sure your investments keep pace with the rate of inflation. That's at the very least. Financial planning is not about staying flat or static. And there is one piece of good news about inflation: it allows you to live in a more expensive neighbourhood without moving out of your home.

As if worrying about inflation wasn't enough. In this country, we have another serious matter to think about before making investment decisions. And that's everybody's favourite thorn: taxes. After I internalized the barrage of bad news about inflation, I had to then face the effects of taxation on this real rate of return. Although guaranteed investments play an important role in your portfolio, because of taxes and inflation you should never have only these types of investments. The key to any successful portfolio is diversification. A little bit of many is better than a few of a little. As usual, nothing was as easy as it seemed. The idea that I could put my money away in a little old bank account and then forget about it was blasted to smithereens.

You need to know your marginal tax rate

Your marginal tax rate is how much tax you pay on the last dollar you earn. In other words, as your income increases, so does your tax rate. Bottom line? Your marginal rate is the highest rate of tax you can pay. This creates a paradox for Canadians, because the more conservative we are with our investments, the more we're taxed. Welcome to the world of our progressive tax system. This is how it works.

Not every dollar you make is taxed the same. Different portions of your income are taxed at different levels. In other words, the tax system is divided into levels or brackets that are based on how much you earn, how you earn it, and what province you live in.

First, there's federal tax. There are four graduated tax brackets. That means that the more money you make, the higher the tax rate on your last dollar. It's calculated by applying a basic rate of 16 percent on the first $32,183 of taxable income. The next portion of $32,185 of taxable income is subjected to a rate of 22 percent. The next $40,280 of income is taxed at 26 percent, and the maximum rate of 29 percent is applied to any excess over $104,648 of taxable income. Basic federal tax is then calculated by subtracting non-refundable tax credits and, if applicable, certain other credits or adjustments. An individual's provincial or territorial tax is based on a percentage of basic federal tax. Some reductions, additions, surtaxes, or flat taxes might also apply.

For example, let's assume you make over $105,000. In Ontario for 2003, your marginal tax rate would be 46.4 percent. Now if you made an extra grand over that, you'd have to pay the government $464. Now let's assume your income is $59,000 a year. Your marginal tax rate on the next $1,000 is 33.0 percent. So you'd only have to pay $330 in tax if you made that extra $1,000.

Federal rates

The federal personal income tax rate brackets and credits are fully indexed each year. Rates are progressive, as shown in the following table.

2003 Federal and Provincial Income Tax for Individuals

Taxable Income	British Columbia	Alberta	Saskatchewan	Manitoba	Ontario	Québec	New Brunswick
20,000	2,666	2,607	3,279	3,282	2,696	3,606	3,060
25,000	3,769	3,907	4,629	4,652	3,799	5,074	4,428
30,000	4,871	5,207	5,979	5,997	4,901	6,658	5,712
35,000	6,247	6,676	7,498	7,689	6,252	8,467	7,310
40,000	7,804	8,276	9,248	9,534	7,810	10,386	9,151
45,000	9,362	9,876	10,998	11,379	9,367	12,304	10,992
50,000	10,919	11,476	12,748	13,224	10,925	14,223	12,833
55,000	12,477	13,076	14,498	15,069	12,482	16,173	14,674
60,000	14,034	14,676	16,248	16,914	14,093	18,292	16,515
70,000	17,545	18,101	19,973	20,954	17,849	22,717	20,518
80,000	21,461	21,701	23,873	25,294	22,189	27,288	24,770
90,000	25,449	25,301	27,773	29,634	26,530	31,859	29,022
100,000	29,519	28,901	31,673	33,974	30,871	36,430	33,274
110,000	33,749	32,661	35,934	38,475	35,373	41,135	37,757
120,000	38,119	36,561	40,334	43,115	40,014	45,957	42,441
130,000	42,489	40,461	44,734	47,755	44,655	50,778	47,125
140,000	46,859	44,361	49,134	52,395	49,296	55,600	51,809
150,000	51,229	48,261	53,534	57,035	53,937	60,421	56,493
200,000	73,079	67,761	75,534	80,235	77,142	84,529	79,913
300,000	116,779	106,761	119,534	126,635	123,551	132,744	126,753
400,000	160,479	145,761	163,534	173,035	169,961	180,959	173,593
500,000	204,179	184,761	207,534	219,435	216,370	229,174	220,433
750,000	313,429	282,261	317,534	335,435	332,394	349,711	337,533
1,000,000	422,679	379,761	427,534	451,435	448,418	470,249	454,633

Top Marginal Rate (%)

	British Columbia	Alberta	Saskatchewan	Manitoba	Ontario	Québec	New Brunswick
Capital Gains	21.85	19.50	22.00	23.20	23.21	24.11	23.42
Dividends	31.58	24.08	28.34	35.08	31.34	32.82	37.26
Other Income	43.70	39.00	44.00	46.40	46.41	48.22	46.84

- This table cannot be used if taxable income includes Canadian dividends.
- Tax was calculated using the information available up to June 12, 2003, the date on which the last provincial budget, Quebec's, was tabled. Tax includes federal and provincial tax (including provincial surtax, where applicable), but excludes minimum tax.
- In 2003, all provinces and territories are using a "Tax-on-Income" system and apply provincial tax rates to taxable income. For purposes of comparison, it is assumed that taxable income is the same for federal and provincial purposes. Tax for non-residents is calculated at 48% of basic federal tax.
- Low-income tax reductions and credits have been considered for provinces that have such incentives.
- In calculating tax, only the basic personal non-refundable credits, both federal and provincial, have been considered. The non-refundable credits for EI and CPP/QPP contributions, the northern resident deduction, and refunds of GST and provincial sales taxes, have not been considered. For Quebec, tax has been calculated under the General Tax System and does not consider the flat amount of $2,870.

Taxable Income	Nova Scotia	Prince Edward Island	Newfound-land and Labrador	Nunavut	Northwest Territories	Yukon	Non-residents
20,000	3,157	3,193	3,290	1,993	2,311	2,671	2,899
25,000	4,495	4,483	4,618	2,918	3,409	3,973	4,083
30,000	5,805	5,773	5,970	3,843	4,506	5,125	5,267
35,000	7,521	7,402	7,747	5,021	5,849	6,520	6,702
40,000	9,369	9,192	9,655	6,396	7,382	8,104	8,330
45,000	11,216	10,982	11,563	7,771	8,914	9,688	9,958
50,000	13,064	12,772	13,471	9,206	10,452	11,272	11,586
55,000	14,911	14,605	15,379	10,656	11,997	12,856	13,214
60,000	16,773	16,464	17,324	12,106	13,542	14,440	14,842
70,000	20,865	20,678	21,713	15,344	16,998	17,933	18,431
80,000	25,140	25,115	26,277	18,844	20,768	21,708	22,279
90,000	29,574	29,552	30,842	22,344	24,538	25,509	26,127
100,000	34,008	33,989	35,406	25,844	28,308	29,310	29,975
110,000	38,602	38,587	40,131	29,638	32,311	33,346	34,061
120,000	43,335	43,324	44,995	33,688	36,516	37,586	38,353
130,000	48,069	48,061	49,859	37,738	40,721	41,826	42,645
140,000	52,803	52,798	54,723	41,788	44,926	46,066	46,937
150,000	57,537	57,535	59,587	45,838	49,131	50,306	51,229
200,000	81,205	81,220	83,908	66,088	70,156	71,505	72,689
300,000	128,542	128,590	132,550	106,588	112,206	113,903	115,609
400,000	175,879	175,960	181,192	147,088	154,256	156,301	158,529
500,000	223,216	223,330	229,834	187,588	196,306	198,699	201,449
750,000	341,559	341,755	351,438	288,838	301,431	304,694	308,749
1,000,000	459,901	460,180	473,043	390,088	406,556	410,689	416,049

Top Marginal Rate (%)							
Capital Gains	23.67	23.69	24.32	20.25	21.03	21.20	21.46
Dividends	31.92	31.96	37.32	28.96	28.40	28.64	28.98
Other Income	47.34	47.37	48.64	40.50	42.05	42.40	42.92

SOURCE: DELOITTE & TOUCHE LLP CANADA. "QUICK TAX FACTS 2003," JULY 2, 2003, <WWW.DELOITTE.COM>

The alternative minimum tax When individuals reduce their taxable income by deducting a significant amount of tax preference items (such as the tax-free portion of capital gains, pension and registered retirement savings plan contributions, and various tax-sheltered deductions), they may be required to pay alternative minimum tax (AMT). This is a parallel calculation to the normal federal income tax calculation—whichever one is higher becomes the basis for calculating your federal taxes that year and therefore your provincial taxes, which are based on the federal. The AMT provisions basically add tax preference items to taxable income. Then the lowest federal marginal tax rate of 16 percent is applied to this adjusted balance after deducting $40,000. The excess of AMT over regular federal income tax represents an income tax prepayment and is refunded to you in a year when the calculation goes the other way.

If I pretended to understand what I just wrote here, I'd be lying.

Provincial rates

The provincial personal income tax rates, which are in addition to the federal tax payable, are shown in the table on page 76. Quebec is the only province in which a separate tax return is prepared. Each of the provinces uses a graduated system on top of the federal tax rates, for a combined rate depending on your province of residence at the end of the calendar year.

So, one of the fundamentals of investment and tax planning is knowing what your marginal tax rate is. Why? Investment income is not created equal. There are three basic types of investment income to consider, all of which are taxed differently. The first is interest income from Canadian sources, such as interest earned on a GIC or Canada Savings Bond. They're fully taxable at your marginal tax rate. Said another way, this interest is taxed at your highest tax rate. The second type of income is what you receive when you own shares in a corporation. Dividends from Canadian corporations, whether paid directly to you or through a mutual fund, are eligible for the dividend tax credit, which effectively reduces the rate of tax paid to lower than interest payments. The third is capital gains, which is simply the gains made on the sale of capital property. Let's say you bought something for $100. It increased in value to $150 by the time you sold it. Presto, a $50 capital gain. This includes real estate, stocks, mutual funds, and precious metals. Capital gains are a better bargain because they're taxed at a lower rate than interest. In fact, only 50 percent of the gain is taxable. I'll explain more about this in chapter 5.

Your marginal tax rate also tells you how much you'll save if you use a tax-deductible investment such as an RRSP. If your marginal tax rate is 39.4 percent (between $64,872 and $67,290 of taxable income) and you

2003 Personal Income Tax Table

Jurisdiction	Tax Brackets	Rate (%)	Surtax
British Columbia	$8,307 to $31,653	6.05	
	$31,653 to $63,308	9.15	
	$63,308 to $72,685	11.70	
	$72,685 to $88,260	13.70	
	$88,260 and higher	14.70	
Alberta	$13,525 and higher	10.00 (flat rate)	
Saskatchewan	$8,000 to $35,000	11.00	
	$35,000 to $100,000	13.00	
	$100,000 and higher	15.00	
Manitoba	$7,634 to $30,544	10.90	
	$30,544 to $65,000	14.90	
	$65,000 and higher	17.40	
Ontario	$7,817 to $32,435	6.05	20% on income tax exceeding $3,747
	$32,435 to $64,871	9.15	Plus
	$64,871 and higher	11.16	36% on income tax exceeding $4,727
Quebec	$6,150 to $27,095	16.00	
	$27,095 to $54,195	20.00	
	$54,195 and higher	24.00	
New Brunswick	$7,756 to $32,183	9.68	
	$32,183 to $64,368	14.82	
	$64,368 to $104,648	16.52	
	$104,648 and higher	17.84	
Nova Scotia	$7,231 to $29,590	9.77	10% on income tax exceeding $10,000
	$29,590 to $59,180	14.95	
	$59,180 and higher	16.67	
Prince Edward Island	$7,412 to $30,754	9.80	10% on income tax exceeding $5,200
	$30,754 to $61,509	13.80	
	$61,509 and higher	16.70	
Newfoundland and Labrador	$7,410 to $29,590	10.57	9% on income tax exceeding $7,032
	$29,590 to $59,180	16.16	
	$59,180 and higher	18.02	
Nunavut	$10,160 to $32,183	4.00	
	$32,183 to $64,368	7.00	
	$64,368 to $104,648	9.00	
	$104,648 and higher	11.50	
Northwest Territories	$11,050 to $32,183	7.20	
	$32,183 to $64,368	9.90	
	$64,368 to $104,648	11.70	
	$104,648 and higher	13.05	
Yukon	$7,756 to $32,183	7.04	5% on income tax exceeding $6,000
	$32,183 to $64,368	9.68	
	$64,368 to $104,648	11.44	
	$104,648 and higher	12.76	
Federal	$7,756 to $32,183	16.00	
	$32,183 to $64,368	22.00	
	$64,368 to $104,648	26.00	
	$104,648 and higher	29.00	

SOURCE: DELOITTE & TOUCHE LLP CANADA. "QUICK TAX FACTS 2003," JUNE 2003, <WWW.DELOITTE.COM>

deduct $1 from your taxable income, you'll save yourself 39 cents in taxes. So when you hear people say they're in a 50 percent tax bracket, that doesn't necessarily mean the government takes exactly half of everything they earn, though it may feel like it. It simply means that everything they earn in excess of a certain amount is taxed at that level. Where this becomes very important is in choosing your investments. You may also change marginal tax brackets based on investment income or amounts deducted from taxable income, so know where the breaks are.

"Ignorance truly is bliss," I groaned. "It seems that in today's world the strong take from the weak, the clever take from the strong, and the government takes away from everybody."

Elaine levelled me one of those looks that said, "Alas, you have much to learn." The craving for M&Ms had never been stronger.

"You've got to admire Canada Revenue Agency." I sighed. "Any organization that makes that much money without advertising deserves respect. So what can people do about inflation and taxes?" I cried.

"Nothing," came the abrupt answer.

I was to learn that you can, however, make investment choices that will work with inflation and taxes. That's because even though over the short term the stock market, compared with guaranteed interest-bearing investments, can rise and fall like a roller coaster, over the long term the TSE 300 Index outperforms both inflation and T-bills.

What's this S&P/TSX we keep hearing about?

Let's talk about what the stock market actually is. Simply put, you go to a flea market to buy, uh, junk. You go to the supermarket to buy food. You go to the stock market to buy stocks or shares in companies.

The index changes as the world changes. The S&P/TSX Composite Index measures the general performance of the largest Canadian public companies. Of course, other companies' stocks are traded on the exchange, but they don't contribute to the calculation of the S&P/TSX Composite Index. The index acts as an indicator of how much money is being invested in and how much is being taken out of the market. Basically, the index provides a snapshot of both Canadian stock market activity and the performance of the different sectors within it.

The Toronto Stock Exchange introduced its first index in 1934 to provide a benchmark for the Canadian market that was distinct from the Dow Jones Index in the United States. In its early days, the index had 60 stocks, which were classified as industrial, gold, or base metals. In 1977, the Toronto Stock Exchange launched the TSE 300, which had exactly 300 stocks.

So what happened to the TSE 300? Early in 2002 the index was renamed and revised. The Toronto Stock Exchange indices are now managed by Standard & Poor's, and the Toronto Stock Exchange changed its branding from TSE to TSX. But the most important change was a new set of rules that defined which stocks are members of the index.

An index has two purposes. The most obvious is to be a benchmark that shows what is happening in the stock market. The other purpose is to be an investment that represents the entire market. For example, a portfolio manager might buy all the stocks that make up the index instead of trying to pick the best stocks. This approach is called passive investing, and many pension funds and mutual funds have used it successfully.

Some of the TSE 300 stocks did not trade very often (which tied in to the debate about what the magic number of companies should be; a debate resolved by the current system, which has the discretion to select a meaningful number of stocks for the index, hence TS"X," "X" being a variable). These stocks were difficult for fund managers to buy or sell because often there were not enough shares available to buy or enough buyers to sell shares to. The rule changes set new minimum criteria as to which stocks should be included in the index, and the new criteria will be adjusted over time as the economy changes. The improved index is no longer a fixed number of stocks, and all stocks that meet the criteria are included. A company can be dropped from the index without any obligation to add a new company if there isn't another one that makes a meaningful contribution. Conversely, as many companies can be added to the index as seems reasonable. There may be 280 companies in the TSX at one time, and 320 at another time. So, it changes as the economy evolves. This makes it easier for fund managers to invest in the index.

Previously, all stocks in the TSE 300 were put into one of 14 sectors that were defined by Statistics Canada in 1977. This has also been changed to a modern standard, the Global Industry Classification Standard (GICS®), which is used throughout the world. This standard makes it easier for analysts to compare the same sectors in different countries. As of April 30, 2004, the new classification system had 10 sectors, aggregated from 24 industry groups, 62 industries, and 132 sub-industries.

When the S&P/TSX Composite Index started up, under the original name TSE 300 Composite Index, the number 1,000 was arbitrarily chosen to represent the value of the index at that time. From then on, every time the value of the companies influencing the index went up or down, it made headlines. To really get you to pay attention to the news, broadcasters and market analysts use choice verbs like *plummeted* or *fell, skyrocketed* or *soared*. We need to keep in mind that the S&P/TSX Composite Index, or any other index,

Slumps and Recoveries in the Canadian Market — 1975 to 2003: S&P/TSX Composite Index

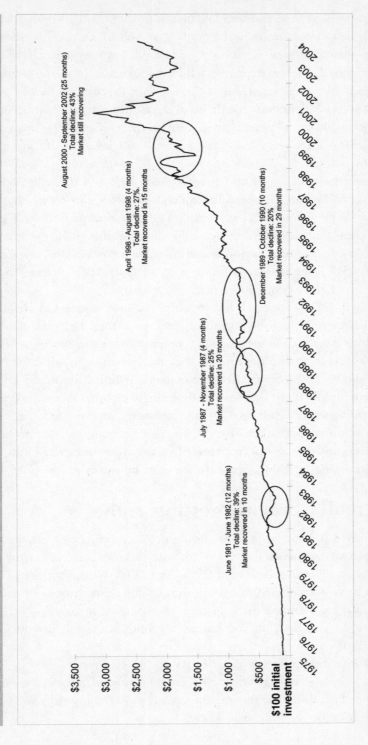

August 2000 - September 2002 (25 months)
Total decline: 43%
Market still recovering

April 1998 - August 1998 (4 months)
Total decline: 27%.
Market recovered in 15 months

December 1989 - October 1990 (10 months)
Total decline: 20%
Market recovered in 29 months

July 1987 - November 1987 (4 months)
Total decline: 25%
Market recovered in 20 months

June 1981 - June 1982 (12 months)
Total decline: 39%
Market recovered in 10 months

$3,500
$3,000
$2,500
$2,000
$1,500
$1,000
$500
$100 initial investment

1975 1976 1977 1978 1979 1980 1981 1982 1983 1984 1985 1986 1987 1988 1989 1990 1991 1992 1993 1994 1995 1996 1997 1998 1999 2000 2001 2002 2003 2004

SOURCE: FIDELITY INVESTMENTS CANADA LIMITED. REPRODUCED WITH PERMISSION. FROM TSX INC. TOTAL RETURNS FOR THE S&P/TSX COMPOSITE INDEX FROM JANUARY 31, 1975 TO DECEMBER 31, 2003. EFFECTIVE MAY 1, 2002, THE TSE 300 COMPOSITE INDEX WAS RETIRED AND REPLACED WITH THE S&P/TSX COMPOSITE INDEX. FOR MORE INFORMATION ON THE CHANGES TO THE INDEX, PLEASE VISIT WWW.TSE.COM. PAST PERFORMANCE IS NO GUARANTEE OF FUTURE RESULTS. IT IS NOT POSSIBLE TO INVEST DIRECTLY IN AN INDEX.

represents only general market movements, not individual stocks. Also, keep in mind that when announcers quote the S&P/TSX Composite Index, they're reporting only on what happened that day, or on the results of the last week or month. If we stepped back and looked at how the market has performed over the long term, we'd see that the overall trend has been upward. So, when you hear that the market has dropped 50 points in one day, it may sound like it's "plummeting." But at the end of 2003, the year-end close of the market was 8,220.89. For long-term investors, it's just another day in the market.

A case in point: during the 47 years between 1956 and 2003, the S&P/TSX Composite Index gained, including dividends, an average of 9.4 percent a year, U.S. stocks came in around 11 percent, and GICs' annual growth was 8 percent for the same time period. To graphically illustrate this: a $1,000 investment maintained over this time period would have given you $27,367 with five-year GICs, $68,512 with S&P/TSX Composite stocks, and $88,897 in U.S. stocks through Standard & Poor's 500 Index.

The light bulb went on. I said to Elaine, "I guess it's a good idea to have your money working for you, not against you. But the stock market?" I groaned. "It gives me the willies. Don't forget it wasn't that long ago I thought the stock market was a place for the disgustingly rich or to sell cattle."

"Wrong on both counts," Elaine countered. "Mutual funds, also known as investment funds, allow the not-so-disgustingly rich, in fact the downright poor and financially challenged, to take advantage of the good, the bad, and the ugly of the stock market. There is, however, an important step to be taken before one runs off half-cocked, blinded by the allure of equity funds." As I'd been discovering, anything worth having must be worth waiting for.

The real secret to getting rich

Elaine leaned forward with a delightful air of conspiracy. "I can make you rich." She had my attention. I was awash with images of tall, dark, wonderfully mysterious men lolling about my palatial estate. This was the bonanza. This was what I'd been waiting for throughout this painfully slow process of deciphering the financial planning maze. Finally, something with sizzle.

She said, "The first bill you pay each month is the bill to yourself. Ten percent. That's the secret."

I was incredulous. Ten percent? That's it?!" I demanded.

"That's it," she quietly affirmed. "Take 10 percent after tax from every paycheque. That should be the minimum you're squirrelling away. You've heard it before. It's called 'getting rich slowly.'"

Then the reality hit me. Actually, 10 percent seemed like a lot to take away from the so-called necessities of life. No, I was sure this was too much. I started to balk.

"Hold on, before you write this notion off completely," she interjected. "We both know how well your stellar financial skills have served you in life, so hear me out." The sarcasm was hard to miss. "Let's say your company came to you and said, 'Sorry, Joanne, we have to lay you off.' However, the suits also say they're prepared to offer you an option. That is, if you take a 10 percent drop in pay, you can keep your job. What's more, they'll invest that 10 percent for you so that when you retire, they will give you a million dollars cash. What would you do?"

"Duh, I'd quit," I shot back. "Of course I'd take the 10 percent drop in pay."

"Okay then Joanne, I want you to fire yourself right now and hire yourself back at 10 percent less."

Ouch. I'd been had. So I decided to try it. If it was going to be too tight, I reasoned, I'd simply stop. Of course you know what happened. I didn't even notice it. The money came out first thing each month and it didn't make a perceptible difference in my lifestyle. I really hated it when Elaine was right. Initially, I put my 10 percent into a special account. I needed to establish a financial cushion first before getting into higher-risk investments. The 10 percent would eventually evolve into "take advantage of whatever comes along" money. Thanks to this 10 percent (and a little help from a personal line of credit), I was able to take a year off to write this book.

If you don't think you can afford it, look for the "black hole" in your financial plan. We all have one. Where does a disproportionate amount of your lifestyle maintenance money go? Mine was easy. Eating out and frittering. I was a world-class fritterer. If you gave me $50 in the morning and asked me before bedtime where the money went, I'd be hard-pressed to tell you. It can be as simple as cutting out your daily coffee and doughnut or chicken wings and beer on Friday nights.

This rule should be adhered to whether you earn $17,000 or $370,000 a year. It's all relative. Oh yes, and ideally this should be over and above your annual RRSP contribution. Your RRSP provides a tax deduction that lowers the amount you have to pay in taxes or, even better, gets you money back. The money you save or get back should be put toward next year's contribution. Remember, the 10 percent rule is something to work up to. If you can afford only 5 percent, that's 5 percent more than you had last year. Every little bit counts. If it's a choice between the two, and you're in a higher tax bracket, go for the RRSP. If it's an emergency fund you're trying to build with your 10 percent, which must also include your RRSP contribution because of budget constraints, still put most if not all of your 10 percent in your RRSP and use the tax refund for the emergency fund. As we'll see in the retirement planning chapter, tax-sheltered interest that you find in an RRSP is so important.

Women in particular need to be sure to implement this strategy. The divorce rate and the fact that they're the primary caregivers make women more financially vulnerable. The catch-22 is that women earn on average less, but often need the financial safety nets more. Most of these suggestions, like emergency funds, mutual funds, or any type of investment, can be started with as little as $50 a month. It doesn't sound like much, but it's a respectable beginning.

I asked Elaine, "So, how does this 10 percent racket work?"

"Next lesson," she offered. "There's only so much even your brain can assimilate." As I took my leave, I shot her a withering glance. She sat back in her chair, grinning broadly.

The lazy person's path to wealth: compound interest

I was settled in for another rousing session of Financial Planning 101. Elaine and I did a quick summary of my financial accomplishments, quick being the operative word here. There was still some distance to travel. Debt gone? Check. Credit reestablished? Check. Personal line of credit/overdraft protection in place? Check. Ten percent savings set up? Check.

"Inquiring minds want to know, Elaine. How can a measly 10 percent make you rich?"

"Rich is a subjective term," Elaine replied. "There are as many definitions of rich as there are people who have them. But to answer your question, it all comes down to compound interest, which needs time to work."

Most of us aren't worried about having money to last us for the rest of our lives. We'd be happy to have it last the rest of the month. But there are two ways to make money. The hard way is to send your body out to work. The other? Send your money out to work. Compounding. It's money multiplying itself and it's not the premise of a weird David Cronenberg movie.

When you save or invest money, you earn income on it. The income grows each year because the amount it's based on grows each year. Admittedly, it's no big deal over the short haul, but over the long term, fasten your seat belt. It's called the rule of 72. What you do is simply divide the number 72 by the annual rate of return, and the number you get will tell you how long it will take for your money to double.

Growth of $1,000

Thousands

$42,972

$6,776

Legend: —T-Bill 91-day — S&P/TSX Comp

SOURCE: INTEGRA PRIVATE INVESTMENT MANAGEMENT. REPRODUCED WITH PERMISSION.

If you invest $1,000 at 11 percent, your money will double in about seven years. Invest the same amount at 15 percent, and it will take just under five years to double. Let's put it in more dramatic terms to really catch your attention. Imagine investing $100 a month at 10 percent. Over 20 years, your principal of $24,000 would be worth over $77,000. If you saved your $100 a month for 30 years, it grows to almost $220,000, over triple the amount. Invested for 40 years, it becomes almost $600,000. Now, let's sweeten the pot. Assume you found an above-average mutual fund that gave you a return of 15 percent instead of 10 percent. Over 40 years, that translates to $2.5 million—a mere difference of 1.9 million.

The following is a classic story of the power of compound interest. Jean and Dianne, twin sisters, were having dinner one night. Over exceedingly decadent cheesecake, they discussed their impending retirement. Dianne had been known for her free-spirited ways in her youth, but she got it together at age 30. She started a monthly savings plan that she adhered to religiously right up to age 65. Dianne began: "Thank God I got on track so many years ago. I'm looking forward to a leisurely yet lavish retirement with no financial headaches. I worked so hard for my money and often couldn't make my RRSP contribution without having to borrow for it. One year I even postponed buying a much-needed winter coat to make my contribution. In fact, there were lots of years like that." She stabbed her cheesecake with a frustrated air. As she looked over her shoulder, she leaned forward toward Jean. She pushed a piece of paper across the table and said in a conspiratorial whisper, "Can you believe I've saved this much! I suppose it's the least I should expect after 35 years of saving." Jean glanced at the statement and smiled benignly.

Dianne went on. "Honey, you're going to be so sorry you didn't look after your retirement all these years. How does it look for you?"

Jean hadn't saved for 35 years. She'd been able to save for only 10 years. Jean started saving when she was 20. When she reached 30, she had to stop as she started her family and became a stay-at-home mom. Since she didn't work in the paid labour force, she couldn't make her own RRSP contributions and qualified for next to nothing with the Canada Pension Plan. She also didn't have access to a private pension plan. Her husband had died the year before, leaving absolutely nothing behind but funeral expenses. Dianne believed she had every reason to be concerned about her sister's future. Jean could easily become one of the 60 percent of women her age living at the poverty line or lower. But what separated Jean from many women in her situation was the nest egg she had tucked away. She'd left that 10 years worth of savings untouched for 35 years.

"I'm ahead of you, Dianne," Jean said. "In fact, about 10 years ahead. I knew I wasn't going to send my body out into the paid workforce, so I decided to send my money out instead. You started at 30 and stopped at 65. I started at 20 and stopped at 30, but didn't touch the money." Jean turned the statement over and wrote down a number. She slid it across the table to her sister and in a quiet voice said, "I'd swallow that cheesecake before you look at this." Dianne looked down. As her eyes widened in disbelief, she started to laugh—a big, hearty belly laugh that comes from immeasurable relief. And shock. Jean had much more money than her sister. In fact, she had almost double what her sister had. After 35 years of consistently investing $2,500 annually and earning a 10 percent return, Dianne had a net worth of $747,817. Jean, on the other hand, could only invest her $2,500, which got 10 percent as well, for 10 years. But she got a 10-year jump on Dianne and ended up with $1,231,671.

That's the power of compound interest.

Once I understood the principle of compound interest, my desire to save was greatly enhanced. After all, easy money appeals to everyone's sense of greed. And it can really help ease the pressure. You work hard for your money; let it take some of the burden. It's never too late to start. Especially given women's life span, you could even start at 65 and still have 15 to 20 years to enjoy the remarkable benefits of compounding.

Emergency funds

"Okay, Elaine. I trust we're finally at the part now where we get to talk about something more exciting. I'm debt free and I'm ready to let you rob me of 10 percent of my hard-earned money," I exclaimed, greedily rubbing my hands together. "I want to talk about something that will give me a really high rate of return each year though be completely liquid so that I can get at it if I need to."

Elaine simply smiled at me. She said, "Tone down your maniacal enthusiasm, Joanne, I have some bad news." That's when my lofty expectations collided with reality. She showed me the dreaded priority pyramid again. "Emergency fund?!" I groaned. "How positively dull." The only thing I knew about emergency funds was the mad money my mother used to make sure I had as an adventurous teenager when I went out with my friends.

I had established my own personal line of credit, but I hadn't yet created a true emergency fund. So the next step I was required to take was to create a safety net for myself. I'd spent so much of my life walking a financial tightrope without protection that at first the idea seemed silly and foreign. I did, however, intuitively understand the need for it. There'd been many times over the years when a little nest egg would have saved me immeasurable heartache and difficulty. But any time I'd saved up an appreciable amount of money, I'd blow it on something necessary like a trip or a gift for someone. I saved money to spend it. The idea of saving money to have "just in case" seemed downright weird. It did, however, make sense that if I was going to create a healthy financial situation for myself, an emergency fund was needed to protect it, and not just for the obvious disasters and pitfalls.

It's hard enough for people to make ends meet with the tangible parts of life, like mortgage or rent payments, kids' clothes, and outrageous food bills. But to try to tuck money away for what *might* go wrong? That often has to wait until the kids' orthodontist's bills get paid. Then the lawyer's bill. And oh yeah, the car insurance is due next month …

Inevitably, however, it's this precise attitude that gets us and keeps us behind the proverbial financial eight ball. Show me one person who hasn't had to deal with a financial emergency of some sort: job loss, becoming sick or injured, the furnace dying, a higher than expected tax bill. And if you have children, the list is exhaustive.

Setting up an emergency fund can be a daunting challenge: conventional wisdom suggests we take three to six months' salary and put it aside into something that's quite accessible. When told this my first reaction was swift and severe: "Are you nuts!!?!" This seemed like an inordinate amount of money going into something like a daily interest savings account where I'd be earning a paltry (if any) interest rate. It's a well-known fact that the easier it is to get at your money, the lower the typical rate of return. The tougher it is to get at or the riskier the investment is, the greater chance you'll have for a better rate of return. Accessibility is a vital characteristic in an emergency fund, but three to six months' salary going into something that wouldn't even keep up with the rate of inflation over the long term? This did not go over well with my highly developed contrarian side. There had to be a way to handle life's little challenges without sacrificing reasonable returns.

The first thing you should do before automatically buying into the old "three to six months' salary" advice is examine your own lifestyle and its possible emergency requirements. If you're single, working at a stable job, and living in an apartment, own a fairly new car and have no serious medical problems, six months of your salary is pretty hefty. Maybe $500 or $1,000 is plenty. However, if you work in a volatile industry, are about to have twins, own your own home (therefore all of its repairs), drive Uncle Gus's Model T, and/or have health problems that could render you unemployed for any appreciable length of time, you'd better resign yourself to the fact that it's imperative to have *no less* than six months of security tucked aside somewhere. Only you can determine the proper amount based on your life's circumstances and your own perpetual anxiety threshold.

The next thing you need to determine after the "how much" is the shorter version of the equation, which is simply "how." An emergency fund has to start somewhere, and $50 a month through preauthorized chequing is as good a place as any. It's a manageable amount by most people's standards, and the fact that it's taken out of your account automatically each month can go a long way toward eliminating the "how" worry. Understand that it may take a while to build up, but anything worth having is worth waiting for.

High-interest savings accounts (from the likes of Manulife Financial, ING Direct, President's Choice Financial) are currently paying 2.25 percent to 2.75 percent and can be one of the best places to sock money away. Your rate of return is higher than a daily interest savings account. There are also no-load money market funds, which are nice and safe because they invest in nothing but cash-type investments like jumbo-term deposits and treasury bills. These funds can also be just as easy to get at as your savings account. The typical return in 2003 for money market funds was approximately 3.0 percent. Talk to your financial institution about this type of mutual fund.

And if your financial institution happens to be a life insurance company, ask about another type of account that could be useful for those of you who have a tendency to qualify that new camera you've been dying for as a good candidate for your emergency fund. Insurance companies offer a kind of savings or investor's account with marginally higher interest rates than the banks offer on equivalent accounts. What makes them particularly attractive to many people with incorrigible saving patterns is the simple fact that you can't write cheques on this type of account, nor can you access it through cash machines. (You can't do either of these with most money market funds either.) It generally takes 7 to 10 working days to get the money out of the account, which is usually enough time to pay for any outstanding emergency you may have—or to talk yourself out of that impulse buy. Since they are with an insurance company, these accounts are generally creditor proof in the event that you declare bankruptcy and also don't get caught in complicated probate proceedings when you die. The money will pass directly and quickly to your named beneficiary.

There's another possible source of emergency funds, but only for those who are credit-savvy. In fact, people who suffer from credit card blues or have taken the trip to credit hell should not, under any circumstances, consider the following suggestion. It can, however, be a godsend to many who understand and treat credit respectfully. This is a line of credit. Now, you should *always* have *some* cash available for day-to-day emergencies. It's never wise to be too credit-dependent. But at least with a line of credit you can be assured access to funds in the event the roof falls in.

The beauty of having an emergency fund in place is that it protects the integrity of your other investments, like an RRSP, for example. I've known people who have used this valuable tax planning tool and retirement savings program as an emergency fund. This is the worst place to have one. Let's say I had an extensive RRSP portfolio but nothing else. If something happened, this would be my only source of revenue. I'd end up damaging the very thing that the investment was supposed to do in the first place: provide for retirement and tax sheltering. Another reason not to dip into your RRSPs before retirement is that Canada Revenue Agency will hold back 30 percent of the value of your withdrawal on amounts of $15,000 and over. That means you get only 70 cents for every dollar. (The holdback is 10 percent for under $5,000 and 15 percent for $5,001 to $14,999; and it's higher in Quebec.) And that's just the beginning. Once you file your tax return, there may be more owing on April 30th depending on what you owe Canada Revenue Agency.

If all your money is in equity mutual funds or the stock market, you can rest assured that your catastrophe will coincide with the day the stock market nosedives. You're then at the mercy of the market. So an emergency fund allows the different investments you make to do what they're supposed to do, whether it be to save for the little one's education or to buy a house. It's like an impact cushion or insurance policy to ensure that the rest of your portfolio grows up to be everything it could possibly be—without any interruptions to fund that broken muffler.

When I started advising women on money matters, I was quick to learn that very few had emergency funds. Having an adequate emergency fund can buy you time for making important decisions that could affect the rest of your life. The worst time to learn about financial planning or to make financial decisions is when you're under tremendous stress. An emergency fund can also buy you the freedom to leave a failed marriage or relationship. Too many women are forced to stay in unhappy or unhealthy situations because of financial dependence or ignorance.

With many women working at the low end of the income continuum, starting an emergency fund can be tough. Often women are forced to spend their earnings on lavish luxuries such as food, shelter, and clothing, with little, if anything, left over for emergency funds. My mother went through much of her life depending on Dad as her emergency fund. At the same time, she managed to squirrel away a little bit here and a little bit there for stuff that the family might need. Mom certainly didn't spend this money on manicures and afternoon teas. In fact, it's safe to say it was never spent on herself. I call this the "teapot syndrome." Women throughout the ages have had emergency funds stashed in their "teapots" to bail out husbands or pay for their kids' summer camp. The focus groups we conducted included an overwhelming majority of women whose mothers saved little bits of money where they could but only spent it on others. Many contemporary women have carried on that trait. The reality of today's world suggests that it's time to break the pattern.

There's no easy answer. Credit can be harder to get for women at the lower end of the earning scale and for those lacking collateral, but that's not to say one shouldn't try. Do try to work up to following the 10 percent rule. Be resigned to the fact that it's going to take time to build up savings. Just getting started, however, gave me a huge psychological boost. The key to building a proper financial plan is to be systematic in your approach. With your 10 percent each month, once your cushion is firmly in place, keep going. That's when you can start to branch out into other investments such as mutual funds, to name one.

Through the miracle of preauthorized chequing and the 10 percent rule, I started an emergency fund in a savings account with surprising ease. A predetermined amount comes out of my chequing account each month and is deposited into a special account that I nicknamed "On Pain of Death Only." Once I had an adequate fund for my purposes (which was almost immediately, because I chose the PLC route until I had three months' salary tucked away), I then started to invest in a long-term, growth-oriented equity mutual fund. I could do so comfortably because I could now afford the risk. If the mutual fund lost money, my lifestyle would still be protected by the emergency fund.

I've learned all of life's lessons the hard way, so take heed. It really doesn't take much to give you financial peace of mind. Simply knowing that your $50 a month is building up and that you have that couple of hundred dollars tucked away can ensure that it's sheep, not loan sharks, you count at night. Remember, when Noah and his wife built the ark, it wasn't raining.

The hilarious world of budgets

I reconciled myself to the fact that there was much to do, not the least of which was to get all this stuff organized. In her naïveté, Elaine suggested a budget. After my howling laughter subsided, she acknowledged she got the point. "Elaine," I countered. "To me, budgets are nervous breakdowns on paper."

Fewer than 10 percent of Canadians do any sort of financial planning, let alone entertain the nasty "B" word. I'm about to utter what's considered veritable heresy in financial planning circles. Budgets don't work. I know budgets don't work from my own experience and that of thousands of people I've dealt with on a professional level. The idea of budgets is sane and credible. There's just one minor detail, however. People don't stick to them. Human nature runs contrary to the very idea of what budgets are about. Budgets are based on needs and wants. The needs (food and shelter) should get priority and attention. We then save or budget for wants (such as a DVD player) afterward. I don't think this is what really happens for most of us. Remember, we live in a "Get it now! Don't pay a cent until 2099!" world. Immediate gratification has become the basis for much of our existence.

Watch how quickly a want becomes a need and throws the delicate balancing act of your budget out the window. I've heard people emphatically state that they need that DVD player so that they can mellow out after a stressful day at the office. Who am I to judge? My approach has always been to justify absolutely anything I wanted. I was brilliant at it. I could justify with the deftness of a senior diplomat the purchase of an $800 suit over a perfectly adequate $400 one in an instant. I'd worry about how to pay later.

The difficulty with budgets comes from the fact that they require us to retrain our money behaviour. This is especially true for the many women who lack financial training or the belief that they need to manage their own money. When I would design a financial plan for people, I told them after their first visit to come back with a budget in hand. Knowing full well how people detest budgets, I described it as an "approximate forecast of the outcome of your spending." I used a very simple one-page form, so it shouldn't have been too daunting a task. Fewer than 20 percent came back with one completed. People fight budgeting. To many, a budget means life is over as they know it. They'll be restricted to eating Kraft Dinner at home and watching *America's Funniest Home Videos*.

In theory, a budget is supposed to be used to allow you to live the way you want. One of my favourite stories is of a woman who had close to $7,000 owing on both of her credit cards. When asked how long she'd been carrying this debt, she replied since her divorce. That wasn't particularly helpful so I pressed on. "When might that have been?" I queried, expecting a year at the most. "Six years ago," she calmly replied. After I picked myself up off the floor, I asked her if she was aware of the monumental interest she'd been paying over the years. She said she was, but had come to accept it as a matter of course. It hadn't bothered her in the least. This woman had gotten caught in the "rob Mary to pay Sally" routine. She'd get a cash advance on her Visa to pay off Mastercard, then switch it around the following month. After impressing upon her the importance of paying off this debt and establishing a healthier form of budgeting, I noticed the familiar "eyes glazing over." I knew I'd lost this soul. I knew she wasn't ready to break out of this insidious trap, and I was right. The idea of budgeting scared her off. I never saw her again.

Abuse of credit cards is the most common way that people sabotage their budgets. There's a well-known story of a woman who took her credit cards and put them in a deep plastic container filled with water. She then put them in the freezer in an effort to stop her impulse buying that regularly threw her budget off. I had a client who, after hearing this story, thought she'd give it a try. She came to realize early on, however, how inane this really was. The minute the first impulse hit, she simply put the container in the microwave for 30 seconds and was off, armed and ready for the next onslaught. Thirty seconds isn't enough time to talk yourself out of your urges. Today, she's happily on the road to financial recovery after discovering that scissors worked infinitely better than ice.

But the real kicker came in the form of one of the most accomplished women I had ever met. Lisette had a Bachelor of Commerce degree, an MBA, and a PhD in organizational management theory. She'd worked as a financial analyst with a major computer company for 10 years analyzing corporate financial trends and developing strategies with immense budgets. Her decisions could affect the company's bottom line in the millions of dollars. When I met her, she had moved on to become a professor at a prestigious university. Lisette had an extraordinary background in finance. Yet this woman could barely manage to pay her rent. In her own words, "I came alive at the poverty line! The idea of having my own money intimidated me to such a degree that I found a way around it; I married an alcoholic so he could spend it for me." Needless to say, this was not an effective money-management technique. Lisette eventually found her way through the maze, but had to experience tremendous pain before she was able to get her money act together. She often said she didn't feel that she "deserved" to have money so didn't pay it much attention, even though she worked like a Trojan and was an extremely skilled woman. How women think about themselves can have a huge impact on their success with budgets, financial planning, and investing.

The vast majority of women I've dealt with, however, do have a pretty good idea of what they can afford to invest. There are a few notable exceptions that I've sent packing to credit counselling. There are also people who could afford to save more but who aren't prepared to make any changes to their lifestyle. An important point to note here is that financial planning shouldn't be painful. It may pinch a bit here and there, but it should never require a radical shift from your present situation—unless, of course, you're in dire financial straits with a strangling debt load. In such circumstances, some drastic measure like credit counselling or, in the ultimate worst case, declaring bankruptcy, may be necessary. If you take on more than you can handle at first, the chances are high that you'll end up dusting the whole notion within six months. Frustration and overzealousness are the two leading causes of the premature deaths of financial plans.

While in private practice, I often suggested starting at half or three-quarters of what the client thought she could afford to save for the first three to six months. It's the "try it on for fit and comfort" method. There's always something people "forget" to include in their budgets. This method often flushes it out. In almost every case, however, people increase their savings and investing to the original, and often a higher, amount.

So, if budgets (in the traditional sense of the word) don't work for most people, what can you do? When you think about it, budgeting is exactly the same as living beyond your means, except now you have a record of it. First of all, let me say straight out that budgets are designed to give you at best a sense of your situation. It's impossible to calculate right down to the penny the comings and goings of your money. If you try, you'll fail. Corporations have a hard enough time at this, and let's not even mention our esteemed governments. It is, however, important to know how much is coming in and going out consistently each month. Things like rent or mortgage, savings, insurance—anything that remains reasonably constant—are easy to account for. Balance these expenditures with your regular income.

Budgeting is about planning for major expenses down the road, not the regular monthly stuff. Budgets help you save for a car. Budgets help you save for annual or semiannual expenses like birthday gifts, Christmas, car insurance, back-to-school clothes for the kids, and car maintenance. Add up how much you spent last year for one-time or unusual expenses, add about 1 percent for inflation, then divide by 12. Start putting money away now in a special savings account.

This is especially important for commissioned salespeople or people who receive bonuses. Base your budget on what you know absolutely is going to come in each month. Commissions and bonuses should be considered gravy. Also try to look at a full year or even a five-year period to get as accurate as possible a handle on your boom and bust cycles and plan accordingly. When you attempt your budget, if you don't have taxes deducted at source, be sure to remember the inevitable tax bill. Setting up and budgeting for a monthly tax account is mandatory in these circumstances. Remember, if you're self-employed or a commissioned salesperson, you can write off only 50 percent of your business meals and entertainment expenses, instead of 80 percent as in previous years. This reduction applies to the goods and services tax credit for business meals and expenses. The self-employed also need to consider budgeting for their own extended health care, life and disability insurance, educational savings plans, and retirement, since pension plans aren't available. Your maximum RRSP contribution amortized over the year should also be a monthly expense.

I found a way to "budget" that worked for incorrigible financial habits like mine—preauthorized chequing and a company payroll deduction plan. These helped me more than anything else to establish an effective working budget. My 10 percent savings, life and disability insurance, RRSP, car payments—everything came out of my account on a predetermined day. The money was out and gone before I could get my hands on it. I was rich for approximately 20 minutes on payday, then preauthorized chequing would wreak hell and havoc on my chequing account. The good news was that I was free to spend guiltlessly whatever was left over. Okay, some months the spending capacity wasn't so good, but I sure slept well at night. I want to stress again, it doesn't matter how much you earn or think you can afford. If you do nothing else but save 10 percent net of your income, the chances are very high that you'll be financially secure. When (and if) you do your budget, right at the top of the list of expenses should be 10 percent savings.

Budgets can be as simple as the scribblings on the back of a napkin (I've seen hundreds of these) or as detailed as a cash flow analysis (I've seen two of these). There's a plethora of budget forms available. Find out what works for you. Financial planners can be very helpful in this area. Remember, budgets are designed to give you the big picture. Don't get hung up on the word. They can actually help to make your money world feel safe again.

Here are some of my favourite budget tips I've collected over the years:

- Make weekly or bi-weekly mortgage payments. This makes it easier to budget using the paycheque method and you'll pay off your house faster.
- Make weekly or monthly RRSP contributions. Ask your employer to reduce the income tax withheld to reflect your tax-deductible contributions.
- Take advantage of the "pay nothing until the next decade" offers, but obviously only if you have the discipline to pay the purchase in full when the bill comes due.
- It's also always good to put the detail person in your household in charge of the budget and to be sure that everyone who's affected by it has input.
- You can always take a budgeting course available through different credit counselling agencies.
- One last budget tip: a good exercise is to write down a wish list. Some people call this goal setting if it's anchored in the real world. Such a list set down on paper does seem to make your financial goal more tangible, so possibly more achievable.

Okay. So now you've come to terms with the real meaning of budgeting. You understand that a proper budget means your money and the month run out together. Now that you've got a handle on some of the basic principles of financial planning, things like tax rates, the power of compound interest, and the importance of emergency funds, let's move on to the next step in the priority pyramid. I had a personal experience that graphically illustrated the absolute necessity of a solid estate plan—life and disability insurance, wills, and powers of attorney. My blood runs cold every time I think of it.

four
Admitting mortality

What is it that bothers me about death so much?
Probably the hours.

WOODY ALLEN

Lynn's story

Lynn and I have been friends for many years. As good friends do, we've shared many a pizza and cheesecake, either celebrating or commiserating. The events of 1989 and 1990 tested Lynn's courage and emotional stamina almost to the breaking point. I was very close to Lynn through this heartbreaking period. The things that happened to her in these two years underline the importance of understanding family law, wills, powers of attorney, life, disability, and health insurance, and tax and estate planning. The important lesson to be learned from her story, however, will be obvious—take financial control of your own life. Lynn is a walking example of a person who waits until catastrophe strikes before waking up to her own financial reality. It's for this reason that she's graciously allowed me to share her story here.

From the outside Lynn's marriage resembled a Norman Rockwell painting, utopian and traditional. Stan was a lawyer with his own thriving practice and Lynn worked in the home raising three rambunctious sons. Before Lynn married, she'd been a secretary to three company presidents. But it was accepted by women and men alike that as soon as a woman married, she traded in her paycheque for an unpaid career in the home. Lynn left her position as an executive secretary and remained out of the paid labour force for over 21 years. She entered into the marriage with no assets other than a stunning wardrobe, believing, however, that her contribution to the home and family made her an equal partner.

In 1968 Lynn and Stan bought a big, beautiful, rambling house in one of Toronto's finest neighbourhoods. Their home was surrounded by almost two acres of impeccably manicured lawns and gardens. The house was in Stan's name, something that didn't even raise the smallest blip on Lynn's radar. The three children they had came in rapid succession. Lynn's life was filled to the brim with her family responsibilities and volunteer work. The financial arrangement was that Stan paid Lynn a monthly housekeeping allowance of $400 (remember, this was 1968) and it was to cover all home- and child-related expenses. Oh yes, and Lynn's own personal expenses were to come out of this as well. Having never learned to drive, she had a charge account with a taxi company as well as accounts with the drugstore and the local grocery store. She had a spouse's credit card, but Stan took that privilege away after she got into trouble with it. The only access to money Lynn had was through the joint bank account she and Stan had, but Stan also had several accounts of his own.

When I asked Lynn if she had saved any of the allowance for her own purposes, like retirement or an emergency fund, she candidly replied, "It never occurred to me that I should save my own money. I came from an era when women married their retirement plans. Even if I'd wanted to, I couldn't. There simply wasn't anything left over." Whenever Lynn approached Stan for an increase in her housekeeping allowance, she could always count on a good argument. Stan never begrudged giving Lynn her allowance, as long as she lived within the amount he determined and doled out. But if she came to him for more money she had to jump through hoops to justify her request. Lynn said she always felt like the "subordinate partner in the relationship." There were the few times when she approached Stan about returning to the paid workforce, if only part time. Again, there would always be a blowup. Stan consistently refused to "allow" her to return to work, his explanation being the $1,200 tax exemption he'd lose if she returned to work outside the home. In the 21 years of their marriage, Lynn had no idea of Stan's income or what he held in assets. Lynn did have a will and life insurance on herself. But the monthly premiums for her policy came out of her housekeeping money. When she started experiencing financial difficulties, she insisted Stan take over the insurance premiums. He finally did but made no bones about his displeasure at doing so.

Part of Stan's problem was that he was trying to build his law practice. His overhead was high, and when he felt financial pressure he resisted spending more money at home. More to the point, however, it was money he had no control over or knowledge of how it was being spent. Not having a clue about the rising cost of children's clothes and food, he assumed Lynn had more than she needed. There's no question that in any marriage it takes two to tango. Lynn believed, however, that Stan had serious issues around needing to be in control of all aspects of their life, in fact to an alarming degree. The marriage began to seriously deteriorate eight years after their walk down the aisle.

Lynn arranged a clandestine meeting with a lawyer to investigate her options for getting out. But she had two experiences that shook her up enough that she shelved her plans to pursue a separation for another 13 years. The first lawyer she went to see told her outright that he wouldn't take her case because "she was too afraid of her husband." He told her that because she had no confidence, her chances of getting remuneration were nil. (This was before family law reforms that ensure equal division of family property.) Lynn's fear was very real. Stan was, after all, a lawyer and would be very tough to beat at his own game. Lynn did eventually manage to find a lawyer who would take her case without a retainer (upfront fee), instead taking a percentage of the spoils. But Lynn knew she was in trouble by the third visit, one she remembers vividly. The lawyer had repeatedly asked her questions about Stan's net worth and income level. "He was drilling me again on Stan's income. I told him that I had no idea. I tried to make it clear to him that Stan never discussed his assets and holdings with me, though I asked many times. The lawyer was looking thoughtfully out the window when he said to no one in particular, 'I can understand that. In his position, I'd do the same thing.'"

That was Lynn's last visit to a lawyer for 13 years. The marriage continued in a backward slide until finally, in 1989, it reached an intolerable level for Lynn. She was devastated by the thought of their children coming from a broken home. But enough was enough. As she put it, "Home was broken, but now I wanted to fix it."

Lynn was still extremely intimidated by the idea of taking on a lawyer. Nevertheless, without Stan's knowledge, she quietly began again to seek advice. She wanted to be sure she and her children would be adequately protected before confronting Stan with her intention to end the marriage. The Family Law Act of Ontario had been in force since 1987, so there was some automatic protection for her in place. Lynn went to a woman lawyer who specialized in family law and was a vocal national spokesperson for women's issues. The first thing this lawyer did was demand a heavy retainer. Lynn was shocked and dismayed, not only because the lawyer refused to take her case without the retainer, but because Lynn had a grand total of $300 to her name after 21 years of marriage and child-rearing.

Lynn then realized she had to get a job somehow to raise the thousands of dollars necessary to pursue the separation. Because of her level of experience before marriage, she did finally manage to get a job as a legal secretary in one of Canada's largest and most prestigious law firms. But Lynn had difficulty adjusting to the new work culture. Technology was everywhere. She did her best to learn, but law firms are very fast-paced and everything is needed yesterday. It was not a patient environment. Also, after three months of the most incredibly inappropriate sexual comments from her boss, Lynn lost her temper and snapped at him. She was fired two days later. Lynn was forced to sell her jewellery, borrow money from a generous friend, and cash in a spousal RRSP to pay her legal fees. After all the years Lynn and Stan had been together, Lynn was flabbergasted to discover that there was only $2,500 in the spousal RRSP.

Once paid, the lawyer began action. When Stan realized that Lynn meant business, he hit the stratosphere. However, after he went off to lick his ego-damaged wounds, he came back agreeing to a new living arrangement. He rented a duplex where he and Lynn stayed in alternate weeks. The week he was at the duplex, Lynn would stay at the family home and vice versa. The children stayed in the family home all the time. It was a dreadful way to live for Lynn and Stan. Having to move every weekend meant their lives never had a sense of settling down. Just when Lynn was sure that things couldn't get worse, they did. Much worse. The negotiation of the separation agreement was acrimonious pretty much 100 percent of the time. The first thing Lynn's lawyer did was slap a matrimonial designation on the house since it was in Stan's name. This action removed any possibility of selling, mortgaging, or otherwise encumbering the house from under Lynn.

Another extremely contentious issue was Lynn's unwavering demand that the house be in joint tenancy. She wanted to be sure that if something happened to Stan, the house would be hers and the children's. She had approached Stan a few times after their marriage began to disintegrate to change this. He'd always refused, with the stunningly brilliant legal explanation that "it simply wasn't necessary." Lynn knew this was part of his control mania. He'd never relinquish control of the house. At her lawyer's suggestion, Lynn had the house and contents appraised. The contents were valued at $100,000. The house, however, was valued at $2 million. Real estate had appreciated dramatically in 21 years. Herein lay much of the problem.

Finally, after an exhausting, gruelling year and a half of vicious fighting back and forth, Stan bitterly agreed to the joint tenancy clause. This was a major move forward and the agreement was very close to being signed.

The agreement was back in Lynn's hands to sign when she noticed a clause that sent her into a rage. She'd be required to pay tax on the child support payments she received from Stan, but he'd be able to use the payments as a tax deduction. (Remember, this was in the late '80s—it's different today. See chapter 9.) She fired the agreement back to Stan's lawyer, challenging it on the grounds that this was unfair and requesting that her payments be increased to compensate her for the extra tax she had to pay. When Stan got word of Lynn's refusal to sign because of the tax clause, he became apoplectic. He refused to discuss the agreement further.

I offered what support I could to Lynn while she went through this agonizing period. My involvement in her life, however, was about to increase dramatically. It was months after the tax issue in the separation agreement exploded. Stan was no closer to budging than he'd been before. I had just completed the licensing requirements to become a financial advisor and was due to start my new job in a week.

At this point, I'd been away visiting the folks in Ottawa for the weekend. It was late Sunday afternoon as I let myself into the house after a long, boring drive home. Out of the corner of my eye I caught the steady, insistent flashing of the red light on my answering machine as I struggled to take the key out of the front door. The display window on the machine flashed "22 messages." I'd only been gone for three days. I started to get an uneasy feeling in the pit of my stomach as I rewound the tape. "Twenty-two messages!" I mused. "I'm sure Michelle Pfeiffer doesn't get this many calls in three days. Who the heck are all these people?" I never got to find out. The first message simply said, "Joanne, Stan Greene was killed in a car accident this afternoon. Thought you might want to know." The message ended. With suitcase still in hand, I immediately turned and ran to my car.

Stan had been killed instantly when he lost control of his car and hit a light standard. Lynn's life turned from bad to nightmarish. The children were completely devastated by the loss of their father. Lynn found herself having to deal with the intense guilt that came as a result of the horrendous shots and slurs that had been slung during the divorce proceedings. But that was only part of her anguish. Because the separation agreement hadn't been signed before Stan's death, the house hadn't been changed to joint tenant status. It was still in Stan's name and it was the only appreciable asset Stan had. Said another way, Lynn had lost control of an asset valued at $2 million. It now belonged to "the estate." The estate was the sum total of Stan's assets and property and, as per the will, was being held in trust for the children until they reached a certain age.

Stan had had the sense to make a tape that outlined what to do in the event of his death. Unfortunately, because of the impending separation, much of what was on the tape had changed, but it did give us a place to start. I began the arduous task of looking for anything that resembled a financial document or insurance policy. Canada Pension Plan offered a small death benefit of about $3,500 to the surviving spouse and a very small monthly pension for each of the children until they graduated from school. We filled out the forms to get this started. It's not easy going through someone's personal papers knowing they've died. We had to go to Stan's office to deal with closing his business affairs. Much to Lynn's surprise it turned out that Stan's business had been in trouble, as evidenced by his mountain of outstanding debts.

It also turned out that there was still a $98,000 mortgage on the house that Lynn knew nothing about. Considering the house had been purchased for $112,000 over 21 years ago, it was obvious that Stan had been dipping into its equity. When we made that discovery, Lynn really began to realize the extent of her vulnerability and financial ignorance. She remarked to me one day, "If Stan had defaulted on the mortgage payments, we would have lost the house. I'd never have known until it was too late." Lynn was beginning to understand the folly of leaving financial matters entirely up to one's partner. Thanks to family law legislation, this can't happen anymore. A spouse can't mortgage a matrimonial home without consent of the other partner.

Because no legal proceeding had been instituted at the time Stan died, Lynn could choose to go under the will or use the Family Law Act. (Note: Be sure to have a lawyer find out if you have the right to make such an election. There are endless permutations as to what's what.) Under family law she'd get half of the house. But Lynn's lawyers strongly advised her as a result of her unique, complex personal situation to go under the will. With the huge debts that Stan had incurred, the proceeds from half the house would be gone in a millisecond. Lynn would fare marginally better, though still not great, under Stan's will. (Note: There are many ways that situations like Lynn's can be handled, so always see a lawyer first. The courts are actually there to help people address inequities due to the Family Law Act.) The will was on file with the trust company, so that part of the situation was simple. The will stipulated that Lynn and the trust company were co-executors, although Stan had made sure that Lynn still wouldn't have control over her financial affairs. Lynn was to receive the contents of the house free and clear, and that was the extent of the assets she could control with no conditions from the trust company. It was dumbfounding to us. Lynn received a house full of furniture as payment for 21 years of being a dedicated mother and wife. Lynn was distraught at the prospect of having to sell the family home. We tried to think of ways around it, but to no avail. We even considered converting the house to take on boarders, but the trust company would never have gone for the idea. Anything Lynn wanted to do with the house had to be approved by them.

I told Lynn that if we could find a life insurance policy that named her as beneficiary, Stan's creditors couldn't touch the money and the trust company would have no control over it. It would be Lynn's exclusively. This was the only fighting chance she'd have at living an independent life. We searched high and low. So did the trust company. There were no life insurance policies to be found anywhere. But Lynn was sure one existed because Stan had been a strong believer in insurance. In one last kick at the can, I began to go through cancelled cheques that Stan had kept, looking for one made payable to an insurance company. I found three stubs that had been written over a year ago to different companies. I called the insurance companies and the worst was confirmed: the policies had all lapsed within the last six months. Two were term life insurance policies and one was a property insurance policy. I also discovered that Stan had let the life insurance policy on Lynn lapse without her knowledge. We all but gave up hope.

It was late Thursday afternoon. Exhausted and bleary-eyed from wading through reams of paper, I leaned back in what used to be Stan's chair in his study. "I just don't get this," I pondered. I picked up Stan and Lynn's wedding picture, now sitting among shards of glass on a pile of unopened mail on Stan's desk. (Lynn had lost her temper during one of the separation agreement nego-tiations and threw the photograph on the floor.) I stared at the young, fresh faces, exuding happiness and hope. Smiling, jubilant faces. "They could never have imagined …" I whispered softly. I felt a wave of profound sadness wash over me. I thought, "What happens to people? Can marriage make people so bitter that they lose all sense?" I thought of the many times I lamented my single status. Having my own family was a major life goal for me. I was at a point in my life when, if I was out walking along a beach and saw a mom, dad, and baby, the stab of pain in my heart would take my breath away. It was becoming too painful to bear. All of a sudden I found myself in a state of swirling, confused emotions. "Maybe I'll never have my own family. Certainly not in the traditional sense." I sighed, looking at the smashed wedding picture. "And maybe that's okay." I smiled to myself as I mentally paraphrased a famous piece of philosophy, "I think, therefore I'm single." I gingerly placed the photograph back on the stack of mail still unopened on Stan's desk. I decided to go through the pile to see if there was anything that needed immediate attention. Anything to get rid of that dull ache in my chest. As I ripped open an unobtrusive-looking envelope, my heart began beating faster with every word I read. By the time the content of the letter had sunk in, I thought my heart was going to burst through my chest. I yelled to Lynn to "get your ass in here as quick as you can." She rushed into the study and I shoved the letter in her hand, grinning like a lunatic. It was a premium overdue notice from an insurance company. The policy would lapse if the overdue premium of $157 was not paid by the 28th of the month. I looked at my watch. It was 4:00 in the afternoon on the 27th.

I said to Lynn, "This is like a very bad TV movie of the week."

I hit the phones with a vengeance. I called the insurance company to get the details of the policy. It turned out to be a substantial accidental death policy. Lynn and I were completely unsure as to what our next move should be. Should we pay the premium and not say anything? We decided to take the high road and call the senior management of the company. I spoke with the insurance company's representative and carefully explained the events leading up to the phone call. As expected, nothing could be done until the legal hacks had a go at it. We were told to "leave it with us." I reminded the woman bluntly that they had to respond immediately, if not sooner. The policy lapsed at 4 p.m. Friday, the very next day. She said she understood. That evening was one of the longest that Lynn and I had ever endured.

At exactly 9:01 the next morning, I called the insurance company. That was the first of a barrage of calls the company received on the hour, every hour. Every call was received with a "No answer yet. Legal hasn't dealt before with someone dying during a grace period so there's no clear policy." The blood of many generations of Irish Italians started to boil in me. It was 2:00 in the afternoon and the insurance company payment office closed at 4:00. Lynn and I were getting very anxious. I called again and this time I uttered the words that would instill fear into the hearts of the coldest and biggest of conglomerates. I said simply, "I will go to the media." This met with the response "I will be back to you in 20 minutes." Forty-five minutes passed. My patience snapped. I called Elaine. "Elaine," I barked, "these guys are trying to stall us until it's too late. Technically, they have to accept the money to reinstate the policy, don't they?" Even Elaine was unsure. It was a pretty unusual situation. Finally Lynn, Elaine, and I came up with a last-ditch plan that we hoped would work.

Lynn and I scrambled to find $157 in cash. It had to be cash because we didn't want the insurance company saying a cheque didn't count because it hadn't been cleared by the bank by the lapse date. It was slightly past 3:00. We leaped into my car and drove furiously through Friday afternoon downtown Toronto traffic. We parked the car at exactly 3:35. There were 25 minutes left to settle everything. We took a moment to compose ourselves before walking up to the wicket. Hand slightly shaking, I passed the overdue notice through the wicket to the young man sitting behind the window. "I'd like to make a payment on this policy, please. The premium is overdue." Lynn said my voice sounded strong and confident. The voice she heard, however, must have come from someone else's body. Inside I felt like a plate of spaghetti.

The young man was very pleasant and eager to please. I passed him the stack of crumpled bills and a handful of coins, turning slightly red in the process. Lynn and I couldn't look at each other. We kept our eyes on the clerk's hands as he counted the money. Then we heard the sound we wanted so desperately to hear: the thud of the stamp imprinting those wonderful words "Paid in Full" on the notice. Very calmly, I asked, "Is that everything you need? Is the policy still in force?"

"Oh yes, ma'am," he replied. "Everything is completely in order."

Only then did I venture a glance at Lynn, whose face had a ghastly pallor. "Good," I replied curtly. "I'd like to make a death claim." With that, I passed him a copy of Stan's death certificate.

He paled visibly. "Uh, excuse me?" he asked in a very confused state. "You're not serious?"

"Get your supervisor down here, please," I said. "We're very serious." It was 3:50, 10 minutes before the business day ended. Lynn and I sat in the reception area, quietly waiting for the fireworks to go off. We were not disappointed.

The representative we'd been dealing with over the last 24 hours miraculously appeared in the reception area no more than five minutes later. She was not smiling. "We would have extended the grace period because of the circumstances. It was unnecessary for you to come all the way down here," she began. "Unfortunately, we still don't know the status of the policy. Oh yes, by the way, Mrs. Greene, my condolences on your loss."

Both Lynn and I bristled at her manner. I stood up. "As of five minutes ago, your legal department has a whole new set of variables to work with. By our standards and that of your company clerk who readily accepted Lynn Greene's money, this policy is technically in force." The woman tried to use a lot of legal manoeuvring to skate around the issue. Both Lynn and I were at our wits' end. Lynn's life and that of her children were at issue here, not some legal precedent. Lynn graciously extended her hand to the woman and said brightly, "I'll have my legal department get in touch with your legal department." She turned and walked away toward the elevators. "Nice one!" I thought to myself. I turned to join her.

I would love to report that everything worked out in Lynn's favour, but it did not. Because the situation got into the hands of the lawyers, it took over three years and $45,000 in legal fees to settle out of court. In the meantime, Lynn was forced to sell the house in order to survive and pay the spiralling legal costs. The will stipulated that Lynn and the family were to live off the interest of the proceeds of the sale of the house. The principal belonged to the estate and was to be managed and controlled by the trust company. Because the principal had to grow, some of the interest had to be reinvested. It worked out that Lynn was to live off of 60 to 65 percent of the interest income. Lynn was very smart. When it became evident she had no option but to sell the house, Lynn refused to budge from her asking price of $2 million. If she had to live off of 65 percent of the interest of whatever the house garnered, she was going to make sure that it would provide a decent living for as long as she was on this earth.

Interest on $2 million sounds like major wealth, but in Lynn's case, it was not. Debts and taxes had to be paid. Even though Stan had died, Canada Revenue Agency still required that a "terminal tax return" be filed for the income he had earned up to that fateful day in September. Even in death, they want their money. Actually, especially in death would be a better way to phrase it. The tax bill upon the death of a family member can come as a great shock to the survivors. You need cash when you die. You're going to be deemed to have disposed of capital assets; in other words, all your assets are considered sold (except those left directly to a partner). There were probate fees, the cost of the funeral, costs of the experts, etc., etc. Often people like Lynn are forced to sell assets just to pay debts and taxes.

Lynn was also concerned that declining interest rates could negatively affect her income. She had repeatedly told these "experts" that she intended to get the maximum she could to protect herself against inflation, taxes, and dropping interest rates. I was impressed at how quickly Lynn was learning. Two million is what she asked for and two million is what she got. Sort of. What was actually left over for the trust company to invest was significantly less because of all the bills. The proceeds from the estate purchased a much smaller but perfectly lovely townhouse for the family to live in. However, a point to note here is that the estate owned the house, not Lynn. Anything she might want to do with it has to be agreed upon, in writing, by her sons.

It's been several years since Stan's accident. All of Lynn's children are working in their own careers, and one even has his own business. Two have gotten married and are looking forward to starting families of their own. But it took almost five years to get their life into a stable routine. Today, Lynn can actually say she recognizes how unbelievably lucky she is. Too many women share her dreadful experience and don't have a large house to fall back on. She's come a long way in understanding money matters. Lynn reads every book and attends seminars. Right after Stan's death I set up savings programs for her children. Today they all maximize their RRSPs even though they're only in their 20s. Lynn and I continually preach to them the importance of financial literacy. There's no way that Lynn will allow them to follow in her footsteps. Oh yes, you may remember I was due to start my new career in financial services. I did start about three weeks later, when the maelstrom died down. Lynn was my first client. Talk about getting your feet wet in a hurry.

Everyone needs a will

It was the first day of my new job. Elaine and I sat in my office trying to make sense of the tax and estate issues in Lynn's case. At one point, Elaine turned to me and said, "I suppose I don't have to ask if you've made a will. I remember you telling me that paying your parking tickets was a big financial step forward." I was quickly learning that honesty doesn't always pay.

Elaine didn't wait for me to answer. "Let's assume you were removed from the picture. Tell me exactly what situation your family would walk into. Would they know what to do? Do you think they'd know what you'd want them to do? And, pray tell, what do you think would happen to all your stuff?"

I pondered Elaine's questions. I imagined the disaster area that was my bedroom. After returning from Lynn's, I hadn't had much time to get organized before starting work. I thought about the mound of dirty laundry on the floor and the unwashed dishes in the sink, but I didn't think that was the kind of thing Elaine was referring to. "What are you really asking me? Obviously, if I died, my family and friends would share the bonanza of my immense estate. That would be after a major blowout at a nondepressing, totally unfuneral-like place like, say, the SkyDome."

"Of course, and standing room only, I assume," Elaine remarked. "My dear, if you die without a will, the government steps in and writes one for you. It's a way to guarantee that the folks you want to get stuff, won't, and those you don't want to get stuff, will. The chances of the government writing a will that's close to what you'd write for yourself are slim to none. They call this dying 'intestate' or 'without a will.' You saw first hand how complicated things can get even with a will."

She had a point there. After being so close to Lynn's trauma, I was, shall we say, eager to meet the next challenge in the priority pyramid. It felt a little strange but I had to face it. Lynn's experience drove home the message of mortality. I was ready to prepare for the day when I would meet my maker. I figured if I was being responsible and looking after my affairs while I was alive, why shouldn't I take responsibility for what would happen when I died? It made sense that I should clean up my own messes or ensure that there weren't any when I died. I made a call to a lawyer specializing in this field.

Having a will is a major, though not the only, part of tax and estate planning. Estate planning doesn't have to be complicated. Be prepared, however—it is time-consuming. Remember also that estate planning isn't for the dead but for the living: survivors such as your mate, business partner, or children. Its purpose is to preserve what you've spent your life accumulating so that it doesn't get chewed up by taxes, probate fees, and bad or uninformed decisions.

It's a way of doing what's right—it's protecting your family. It's part of the foundation of your financial plan. While I made my living as a financial advisor, I learned much about human nature. There's a prevalent "head in the sand" attitude when it comes to admitting we're going to die. Oh sure, we all know it, but we act like death really isn't possible. At least not today. And certainly not tomorrow. Consider the following true example of a couple who seriously need a will. But do they have one? No-o-o!

These are two of my oldest friends. They've been married forever, and have three children (the twins are my goddaughters) under the age of 12. They own a beautiful big house and lots of assets. Laura is a very successful account executive in the computer industry (I worked with her for many years) and, wait for it, Hans is a lawyer. Not only is Laura's husband a lawyer, so are her father and her sister. I hound these good people about getting a will almost every time I see them. And each time they enthusiastically agree I'm right. Every time we talk about it they promise to do something. They've been promising for eight years now. I yell at the lawyer of the two: "For heaven's sake, all you have to do is stumble out of your cushy little office and walk three feet! Everything you need is right at your fingertips." To which Hans invariably responds, "I'll have you know I have to take the elevator down three floors. It's not as easy as you think."

Then the banter begins. I counter, "Name one good reason why you two bright people don't have a will."

He says, "Uh ... we aren't going to die ...?!?? Okay, Joanne, I think maybe if I do the will thing, that's when it will happen. Show me one person who's signed a will who hasn't died!" Don't laugh. I've heard this many times. Whether consciously or unconsciously, some people are afraid to get a will or own life insurance. To do so is an active step toward acknowledging one's mortality.

Here's an indication of the depth of the problem. The Trust Companies Association of Canada did an extensive national survey and discovered that only half of Canadians have made wills. The survey revealed other disturbing news. Of those who had wills, only one in three had discussed what was in the will with the executor, the very person who was going to be administering their last wishes. A staggering 44 percent were completely unaware that their executor could be financially responsible for any "negligence"—mistakes made while the will was being settled. Here are some other findings: 77 percent named an immediate family member as their executor while only 6 percent named a professional. Eighty-three percent of Canadians who had wills had had them drawn up by a professional (lawyer or trust company) and 13 percent had holograph wills (written in their own handwriting, dated, and signed, but not necessarily witnessed). Of those who didn't have a will, three-quarters thought they might know who would inherit their assets. One-quarter had no idea what would happen to their property, cash, or personal belongings.[1]

Take a look at the following StatsCan figures based on the 2001 census. There are almost 1.5 million people widowed in Canada. Eighty-two percent are widows and 18 percent are widowers. The average age at which women lose their partner during divorce is 39 (the age for men is 41). The writing on the wall is very clear. Women can and will be on their own at some point in their lives. When you consider that one out of three widows lives at or below the poverty line (and two out of three when they reach age 75), it's obvious that people aren't paying attention to this important part of life.[2]

Dying without a will can leave one's family dangerously exposed. There's enough grief and anguish to handle during this time without the necessity of dealing with an added financial mess. The ability of the surviving family members to make appropriate decisions is often hindered by their emotional state. Outlining your final requests in a will not only makes the transition immeasurably easier, but it can reduce costs and minimize delays as well. Many an estate planning lawyer has shared with me stories of how not having a will has caused families that were normally friendly toward each other to fight over assets. If you die without a will, it's called an intestacy, and it's significantly harder to administer than if you had a will. Your assets could be frozen so there'd be no cash to help wind up your affairs or for your family to live on until your estate is administered. However, there will always be money to bury somebody. If you show up at a bank with a funeral director's certificate of death and an account from the funeral home, the bank will pay it.

My discussions with Hans and Laura on this topic were always lively. Our last chat started off with Hans's declaration, "You say we need a will, but do we really? We own life insurance and we've named each other as beneficiary so the policies bypass probate; we've also done that with our RRSPs and other investments. Our house is jointly owned and so are our bank accounts, so we'll automatically receive each other's share. We aren't as badly off as you think."

I then launched into my speech. "You're forgetting something, Hans. What if you die together? This is called common disaster. If no one's sure who died first, the law in Ontario, for example, will presume that you predeceased each other. What this means is that, without a will, your stake in the house and RRSPs that are jointly owned passes to beneficiaries other than Laura. And vice versa. Who chooses these beneficiaries? The law, Hans. Doesn't that make you feel warm and fuzzy? You lose control over who receives your estate."

I was just warming up. "When you go out for the evening, I know you always make sure the babysitter knows where you are, who to call if there's an emergency, and where everything is to ensure the kids are properly looked after. All this attention to detail and you're only going to a two-hour movie. Please explain to me why you don't have plans in place in case you don't come back from that movie. Does that mean you want me to raise your kids? Some of your family members might have something to say about that. You need to name a legal guardian or there'll be hell to pay among your family. Even if you do name a guardian for your kids in the will, that doesn't necessarily mean that the court will honour your request. Though rare, if someone comes up with a good enough reason not to honour your choice, your request can be over-turned. But it's still much better to name one in your will. If the custodian or guardian is named in your will, that fact can be very persuasive in the event of a dispute.

"You've already decided your first-born is brilliant and is going to be a judge or surgeon. What if she excels and wants to go to an expensive specialty school before the age of 18? Her guardian would need to go before a judge to convince her that this money is needed. It's a proper pain in the butt. Or worse, what if she turns out to be a disaster with money and blows her entire share by sundown the day after her 18th birthday? Establishing a trust would take care of these issues. You could choose a trustee, who's often your executor, to manage how much and when." By now Hans was staring at his shoes and shifting uncomfortably in his chair.

"Now let's assume the worst and everything wasn't held jointly and you died before Laura. Most people assume that their partners will get everything because that's what you want to happen. Forget that pipe dream. Depending on which province you live in, the government will divvy up your estate according to strict guidelines. You and Laura live in Ontario. That means Laura receives the first $200,000 of your estate, and the residual amount is divided between her and the kids. Laura will get one-third of the amount left over after the first $200,000 is paid out. Since all three of your children are under 18, if you died now, their portion would be held in trust for them by the court until they reach the age of majority or until Laura makes the application to be a trustee, which is very expensive. You lose the flexibility to set up a trust to reflect your own personal situation. What if you wanted the kids to receive certain amounts of money staggered at different ages? Without a will, you blow any chance of having the ability to take into consideration any special needs of other family members."

Feigning self-righteous indignation, I continued on. "I'm single, for heaven's sake, and I have a will. If I didn't, my parents would get everything. If they died before me, then it would be my brother and sister and so on down the line. Now, I want my parents to be looked after well enough, but I also have twin nieces that I'd like to see get a good start in life. My university alma mater is always looking for money because of the drastic cutbacks in the government's education funding. I'd like to leave a donation to breast cancer research. These are all near and dear to my heart. But if I didn't have a will, I couldn't do these things. I'd lose my ability to choose who benefits from my life's work.

"And Hans, there's something else I'll bet you haven't thought of. I know how much you love the taxes you have to pay. Your accountant receives big dollars to make sure you don't have to pay anything unnecessarily. If you take the time to draw up a proper will, you can save a bundle in taxes at the time of your death. But if you meet your maker without proper planning, your death will trigger a domino effect that will cost you plenty. Your cottage, common stocks, and that headache you call investment real estate will automatically be taxed as though you'd sold them. Welcome to the wonderful world of capital gains tax. You know that RRSP and pension plan you relish so much because you don't have to pay tax until you cash it in? Well, consider it cashed in. It will be taxed as income in the year you die. Assuming you have the good sense to wait until the kids are grown and the mortgage is paid off before you die, you'll have accumulated significant RRSP holdings which will be rolled into your income. The result will be a lot of tax to pay." Hans was turning the most unusual shade of green.

"Although actually, Hans," I said, not able to stand to see him cry, "even without a will, pensions and RRSPs can be rolled over to Laura's RRSP tax free until she decides to use the money. In fact, anything you leave to Laura won't be taxed if she hasn't died before you. This is an automatic provision since the government considers a couple as one person. No tax need be paid until the last of you two die or cash the assets in. But remember, at best you can only hope to postpone paying the tax, you'll never eliminate it. The other consideration is that Canada Savings Bonds (except for the interest portion), cash, and proceeds from life insurance have absolutely no income tax implications. Cash and non-growth-type assets are considered income on which the taxes are already paid. Apart from these assets you'd pay tax on just about everything else.

"You and Laura are fiscally responsible. You wouldn't have acquired all that you have at such a young age without some savvy. The term 'estate' sounds like you must have a lot of assets, but in fact if you leave even $10 when you die it's still called an estate. And you know darn well there's no such thing as a free lunch. To administer your estate costs money. It'll cost even more if there's no will. Your estate is administered if you die without a will. It's probated or validated if there is a will. In Ontario, administration and probate fees are half of

1 percent on the first $50,000 and 1.5 percent on everything above $50,000. Probate fees vary depending on the province you live in. There are ways to lower the fees if you're proactive. Some of the things you and Laura are doing now. Have all your real estate holdings in 'joint tenancy with the right of survivorship' so that they go directly to Laura, and vice versa, rather than becoming part of 'the estate.' Mind you, one cannot neglect the point that there are often good reasons to have property in one person's name. You may read plenty of articles about ways to bypass probate, but one should tread carefully. There may be very sound business reasons why assets are held by individuals in a relationship. If one of the people in a marriage is involved in a high-risk business, and all the assets are held by that individual or held jointly, those assets could be at risk in the event the business went under.

"You've already made sure that Laura is the named beneficiary of your insurance policy, as you should be on hers. This is very good. If you named the estate, the creditors get paid first and your family gets what's left over. If a person is named directly as a beneficiary, the proceeds from the insurance bypass probate and the estate. The same principle applies to your RRSPs. You bought your RRSP through an insurance company so you can name anyone as your beneficiary and not have the proceeds form part of your estate, so again, fewer probate fees.'

"Now Hans, do you know what you'd like to have done with your body when you die? Do you want to be buried or cremated?"

Hans was feeling a little beat up at this point. He mumbled something that sounded like "… cremated, I guess."

"Okay, who else besides you knows this?" I inquired.

"Uh, no one. Just me."

"Does that mean you want us to guess? Would it bother you too much if Laura goofed and made the wrong choice?" I was intent on hammering my point home.

Hans blanched. "Okay, okay, tell Laura and put it in the will. I'm getting it. God, I hate feeling like a doofus. Go home, Joanne."

He wasn't kidding. He was quick to see the theme developing here. "I never thought of it, but the best reason to have a will is to protect yourself against what would happen if you died without one," he sighed. "It doesn't only tell people who gets what, but it tells the world who should be dealing with my estate."

Bingo.

What a will really does is guarantee order and timeliness. A will distributes, according to your wishes, your DVD and your RRSP. That's why it's very important to put together a list of all your assets. This exercise will help you to figure out a fair distribution of those assets to your loved ones. Examples of the most common assets include your home, jewellery, household furniture, investments, life insurance, pension plans, RRSPs, and any interest in a business. Be careful in naming assets. If someone lists furniture as going to "Uncle Bob" there can be an issue over whether the deceased meant the furniture at the date of the will being signed or any new furniture acquired after that time. You must specify "I will give Uncle Bob any furniture owned by me at the time of my death." Sometimes by listing assets, someone intended as a beneficiary can get nothing. For example, you promised a painting to a friend because of its sentimental value, but it's damaged beyond repair while moving. Your friend gets nothing. And don't forget your liabilities. All your debts must be paid immediately upon death. That's why it's important to insure your mortgage and any substantial loans you might have. A tax return has to be filed and income tax paid on the amount you earned in the year of your death. Canada has no specific death taxes. However, if you own real estate or have holdings in other countries, such as the United Kingdom, your estate will have to pay tax according to the laws of that country. Once all your creditors have been satisfied, whatever's left over will be distributed by your executor according to your instructions.

Choosing an executor

Being an executor can be a very big job. Naming the executor doesn't mean they have to act. They can refuse. In Canada, the vast majority of people choose friends or family members as their executors. Intuitively, this makes sense. But remember, the role executors play is very time-consuming and, depending on the estate, complex. Be sure your executors are emotionally capable of handling the responsibility, especially considering that they'll be grieving while going through the process. Few people know that your executor can be held financially responsible for negligent mistakes made relating to your will. Can they afford to pay? There's some protection for them, however. You can have a clause in your will giving them discretion as your power of attorney and protecting that discretion. Your executor may be paid, usually a percentage of the value of the estate. This fee, called the executor's fee, is established by the court and varies from province to province.

Your executor should be knowledgeable in the area of tax and estate planning or have access to resources in this area. Trust companies have tremendous expertise in estate planning and are often used for large estates, although they can wield an iron grip (ask Lynn) and will want everything appraised and counted before they distribute assets. This can add significant costs. It's not a bad idea to name an alternative executor in the event your first choice is unable to do it.

An executor is the mind, voice, and hands of the deceased and takes direction and authority from the will. The job includes a variety of tasks. My lawyer insisted that I have my mother as co-executor since he didn't want the responsibility of "looking in my top drawer and going through my unmentionables." Because my mother lives in a different city, I chose her plus another co-executor who lives in the same city as I do, thus making life much easier for everyone.

Here are some of the tasks executors must perform:

- Find the will and act on it. It's obviously important that your executor know where the will is.
- Make the phone calls to your lawyer, banker, broker, insurance agent, and next of kin, not necessarily in that order.
- Arrange your funeral according to your wishes. (This is often done by family members. Make sure they know what special wishes you have. Don't take those wishes to the grave with you.)
- Arrange payment for the funeral, outstanding debts, and taxes. (The money for these payments usually comes out of the estate.)
- Prepare a statement of assets and liabilities.
- Find someone qualified to file your final tax return.
- Fill out forms for life insurance and Canada Pension Plan survivor benefits.
- Sell your property or any asset as you specified in the will.
- Manage the estate if necessary prior to distribution. Not all assets get distributed immediately, like investments, rental properties, and so on.
- Distribute your estate to the heirs and see that any cash legacies, like donations to universities or charities, are carried out.
- Transfer assets or money to any trusts established under your will.

The situation will be made infinitely simpler if your executor knows who the key players are and how to reach them. Do as Stan did and make a tape to go with the will. Remember this is a very tough time for your survivors. Make it as easy on them as you can.

How do I make a will?

The experts agree that a will isn't something to skimp on. Far too much is riding on it, and it may be complicated. Any mistakes may be very costly. Let the lawyers do it. They'll charge you anywhere from $100 to $700 for a basic will. Holograph wills, as described below, are wills written in your own handwriting, dated, and signed, but not necessarily witnessed. They're the do-it-yourself home version of what lawyers typically do. Form wills from the drugstore or the Internet can create many problems. Even those packages created by lawyers usually have complex instructions or provide instructions for only the most basic of distributions. And even where instructions are clear and proper, half the people still interpret them incorrectly and end up drafting an invalid will. For instance, if the spouse of a beneficiary signs as a witness, the beneficiary loses his/her entitlement—all of it. Although legally binding, wills are more trouble than they're worth if there's a mistake or misunderstanding. I doubt that most of us are qualified to write our own wills, since there are variables we probably aren't even aware of that could dramatically affect the lives of our survivors. Lawyers go to school for many years to learn these things.

Review your will at least every three years. Remember that the minute you marry, your old will is rendered null and void. It's important that your will reflect any major changes in your life, such as births, deaths, marriages, divorces, and new business arrangements. You can have a marriage contract that will exempt you from any provincial laws concerning the distribution of assets. You do, however, have to leave your spouse some share of your estate, unless you have a domestic contract. Many people arrange to leave their assets to their own respective children if they're in a blended arrangement. Have your own lawyer review your domestic contract very carefully. The Family Law Act of Ontario, one of the most comprehensive in the country, guarantees that the spouses share evenly in the growth of the value of the property acquired after the marriage, regardless of what the will stipulates, again depending on whether or not there's a marriage contract. However, family law does vary among provinces.

One final note. Be sure to keep your will where it can easily be found. Usually the original stays with your lawyer, but keep your copy where your family and executor can get to it without difficulty.

Holograph wills

In 1948 a Saskatchewan farmer, Cecil Harris, lay in his field, impaled on a metal shaft from the tire rim of his tractor. It was a freak accident, and while he lay there dying, he slipped a knife from his pocket and painstakingly carved into the fender his last written words. They said simply, "In case I die in this mess I leave it all to my wife." Two days later, he died in hospital. Later the tractor fender was brought into court where a judge ruled that it met all the criteria of a holographic will. A holographic will is a legal document and, as the farmer's case proved, it can be written on anything. As long as it's written and signed by the deceased and shows intention to divide property upon death, it is indeed legal. Legal but dumb.

Holograph wills should only be made in an emergency situation. The law requires a certain format and a mistake in this format will invalidate the will.

Powers of attorney

There are two types of powers of attorney. One is for property, the other is for personal care. Let's start with the one for property. I'll illustrate why you need one with a brief story.

Power of attorney for property

I took up rollerblading. I'd skate for hours, letting my mind wander, coming up with ideas that I could use to help my clients. I blew off a lot of steam while waiting for moments of inspiration to hit. One day, it wasn't inspiration that hit. It was me, meeting the highway in an intimate sort of way. A cyclist who had ridden by earlier had yelled to me that he'd clocked me going 80 kilometres an hour. (I was skating flat-out down a reasonably significant hill.) No more than two minutes later, my blade caught a pebble. I was in the customary posture, leaning forward over slightly bent knees. This contributed greatly to the velocity I experienced as I became airborne. The good news is that I was only in the air a matter of seconds. The bad news is that I dived and hit the pavement chest first, head second. Hard. Thankfully I'm not as stupid as I look. I wear protective gear: a helmet and knee, elbow, and wrist pads. These newfangled wrist guards have a curved plastic piece that fits in the palm so that if you do wipe out, it allows you to slide instead of coming to an abrupt, dead stop.

Well, slide I did. Right across the paved highway. On my chest. With my hands stretched out in front of me. It was like high-speed body surfing—on pavement. I came to a stop when I hit the loose shoulder on the opposite side of the road. The only thing I could think of was that I should be dead or permanently damaged. My grey matter was rattling around in my skull from the impact of my not-so-graceful swan dive. My brain did function enough to realize I should stand up as quickly as possible to avoid contact with the steady stream of gravel trucks that used this piece of road. I leaped to my feet as gracefully as anyone could who's just been knocked silly and was wearing rollerblades. I did a quick mental check of all my body parts and discovered, much to my surprise, everything intact. Shaken, but intact. My T-shirt was the only thing that suffered. The decal on the front had been completely worn away.

When I related this harrowing experience to a friend, he comforted me by saying, "You came very close to becoming a nice little turnip." Bad humour aside, I started to think about how close I had come to disaster. The accident wouldn't have been enough to kill me, that was certain. But without that protective gear, and at the speed I was travelling, I would have sustained serious head injuries and God knows what else. I would have been out of the loop for a very long time. The long-term consequences could have been grave. If I wasn't able to make decisions for myself because I was in a coma, what would happen to my stuff? My investments? Who would pay my bills so that I wouldn't lose my possessions, my car for instance? I knew a woman who couldn't sell her house without her husband's signature because the property was owned jointly. He became incapacitated and wasn't able to sign anything.

As if all of this isn't enough to worry about, women need to be acutely aware of what happens when one becomes incapacitated, for whatever reason. It comes down to the fact that we live longer and do most of the elder care in this society. We need to worry because of what may happen to us personally and to the people who eventually become our charge. Women are much more likely to be disabled for a significant period of time before age 65 than are men. Women are, at least according to Arthur Fish, an estate lawyer with the Toronto-based law firm Borden Ladner Gervais LLP, the proverbial ham in the sandwich. They get stuck between the needs of their children and the needs of their parents. As Fish says, "Women need to learn about this stuff, not only to ensure their own financial base is solid, but for their parents as well. In reality, the chances are good that women will be dealing with powers of attorney issues with them long before they need to deal with them on their own ground." Unless, of course, your rollerblading skills equal mine.

I wanted to know specifically what would happen if I'd tangled with a truck and found myself in a hospital unable to make any decisions for myself. It turns out it's a pretty big job. Your attorney for property acts for you, managing your assets, property, financial affairs, and so on until you can act for yourself again.

There are primarily three situations in which people generally get motivated to get powers of attorney for property. The first is when you're of sound mind and body and recognize the general importance of having a power of attorney for property in place to cover any kind of worse-case scenarios, kind of like what I should have done before embarking on my short-lived blading career.

A second common scenario is that you don't have one and you can't or won't make one. This is often the situation with people suffering from some kind of dementia. For example, in Ontario this may well lead to what's called statutory guardianship, which can be created in one of two ways. The first is if you become an in-patient in a psychiatric facility. Your physician can certify you as being incapable and is authorized to assign the Office of the Public Guardian and Trustee as your guardian. The second situation could be that you still live in the community. Any person might request that you receive an assessment of your financial competency, which would be conducted by a licensed assessor of capacity. You can say no, however. If you say yes, this person has the power of certifying you as being incapable of managing your property. In either case, the net result is the Office of the Public Guardian and Trustee becomes the statutory guardian of your property.

Having the Office of the Public Guardian and Trustee as your statutory guardian isn't necessarily set in stone, however, as the guardianship can be removed the same way it was created. If you had a continuing power of attorney that no one knew about, it would be very easy for your attorney to terminate the statutory guardianship. If you didn't have powers of attorney, a spouse/partner or relative could apply to replace the Public Guardian and Trustee as your statutory guardian. They'd need a plan that was acceptable to the court for the management of your property and a bond equal to the value of the estate.

The third and last scenario in which a power of attorney for property comes into play is in the realm of court-appointed guardianship. Let's say the wrong person applies to a court to become your court-appointed guardian of property. A judge might decide that no guardianship is necessary, because your attorney for property, the person you've chosen, should be allowed to look after you. All you have to do is watch TV to understand this scenario. A classic movie-of-the-week story line would be an aging man getting lonely and taking up with his caretaker. She's unscrupulous and is trying to go after his money. Arthur Fish says he sees cases like this at least twice a year.

It's important to know that if the Public Guardian and Trustee becomes your statutory guardian, any one of the following people can apply to replace the officer:

• a spouse or partner, including same-sex partners
• any relative
• a trust company, should a spouse or partner consent to the application

According to Fish, in-patients in a psychiatric hospital are at the highest risk. Even so, Fish says it's still a very good idea for most people to have continuing powers of attorney for property, especially for people who have dependents. One of the main purposes of these documents is to protect your dependents. When they need your money, they have to have access to the bucks.

Fish warns, "Powers of attorneys are not a benign intervention and should be handled with extreme care. People can take advantage of others, most often out of ignorance, but also out of malice. They have been sold as a panacea and they aren't. Your attorney can misuse the power given them."

Janet Freedman, co-author of *Hit by an Iceberg: Coping with Disability in Mid-Career,* tells a story of a friend of hers in a second marriage in later life. She encountered serious problems when her partner suffered a stroke. The children had power of attorney and instructed the hospital not to allow her into his room. According to Freedman, this is before the courts and is entering its fourth year. It has cost thousands of dollars in legal fees. The moral of the story: Be very careful to whom you give power of attorney.

Freedman herself encountered a devastating disability when she slipped on the front steps of her house and ended up with a C6 spinal fracture. Her co-author, Marie Howes, had power of attorney for Janet. Freedman says, "Thank God because I was on a ventilator for three weeks and completely out of it. I also had a tracheotomy and nobody could understand me unless they could lip-read! But at least I knew that they were looking after things."

You really need to think about how that power comes into force. Consider leaving the power of attorney at the lawyer's office and have a detailed discussion on what has to happen before the details are released to the world at large.

As to whom you should choose, people tend to stay with family. This is fine in most cases, but be aware of the fact that these people have pretty much the same rights over your financial affairs as you do. Make sure you trust the person, whether it be a partner, child, or parent, to make the right financial decisions for you. The person who has your power of attorney will be responsible for doing your banking, making investment choices, selling your house if necessary, and so on. Ask yourself if he or she understands the mechanics of making such decisions. While I was single, my mother, in partnership with my lawyer (who was also a personal friend), acted as my attorney. My lawyer was the alternative attorney, which is always wise to have. If you're single, brothers, sisters, lifelong and trusted friends, even parents, depending on their age, are all worthy of consideration. Older people should consider the possibility that they and their spouse will become incapacitated simultaneously.

Be sure the power of attorney you make is continuing and enduring, which means it will remain valid even if you become mentally incapable. The good news is that even people who are incapable of managing their property are still sometimes capable of making a continuing power of attorney. A power of attorney has other practical uses as well. Let's say you decide to "do Europe" for a year. You could designate an attorney to handle things for you, but only for the time you're away.

Many people worry about giving someone too much power over their affairs. A simple way around this is to appoint two attorneys who must act jointly, or leave your power of attorney with your lawyer along with written instructions on when to release it. Your stand-in can't act without the physical document. There is, however, a balance that is necessary here. Try not to make the document too restrictive, since that will defeat the purpose of having a power of attorney in the first place. It's remarkably easy to revoke. If the document hasn't been distributed, simply tear it up. The more appropriate route, however, is to inform your attorney(s) in writing and retrieve all original copies.

These are some reasons why I now have a power of attorney for property. I want to have someone I know and trust look after my financial affairs. That's precisely what a power of attorney does.

Power of attorney for personal care

Powers of attorney for personal care (known in Quebec as a health care or advance directive, or a mandate) are as important as powers of attorney for property. Some people suggest that you're more at risk on the personal care side of the equation than on the money side. The big advantage is this: if I had sustained a brain injury but wanted to live in the community, this can give me the mechanism to ensure that I get to stay there. It helps with the decision of whether or not you get to go home or if you have to stay in a long-care nursing home. Consent to treatment legislation typically doesn't cover all the decisions that have to be made for an incapable person living alone in the community.

Another function it has is to make health care decisions for you when you can't or to ensure your wishes are carried out regarding the very personal issue of how you die. Advances in medical technology have made it possible to sustain life, even in the face of life-threatening illness. In North America there are over 10,000 people in chronic vegetative states being kept alive by life-support systems. In almost all of these cases, the patients had no part in the decision that maintains them in this state.[3]

Let's go back to my rollerblading accident. Let's assume that the injuries I almost sustained had been serious enough that I should have died but didn't because of technology. Let's also assume that the chances of my recovering were nil, but that I was kept alive by the respirator which breathed for me. This situation would have been completely unacceptable to me. But where would my voice have been? How could I have made my wishes known? I couldn't. That's why I have a power of attorney for personal care. I can include what are termed "wishes." It takes the painful decision out of the hands of friends and family and informs the doctors that I don't want to be kept alive through artificial means or heroic measures.

However, it's important to know that once you've become incapable, the wishes are binding. Arthur Fish has had considerable experience in this area. He's seen clients who are living their deaths, whether they be AIDS patients or people with terminal cancer. His point is that these people are very clear about what their wishes are in terms of reasonable measures. Young and/or well people don't know really what to wish for because they aren't there. His advice? Go slowly and cautiously. The most valuable thing you can do is talk to your attorney. Verbal wishes are also binding. Ask them, "Can you let me go? Are you able to do that for me?" If they say yes, Fish says you can actually be better off than having a written document. Always speak to your spiritual advisor on this sensitive subject, whether it be a rabbi, priest, minister, or 12-step sponsor. There isn't a substitute for communication.

For years, people have been attempting to have powers of attorney for personal care legally recognized, putting forth the argument that quality of death is as important as quality of life. These powers are simply an expression of your wishes to your family and the medical community regarding the manner in which you die. Until recently, there was no way of really knowing if your final wishes regarding your death would ever be carried out. However, more and more doctors and lawyers are beginning to recognize their moral obligation to ensure quality of life and death, and seem to be moving away from the "save life at all costs" philosophy.

My grandfather, who lived in Montreal, had a massive cerebral hemorrhage at the age of 79. He suffered so much brain damage that he had absolutely no hope of a decent life. Although Granddad didn't have a power of attorney for personal care or mandate, as it's known in Quebec, the doctor took the family aside and said, "If it were my father, I'd never want him to live like this." With the support of the hospital and staff, we let him go quietly. The point to be made here is that we were very lucky to have a like-minded physician, but you can't depend on this as a matter of course. The only way to ensure death with dignity is to write your wishes down.

Several provinces have decided to leap out of the dark ages, recognizing the urgent need for legislation in this area. Nova Scotia, Ontario, Quebec, British Columbia, and Manitoba have made living wills legally binding or are in the process of doing so. You can take advantage of commercial kits, ranging in price from $10 to $40, available through provincial government offices like the Office of the Public Guardian and Trustee in Ontario, for example. Vancouver-based Self-Counsel Press publishes kits for all provinces. You can also buy 50-cent stationery store versions of a power of attorney for property and living wills, but because the rules are complicated and vary from province to province, it's always wise to seek legal advice before signing anything. All these options have flaws, however. They're either too simple or don't address setting up an alternative attorney if something happened to your first choice. In Ontario, the law stipulates that your attorney can be paid. Commercial kits don't address the compensation issue. One need not have a vivid imagination to visualize the potential family squabbles that could ensue. Couples who have no adult children might rule out compensation for themselves, but not for a friend, for example.

Lawyers are getting very marketing oriented these days. Some are offering wills and power of attorney kits that you fill in for yourself. These are perfectly legal and can save time and money. I would strongly advise, however, that you use these lawyer-provided kits only if your situation is very straightforward. Fish notes, however, "If you're not a lawyer, how do you know if your situation is straightforward? There are no choices in this kind of power of attorney other than name and address. This is why these should only be used in clear-cut, simple situations. However, these are much safer than the stationery store versions. Too much could go wrong with this latter type because there are too many choices you can make, which increases the possibility of error. You may save a few dollars up front, but end up paying thousands later in legal fees trying to regain control of your assets should something go wrong."

If you want to tailor your power of attorney to your own specifications, you have no option but to go to a lawyer. I believe it's always important to get your lawyer's advice on your power of attorney, for both personal care and property, just as it is with your will. Both are very powerful documents. You can amend, add, or adjust anything in your health care directive should you want to, though most come with boilerplate clauses that provide a good starting point. It's really important not to be too vague, like saying, for example, "Please avoid using heroic measures or life-support systems," because this wouldn't be of much use to the doctor. What's heroic to one physician may be standard procedure to another. I have very definite feelings about the kind of treatment I want and don't want. The term heroic measures scares me silly and conjures up images that scaremeister Wes Craven could do justice to. I want to leave this world as naturally as I came into it. Power of attorney for personal care and health care directives, and Quebec's mandate, are, in fact, sophisticated versions of the living will and more. They're not restricted to terminal conditions; they also allow you to name specific medical treatments you want applied in specific circumstances. Do you want a cardiac resuscitation or organ transplant, for example? A discussion with your partner and medical practitioner is always recommended so that your living will can be tailored to fit your own health circumstances. Make sure you make copies for your doctor, lawyer, and family. Look to pay around $50 to $150 for powers of attorney done by a lawyer, always the recommended option. You can save money by shopping around and comparing fees. Many provincial law societies operate lawyer referral services that give you the first half-hour of legal advice free.

Office of the Public Guardian and Trustee

Trudy Spinks, a lawyer with the Office of the Public Guardian and Trustee in Ontario, believes that there's a lot of misinformation about what her office really does. "If the Public Guardian and Trustee is appointed, there is a mechanism which enables family members who don't already have a power of attorney to be appointed as guardian directly by the Office of the Public Guardian and Trustee rather than having to go through the court. This process is much more expeditious and inexpensive (cost: $400) than a court proceeding and has been well received. However, if there's a preexisting power of attorney this process is unnecessary, as the power of attorney has automatic precedence.

"The governing legislation and the policies of the Office of the Public Guardian and Trustee both emphasize the 'last resort' nature of the office's role. Immediately upon being appointed, the first step our office takes is to search for family who may wish to act. We do this before taking any steps in respect of the person's money or property. If a family member does wish to become guardian, we work co-operatively with that person while the application is being processed to ensure that essential items (e.g., insurance premium and mortgage payments) are dealt with in order to protect the person's financial status. Contrary to popular perception, our office does not freeze anyone's assets unless it is determined that the Office of the Public Guardian and Trustee will assume active management as there is no alternative guardian. In that case, we do not 'freeze' it but assume management for the benefit of the incapable person. Even so, if an account is held jointly by the incapable person and another individual, the other joint holder retains full rights and we do not have any special authority to freeze his or her assets. Another point which may also be of interest is that our current rate of interest, payable to our clients on their accounts, is 5 percent, which is significantly higher than that provided through private financial institutions."

So, there it is. There shouldn't be much more convincing needed as to the importance of powers of attorney in your financial plan.

Life and health insurance

"I detest life insurance agents. They always argue that I shall one day die, which is not so." —Stephen Leacock, Canadian humorist

I was staring absent-mindedly out of Elaine's window, slumped in one of her stuffed chairs, which I propelled aimlessly back and forth with one hand against her desk. I was feeling introspective. I was still living on a daily basis with Lynn's ongoing nightmare. Between her situation and Elaine's insistence that I consider preparing for my death, I found my thoughts eventually meandering over to life insurance. I had a will and powers of attorney in place. Investigating whether I needed life insurance seemed the obvious next step. "Elaine," I asked, "should I get some life insurance?"

"I think life insurance is one of the best things you can do for your survivors, Joanne."

"Why? So they can grieve in Tahiti?" I cracked.

"What do you want it for?" she asked, smiling.

"For sure I want money for funeral expenses. They'll be costly. The SkyDome doesn't come cheap," I joked. "Seriously though, Elaine, after witnessing Lynn's trauma I've come to the conclusion that there's nothing like a funeral to put the cost of living into perspective. Lynn and I were shocked at how expensive it is to die. People think more about buying their car, yet funeral services can cost as much. I was dumbfounded to learn that it costs anywhere from $4,000 to $10,000 to bury someone. Stan's funeral was close to $10,000. I always figured, you know, a box, a hole in the ground, some flowers, and a minister. How much could that cost? The guy at the funeral home said $10,000 was the average amount that people pay, though there are less expensive options, like cremation."

"Actually, these days there are more and more less expensive options," Elaine offered. "If you have your heart set on a full-service funeral but still want to keep costs down, shopping around can chop at least 25 to 30 percent off the cost. Frankly, as morbid as this sounds, prearranging your funeral is quick, doesn't cost anything, and will save your friends and family time, money, and a lot of unwanted grief. This guy Donald Flynn wrote a book called *The Truth About Funerals*."[4]

"Someone wrote a book about funerals? I bet he'd be a blast on a date."

"At least he can get one," Elaine shot back. "The book is a kind of detailed insider's guide on beating the high cost of dying. I love some of the ideas he has."

Pretending to be bruised, I sniffed, "Like?"

"Like, asking if the funeral home is independent or owned by a large corporation. It turns out that independents tend to be more flexible with prices. And, if you take the time to prearrange, you have the luxury of being able to speak with at least three funeral homes for comparison purposes. Speak directly with the owners if possible, because they can make deals on the spot. Also make sure the funeral homes know you're shopping around. That's a pretty standard negotiation tactic. Frankly, prices really vary and in certain areas of the industry, they're going up all the time."

"Elaine," I interrupted, not able to resist a shot, "don't you find it just a little ironic that cemeteries can raise their prices and blame it on the cost of living?"

Shaking her head, Elaine continued undaunted. "There are even third-party sellers of caskets that can save you several hundred dollars. I've even heard of paper caskets."

"Paper, eh? Yikes, images of wailing, grief-stricken family prostrate across the casket come to mind. Could get messy. Obviously a cremation thing," I ventured.

"Probably. But research the company, because many of these no-frills funeral varieties have sprouted up lately. Flynn also says don't rent a casket."

"Rent a casket? You can do that?" I asked, shuddering. "That is so seriously gross. Like I really want to cozy up in a casket where untold numbers of other dead folk have napped." I suspected my jocular approach to the topic had more to do with discomfort than sensitivity, or lack thereof.

Elaine laughed. "That, and you don't save that much. A less expensive casket with a flag or pall draped over it is a good alternative. He also suggests that when buying a family cemetery plot, make sure there's a buy-back clause. A divorce could leave you with unwanted real estate. Remember as well that a funeral plot is not a commodity. You don't get its present worth, only what you paid for it. It's not an investment. So in a divorce, if you paid $800 for a plot and now the cemetery is full and they're selling them for $5,000, you still only get $800."

"With great respect Elaine, this is wa-a-ay too much information," I muttered. "I'm just a young pup. Life insurance is one thing, but picking out a casket is something else entirely."

Elaine nodded with understanding. "I hear you. But what's so amazing to me is that people take a year to arrange a wedding but are expected to put a funeral together in two or three hours. Don't you think it makes sense to think about it now while you can still be relatively detached from it?"

"Yeah, when you put it that way. You want to know something hilarious? My mother did exactly what you're talking about, she prearranged her and Dad's funeral. How I came to know this was as a result of a bizarre conversation we had one day. She started off by asking, 'Is it easier for you to visit us in Montreal or Ottawa?' Since my parents already live in Ottawa, I innocently replied, 'Why, are you guys thinking of moving?' She said, 'I guess you could say that. I'm trying to decide where your Dad and I should be buried.' I remember the water I was drinking at the time shot through my nose as I started to choke.

"Mom felt compelled to inform me of her progress, every step of the way. She spent a good couple of months narrowing her choice of funeral homes. I got another call from her announcing that she'd finally made her decision and virtually everything was done. She went into great detail about how reasonable the cost of the funeral and the plots were, how happy she and Dad were going to be being out in the country, and so on. I couldn't believe the painstaking care she took in covering off everything. Teasing her, I mustered as much sarcasm as I possibly could and asked her, 'So what are we eating at the party?' My mouth fell open as she detailed the menu. She even had the catering decided. When one or both parents die, all I have to do is make one phone call and presto! lunch is served. The reassuring thing about all of this, I must admit, is that I can be sure the funeral they get will be the funeral they want, right down to the paté."

"Did your parents prepay the funeral service?" Elaine asked.

"No way. I told Mom prepaying for her funeral services didn't make good business sense. She'd be better off putting the money in an RRSP or some other investment. She did have to pay up front for the cemetery plots, though. That makes sense because they're tangible assets."

"Your mom is pretty savvy. But the cost of funerals is really only part of the cost of dying. People always forget things like legal fees and medical bills for things that aren't covered by a health plan. There are so many hidden or unexpected costs that often the survivors are caught by surprise," Elaine offered. "Back to you now. You said you want money to pay for your funeral and other death-related expenses. What else?"

"Well," I pondered, "I don't have dependents, but I'd like to provide the tuition for med school for my twin nieces."

"Medical school?" Elaine said, raising her eyebrows and smiling.

"They're going to be Chiefs of Thoracic Surgery at Toronto's Hospital for Sick Children. I know because they told me," I said matter-of-factly.

"They actually said the word 'thoracic'?" Elaine rolled her eyes.

"They're quite brilliant. Just the other day they chose, out of two forks, the proper one for their salad without even being told which one to use," I said, eyes wide in amazement.

"You're right," Elaine said. "They obviously show great aptitude for surgery. Or eating."

"Think big, Elaine," I said, brushing off her shot. "Imagine what it will cost to go to university 15 years from now. Financial advisors will be asking parents, 'Do you want to buy a home or do you want to put your kids through school?' Higher education is going to cost more than $30,000 a year. Expensive stuff. I'd also like to leave something for my folks. They're playing catch-up because of the bankruptcy, so I'd like to help their retirement."

"Funeral, twins, parents—all valid reasons. What else?" Elaine asked.

"I'm concerned about the tax problems should I ever own my own incorporated business. Let's assume that when I'm 35 years old, the business is worth $50,000. Provided that famine and pestilence don't hit, let's say it grows at 10 percent a year. If I have an early demise and die at 65, my business will be worth a whopping $872,450. Canada Revenue Agency generously allows my business to earn $500,000 in profit before it taxes me, for the moment anyway. They're trying to change the legislation. Considering it was worth $50,000 when I was 35, that leaves me with a gain of $322,450. Fifty percent of this will be taxable at my tax rate of approximately 50 percent. By my calculations, my tax bill will be a staggering $80,613.

"And it's not only business taxes I'm worried about. By the time I'm 40, I plan on owning a cottage on a lake approximately 60 miles north of nowhere. Since this place would be a second property after my principal residence, which I also plan to own by 40, my estate could have to deal with another serious tax bill. Let's say, Elaine, I work really hard and manage to achieve my goal to buy this dream cottage for $100,000. If I'm lucky, this property will grow in value maybe 7 percent a year. If I die when I reach 80, my little dream spot will be worth almost $1.5 million. My tax bill, just on the cottage alone, will be over half a million dollars.

"I don't want my family to have to sell my business or that country estate of mine when I die just to pay a tax bill. I want my insurance to pay my tax bill so my business and personal stuff can go directly to my family. It seems to me I have a choice of paying, say, 3 cents on every dollar in advance to pay my tax bill by using the tax-free death benefit from an insurance policy. Or, the other option is to pay 50 cents on the dollar for my tax bill if I don't have insurance when I die. I know what makes more sense to me."

"You've been doing your homework," Elaine said with mock surprise in her tone. "Your tax reason is a good one. And you don't have to be rich to be concerned about it. Almost everyone, at all income levels, especially business owners, should think about the tax implications of death. It's funny, though— almost no one does. It's said that the only two things in life that are certain are death and taxes. These two go together more than people realize. The one thing you haven't considered, though, is that you might find some poor, unsuspecting fellow who marries you and manages to stay alive until after you die. If the cottage is in joint tenancy he'll get it rolled over to him with no tax problems. That is, of course, unless he sells it; then he'll be hit. Canada Revenue Agency will allow you to pass on your belongings and investments to your legally married or common-law spouse and defer the tax load to that person. They're very generous that way. Remember, in this country, there's no such thing as tax free, with the exception of the sale of your principal residence. There's simply tax postponement. If there's no spouse to pass this stuff on to, then yes, your estate is going to have a serious tax bill to contend with. Insurance can be the least expensive way to pay these bills. Good one, Joanne. And to think your high school algebra teacher said you couldn't add."

"Let's see," I mused. "Another reason is my health. I'm in the pink at the moment, but as my rollerblading record will attest, that may not always be so. The cost of insurance goes up every birthday. I'd certainly never let my good health and young age be the only reasons to buy insurance, but they do contribute another positive element to the equation."

Elaine only partially agreed. "Those are your personal choices. They definitely shouldn't be primary reasons to buy insurance. Naturally, once you're married and start a family, the reasons become self-evident."

"Absolutely. I only need to find a date first," I deadpanned.

It is my considered opinion that, if you're single, insurance needn't be a priority in your financial plan unless you have personal, business, or tax planning reasons to want it. I wouldn't be caught dead without it. (Pardon the pun.) There are, however, single people out there who wouldn't be caught dead with it. If you have enough assets to cover the winding down of your affairs and have no business concerns, you won't need it. Unless of course, like me, you want to leave a legacy behind. Either way is perfectly acceptable, as long as your survivors aren't saddled with the financial responsibility of cleaning up your messes. Debt should never last longer than the person who created it.

Do you need insurance? Absolutely no one can answer that question except you—with the help of a financial advisor. Joe Chisholm, partner in the Toronto-based Queensbury Insurance Brokers, says, "Nobody objects to life insurance, it's life insurance premiums that people resist. If it was free, who wouldn't get as much as they can? But the reality of it is that everyone has to evaluate their need and what is affordable."

I tend to think of it as a "repositioning of assets"—you either pay the premium cost or the tax cost.

Having been in the insurance business and having spent a few years talking to people about their insurance needs, I know two things for sure. One: people are emotional about this topic. They either love it or hate it. Two: there are no hard and fast rules. There are as many different answers to what you should do about life insurance as there are people who have opinions. People buy life insurance for many reasons, but its number one function is to provide financial protection in the event that you die prematurely. A person creates an estate, or adds to one, with an insurance policy. The decision as to what kind and how much to buy won't be an easy one. The world of life insurance is a baffling, controversial, and often complicated one. I'll try to steer you through the maze, but I can't tell you what or how much to buy. Get enough facts to develop a working knowledge and then seek advice from a qualified financial advisor licensed to sell insurance.

It's been my experience that only part of the life insurance decision-making process is about math. There's also a very important human side. There are emotional considerations that come from a person's life experiences that must be taken into account when developing a life insurance portfolio. Moreover, this is a very sensitive subject: a person's mortality and their wish to provide financially for their family. At the same time, it's important to be on guard against those few who use an emotional sales pitch to sell this product. If you find yourself wanting to weep uncontrollably during your first visit with a new agent, get that agent out of your house or office as fast as you can.

Get the facts and apply them to your own personal requirements. Then, and only then, will you be equipped to make an informed decision about your life insurance needs. Your life insurance portfolio can be part of a very sophisticated and complex estate plan. Or it can be as simple as "pay my beneficiary something when I die."

There are only two types of life insurance—term and permanent (cash value). Anything else is a variation of these two. In fact, term and permanent insurance are essentially the same thing. They're just different ways of paying for a death benefit. A death benefit is no more than what gets paid out to your survivors after you meet your maker. The amount depends on the size of the life insurance policy you bought. Term refers to coverage for a specific time frame or term. Permanent is permanent coverage until you die.

Term insurance

Term insurance takes three seconds to explain. If you die while it's in force, it will pay your survivors a tax-free death benefit. That's pretty much it. It's the cheapest, simplest, purest form of insurance there is. That's not to say, however, that it's the easiest to buy. You can buy it in 1-, 5-, 10-, and 20-year chunks, depending on the nature of the responsibility you want to insure. The cost of coverage increases at each renewal according to your age at the time of renewal. This type of insurance is used to cover obligations that will eventually disappear—things like mortgages, children (who eventually grow up and move out—with any luck), and major debts or business loans.

The only kind of term insurance you should buy is the renewable and convertible variety. This type of insurance allows you to convert to a permanent form of coverage should you decide you need it later in life. You also won't need to fess up to any health problems you may have encountered during the period you were covered by the term insurance.

The key with term insurance is to be sure that you find out how much it will cost to have yourself insured for at least 25 years. The cost may be unbelievably inexpensive today, but it could be much higher in 5, 10, or 20 years, depending on your age, since you need to renew it after each term expires. It's interesting to note that the Canadian Life and Health Insurance Association says that fewer than 1 percent of term policies stay in force long enough to pay death benefits. Almost all term insurance gets dropped without paying out any death benefit. Be sure to ask if there's a cost to convert your term coverage to permanent insurance. The cost of term can vary dramatically from institution to institution. It pays to shop around and compare prices. Insurance brokers subscribe to a computer service that accesses most companies and can compare many types of policies. Let their computer do the walking.

Permanent insurance

Get comfortable. This form of insurance needs some explanation because it does more than term insurance.

During the '70s and '80s inflation reached alarming proportions, running at a double-digit level for almost an entire decade. Because of this inflationary pressure, interest rates on investments like Canada Savings Bonds skyrocketed to unheard-of heights of 18 percent. The rates of return on whole life or permanent policies were regulated and based on portfolio rates of 7 to 8 percent for the life of the contract. Consequently, these policies became uncompetitive. The old way of doing things was no longer adequate.

For insurance companies to survive, they had to begin to develop interest-sensitive products to compete effectively in this new world of extraordinarily high interest rates. It was around this time that insurance companies also began to unbundle their policies and to identify all the separate components of a policy. Examples are the nonsmoker and gender-specific policies that were introduced in 1981. Universal life policies came soon after, which let the investor separate the investment part of the insurance contract from the insurance part of the contract.

With permanent insurance, your insurance premium (the monthly or annual amount you pay) is based on your contributions, the income the company makes on its investments, the cost of doing business, and the mortality tables. Mortality tables, as evidenced by their name, tell the insurance company how many people are going to die in a given year. There are events that impact the mortality rates. For example, AIDS has greatly affected the way insurance companies do business today. Anyone applying for a minimum of $100,000 worth of coverage will likely be given an AIDS test. These tests are becoming more and more customer friendly. Many companies are using saliva tests that are administered by the agents themselves right at point of sale. These are much less intrusive than blood or urine tests and take much less time to determine the results. It's interesting to note that less than 3 percent of insurance applications are actually turned down for health reasons.

Your contributions, minus the company's expenses and mortality charges, are held in an account. The income on the investments the company makes with your contributions and time help the account to grow. As long as the size of the account and the size of the death benefit that the cash value is supporting meet a predetermined benchmark (set by the government), the cash in the policy accumulates on a tax-sheltered basis. If the cash value exceeds this benchmark or you surrender the policy, tax then becomes payable. One of the purposes of the cash value in a permanent policy is that it will pay for itself when the costs of insurance become prohibitive in later years. The older you get, the more expensive insurance is. The premiums charged in the earlier years are actually higher than the cost of the insurance. The cash value begins to grow when the costs of the insurance are looked after.

Here are the three types of permanent insurance:

Term to 100 Up until recently, this form of insurance was what it said it was—permanent coverage with no cash value up to the age of 100. Now it offers cash value and paid-up value at the same premium price as "pure" term insurance. The paid up portion can actually carry you past the age of 100.

Whole life With whole life, you pay level premiums for a specified number of years. In the early years of the policy, of course, the chances that you'll die are low. Essentially, the premiums you pay in the early years exceed the actual cost of covering you. The insurance company invests these excess payments to cover the increasing cost of insuring you as you get older.

It works like this: the part of your premium that isn't used by the company to pay expenses and death benefits is socked back into your insurance plan in the form of dividends. These aren't the same as stock dividends, which represent shares in a company's profits. Insurance dividends are a return of the unused part of your premium. These dividends can be used to automatically "buy" additional coverage in your existing plan, which makes sure your coverage keeps pace with inflation. Even though your premiums stay the same year after year, your coverage will actually increase by the dividend amount paid into the policy each year. This is what's often referred to as the "savings" portion of the plan.

The rates of return on the "savings" portion of permanent insurance policies vary depending on a company's expenses, how much it's had to pay in death claims, and what the company has earned on its investment portfolio. In most whole life policies there's no cash value until usually the third or fourth year, and it's at this point that you may begin to borrow from your policy, up to 85 percent of the cash value. (Some plans have cash value starting in the first year of the plan that amounts to 40 percent to 60 percent of the premium you've paid.) Until the costs of providing the insurance for life are recovered, the cash value remains quite low for a number of years, at least 8 to 10.

Even though you can access these "savings" by borrowing from the policy, what you're actually borrowing is the death benefit. And what you're borrowing actually belongs to the insurance company, not you. If you do borrow from your policy, be sure to pay it back or you may lose the valuable financial resources your family will need after your death. The cash value in these plans is accessible as soon as your policy is in a positive cash value position, and can act as emergency funds as long as you pay the loan back. It can also bolster your retirement planning if you find you get to your golden years and don't need as much death benefit as you had anticipated. You can access the cash value in your policy to supplement your RRSP and other retirement savings, but you'll pay interest on whatever you "borrow." The loan rate is usually the same as what banks charge on term loans. If you don't pay the loan back, your survivor's death benefit is decreased by the amount of the loan. Stan had borrowed from his policy, and when he died the outstanding loan had to be deducted from the death benefit but the basic death benefit was still there.

You can take advantage of what's called a "vanishing premium," which is available on whole life plans. Provided that the cash value generates enough interest earnings, you can pay up your policy in 7 to 10 years. Be very careful, however. With declining interest rates many people are now finding themselves having to pay over a much longer period than was originally forecasted by the insurance companies.

One of the major criticisms of this kind of insurance is that you have no say over where the savings component of your premium goes. Hence the introduction of universal life.

Universal life Universal life insurance is a variation of whole life. In whole life the insurance and savings portion of the premium are merged, making it impossible to determine the return on the "savings" element of the policy and making the policy more difficult to understand. This is the main reason that has prompted many consumers to switch to a universal life policy, in which the "insurance" and the "savings" elements are clearly separated and the policy owner is given a choice of several investment options for the savings portion of the premium. You—not the insurance company—own the cash value in the policy. You can invest the cash as you see fit. However, it is now proven that if the market "goes in the toilet" so does your universal life policy. Al Hardy of Hardy Financial has been in the insurance business two years longer than God. He calls universal life "toilet bowl insurance."

With universal life, you get to choose the premium level and payment period based on your life situation (and an assumed rate of return). The minimum you can pay will be set in order to be sufficient to provide coverage for life. Any money you put in over and above that minimum is deposited to the investment account that you've chosen. Most policies offer a wide range of investment options, including savings accounts, GICs, and mutual fund indexes. It's important to understand that you don't actually get shares in a mutual fund. The insurance company agrees to pay the equivalent, or close to it, of the chosen index's performance out of a pool of investments set up for this purpose. Normally, there's a guaranteed minimum interest rate applied to the policy. No matter how badly the investments fare with the insurance company, you're guaranteed a certain minimum return on the cash portion. The GIC option generally offers a 3 percent minimum return, but if you are invested in indexes or funds, you have 100 percent market exposure (risk) on every dollar above the cost of the insurance which is drawn out of premiums before the investment is made. If the insurance company does well with its investments, the interest return on the cash portion will go up.

What I particularly like about keeping the insurance and investment separate is the flexibility it can give you. In years when your earnings are good, you can put more money in the cash portion of the policy and get a faster buildup of the cash value. In years when your earnings aren't so good, you may skip paying the premium altogether or pay less than the total premium. For instance, should baby number four come along unexpectedly in the form of triplets, you can take what's called a premium holiday. It can be a month, 12, or in some cases forever, as long as there's enough cash built up in the policy to cover the insurance costs under the plan.

You can control the cost of the insurance by increasing or decreasing the death benefit. However, if you want to increase the coverage, expect to take a medical examination. The insurance costs do fluctuate as a result of changes in interest rates. The insurance company can also change the amount it charges for the actual insurance up to a certain maximum. If the costs of the insurance component rise and you don't add more cash to the policy, the amount of insurance coverage you have will subsequently be reduced. Be careful—there's a risk you could end up with less insurance than you really need.

Be sure you understand that deposits to a universal life policy aren't tax deductible. But the money you have growing in the investment component does so tax deferred. As with all good things in life, there are ceilings. Canada Revenue Agency has a formula that tells you how much you can put in, which varies according to individual circumstances. Cash value insurance has the primary purpose of providing a death benefit for your survivors and keeping your insurance costs manageable in later years should you need coverage past age 70. This is precisely why the cash value inside permanent policies enjoys tax-sheltered status. The government made sure in MacEachen's 1981 budget that no one could pour large amounts of cash into their policies and thereby avoid paying tax. That's when they set this benchmark that determined anything over this particular line is subject to tax. Cash value withdrawals are taxed as income. You're taxed on the difference between the cost of the insurance and the amount of cash you withdraw.

Universal life policies aren't for everyone. However, for those concerned with estate planning, and who are at a stage in life where preservation of capital is becoming important, universal life has advantages. Because the investment component grows tax deferred, those of you (all three of you) who have maxed your RRSPs and are looking for another place to part with extra money without Canada Revenue Agency getting their paws all over it can consider this as an option. The truth is that the tax advantages of universal life policies are more beneficial to those who reside in high tax brackets than those in low- or middle-income brackets. Although the money you take out may not be totally tax exempt, you get to choose how much and when. So you can, in essence, defer income until retirement, thereby reducing what you have to pay in taxes. It's the same principle behind RRSPs. Naturally, if you don't use the cash component, it gets paid out as part of the tax-free benefit to your beneficiaries.

In short, this is what universal life does:

- pays a death benefit to the beneficiary you name
- offers a tax-deferred, low-risk cash value account earning market rates
- offers the ability to borrow or withdraw from the policy during your lifetime

- allows flexibility in premium payments
- has the ability to vary the amount of policy coverage
- in an annual statement, breaks down your policy by components—the charges, credits, and insurance aspects—which makes it much easier to compare different company policies.

When buying a universal life policy, make sure you're comfortable with the soundness of the insurance company. Look at annual administration and management fees, and possible tax penalties if you decide to change.

One thing everyone agrees on is that if you're going to use permanent insurance as a savings vehicle, it's imperative that you have your debts paid off, emergency fund intact, and your RRSP maximized. Remember, insurance is insurance no matter how you try to dress it up. Use it as protection first, and, if you choose to, as an investment second.

Who needs permanent insurance?

My view? People who earn a living. And those who don't ...

- First and foremost, people who have concerns about estate taxes. If you want to keep your estate intact so that it will be passed on to your survivors without having been annihilated by Canada Revenue Agency, permanent insurance will provide the funds to pay your tax bill upon your death.
- If you're a woman who works unpaid in the home raising a family while your partner works in the paid labour force, you need proper coverage to make up for pension inequities. This also applies to women who work part-time or in jobs that don't provide pension plans. There's a serious problem these days of people outliving their capital. Make sure you'll be financially looked after should you live to 100.
- More and more people are having children later in life and in second and third marriages. If your insurance requirements will extend past a certain age, say 65 or 70, permanent insurance will be necessary.
- You need permanent insurance to protect your privately incorporated business, especially if it's a family business that you want to pass on to your next of kin. Your business could be hit with a tax bill so prohibitive that it could force liquidation of the company. Your family's source of revenue could, as a result, dry up. The good news is that there's a $500,000 business capital gains exemption that will ease the burden somewhat. But if the business is a thriving one, the exemption may not be enough to protect your family's interests.
- If you have an RRSP, adequate emergency funds, and no (read: manageable) debt, you can use permanent insurance as a savings tool, though there are much better investment options.

If you're young, have a limited budget, and need a lot of coverage, you should look at purchasing term protection. People have come to me who have two children, a mortgage, no RRSP or savings to speak of, and owning $50,000 of permanent insurance. Their intention was to start a savings program at the same time as having their insurance needs addressed. This is nothing short of criminal. It not only doesn't provide anywhere near enough protection, but the savings element is so inconsequential for the first few years that it's virtually useless. If protection for your family is your main concern, get as much term as possible for your money. Term can always be converted to permanent later when you have more financial resources and, obviously, if you need it. Take the few dollars left over and sock them away into an RRSP.

Group and association insurance

Group insurance is the stuff your employer is kind enough to lend you while you work for the company. But it's kind of like living with your parents— chances are exceedingly high that you'll have to move out eventually. Employers never expected to replace the need for their employees to have their own insurance. One or two times earnings through a company plan was always meant to be a supplement to an employee's own personal plan. And in today's economy, job security is a thing of the past. No matter what happens in your work life, a privately owned plan will always be yours and completely transportable. Group insurance is a great way to augment your core insurance plan. I would suggest to you, however, that it isn't secure enough to be the only coverage you have. When you leave your job, it disappears. Even if you're lucky enough to get another job that offers group life insurance, it may not be enough. The amount of coverage varies from plan to plan. If you're unable to afford your own plan, your group coverage is at least something. The government has recently taxed life insurance group benefits over $25,000 if your employer pays for this benefit.

Association insurance works much like group, but it's provided by a professional organization or a university alumni. This type of coverage is a very inexpensive alternative but should be used only to supplement your privately owned coverage. It's subject to price increases and possible cancellation if the organization can't afford to offer it any longer.

Insurance riders

Buying an insurance policy is like buying a car. You can add on features to tailor it to your own needs. It's important to know exactly what you're getting.

Waiver of premium If you become completely disabled and unable to work at all, the insurance company will pay your premium for you. Now, we're talking down for the count, not a part-time problem. This is designed to help out only in the worst possible scenario. You also have to be off work for a minimum of six months before this benefit kicks in. The insurance company will pay those six months of premiums retroactively, however. Under no circumstances is this to replace a disability insurance, since they're two totally different animals. Buy this only if you're really flush cash-wise. It's not an essential part of the equation.

Accidental death benefit This will double the benefit paid to your survivors if you're killed in an accident. This is a rarely used option. You should buy insurance based on your need for it, not on the way you die.

Guaranteed insurability option This allows you to buy additional chunks of insurance every three years up to age 40 to 45, regardless of your health. This is a good idea if you think you're going to need additional coverage later in life. It can be expensive, though. You're paying to guarantee coverage even if you become terminally ill. This does not come cheap.

Women and insurance

Women have made important moves forward since the days when a woman's life was thought not to have any monetary value. It's still perplexing to me, however, that so few women own their own life insurance or that, if they do, it's usually what Gram and Grandad gave them when they were born. It would barely be enough to bury them. Our research has also shown that as women grow older or get married, their frequency of purchasing life insurance declines notably. LIMRA, a life insurance industry research association, gives the following eye-opening stats:

- Women are more favourably disposed to the insurance industry than men— 49 percent versus 42 percent.
- Fifty-eight percent of women say that protecting their family in the event of death is important, but only 38 percent have permanent insurance. Generally, most women are underinsured.
- More than 50 percent of couples who look at life insurance never consider adequate coverage for the wife.
- The average coverage of men is twice that of women.
- Women buy very little life insurance because they're sold very little life insurance. Thirty-eight percent of those who said they owned it contacted the company themselves.

Enough said.

There's a disconcerting number of women who assume they have life insurance because they're the beneficiary of their partner's policy. This is not owning your own insurance. When life insurance agents or brokers do a life insurance analysis, it's standard practice to evaluate the cost of replacing the work that women do unpaid in the home. Many insurance companies use in the neighbourhood of $18,000 a year as the minimum average amount that it would cost to replace the services of someone who works at home. (I've seen replacement values as high as $25,000.) There's an old insurance industry adage: "There are two types of people who need insurance. Those who earn a living, and those who don't." There's more than an element of truth here, especially for homemakers who work in the unpaid labour force.

As was seen in a Statistics Canada study, women working in the paid labour force are still solely responsible for child and home care in the majority of Canadian households. It's essential to include the cost of replacing the unpaid work women do in the home in their life insurance analysis, since the amount can be staggering.

If we look back over the years, we see that many experts, then and now, have been advising their clients to buy insurance with the eventual intent of becoming "self-insured." This means that you'll have accumulated enough assets that you won't need insurance anymore. If this advice has been so sound, then please explain to me why so many women between 60 and 65 today live at or below the poverty line. It's safe to say that these women aren't living at this level because their partners were "self-insured." More likely it's because there are very few assets and little life insurance. Today women are taking control of their own financial destinies, so the need for widows to depend solely on their partner's life insurance will diminish accordingly. Another point to consider: if you accumulate enough assets to be technically "self-insured," the chances are good that you'll need life insurance to pay your tax bill.

General rules

There are some general principles you should follow before making any insurance decisions.

- First and foremost, never buy life insurance before having a proper need analysis done. And have one done often. There are standard formulas for how much coverage you need, such as 10 to 12 times your salary, but these are too loose and general. The worst time to find out you don't have enough is when it's too late. You could also be paying for insurance that you don't need.

- Never buy life insurance based on what you think you need. I've done more life insurance analyses where the absolute minimum amount required was triple what the people thought they needed. People are always shocked at how much is really required. Canadians like life insurance, but remain woefully under-insured as a group.
- A proper life insurance analysis doesn't mean the agent or broker determines the amount of coverage for you. The agent will ask you a series of questions about your financial requirements. You decide, with the guidance of your advisor, the costs you think will be incurred for funeral, medical, legal, and other expenses. Things to be factored into the analysis include mortgages to be paid off or rent payment funds to be established, childcare, debts, education costs, salary replacement to provide an ongoing income, retirement planning, and inflation.
- If you're single, or just want enough to bury you, a comprehensive analysis isn't quite as important. But if you have a family or business obligations, you must know exactly how much you'll need. And always take into account the potentially negative impact of inflation. Since life insurance is about a lifetime, be sure to consider carefully your death benefit's future buying power.
- Don't be influenced by what your neighbour or accountant has done. Every person's requirements will be different.
- You'll often hear that life insurance makes a lousy investment. But please remember, investments make lousy life insurance.
- All insurance company products, not just life insurance, are creditor proof in the event of bankruptcy. You can name a beneficiary on anything from a term deposit to a mutual fund so that it will bypass probate and go directly to your beneficiary.
- Should you ever leave your place of employment and you're uninsurable, be sure to take advantage of the opportunity to convert your group plan into personally owned insurance. Most group policies have a 30-day conversion clause that allows you to do this, and you don't have to prove your insurability. It may be the only chance you get to own your own coverage.
- Insurance companies all adhere to the same mortality tables, so the cost of the actual insurance is basically the same. Where costs begin to differ is in how well the company is run and its overhead. Costs will vary, so it pays to comparison shop.
- Never let another agent talk you out of your existing insurance plan and into a "new and improved" version until you're absolutely sure you've been medically approved by the new company. Be sure that it's in your best inter-

est to change plans. (This generally refers to replacing one cash value policy with another.) Don't be fooled by agents telling you that the rate of return on their policy will be better than the one you currently have. Remember, the projections are based on an assumed interest rate. If you've had a cash value plan for a long time, say five or more years, and someone is suggesting you cancel it and buy term, be very, very careful. Sometimes replacing an improperly sold policy may be the correct decision, but work out the losses in cash value, the now higher cost to insure yourself because you're older, and whether you'll need coverage for life before making your decision. Replacing an insurance policy that's already been sold is very serious business in the industry. Be prepared, the first agent will obviously try to resell you. This isn't a bad thing, and I'd encourage you to always give the original person a chance. Review with this agent your reasons for buying their plan in the first place.

- There's a common belief that insurance agents and brokers only sell expensive permanent policies to make a whopping commission. If your agent offers whole life without mention of other possible options as a solution to your insurance requirements, you have a right to become wary. Look for a broker or a career agent (one who's been in the business a long time and has or is working toward insurance industry designations such as chartered life underwriter or chartered financial planner). If they plan on being in the business for a long time, your chances of getting an improperly sold policy decrease.
- Let's assume the man of your dreams—let's call him Lance—comes into your life and sweeps you off your feet. He puts that incredible diamond ring on your finger. What's the first thing we're often compelled to do? We insure the ring. Forget the ring. Insure Lance.

Disability insurance

Oh, how I'd love to say it was skiing. Or the ever-exotic parasailing. Or even a lowly car accident. Alas, I was clowning around, lost my footing, and fell off a 15-foot ledge. As I was in the heyday of my youth when reflexes are sharp but judgment less so, I landed on my feet. And broke my ankle in three places. My ankle was rebuilt with the latest technology, involving plates, pins, screws, and wire. The whole ordeal meant emergency surgery, two weeks in the hospital, three months on crutches, nine months recovery, and one ankle scarred for life.

I was 25 years old, working for a dealership flogging photocopiers door to door in downtown Vancouver. It was a small operation, so there were no benefits and I was strictly on commission. I suppose I could have used the crutches and the cast to elicit sympathy and increase my sales, but the doctor wouldn't hear of it. This was most distressing because if I couldn't sell, I wouldn't have a job. So, I was now unemployed. I had no disability coverage, savings, or means to earn an income. Ironically, my car was insured, as were my house and possessions, but not the income that paid for all these things.

Disability doesn't wait for a convenient time to strike. It seems to pounce at the worst possible moment. My relationship with the man I then shared a house with was deteriorating. We'd been talking for some time about each getting our own addresses when this disaster struck. Nevertheless, he graciously offered to cover all expenses until I got back on my feet, as it were. The humiliating part of it was that, other than moving back to Mom and Dad, I had no options. It was hell. Two months later, we finally decided to call it quits. I may have been somewhat irresponsible with my own money, but my pride wouldn't let me live off someone else. Parents, however, don't fall into the same category. After a phone call to the folks, I boarded a plane—cast, crutches, and all—and headed home to an anxiously awaiting family. Bill Cosby says that human beings are the only species in the world who let their children move back home. Thank God.

Granted, there's no shortage of stories like mine and many that are much worse. People have lost homes and businesses because of an unprepared-for disability. Families dependent on a single income have suffered immeasurably when this income is interrupted. My accident is a good example of how easy it is to become sick or injured. I lost my biggest asset: my earning ability. My exciting adventure of living in a new city filled with career opportunities was abruptly called to a halt and I became dependent on the charity of others.

Usually it's only after something happens to us or a loved one that we begin to pay attention to our own fragility. I had tons of clients who ignored reality until it came up behind them and bit them. The problem is we don't believe that it could ever happen to us. Evidence to the contrary abounds, however. Hospitals are overcrowded, and wheelchair ramps and handicapped parking are available in most places. Yet we remain blind to the obvious. Great West Life Insurance Co. points out that almost half of all mortgage foreclosures in Canada occur because of disability.

As Freedman says, "It used to be said that people should buy life insurance because 'What will happen to my loved ones if I should die?' With advances in medical science, many more people are surviving accidents and illnesses that would have killed them 50 years ago. So now the question really needs to be 'What happens to my loved ones and me if I survive and become disabled?'"

The Commissioners Disability Table illustrates this point:

In a year:

1 in 106 people die.

1 in 88 homes catch fire.

1 in 8 people become disabled.

It's not uncommon for people to insure their possessions but not the income that guarantees their lifestyle. It's foolish to spend your money on life insurance or RRSPs but not take into account what will happen if you become sick or hurt and lose your earning ability. While in practice, I saw a disconcerting number of women who owned life insurance that would take care of others when they die, but had no disability coverage to look after them if they became sick or hurt. The majority of women's jobs are concentrated in the service sector, which rarely provides company benefits. There's an explosion of women leaving corporate Canada and the security of company-sponsored plans to go into business for themselves. Canada has the highest percentage of women entrepreneurs in the industrialized world. Many of these women are in the service field and rely entirely on their skills. If a woman becomes disabled for a long period, the business will surely fail. Canada Pension Plan does offer a disability benefit for everyone who has contributed to the plan for four out of the last six years, but to qualify the injury or illness must meet the definition of "permanent and severe." CPP was only ever designed to provide a maximum of 25 percent of the average industrial wage as a benefit. This is not to be relied on except in the worst situations. But most insurance companies will insist that plan beneficiaries apply for CPP disability benefits even if they don't meet the definition of prolonged and severe. Not only that, they will also insist that claimants exhaust all avenues of appeal or risk being cut off. This is because most group plans reduce payments by CPP benefits received.

Consider the following: a 35-year-old woman is seven times more likely to face disability than death before she reaches 65. A man is three times more likely to be disabled than die before age 65. Whereas two out of every five men become disabled, one out of every two women will experience a disability lasting 91 days or longer.[5] If two women are out having dinner, these statistics suggest that one of them had better be very careful driving home.

Because women are disabled more frequently than their male counterparts, they pay significantly higher premiums. (However, it's also worth noting that women have a greater life expectancy than men and their life insurance is cheaper.) Women between the ages of 25 and 40 (the childbearing years) pay an additional 15 percent (30 percent if they smoke) right across the board.

What happens to a woman's career possibilities and income level if she becomes disabled? The picture gets grim. The unemployment rate for physically challenged women is 16 percent; for physically challenged men the rate is 13.2 percent. Physically challenged women are paid on average 47 percent of what their male equivalents are paid, and 36 percent of what a non-disabled man receives.[6]

I had a good friend who owned her own computer consulting business. She'd been in business for seven years. Jill hadn't escaped my haranguing about protecting herself, her family, and her business. She was like everyone else— she saw the wisdom of income protection but "didn't have the time or the money at the moment." Besides, she was in no big rush. Jill would say she was "unbearably healthy," to which I would invariably respond, "Yeah, but have you seen an empty hospital lately?" She called me one day at the office.

"Joanne," she began, "I swear, if you laugh when I tell you what I have to tell you, I'll never talk to you again. I might just have to kill you." We were very close. It couldn't be that serious if I was receiving death threats for laughing, so I relaxed. "What's up, Jill?"

"It's Michael," she said. "He, uh, hurt himself yesterday. Nothing too serious, but it looks like he could be off work for six to eight weeks. Maybe longer."

I sat straight up in my chair. "What happened?" Michael is a litigation lawyer and had recently become a new partner at a very busy law firm.

Jill explained. "You and I both know that Michael's talent is his gift of gab in the court room. It's in everyone's best interest that I do the handy work around the house and keep him as far away as possible from a ladder or anything with sharp edges. But yesterday was such a beautiful day, he wanted to putter around in the yard. I thought to myself, 'Michael rarely gets a chance to work outside. What trouble could he get into trimming an odd hedge or two?' About an hour later, I heard a yell they're still talking about in Iceland. I ran out to the backyard and found Michael lying face down with that damned ladder beside him. He'd lost his balance and fallen while cleaning out the eavestrough. I called an ambulance even though he was still conscious. I don't think I've ever seen anyone in so much pain."

"This is dreadful, Jill. What's the damage? Before you answer, I can't believe you'd think I'd find this funny. This is very serious!" I exclaimed.

"I haven't come to the punch line yet," she responded. "He'll be fine, Joanne, really. His body is covered with bruises, but none that rival the bruise his ego received. Oh, did I mention he broke his jaw and it has to be wired shut for several weeks?"

I completely lost it. As I struggled to regain my composure, I heard Jill sigh with resignation and quietly mumble, "I guess I'd better get used to this reaction." She continued, "The people at Michael's office were very sympathetic but also couldn't help laughing. You'll be interested to know that Michael is covered for the time he's off with the insurance he has through the Canadian Bar Association. I want to come and talk to you next week about something for me."

After I hung up the phone, I sat back and thought about how shocking it is when this kind of thing happens, even if you think you're prepared for it. "Elaine!" I bellowed from deep within my office. "How do I find out how much the company pays me if I'm rendered useless and can't earn a living because I'm hit by a runaway lawnmower or stressed out from being over-worked?"

Elaine's response dripped with sarcasm. "You poor dear," she shot back in mock sympathy as I entered her office. "It's a serious consideration for people like you whose work schedule starts every day at the crack of noon!" (My alarm went off every morning at 5:45.)

Ignoring her, I plunked myself down in a chair and told her about the phone call. She wasn't surprised and pointed out that that was how most disability insurance policies are sold. The injury or illness of a close family member usually prompts people into action. "What a coincidence," she continued. "If you take a gander at your trusty priority pyramid, you'll see this was next on our agenda." She pulled out a copy of the company's benefit plan from her desk drawer. "You were given this the day you were hired and told to read it carefully. I'm delighted to see that you follow instructions to the letter.

"Now answer the following questions," she continued. "Are you the owner of the plan or is the company? Do you pay tax on the monthly amount you receive if you're sick or hurt? How does the company define 'disability'? Is it flat out and down for the count or can a broken baby finger qualify? Will it pay anything if you're only partially disabled? How long will the company pay the monthly amount? Does it take into consideration inflation? What happens if you're well enough to work, but not at the job you had before your illness or injury took you out of the game? When can you start receiving the money? Can the benefits be reduced or cut off for any reason? Will the company help you become rehabilitated, and how much will they pay you while you're on a program? I don't get it," she concluded. "Why is it that people only care about 'how much'?"

"Okay! Okay!" I cried. "Message received. I'll read the booklet." I snatched it out of her hand and headed back to my own office.

I'd worked for many companies in my lifetime, but I don't think I ever knew the details of the benefits they provided. The only time I made the effort to find out was during my experience of being hurt and unable to work, only to discover I had no coverage. On reading the booklet, I made a startling revelation. I didn't have enough insurance. As I returned it to Elaine, I told her I'd better bump up my coverage in a hurry. If I couldn't work, the monthly benefit would be substantially less than my current income. Elaine was impressed that I'd found out earlier rather than later, but promptly said, "You can't."

"Excuse me?"

"You're new to the business and you're classified as an independent contractor. It's like being self-employed, but because your licences are sponsored by a company, you'll have some company coverage. But as you found out, not enough. You have to wait a full year to be able to get some of your own insurance. In fact, anyone who starts up a new business has to wait a year. The only exception might be if you start up a business that's similar to your last job, but there are certainly no guarantees. The insurance company wants to be sure you're not a financial deadbeat and you have a modicum of stability. In the meantime, be thankful you at least have the company plan, such as it is."

I was stunned. The company plan might have been all right for some who worked there, but it certainly didn't cover my needs. Group benefits are pretty much the same for all who work at a company, regardless of how much they each earn. Some people may end up earning too much to be adequately covered. The most coverage you can expect to receive, whether from group, association, private, or government plans like workers' compensation, is from 60 to 85 percent of your total earnings. If you decide to buy private insurance in addition to a group policy at work, your benefits will be coordinated so as not to exceed your normal income. I was eventually able to take advantage of a privately owned plan to make up the shortfall from the company plan and still be within that 60 to 85 percent range. Topping up your group plan is often hard to do, though, because this ceiling takes workers' compensation and employment insurance (EI) into account. This reduces the amount you're able to buy on your own. Because I was technically self-employed, I didn't have any government benefits to rely on so I had some breathing room. But then came another revelation. The amount of disability insurance you can qualify for depends entirely on how much income you earn. I couldn't go to the insurance company and say, "Give me coverage worth $8,000 a month" if I only earned $40,000 a year. Your income justifies the benefit amount.

Joe Chisholm provides an interesting take. He points out that some disability insurance coverage is adjudicated at the point of claim and some at underwriting. If you have $500,000 of life insurance and you die, that's what the insurance company pays. But just because you have $4,000 per month of disability insurance, that doesn't ensure that you will get the full $4,000 each month. Disability insurance is more like car insurance. Just because you are in an accident doesn't mean that the insurer pays you $1 million simply because that's how much coverage you have. They assess the benefit at point of claim based on the loss up to and not exceeding the threshold. Most non-cancellable policies are financially underwritten at point of application and within limitations so that you won't have to haggle with the insurer about how much you are entitled to. This is a good thing. Who wants to be fighting with an insurance company when they are in a state of illness or injury?

Of particular concern is people who are self-employed. If you aggressively deduct every expense imaginable to make a $100,000 income look like $25,000, this will save taxes now but might come back to haunt you when you make a disability claim. You want the claim to be based on $100,000 of income, but if the financial underwriting is done at point of claim, the insurer may reasonably process the claim based on the $25,000 claimed as income.

I must admit, after learning about disability insurance, I spent the next 11 months being extra careful about looking both ways before I crossed the street. When I was finally able to apply for additional coverage, I was surprised at the differences between my company plan and the one that I now owned personally. The good news about the group plan is that it costs very little. But if the company pays the whole shot or even part of the premiums, the monthly benefits are taxable. If I pay the premiums myself, the benefits are tax free. The other good news about company plans is that the state of your health is incidental, providing that you started with the company after the plan was implemented. If you can't get disability insurance privately for health or financial reasons, you can still take advantage of your group coverage through work. The major downside is that when you go, you lose it. It's like rented insurance. You're entirely dependent on the generosity of your employer.

The other pitfall to watch for with company plans is their definition of disability. This is the heart and soul of your plan. At one end are the private plans, which tend to have the most generous definition, and at the other end is the Canada Pension Plan with its stringent and severe definition. Group plans may fall anywhere along the continuum but tend more toward the strict definition. Be very careful of the clause regarding "own or any occupation." If the policy says "any occupation," it can cut you off benefits once you're well enough to work in any job. If, for example, this had been the clause in Michael's policy, his benefits could be cut off (generally after two years) if he were fit to work as a gardener but not able to practise law. Get a plan that's good until you're 65. And finally, be sure your policy is guaranteed renewable and non-cancellable to age 65 at the same premium as when you bought it.

Even if you become uninsurable or unemployed after you bought the policy, the insurance company can't take it back. It's good for the length of the contract as long as you continue to pay the premiums.

Many professional associations, university alumni organizations, and business groups offer disability insurance to their members. Association plans are often very useful for self-employed people or for people looking to top up their group benefits or to continue coverage if they're changing jobs (provided you're still a member of that group or association). It's important to realize, however, that association coverage is much like group or company plans. The association owns it, not you. Recently, certain associations experienced significant premium hikes because of increased claims. Because this type of insurance isn't actually yours, the premiums can increase as you get older and the policy has to be renewed every few years. This means you'll have to be "in the pink" healthwise or your insurance may be discontinued. Also, if you leave the association or group, your coverage stays behind. If you've become uninsurable during that time, you'll be out of luck trying to replace it. Association coverage has more of a "group" flavour to it when it comes to the definition of disability. It tends to be a more restrictive definition, but it's still an excellent option. Just be aware of the restrictions.

Here's something interesting: there's now disability insurance specifically to insure a child or spousal support obligation. The amount declines as the obligation does.

Having appropriate disability coverage through whatever means you choose is one of the first steps toward creating a solid and responsible financial plan. It's disconcerting to me that so few people have proper disability insurance or know the details of their coverage if they're part of a company plan. Every birthday you celebrate increases the cost of disability insurance. If you're one of the few remaining souls bent on slow suicide who still smokes, brace yourself to pay up to 20 percent more.

The cost of disability insurance can itself give you a heart attack, as both Jill and I found out. However, insurance companies use an "unbundled option" approach that allows you to control the costs to some degree. There are several features available so that you can build the plan most suitable to your own needs and budget. Jill was a 35-year-old nonsmoker who earned $40,000 last year. She was given certain options that would reduce (or increase) her premiums. The biggest impact on cost was when the plan would actually kick in and start paying the monthly benefit. Jill could choose from having her benefit start 61, 91, or 121 days after her illness or injury instead of 31 days. These choices would significantly reduce her monthly premium. She opted to pay $130.62 for a $2,100 tax-free monthly benefit that will last until she reaches age 65. The $2,100 monthly benefit starts on the 31st day after the disability occurs. If she waited 61 days for the benefit to start, it would cost $91.03; 91 days, $74.17, and so on. I recommended that she stay with the 31-day option because her cash flow was so tight her company wouldn't survive for 61 days without some income. She balked at the price, as everyone does, until I put it to her this way: she could live on $40,000 a year and have no income if something happened, or manage on $38,499 and receive a tax-free benefit of $25,200 if she got hurt or sick. It didn't take a rocket scientist to figure out the better option.

I was very lucky. Even while working for an employer, I owned my own disability and life insurance. When I left corporate Canada my privately owned plan came with me. I chose to own my own plan, not because I knew I'd be self-employed someday, but because I like having control of my own affairs. Today I live worry free (as do my staff and creditors), secure in the knowledge that if I'm sick or hurt, there will be income to ensure the bills get paid.

Remember: health buys insurance. Money only pays for it. Think of disability insurance as a parachute. You should always have one, but pray like crazy that you'll never need it. Disability insurance is a very complex area, and this is by no means a definitive discussion of the subject. It's designed only to give you some highlights and to get you thinking about it. Remember that whatever reason you may have now for not buying disability insurance will sound hollow when you're sick or hurt and unable to work.

Freedman uses the analogy of car insurance. "You don't buy car insurance because you expect to have an accident—it's just in case. And disability insurance is often significantly less on a monthly basis than car insurance. The first thing all my clients asked me upon hearing of my accident was if I had disability insurance. They all knew that I had preached about it for years and it was the first thing I did when I started my business. I totalled up the amount I had paid in premiums over 15 years and I had recouped all that money and more within 15 months of my accident. In addition, I have residual income benefits, which means that while I can work part-time, the insurance company continues to pay me as long as I am earning at least 20 percent less each month than I was before the accident."

Talk to a disability insurance expert, one who deals in it extensively, if not exclusively. These experts will be able to tell you the claim payment history of each company and describe the myriad options these policies offer. Furthermore, any financial advisor will be glad to sit down and review your group benefits with you. Spend 10 minutes rooting around in your desk to find your benefits booklet. You won't regret it.

Critical illness insurance

This product, new to the Canadian marketplace, fills a gap that exists between life and disability insurance. Critical illness insurance pays cash—between $25,000 and $2 million—in the event that the insured is diagnosed with any number or conditions including cancer, multiple sclerosis, stroke or heart attack, and many others. With some plans, as well as receiving a cash payment you can use a program called Best Doctors. Best Doctors gives you access to leading medical professionals in North America for the purpose of diagnosis and treatment. Furthermore, you get "first in line" treatment that is usually reserved for professional athletes or other medical professionals. However, the more common critical illness policies pay out the lump sum on diagnosis without U.S. medical care being a component at all, even though this type of plan is the one that is most often marketed.

Why would you want this insurance? Chisholm has this to say: "Let's say you owned life and disability insurance and were told you have cancer. It will eventually kill you, but today your life insurance pays you nothing. It will eventually disable you, but your disability won't pay until you actually are incapable of returning to work. Once you are disabled from cancer, your disability pays a percentage of your income, although with added health care costs, you may need more than your normal income to get by. Critical illness pays you today—upon diagnosis."

However, as Freedman points out, "Only if it is life threatening. Breast or prostate cancer, for example, will not pay out in the vast majority of plans unless it has metastasized. This is never 'obvious' in the policy."

She also asks about people who do not work. What about those who are out of the workforce because they are caring for a child or another family member with a disability? What about those who are homemakers or who are retired? Or those who are not yet eligible for disability insurance, such as new business owners? What about large, lump-sum expenses, which even people covered by disability income payments cannot cover out of cash flow? Her take? Critical illness insurance may be an option.

I believe this is a great alternative for a non-earning spouse (read: mostly women). If she became ill, there would be a financial loss to the household, yet disability insurers won't cover them because there is no loss of income. Critical care insurance won't cover all the conditions that disability insurance will, but it is a good alternative to insuring this specific need. Critical care insurance policies offer child riders as well. Chisholm says, "Consider if you have children who became sick: the chances are excellent that you would go to any lengths to care for them. This will have a price tag connected to it in terms of your time away from work and possible travel if needed for superior health care. A child rider can pay you cash if health disaster inflicted your family."

Here's how it works. When you buy a policy, you decide what amount of coverage you want. The more you apply for, the more it will cost. Again, your health determines whether you qualify for this insurance. Underwriters will be more interested in family history for this type of insurance—what ailments your parents have had or what hereditary diseases there are in your family. Some applications are declined. Some have exclusions, based on your health or family medical history. It is always possible to be approved for one or two of life insurance, disability insurance, or critical illness insurance and not be underwritten for others, as each has different criteria.

In Freedman's book, she explains that the funds paid out from a critical illness insurance policy can be used as the policyholder sees fit. The exception is *medical treatment critical illness policies* that enable policyholders to obtain more expensive treatment (often in the United States) up to a certain dollar value instead of a lump-sum payout on diagnosis. Although the premiums in the latter type of policy may be lower than a regular critical illness policy, the flexibility and, indeed, the necessity for payout may be lower, too.

Benefits received from a regular critical illness policy have no restrictions on how they can be spent. They can be used to

- pay off the mortgage or other personal debt
- pay for medical treatments not covered by government or private health insurance
- pay for renovations to the home required as a result of the illness
- pay for modifications to a motor vehicle
- replace income lost as a result of time off work
- ensure the survival of a small business
- pay for a vacation, children's education, or any other goals

Insurance companies have a list of basic ailments that are covered. These usually include

- cancer
- heart attack
- stroke

Additional conditions, normally found in *enhanced critical illness* policies, vary according to the insurance companies' policies. These conditions may include the following:

- organ transplants; organ failure
- heart bypass surgery
- kidney failure
- paralysis
- multiple sclerosis
- blindness
- deafness
- Alzheimer's disease
- Parkinson's disease
- coma
- speech loss
- loss of limbs
- major burns
- brain tumours (benign)

It is very important to understand the *definition* of the particular medical condition covered under the policy. Each insurance company will have its own definition of the condition that leads to a successful claim. The chart below illustrates the definition of *heart attack* by three different insurance companies.

Illness	Company 1	Company 2	Company 3
Heart attack	Yes, covered	Yes, as shown by ECG changes and elevation of cardiac enzymes	Yes, as shown by ECG changes, elevation of cardiac enzymes, and chest pain

The point to remember is this: know what the definitions of each medical condition are in the policy you take out. As insurance companies' experience with critical illness insurance matures, many specialists predict that there will be standardized definitions for critical illness insurance policies that will be updated by distributors every few years, as is the case in the United Kingdom.

Freedman makes this argument: "Some insurance agents are recommending that people take out [critical illness] coverage instead of [disability insurance]. If I had followed this advice, I would now be bankrupt. [Critical illness] would not have paid out as I would have needed to be completely paralyzed for 90 or 180 days depending on the policy and I was starting to walk again by then. If you receive a [disability insurance] benefit of $25,000 per year, [four] years of disability would mean payments of $100,000. But most people would purchase $50 [to] [$]100,000 of [critical illness] coverage that would have been exhausted long before [disability insurance] would run out. [Disability insurance] can run to age 65—if you are 50 at the time of onset, the amount of [critical illness] to see you to age 65 would be astronomical. A better solution is to combine [critical illness] with [life insurance]. While some life insurance policies already have a terminal illness clause whereby upon diagnosis of a terminal illness a portion of the benefit may be paid out, we are starting to see product on the market now which is specifically [critical illness] and [life insurance]. So for example, you buy $100,000 of [term life insurance] and can designate from 25 [to] 75 percent of the face value as [critical illness]. [Critical illness] will pay out and if it is not needed will continue as [life insurance]. If [critical illness] is paid out, the balance would continue as [life insurance] until death."

So much to learn, so little time. If you are anything like me, right about now you should be getting pretty antsy to get to the sexy part where we can start to learn how to make some money. One day Elaine grandly announced that the moment had finally arrived. It was time to learn the basics of investing.

five

The golden years

Retirement means twice as much husband on half as much money.

My GRANDMOTHER

I was on my way to another session with Elaine. I started to think about the tremendous progress I was making in understanding personal finance. In fact, I was beginning to feel downright cocky. "Today," I thought to myself as I took the elevator up to the 26th floor, "the roof could fall in on my house, I could break a leg rollerblading or die in a daring rescue attempt and my financial affairs would be in order. Life is so much less nerve-racking this way."

I'd also begun to notice that the very vocal committee that had taken up permanent residence in my head was actually beginning to quiet down. The fast and furious internal debates brought on by anxiety about money were lessening to a noteworthy degree. Being financially organized resulted in some blessed relief from the interminable chatter going on in my brain.

Meanwhile, back at the ranch, Elaine was about to attempt another psychological breakthrough with me. She was going to try to get my head out of today and into the future—like, 35 years into the future. As I settled into one of the comfortable armchairs, Elaine asked me one of her characteristically tough questions, one that I've subsequently asked many women. "Joanne, what is your greatest fear?"

"That the milkman will find out about the pool guy." This met with the standard lack of appreciation of my rapier wit. "Uh, that's not what you meant. Okay, I'd have to say being financially dependent on someone else, including the government. The general scuttlebutt is that the Canada/Quebec Pension Plan (C/QPP) will be a vague memory by the time I reach 65. And even if it isn't, it won't come close to supporting me in the lifestyle to which I plan on becoming accustomed. [QPP is essentially the same as CPP except that the

Quebec government administers QPP for its workers whereas the federal government administers CPP for the rest of the country.] As I understand it, C/QPP provides barely a meagre existence now. The reality is, Elaine, I don't want to end up a bag lady—even if the bags are from Holt Renfrew."

Elaine nodded in agreement. "Too many women, particularly women our mothers' age, married their retirement plan. The truth is that people die and people leave you. You need to be in complete control of your own financial present and future. It's my belief that retirement planning should start no later than age 30 if it's to remain painless. You're only a year behind. Your retirement dream should start, uh—how about today?"

"Retirement planning?!" I exclaimed. "I'm just getting used to seeing a positive balance in my bank account. You want me to jump ahead and start to plan for something 35 years away?" I was beginning to think this state of incredulity was going to be permanent.

"Get used to it, kiddo," Elaine replied. "Besides a house, your retirement is going to be the most expensive thing you'll have to pay for. Remember, we want compound interest to do much of the work for you. In order for that to happen, you need time. And lots of it. Look at the priority pyramid. RRSPs are your next step. Actually, you take this step at the same time as or before you start your 10 percent savings plan, depending on your financial situation. In reality, Joanne, the entire base of the pyramid should be set up simultaneously. At the same time that you start your emergency fund, you should be starting your retirement fund."

I couldn't get over it. I was 31 years old, trying to figure out how I wanted to live 35 years later. I had a hard enough time figuring what I wanted to do for the weekend. Still, I knew I had to follow Elaine's advice, if for no other reason than that I was afraid of her. She had got me thinking. Visions of many women I knew came to mind. About a dozen who were over 65 struggled for even their most basic requirements. My own mother will have a challenging time ahead of her. One of my closest friends is a 76-year-old woman who still must work to stay financially afloat. She was a traditional stay-at-home mother who raised five children. Her husband died after a long, protracted illness, leaving her nothing. Not exactly an appropriate reward for her life's work. Maybe retirement planning at my age wasn't so far-fetched after all.

It wasn't until I'd talked to hundreds of women of all ages as a financial advisor that I really began to understand the soundness of an early start. Although it's never too late, the earlier the better. Almost every woman I talked to shared the same concern: being poor at retirement. The comment I heard most frequently was "I don't want to become a bag lady." Women need to be acutely aware of the reality of what their lives could be like when they get older. A generation ago, it wasn't a pretty picture. Even today, it's alarming to see that, statistically, the older many women get the poorer they're liable to be. Many of these bag ladies whom we so often glibly refer to are wives and mothers who were left destitute by the death of their spouse or abandonment by spouse or family. At the turn of the century, Elizabeth Cady Stanton astutely pointed out: "Woman will always be dependent until she holds a purse of her own." The statistics show that women haven't been able to follow this advice.

According to the 1996 StatsCan census, 38 percent of women aged 65 and over, versus 12 percent of men that age, are living alone. My mother works with senior citizens in the Ottawa area. She shocked me one day when she told me that three out of four nursing home residents are women. Women over 85 comprise nearly 90 percent of the total population in these homes. At this end of the age spectrum, it's literally a woman's world. Half of these women have incomes averaging $16,070. This is only 61.4 percent of the average elderly man's income.

What's so distressing is that many of these women now living below the poverty level weren't before they lost their husbands. Because of women's longer life span, it's entirely possible that their retirement will last longer than their careers. This can be quite a problem because many women don't earn enough to be able to save for retirement. Women are still predominantly responsible for both childcare and home care, which means they must often work in the service sector or in that part of the labour force that allows for occasional work. These jobs typically don't provide pensions and pay significantly less than the average income that men receive. Of women who are already retired, 80 percent aren't eligible for pension benefits.

There are financial penalties affecting women's retirement that derive from the fact that we are the child bearers. Because they're income based, RRSPs, C/QPP, and private company pensions are diminished or, worse, eliminated while you're off having children. Women have this fact as well as the actual interrupted earnings to contend with. If you look at the situation of a woman in the paid labour force as compared to that of her husband, you will see quite a difference in the C/QPP payout. Let's take the case of a woman who earns less than her husband and has lost five years in total due to child rearing. Her C/QPP at age 65 will be $345.39 per month. His will be $543.06. The contributory period for CPP is based on earnings between 18 and retirement age. It's important to note, however, that the months of zero or low earnings while caring for a child under the age of seven are excluded or dropped out in calculating pension benefits. This can positively affect the benefit paid to some mothers, since the low- to no-income earning years won't pull down the overall average. The mothers who work in the home after the child is seven will not benefit from the drop out. This system tries to balance out some of the inequities women experience as the primary caregivers. (Actually, for anyone who experiences periods of zero or low earnings, up to 15 percent of that person's contributory period may be dropped out in calculating the retirement pension. This 15 percent drop-out feature does not replace, but is actually in addition to, the child rearing drop-out provision.) Although these two contributors worked in the same industry, the woman's contributions were erratic because of child rearing. Also, because she earned less than her husband, her contributions were less. As you can see, the effect on her pension is dramatic. Women also leave the workforce more frequently, not only because of child rearing, but to relocate with their husbands. It's sobering to see how severely pension payouts are affected by interrupted careers. Really, CPP represents such a small amount of money that it should only be looked upon as "extra" funds available at retirement on top of what's been saved.

An RRSP is an option for anyone who earns an income, but the amount you can sock away depends on how much you make. Since women on average earn less, they have smaller RRSPs, although RRSP contribution levels have almost doubled since 1990. Women comprise the fastest-growing group in Canada taking advantage of RRSPs. According to Statistics Canada, in 1979 women contributed $700 million to RRSPs, and in 2002, 2.8 million women contributed a total of $10.6 billion.

The other factor that may have a negative effect on retirement planning is divorce. For the most part, women fare much worse financially after divorce than men do. The divorce rate is close to one out of every three marriages. Statistics Canada recently released a report, based on tax returns, which showed that of the single-parent, female heads of households with children under 18, only 56 percent receive support from their departed partner. Sixty percent of single-parent families live below the poverty line. How do these women plan for retirement? They don't. They're too busy trying to stay above water.

The reality can be pretty grim for many older women, but the picture is getting significantly brighter. Women today who are approaching retirement are healthier and more affluent than they were even 10 years ago. They're certainly in a better economic position than the previous generation of women. Women are beginning to gain significant economic power since they're working long enough to be entitled to some pension benefits. Their longer life span can also mean ultimate control over the family's assets, if there are any. Statistics Canada says the number of women receiving the full Guaranteed Income Supplement benefit, which is for people with little or no income, fell 50 percent between 1979 and 1989. The number of women receiving C/QPP benefits, which are based on earned income, rose from 22 percent to 45 percent between 1979 and 1989. This is mainly because of the growth in the number of women in the paid workforce. In 1979, fewer than 14 percent of the women who paid income tax contributed to an RRSP. By 1999, that rate had increased to 44 percent. The percentage of women participating in company pension plans (registered pension plans, or RPPs) also increased four percentage points to 36 percent during the same time period.[1]

The older women of the future will have much more financial savvy and be more knowledgeable about money than many older women are now. Society is beginning to encourage women to think and talk about money. The old adages "Never talk about money. It isn't ladylike" or "Money is toxic and immoral" are, thankfully, dead and buried. If she were alive today, my grand-mother would be having a tough go in her retirement. My mother will also be challenged, but her situation is a shade better than was her mother's. At least Mom recognizes where the buck stops. As for me, I have no intention of depending on anyone, Lance or the government, to ensure that I'll live with dignity and integrity in my twilight years. Fortunately, I have many more options than the previous generations of women in my family, and for that I'm thankful.

In looking at my own family, I see the trend line moving in a positive direction. My grandmother Pearl was a full-time mother and homemaker right up to the day she died at age 70. She was never able to qualify for QPP (she lived in Quebec) since she hadn't received an income for her labour at home. Pearl certainly didn't have a private company pension plan and she depended almost entirely on my grandfather for her retirement needs. At 65 she did receive a small sum from the Old Age Security program, but that basically was it.

Now my mother, who represents the next generation, has fared somewhat better. Although Mom was 40 when she took her first paid full-time job outside of the home, she'll be able to receive some CPP benefit. It won't be much, since she was in the paid labour force for a much shorter time and was paid far less than was my father, for example. My mother is also able to take advantage of RRSPs, but can't contribute much because her income is low. But it will help. She's in the middle generation between women who are living below the poverty line because of non-existent retirement planning options and women of my generation who are beginning to have significantly more income, choices, and control. I'll qualify for CPP, provided it's still around when I retire. Because I work in the paid labour force, there's a better chance that I have access to, or could have in the future, a company pension plan. (Since I'm currently self-employed, I don't have access to a company plan.) I can also make RRSP contributions. I earn more money and have been in the workforce longer than my mother. These factors will have a favourable impact on what my retirement will look like. As we'll see later, women still have a long way to go, but things are definitely looking up.

The retirement choices

There are three principal sources of retirement income in Canada: the government, your company, and you. There's a great debate going on at the moment as to whether the government will even be part of the picture by the time the baby boomers reach retirement age and exhaust the system. The odds are that if you were born after 1950, you'll have to count exclusively on your own resources for a secure retirement. It's estimated that in the year 2015, six million Canadians will reach 65. That's a lot of baby boomers hitting retirement age at once. It's expected that Canada's social welfare system will be greatly affected by this wave, and that it will be hit the hardest between the years 2015 and 2045.

Many of our existing social programs were developed during a time when Canada was experiencing high birth rates, from the beginning of the baby boom after the Second World War up to the '60s. Because of costly benefit enhancements over the years and a subsequent baby bust, the cost of continuing to provide C/QPP is going to have to rise dramatically over the next 30 to 40 years. One factor that has helped keep the cost of C/QPP from going through the roof is women's relatively recent increased participation in the labour force. They've added a whole new raft of contributors to the C/QPP net, and they're still too young to be drawing off any of the benefits. At this point, the contributions they make are higher than the cost of paying the benefits.

In its *Canadian Retirement Income Social Security Programs* report, the Canadian Institute of Actuaries states that C/QPP offers important advantages that should provide an incentive for Canadians to keep it around. The report says that C/QPP offers "virtually full coverage of the working population." (My grandmother and mother who worked unpaid in the home might object to not being considered part of the so-called working population. Watching soaps and eating bon-bons weren't high on their list of priorities.) The report goes on to explain that the benefits are portable and indexed against inflation, as well as having relatively low administrative costs. But here's the basis of the C/QPP controversy: In 1994, the combined employee/employer C/QPP contribution level was 5.2 percent of your earnings up to $34,400. By the year 2035, it's estimated that the C/QPP contribution will rise to 13.25 percent.[2]

Will Canadians be prepared to pay this? Only time will tell. If they are, then C/QPP should continue.

Nevertheless, it's always been my advice that you should never count on the government's ability to fund your retirement. One thing is for sure: C/QPP isn't likely to be around in its present form. Government-sponsored pension plans provide only a small part of your total retirement income—39 percent on average, as the Canadian Institute of Actuaries report points out. C/QPP was a much better deal for our grandparents and parents than it will be for baby boomers and those younger. A recent study done by the QPP actuary is quite interesting. It was concluded that a man born in 1920 would receive benefits worth 7 times what was contributed on his behalf. A man born in 1960 would receive benefits with a value of 2.6 times his total contributions. A male contributor born in 1980 could, at best, expect to break even. The actuary also projected that someone born in the year 2000 would receive only 80 percent of the value of total projected contributions. It's a good idea to plan for your retirement as though government benefits won't be an option for you. If C/QPP is around, consider the income you receive from it as gravy, albeit less than $9,000 worth of gravy annually.[3]

How much is enough?

The key to a happy retirement is to have enough money to live on but not enough to worry about. A friend of mine told me his Dad's motto was "If I die with $20 in my pocket, I worked an hour too long." Now, there are no hard and fast rules about how much a person has to save to retire comfortably. Instead of asking how much you need to save, think about how much you want to spend, and what your financial resources are going to be. What sort of carefree lifestyle do you plan to lead? Is it important to you to leave a huge estate for your kids? (Being someone's kid, I personally endorse this plan.) Or is a Hawaiian beach the Parthenon in your future? Do you plan to sell your house and move to the country? How much will your pension be? Keep in mind that dry-cleaning costs are sure to go down, along with a number of other costs.

Once you have a handle on what you're actually going to spend, then you can start thinking about how to invest your retirement nest egg. Conventional wisdom suggests an age rule: if you're 40, 40 percent should be in conservative stuff and 60 percent in growth investments. This is an okay guideline, but the real numbers depend on your goals, risk tolerance, time frame you have to invest, and size of portfolio. There are some seniors whose financial diligence has paid off. They'll never spend all they've saved. They're really managing it for their kids, who may not get to touch it for another 20 years. They can afford to take a higher risk, whereas someone with a smaller nest egg may not be able to afford to do so.

A quick, easy guideline is that you need to set aside 15 to 18 percent of your salary for 35 years. Increase that to 20 percent if you're like most people and haven't started thinking of retirement planning until your 45th birthday. Don't panic. This does include your RRSP and company pension plan contribution. If you're using your house as part of a retirement plan, its value can be included as well. The ideal is to be sure you'll have 70 to 80 percent of your current income coming in and sustained during the length of your retirement in order to maintain your existing standard of living. This is no small feat. The following are your possible sources of retirement income to ensure your future security.

Old Age Security

Established in 1952, Old Age Security (OAS) is a universal program that applies to everyone, whether they work in the paid labour force or not. The OAS program consists of the Old Age Security pension, the Guaranteed Income Supplement (GIS), and the Allowance for Survivor. The OAS pension is for anyone over 65 who's a resident of Canada (subject to length of residence). The GIS is for people receiving OAS who have little or no income. The Allowance for Survivor is given to spouses aged 60 to 64 of OAS pensioners or to widows or widowers whose family income doesn't exceed a certain limit. You don't have to be a member of the paid labour force to qualify for these plans.

Despite pension reforms to programs such as RRSPs, women still rely to a large extent on the government for their retirement needs. Government programs such as the OAS and GIS are extremely important for women who are in the unpaid labour force or who have only sporadic paid employment. The maximum amount available from these two programs is considerably below the poverty line for an individual. Based on current increases in the consumer price index, in 2003, the maximum OAS benefit is $5,497.62 a year. At best, these plans reflect only 14 percent of the average annual lifetime earnings. The GIS maximum is $4,255.83 a year for a married person and $6,532.17 for someone who is single. The OAS and GIS make up 40 percent of single elderly women's total income. The comparable figure for single elderly men is 25 percent. OAS and GIS represent 75 percent of total income for those at or below the poverty line; this figure increases to 87 percent when you factor in C/QPP. When your income reaches a certain level (over $5,879), you have to start paying your OAS back at tax time, which is known as a clawback. Full repayment of the benefit is required when your income exceeds $94,119.

Canada/Quebec Pension Plan

You contribute to these plans according to your earnings. You must be salaried or self-employed, aged 18 to 70, and have an annual income that exceeds a minimum threshold, which is adjusted each year. It's important to note that on or after January 1, 1987, CPP provides for mandatory credit-splitting upon divorce, but this splitting isn't always done. Historically, fewer than 1 in 20 divorced women ever exercise their legal right to their share of their ex's C/QPP credits. This failure to claim what's rightfully theirs was the result of a lack of education. The story is much different today—nearly 100 percent claim their credits because of greater awareness.

Retirement savings plans

Registered pension plans are tax-advantaged plans and are available to you through your company. Registered retirement savings plans are privately owned pension plans that you control. RRSPs came into being in 1957 and were designed to help those people who don't have a pension plan through work.

Employer-sponsored pension plans are far from homogeneous. Some are very generous, some are not. Pension plans are far more prevalent in some industries than in others, and are more common in the public than in the private sector. Full-time and unionized workers are much more likely to have pension plans than workers who are part-time and non-unionized. Big companies offer pension plans more frequently than do small- to medium-sized companies. We begin to see, then, why women aren't covered by employer-sponsored plans as much as men. Women concentrate more in the business and service sectors that typically offer less pension coverage; and women are far more likely to work part-time. Even though the coverage rate in these areas is only 20 percent, their employment increased 40 percent in the 10-year period between 1981 and 1991, reflecting the significant rate at which women are entering these particular sectors. On the other hand, during the same period significant job losses occurred in manufacturing and other industries that have always had high pension plan coverage.[4] Then there's the proliferation of women entrepreneurs who are no longer able to depend on their employers for pension plans. The world is indeed changing.

That's why group and individual RRSPs have experienced such dramatic growth in recent years. They provide a way to compensate for the inadequacy of pension coverage. The late '80s did bring about certain long-awaited and significant pension reforms. One of the most significant changes is that pension benefit legislation has now expanded the definition of spouse to include a common-law spouse for the purpose of designating survivor benefits. There's federal legislation in effect that gives same-sex couples working for the federal government survivor pension benefits. Quebec has passed omnibus legislation redefining "spouse" in 39 statutes, including private and provincial pensions. Other provinces may or may not follow suit.

Traditionally, there have been two main types of company pension plans: defined benefit and defined contribution.

Defined benefit plans

This type of company pension plan is the most common. It promises to pay a specific amount of pension income based on your years of service to the company and how much money you earned. Here's a typical example: Your employer pays you 2 percent of your best three to five years of earnings multiplied by the number of years you've been on the plan. Let's say you've been with Bell Canada as a telephone operator for 30 years, and your best three years of income averaged $30,000. Using the above formula, your pension will be $18,000 a year (2 percent of $30,000 times 30 years), which comes to 60 percent of $30,000. This type of pension plan is becoming less common in recent years since it's become too expensive for corporate Canada. Pretty much only the government and public sector offer them these days.

Sometimes these pension plans are indexed, which means they attempt to keep up with cost of living increases (inflation). You should also check to see if your (or your partner's) pension plan has survivor benefits. If you die, wouldn't it be appropriate for your partner to continue receiving at least a portion of your pension? Survivor benefits are often worth only 60 percent of the original pension. There is also a pre-retirement earnings threshold to consider, which, in 2004, is $91,650.

Defined contribution plans

These plans are also known as money purchase plans. You and your employer make a specific contribution to an account each year based on your earnings. What you've accumulated over the years through these contributions and the interest they generate is what you use to buy your pension. Your retirement income is actually unknown until the day you retire.

There used to be only these two choices. Nowadays, companies are becoming infinitely more flexible and are beginning to offer one, the other, a hybrid of both, or none at all. The idea behind this new-found flexibility is to give people more room to contribute to their RRSPs. With RRSP contribution levels going up so much (they've doubled in the last few years), people want the freedom to control their own pension planning. (The RRSP maximum contribution is $15,500 in 2004, or up to 18 percent of earned income for 2003. More on this later.)

Group RRSPs

Some employers will set up a group RRSP in lieu of a pension plan. A group RRSP is essentially a combination of individual RRSPs. Under these plans a single trust or contract is established for employees of a company. Individual RRSP contracts are registered for all participants, but their contributions are pooled and invested accordingly.

Here are some key questions to ask when investigating if you have a pension at work and, if so, what kind:

1. Is the plan comprehensive enough to include benefit indexing? In other words, will it attempt to keep pace with inflation?
2. What happens in the following situations: you die, your partner dies, you divorce, you retire early, you become disabled, or you quit or your employment is terminated? It can be quite a shock to the system to discover that since you decided to retire at 55, you now get only 50 percent of the pension. Or your spouse dies and you discover that 60 percent of his pension isn't enough to live on. In the early '90s almost half (46 percent) of the men who participated in pension plans were in plans that had no benefits to the surviving spouse. New pension legislation states that there must be at a minimum 60 percent survivor benefit, unless the other spouse has signed away their rights.
3. Be sure to find out if you can take the pension with you if you quit or your employment is terminated. What is its "commuted value" in this case? How will actuaries value the expected benefit?
4. If your company offers a variety of plans, ask if you can transfer between plans and how often.
5. Usually you have to be with a company for two years before you're eligible for its pension plan. This is known as vesting. As part of your initial negotiations for employment, you might consider asking if you can join the pension plan right away.

RRSPs

After doing some research, it was easy to conclude that Elaine was right about the prohibitive cost of retiring. "Okay, let's do it then," I said to her shortly after our retirement discussion. Quite frankly, I wasn't entirely sure what *it* even was.

Elaine picked up the ball. "What we need to do is start an RRSP for you. As a self-employed person you don't have access to a company pension plan, so you're on your own. That's why RRSPs exist in the first place, to give people like you a chance to secure your future. They're like personal pension plans. What type would you like it to be? I have a suggestion, but you go first."

Puzzled, I replied, "Type? Like it to be? Like what to be?"

"Your RRSP," Elaine stated matter-of-factly.

"Oh, brother," I thought. "Are we back to the running shoe school of finance again? I have to choose a type?!" I finally answered, "Elaine, I thought when you bought an RRSP, you bought an RRSP. You've lost me here. What do you mean by type?"

Like thousands of other unsuspecting Canadians, I fell into the trap of assuming an RRSP is a product unto itself. I was quick to learn that it's not. The key word in "registered retirement savings plan" is "plan." You can open more than one. In fact, it's advisable to diversify your RRSP portfolio just as you do with the other elements of your financial plan. You also get to pick and choose what to put into your RRSP. The investments you can choose from include daily interest savings accounts, GICs, mutual funds, stocks, and a variety of bonds, including Canada Savings Bonds, municipal, provincial, and federal bonds, treasury bills, and certain types of mortgages, including your own (if certain conditions are met). You can also have limited partnership units that are available on Canadian stock exchanges (which is considered foreign content), certain warrants and bankers acceptances, shares of a qualified small business corporation up to a limit of 100 percent of your RRSP, debt instruments issued by public corporations not listed on Canadian stock exchanges, and debt instruments of foreign governments. There are other options that you can discuss with your financial advisor.

Once you've made your decision as to which investment or investments you want inside your RRSP, you fill out a form with your financial advisor, if the advisor sells financial products, or at the financial institution of your choice. This form will be identical to the form you'd fill out if you were buying a regular GIC or mutual fund, or opening a daily interest savings account. The only difference is that when you get to the box that says, "Do you wish this plan to be registered?" you check off yes. Your GIC now becomes part of your RRSP. This means that you get to enjoy watching your investment grow in value and you don't have to pay any tax on that interest as long as it is within the registered account. (If the plan wasn't registered but was just a regular GIC or daily interest savings account, you'd have to pay tax on the interest it earned every single year whether or not you cashed in the GIC.) If you don't pay tax on an investment until you cash it in, years down the road you'll end up with much more money in your pocket than if you'd paid tax on it every April. This is why it's important to defer your taxes whenever you can. The retirement income option you choose after collapsing your RRSP will determine when the money will be taxed.

The way it works is pretty simple. If, let's say for simple math, you're enjoying (?!) a 50 percent marginal tax rate and have $1,000 in a GIC earning 10 percent interest, you'll earn $100 in interest in a year. (Remember, though, that the marginal tax rate isn't really 50 percent, it just feels like it is. The top marginal tax rate in Canada is Newfoundland and Labrador's, at 48.6 percent. Ontario's is 46.4 percent, and Alberta's is 39 percent, the lowest in Canada.) But because your tax bracket is what it is, you'll have to give $50 of that $100 interest to our friends at Canada Revenue Agency. Therefore, the following year you'll be investing only $1,050, since you had to pay $50 in tax on the interest from the previous year. Now, if that $1,000 GIC were in an RRSP, you wouldn't have to pay tax on the interest until you cashed the RRSP out at retirement. The entire $100 of interest will be reinvested the following year. In other words, you'll be investing $1,100 instead of $1,050. The interest is tax sheltered, which is one reason why an RRSP is an essential part of your tax and retirement planning. Even though you'll have to pay tax on the investment at whatever your marginal tax rate is when you collapse (cash in) your RRSP, you'll be much further ahead than if you'd paid tax on the interest every year. The other tax advantage to an RRSP is that your contributions are tax deductible at the same rate. If you have a 50 percent marginal tax rate, a contribution of $5,000 to your RRSP will result in a tax refund of $2,500. Humans aren't like other animals. Animals have instincts. We have taxes. That's why we need RRSPs. More on this a little later in the chapter.

Another point: RRSPs truly benefit people who have higher tax rates. Other than the tax-sheltered savings opportunity, these marvellous creatures lose their shine the less money you make. There's a whole constituency of women out there who don't make enough money to reap the considerable tax benefits that everyone lauds. However, even though the tax-deductible side is not great, the ability to save without having to pay tax on the gain in your investment is terrific, no matter where you are on the tax scale.

You can also put mutual funds inside your RRSP. They work much the same as other investments, but because many mutual funds are already tax advantaged, the reasons for having them in a tax-sheltered retirement savings plan are different from the reasons for having a GIC, for example, in your RRSP. Perhaps it seems redundant to put an investment that's already receiving tax-favoured treatment into a tax shelter. But guaranteed products like GICs don't experience the growth one needs in the long run to counterbalance the impact of inflation and taxes. Even though the interest on your guaranteed investments will accumulate tax sheltered, balanced funds and, in particular, equity funds can provide a more significant growth opportunity. The idea behind an RRSP is long-term: to provide for retirement. Equity funds are also long-term. It seems to me they form a perfect marriage, since their goals are essentially the same. Ideally, what people need is to do both: have a portion of their RRSP portfolio in equity mutual funds for maximum growth potential and invest in equity mutual funds outside their RRSP, say, in their 10 percent savings plan, to take further advantage of the tax benefit these funds offer. If you have only a limited amount of money to invest, putting equity mutual funds inside your RRSP definitely makes sense.

Seventy percent of the stocks and bonds that make up an equity fund in your RRSP have to be Canadian. This rule is in place because it's a Canadian tax break you're getting. Be sure that you take advantage of the 30 percent foreign content that you're allowed to have. Segregated funds, offered by life insurance companies, don't have this limitation. One hundred percent of your segregated funds can be foreign. New RRSP funds allow the investor to benefit from the returns outside of Canada while not going over the 30 percent threshold (more on this in the next chapter). These 100 percent RRSP-eligible funds use futures/derivatives while keeping 70 percent (many also hold up to 100 percent) of the money invested in Canadian T-bills. Global Strategy has had its fund for a number of years, and more and more mutual fund companies, such as Mackenzie, CI, Investors Group, TD, and Royal Mutual Funds are offering their own versions.

At the time of writing, I am 47 years old. My RRSP is predominantly in international equity mutual funds. This strategy reflects my goals and risk tolerance level. My plan is to diversify into other types of investments, including guaranteed investments, by the time I'm 60. Some advisors suggest that as you approach retirement you should begin to shift out of the more volatile mutual funds entirely and start converting to guaranteed investments like GICs. I absolutely disagree. We're living, on average, to over age 80. If you retire at 65, there are still 15 years plus to plan for financially. You still have to make your money work hard. Shifting the mutual fund portion of your RRSP to a balanced fund might make more sense, since a balanced fund will still give you the growth you need but in a more stable pattern. The guaranteed investment part of your RRSP should have staggered maturity dates so that you're always able to take advantage of the best investment opportunity at the time of their maturity. Remember the very loose guideline I mentioned earlier, called the age rule? (If you're 35, 35 percent of your portfolio should be in low-volatility, more stable investments like GICs and mortgage mutual funds, and 65 percent should be in growth-oriented investments like equity mutual funds. If you're 50, then it should be 50/50, and so on.) This is by no means totally accurate, since asset allocation depends on such things as individual goals and risk tolerance. But what it does do is illustrate how important it is to continually monitor your portfolio, RRSP and otherwise, as you age. You can't make an investment choice and assume it will serve your purposes for the duration of your lifetime. You need to diversify on an ongoing basis. A financial advisor should review your plan every year and recommend any changes that may be in your best interest.

Your retirement plan should be set up in phases. Phase one is what money you use between the ages of 60 and 65, if that's when you choose to retire. This phase would include the cash assets you've accumulated. Phase two could start at 69 when you must begin accessing the funds in your RRSP. You can't, by law, hold RRSPs past age 69. At this point you can convert your RRSP into a Registered Retirement Income Fund (RRIF) and/or an annuity, both of which can pay out income on a monthly basis. Phase three, perhaps at age 75 or 80, could be the proceeds from the sale of your house. (It's interesting to note, however, that the majority of Canadians don't sell their home the day they retire.) These phases suggest a very loose guideline, but the point is that you don't have to cash in your RRSP the day after you retire. The longer you let your money sit in a tax-sheltered investment, the more powerful the effects of compound interest will be. Before you decide what goes where, be sure to talk to a financial advisor to help you determine what you want to do.

As I illustrated earlier, the other significant advantage to RRSPs is that the amount you contribute is tax deductible. This simply means that your contribution will reduce the amount of income tax you have to pay. Having an RRSP may make the difference between paying more taxes and getting a tax refund.

A case in point: Sybilla is a physician in the top tax bracket. She decides to invest $5,000 a year in an RRSP. She's consistent and carries this on for 25 years, earning 8 percent interest each year. On the other hand, Nada, also a physician in the top tax bracket, invests her $5,000 a year in a non-tax-sheltered GIC, which earns the same interest rate as Sybilla's investment. Because Nada's $5,000 isn't tax deductible, she really ends up investing only $2,500. Now the double whammy: the interest she earns on this $2,500 is also taxed at close to 50 percent every year. So much for the 8 percent interest; in reality, Nada is earning only 4 percent. At the end of the 25 years, Sybilla will end up with $286,493 more than Nada. Even if Sybilla cashed out her entire

RRSP in a lump sum in the 25th year and had to pay out half of the entire amount of just under $400,000 in tax, she'd still have over $190,000, or 82 percent more than Nada's savings of $108,279. It's pretty easy to see why RRSPs make sense.

RRSPs have evolved, almost by default, into the most important tax and retirement planning tool available. The government has, for all intents and purposes, choked off just about everything else. RRSPs do have a drawback, however. Remember, they're a tax-deferral mechanism. If an emergency arises and you find yourself with no other option than to cash in your RRSP, expect a hefty tax bill upon collapsing the investment. You'll have to pay tax on the amount you take out, the tax you haven't been paying all along. As emphatically stated earlier, RRSPs should not be considered as a source of emergency funds.

Who can buy an RRSP?

Anyone who has earned income and a social insurance number can buy an RRSP. There's no minimum age as long as you're earning an income.

What qualifies as earned income for an RRSP?

Here's a list of types of income that qualify for RRSP contribution purposes:

- income (less most employment-related deductions) from employment, whether you work for a company or are self-employed
- net rental income
- disability benefits, if taxable
- supplementary unemployment insurance benefits
- royalties
- research grants

The following don't qualify but are often assumed to:

- investment income
- employment insurance benefits
- pension income
- post–May 1997 child support agreements
- retiring allowances
- death benefits
- scholarships
- C/QPP benefits
- OAS

How much can I put in?

As stated earlier, RRSPs were developed to help give people with no company pension plans a break. The idea was to try to equalize retirement savings opportunities. Therefore, people with pension plans at work can't contribute the same amount to an RRSP as those who don't have one. That wouldn't be fair. Let's say Nada has a pension plan through the hospital where she works. After reading this book, she realizes she's missing a significant opportunity and decides to start investing in RRSPs. Sybilla, on the other hand, is in private practice and doesn't have access to a company plan. Although they earn the same income, it wouldn't be right for Nada to be able to put the same amount into her RRSP as Sybilla. For Nada to determine how much she can contribute to her RRSP, she (actually her employer) needs to calculate the value of her pension benefit accrued under the hospital pension plan in the previous year and subtract that amount from 18 percent of her previous year's earned income or $15,500 (the maximum contribution level as of 2005), whichever is less. This is called a pension adjustment and is used to determine your contribution limit.

Now that I've gone to great pains to help you understand how your RRSP contribution is calculated, you can promptly forget about it. Canada Revenue Agency does all this for you. Your annual income tax Notice of Assessment tells you exactly what you can contribute. They've taken all the guesswork out of this exercise. It's one less task for our already overworked grey matter to contend with.

There are situations in which you can contribute more than your basic contribution limit. You can transfer payments of certain types of pension income to an RRSP. If you leave your company or it folds and you've accumulated a pension, these funds, known as the commuted value, may be transferred to a locked-in RRSP. These funds are available by age 55 or sooner, if your pension plan allows. Between then and age 69, you can convert a locked-in RRSP to a Life Income Fund (LIF, or LRIF in certain provinces), which is similar to a RRIF except that it has a maximum as well as a minimum annual withdrawal. As well, in certain provinces an LIF must be used to purchase a life annuity at age 80. However, this requirement is gradually being removed.

You can also over-contribute to your RSP up to $2,000 over the course of your lifetime. This cushion is for the mathematically challenged who accidentally contribute too much. It can also help those whose defined benefit pension plan has been upgraded retroactively, which may mean they over-contributed inadvertently. Canada Revenue Agency watches over-contributions carefully. If you over-contribute to your over-contribution, there's a 1 percent per month tax penalty on the amount by which you've exceeded your limit.

If you've left a company with a defined benefit pension plan or a deferred profit sharing plan after December 31, 1996, but before your retirement, you may be eligible for a Pension Adjustment Reversal. This may restore some contribution room listed on your Notice of Assessment. Contact your former employer or Canada Revenue Agency to find out more. Your employer should send you a notice about this.

How much can I take out?

In a perfect world, your RRSP should stay intact until the day you blow out the candles at your 69th birthday party. (Actually, you have until December 31 of the year in which you turn 69.) Unfortunately, a perfect world it ain't. If you find yourself in the unpalatable situation where you have to tap into your RRSP before its time, this is what you need to know. The law states that the financial institution is required to hold back some of your money, which is called a withholding tax. The more you take out, the higher the amount set aside for Canada Revenue Agency. If you take out anything under $5,000, the withholding tax is 10 percent. Anything from $5,000 to $15,000, the financial institution holds back 20 percent. Over $15,000, it's 30 percent. For obvious reasons, it's a good idea to avoid taking out more than $5,000 at any one time. Let's say you need $20,000 dollars. If you took it out in one fell swoop, your trustee would have to withhold 39 percent or $6,000. That leaves you with only $14,000 in your pocket. Broken up into four withdrawals of $5,000, you'd have only $2,000 withheld. Remember though, that the following April you'll have to pay tax on your full income, and that might mean a large cheque to send back to the government.

Sound too good to be true? It might be. Some institutions may limit the number of RRSP withdrawals that you can make. But this is often negotiable if you're a valued client, so be sure to ask about their policy. It's also important to know that the withholding tax doesn't necessarily take care of all your tax obligations. Always go over these decisions with a tax advisor. And even though money can't buy health, happiness, or what it did last year, you need to look after it with care.

What if I don't work or have a sporadic work history?

Spousal RRSPs are an excellent way of addressing the situation of women who are working unpaid in the home or who earn less than their partner. Spousal RRSPs can be the great financial equalizer. If you don't have a pension plan but your partner does, this is another reason to consider a spousal

RRSP. The main purpose of a spousal RRSP is to split retirement income more evenly between partners. Women who would otherwise have little or no retirement income will enjoy some peace of mind through this arrangement.

A spousal RRSP is essentially the same as a regular RRSP except that it's registered in the name of the spouse who owns the investment part of the plan while the contributing spouse takes a full deduction for all the contributions made to the spousal plan. The total contribution by the contributor or non-annuitant can't exceed his or her own personal contribution level. You also have to be sure that there are no withdrawals made for three years after the contributions have been made, or the withdrawals, up to the amount contributed by the non-annuitant, will be taxed in the contributor's hands. Chances are the marginal tax rate of the spouse owning the spousal RRSP will be lower than that of the contributor, so there'll be less tax to pay when the spouse takes the money out.

Remember Lynn's story? She was a stay-at-home mom who had no income, while her husband Stan earned a substantial living as a lawyer. This would have been the ideal scenario for a spousal RRSP. One year, Stan did take out a small one ($2,500) for Lynn. She owned the RRSP (which she eventually had to use to pay legal fees), while Stan got to use his contribution to the spousal RRSP as a tax deduction. If he'd done this regularly, Lynn could have been guaranteed a dignified retirement with some security. However, had their separation been finalized before Stan's death, in the division of their property Lynn and Stan would have had to divide the assets inside the spousal RRSP. If withdrawal from the plan had been necessary, they would have split the tax between the two of them. Where no alternative to collapsing the plan exists, each partner can roll his or her share over to a new plan without incurring taxes if sanctioned by the courts.

Common-law spouses are treated, for tax purposes, the same as traditionally married couples. What this means is that common-law spouses now qualify for spousal RRSPs. You have to have been living together for at least a year or have a child together. One other point: it's always wise to name your partner as the beneficiary of your RRSP so that the money can automatically roll over tax deferred into your partner's RRSP when you die. This is to avoid having to pay probate taxes on the value of the RRSP that comes from having RRSP assets pass through the will.

What about non-Canadian investments?

You know it's a small world once you've made that long trip to the airport. The good news? Canadians are really getting this when it comes to taking advantage of the foreign content in their RRSPs. As I mentioned earlier, although RRSPs are a Canadian tax break, the government does allow us to put 30 percent of our RRSP in foreign investments. And we need to. Although Canada does offer excellent investment opportunities, it's still only 3 percent of the world's capital markets. Translation? Pretty small. Investments outside of Canada have often outperformed Canadian investments, so it's a good idea to take advantage of the bigger pond and diversify to the extent that you can. I should also mention, however, that while increasing foreign equity content makes sense, it does increase currency risk as we witnessed in 2003 with the Canadian versus the weak U.S. dollar.

This 30 percent limit is based on the book value or original purchase price that you paid when you acquired each investment. Since you're receiving a Canadian tax break, you can't go above this percentage without incurring a hefty penalty.

International investing may reduce risk through diversification. More tightly concentrated international investing offers additional opportunities for growth as well. Here are some ways to boost foreign content without exceeding the 30 percent limit, up to a theoretical 51 percent:

- Buy RRSP-eligible Canadian mutual funds that are using their own 30 percent foreign content limits. Check out the mutual fund performance tables in the newspaper. It shows each fund's level of foreign content.
- Clone funds are mutual funds that are 100 percent Canadian content but mirror foreign equity and/or bond funds. For instance, the Fidelity International fund is eligible for the 30 percent foreign content. Fidelity also has an International RSP fund which has a slightly higher management cost to operate than the non-RSP version, but is 100 percent Canadian content.
- Segregated funds, like mutual funds, have varying mandates to hold and trade equity and fixed-income investments on behalf of the unit holders (investors). They are managed by insurance companies and fall under the Insurance Act—not the Bank Act—and don't have the 30 percent foreign limit. They are all 100 percent Canadian content, regardless of the underlying assets.
- Some funds are almost or entirely foreign yet still qualify as Canadian property. For example, some buy Canadian-issued securities that are denominated in foreign currencies.
- Buy Canadian-issued foreign pay-bonds on your own. Most investment dealers offer strip and ordinary bonds payable in U.S. dollars or other currency. They come from federal and provincial governments and utilities such as Ontario Hydro. Bonds issued by the World Bank get the same treatment.

- Remember as well that any Canadian mutual funds in your portfolio that take advantage of this 30 percent rule themselves don't have to be included in your individual 30 percent calculation. This translates into an easy way to increase the actual amount of your foreign holdings beyond the 30 percent limit.

Considering its age, this is a mighty fast world. It's tough to keep abreast of the hot and cold spots, which is essential in international investing. That's why it's always smart to talk with a pro before jumping into this. And don't be afraid to go out on a limb. That's where the fruit is.

Can I change institutions?

No problem. You can transfer from one institution to another by filling out a special form provided by the institution to which you're transferring. This way the RRSP isn't collapsed and you don't trigger any of the tax implications. There's no limit on the number of times you can change. Some institutions will charge an administrative fee in the neighbourhood of $150 for doing this, however. Check first.

Self-directed RRSPs

These are typically for the well-heeled investor. You make the ongoing investment choices for your plan yourself with the help of a financial advisor. There's usually an annual administration fee for handling a self-directed RRSP, which ranges from $90 to $200, but they're usually around the $100 mark. I've seen it recommended that you have anywhere from $10,000 to $75,000 in your portfolio before going the self-directed route. If you have a multitude of plans in a multitude of institutions, a self-directed plan will organize them all into one statement from one financial institution, for example a brokerage company. You don't have to deal with several financial institutions in order to have several investments in one plan. Self-directed RRSPs tend to be more flexible, but you'd better be sure you're comfortable with the principles and language of investing before taking one on.

What if I can't afford to make my contribution?

I had a client, a 30-year-old woman, who tried to beg off a particular year's contribution of $5,000. I've heard it so often: "I can't afford it this year. I've got a car bill to pay …" When I explained to this woman that postponing a $5,000 contribution at age 30 meant taking as much as $85,000 out of her pocket at retirement, she capitulated.

If you're financially short and find yourself unable to make your contribution, you do have an option. It used to be that if you missed your contribution, you missed your contribution—there was no way to make it up. But the rules were changed to give us folks a bit of a break. On your Notice of Assessment, your contribution eligibility will include your basic contribution plus what you didn't use in previous years. If you have a banner year, you can make up all or part. This is called carry forward.

What about borrowing to make my contribution?

The reward for saving money is being able to pay your taxes without borrowing. Herein lies the irony. If you want to reduce the taxes you have to pay and have a secure long-term future, but you don't have the cash, borrowing is exactly the right thing to do.

Remember the good debt and bad debt scenario? Bad debt is going into hock for a camera you don't need. Good debt, like an RRSP loan, can make a significant difference in your quality of life in the future.

It makes sense to borrow to make your contribution, even though the interest on the loan isn't tax deductible. The benefits of tax-sheltered compound interest will outweigh the costs of borrowing if you pay the loan off within the year. In fact, in most cases I'd recommend that you borrow as opposed to carrying forward your unused contributions. Many of us find it hard enough to save for retirement without tempting fate by postponing our contribution. Procrastination is the greatest enemy of financial and retirement planning. If it was hard to come up with $5,000 this year, how much easier will it be to come up with $10,000 next year? We've already seen what postponing your contribution one year can mean in terms of tax-sheltered compound interest.

Most financial institutions will give you an RRSP loan at prime as long as you buy their products. It can be prime plus 1 percent if you borrow third-party products. It could be as high as prime plus 2 percent or 3 percent if it is financed for a period of over a year. Loans are available up to $15,500, the maximum RRSP contribution that's allowed starting in 2005. There are also catch-up loans that allow you to borrow in excess of $50,000 if you haven't been in the position to maximize your contribution. These make me nervous. The cost of the interest may outweigh the tax-sheltered benefit. With a one-year RRSP loan, the math is simple. It almost always pays off to borrow. Be sure to do the math on the big catch-up loans.

Some institutions don't require the first payment until 120 days after the loan has been made. That gives you time to get your tax refund. The idea is to then use it to either make the first payment or pay off the whole loan. The deadline for applying for loans is usually a few days before the usual March 1 RRSP contribution deadline. And getting a loan has never been so easy. Pick up the phone, get online, or go visit your advisor. So, not having money is no excuse not to try to save money. You really should. Someday it may be valuable again.

Should I pay off my RRSP loan with my tax refund?

There are several things you can do with your tax refund. You could pay off your credit card debt first. These have extremely high interest rates that any investment could only dream of attaining. You shouldn't be financing any long-term debt with them. Or you could pay off your RRSP loan. If you took a loan out, it makes sense to pay it off the minute your refund hits your bank account. If you don't, it becomes a lot harder to catch up next year, especially if you end up having to borrow again for your RRSP. Or you could pay off your mortgage. A lot of refunds fall into the $1,500 range, which for many people makes a nice little monthly mortgage payment. And many mortgages now allow you this flexibility. Another idea—put your money to work for you. With mortgage rates at near-historical lows, investing your money in a basket of funds may be better than paying off your mortgage.

Or how about making next year's RRSP contribution now? As we've seen, money invested in an RRSP grows exponentially, so putting money in at the beginning of each year, rather than waiting more than a year for the March 1 deadline, could potentially put you hundreds of thousands of dollars ahead by the time you're 65 or 70 years old. Eighty percent of RRSP owners make their contributions in the last two weeks of February. Because of the power of tax-sheltered compound interest, you could earn almost $60,000 more in your RRSP if you contributed $5,000 on January 1 of each year for 30 years (assuming an 8 percent interest rate) rather than on March 1 of the following year. This is one situation where sooner is definitely better than later. Remember, you can be young without money but you can't be old without it.

What happens to my RRSP if I die?

If I die tomorrow and I'm single, my RRSP proceeds will be counted as income in the year of my death and will be fully taxable. If I'm married or have moved in with Lance, the money would be rolled over into his RRSP and continue along just as it did in mine. Lance, however, gets to pay the tax when he accesses the money. If my estate and beneficiaries wish, the funds could also pass directly to a child or grandchild who is financially dependent on me. The money from my RRSP can be rolled over to the child and taxed in her hands instead of my estate. If my daughter is a minor, a special annuity will be purchased that will pay equal annual payments until she's 18.

How to "buy" your RRSP

Here's the typical Canadian scenario: It's the RRSP deadline, March 1. The lunchtime crowd at the bank is immense. The lineups stretch around the block as last-minute procrastinators converge on frazzled bank tellers. The tellers' eyes have glazed over and their voices have a monotonous, robot-like quality. Bank managers, sequestered at the back of the branch, are rapidly darting about putting out numerous administrative fires. People are fidgeting under the weight of their heavy winter coats and standing in little puddles of grimy water as the snow melts from the body heat. Kids are squalling, mothers are shushing, and business people anxiously look at their watches every 2 minutes. Everyone's been standing in line at least 30 minutes.

Sound familiar?

The banks do their best to prepare for the inevitable onslaught of last-minute contributors, but at the last minute you won't get the advice you need. If you go in advance and talk to one of the mutual fund representatives, maybe. But not the last day of RRSP season. You don't have to subject yourself to this cruel and inhuman punishment, you know. You can invest in an RRSP in a way that's reasonably painless and effortless. You can be the person walking smugly past the bank at noon on March 1 as you make your way to a nice, quiet restaurant for a relaxing lunch, shaking your head and tsk-tsking at the sweltering mass of humanity waiting impatiently to do what you've already done.

Where can you open an RRSP and invest in products for it? Anywhere, everywhere. Banks, credit unions, insurance companies, trust companies, mutual fund companies, stockbrokers, they all offer them. You might be able to set one up through work if your company offers group RRSPs. They're the same as regular RRSPs except that your employer deducts your contribution directly from your salary. Be sure, however, that you agree with the investment philosophy of your company. Some companies will offer a choice of investments for your RRSP. Don't sign on the dotted line until you know where your money is going.

For those of you who work for an employer, there's a little-known but highly effective way of making your RRSP contribution. You have to go through your local Canada Revenue Agency district office, but it's well worth the effort. You need to get a Request for Reduction of Deduction at Source, or Tax Deduction Waiver. You fill out this form and bring a copy of the form you filled out to open your RRSP as proof of purchase. You then submit these directly to Canada Revenue Agency. The tax deduction benefit that you usually don't get until after your taxes are filed is available immediately and appears regularly on your paycheque. Let's say you make a monthly $200 contribution to your RRSP and you're in the top tax bracket. This means you will in effect receive a refund of $100 for every $200 you contribute. Instead of having to wait until May or June for Canada Revenue Agency to send back the tax refund owed you, you'll see an extra $100 every month on your paycheque. Not only will you end up with extra money every month, you'll also enjoy the advantage of having your RRSP bought and paid for by the time the deadline rolls around. I think this is a superlative idea for those who contribute to their RRSP monthly. But, be aware that companies have been known to refuse to do this.

We'll talk about the power of dollar cost averaging in purchasing mutual funds in the next chapter. Since I'm self-employed, I divide my annual RRSP contribution by 12 and make monthly deposits into my plan. That way, by March 1 my contribution is taken care of in full and I've enjoyed the benefits of dollar cost averaging.

"Lumpers" are people who contribute everything at the end of the year. There's a clear disadvantage to doing it this way, because although they might have been able to make their lump-sum payments in the past, the habit can be disrupted by unexpected one-time costs, like car repairs. The research company Compas conducted a survey showing that men tend to be lumpers more so than women—39 percent compared with 28 percent. David MacDonald, assistant vice president of Compas, says, "In many instances in the survey, women showed they were more methodical." He also noted that the clear gender differences may make for marketing openings for advisors.

How do I make my retirement income stretch?

In the old days, retirement security meant making sure all doors were locked before going to bed. But living longer and low interest rates mean we have to find ways to make our retirement income stretch. Here are four things to consider as you set up your retirement savings plans:

1. When rates are down, don't lock in a large percentage of your retirement capital for the long term. Try staggering the maturity dates on investments like GICs and bonds so that approximately 20 percent of your holdings mature each year. This ensures that you'll have some money to reinvest if interest rates rise.
2. The second strategy is to diversify your investments. For example, in the summer of 1990, five-year GICs were paying 12 percent. In July of

1999, you were lucky if you got a third of that. Investors who sank a large portion of their retirement savings into five-year GICs in the mid-80s enjoyed several years of excellent returns. But when it came time to renew, their income dropped like a stone. Diversifying helps to avoid that. Look at things like mortgage, bond, and dividend funds. Don't forget money market funds and some equity funds for growth.

3. Consider how your investments are taxed. Interest income tops the list as the highest. Canadian dividend income and capital gains are treated far more favourably.

4. If you're investing in RRIFs, choose your payment schedule carefully. How you take your payments can make a big difference in the amount of income you receive and how long your RRIF will last. You don't want a retirement where the living is easy but the payments are hard.

Everyone, especially women, should be taking advantage of RRSPs to help overcome the financial challenges of lengthy retirements and less income to provide for them. Statistics Canada shows that 48 percent of women between the ages of 60 and 65 live on $10,000 a year or less. Only 18 percent of men fall into this category. You remember the story of Lynn and Stan, their messy separation, and Stan's untimely death. As dreadful as this may be to say, had Stan not died when he did, Lynn could have become one of the poverty statistics in her retirement. She couldn't contribute directly to an RRSP. Stan wasn't receptive to the idea of setting up a spousal RRSP. She didn't qualify for CPP benefits since she worked unpaid in the home. Stan was self-employed and had no company pension from which Lynn could get survivor benefits. She would have been entirely dependent on Old Age Security and whatever Stan had arranged for her. She was very vulnerable.

As women's financial literacy improves along with their own burgeoning economic power, the Lynns of the world will become a minority. RRSPs can ensure that our golden years will, indeed, be golden.

six

Demystifying mutual funds

I've been rich and I've been poor. Rich is better.

SOPHIE TUCKER, 1884–1966

I was gloomily sitting in Elaine's office, having just received a call from Lynn updating me on the lawyer's latest antics. It got me reflecting on my progress over the past few weeks. I'd finally dealt with my estate planning and insurance needs. That had meant visits to lawyers, painful discussions of death, intensely personal questions on applications for life and disability insurance, and the anxious waiting to see if I was insurable. I had even started planning for my life as an old person. I was beginning to think this whole idea of being financially responsible was far too depressing for such a free spirit.

Elaine sensed my mood. She started off in a sympathetic tone, "This stuff ain't easy. Building a decent financial base can be especially disturbing if you're uncomfortable with some of life's realities, like death and disability. But the good news is now your debt is paid off, your emergency fund is intact and growing, your estate planning and insurance needs are in place, and you've started to plan for your retirement. So, your base of the priority pyramid is pretty solid. You've done well, kiddo. Now we get to move on to the rewards. You know, the 'actually-making-money' part of the equation."

Finally. Something with a little pizzazz.

I was elated. "It's about time, Elaine. I need to make lots of money. You know, in case I don't die."

Elaine smiled. "I suspect that making money will become a hobby that will complement the other hobbies you have beautifully. However, my grandmother had an expression you'd do well to remember: 'No just person became quickly rich.' The only thing wealth does for some people is to make them worry about losing it."

"I can only wish I had that problem," I sighed. "I know money can't buy happiness. It can, however, rent it. But in heaven's name, where do I start?

I have what can only be described as a sobering lack of knowledge and experience in this area."

"You and millions of others," Elaine concurred.

"Let me tell you a true story to illustrate my point," I said.

"Elaine, picture this scene: I'm at a dinner party. I'm surrounded by people casually chatting about their different investments. To my ears, it sounds like Arabic. 'My bond fund did well last quarter thanks to interest rates dropping.' 'I'm so glad it seems like we've beat the bear.' 'I've had a nice pickup in my international equities—it seems like the global economic recovery is picking up steam.' 'If only we knew when the Fed was going to move on interest rates ...'

"As I stood there, I smiled brightly pretending to be intelligent, nodding my head every so often to create the illusion that I actually had a clue. Inside, I was feeling nothing short of sheer panic in case someone asked me something.

"As you can guess, Elaine, my worst fear was realized. Someone uttered the fateful words, 'So, Joanne, what's your money in these days?' My smile froze for an instant but I recovered quickly. My response was divinely inspired. I stammered, 'The banks. Ah ... yes, most of my money goes into, uh, banks.' I smiled directly at my inquisitor in triumph. I hadn't lied. Most of my money went directly to two banks. The ones that offered Visa and Mastercard.

"It was then I realized I was becoming remarkably adept at faking knowing something when I didn't. Frankly, men had been teaching me this trick for years."

Elaine cracked up at the vivid image of a grown woman squirming in public. Especially this particular one. "Woman, you are too much. Methinks it's time you actually had some real investments to talk about at dinner parties."

"Yeah, but if I was nervous about learning the basics of financial planning, the thought of investments like mutual funds throws me right into the realm of outright fear. Criminy, I don't even know what questions to ask." I moaned for effect.

"I'm always surprised at people's level of anxiety about mutual funds and investing in the stock market," Elaine said thoughtfully. "Mutual funds, especially the stock market variety, seem to intimidate people; they often think you need a fortune to get into them. I always think of Mark Twain's take on the stock market. He said, 'October. This is one of the peculiarly dangerous months to speculate in stocks. The others are July, January, September, April, November, May, March, June, December, August, and February.'"

"Yet, the freedom to make a fortune on the stock exchange has been made to sound more alluring than freedom of speech," I replied.

"Don't despair. It's not all that complex. I'd be surprised if there were more than 50 funds in Canada that are worth buying. Many of the 4,800 or so available, which includes funds like segregated funds, are identical, with the only distinction being their name.

(Author's note: That being said, there has been a lot of consolidation in the fund industry recently. Originally there were 80 fund companies, now there are 57. CI bought BPI and Synergy. Strategic Nova [previously O'Donnell] was bought by Dynamic. Aim and Trimark merged. There was a big drop in players, but with the advent of different classes of mutual funds—for example, F-class, corporate class structure, clone, and segregated—there are more funds than ever before.)

"The challenge is figuring out which ones you want. No matter what kind of investor you are, whether the ultra-nervous type or the aggressive, guerrilla type, you can find a fund that's right for you. And you don't need a lot of funds. You can put together a really well-diversified portfolio with a half a dozen or less. If you don't expect miracles, you'll be fine. Remember how I hammered home the importance of socking away that 10 percent of your after-tax income? You know, your palatial estate and lolling, dark, mysterious men fund?"

"I know exactly what you're going to say," I quickly replied, anxious to impress. "Mutual funds. I'm going to put my 10 percent in mutual funds where it will go forth and multiply at a breathtaking rate, right?"

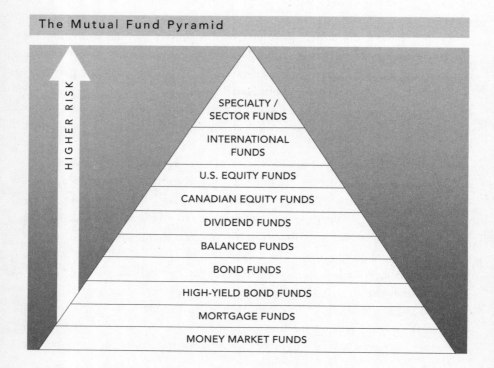

The Mutual Fund Pyramid

HIGHER RISK

SPECIALTY /
SECTOR FUNDS

INTERNATIONAL
FUNDS

U.S. EQUITY FUNDS

CANADIAN EQUITY FUNDS

DIVIDEND FUNDS

BALANCED FUNDS

BOND FUNDS

HIGH-YIELD BOND FUNDS

MORTGAGE FUNDS

MONEY MARKET FUNDS

"In a word," she replied, "no. You know how your beloved priority pyramid is built according to risk. The base is the safest but the pyramid gets progressively more risky right up to the top where art enjoys the most speculative of positions. It's the same with mutual funds. You'll be delighted to see that I have another pyramid that illustrates this point." Elaine pushed a piece of paper across her desk at me.

It looked like the priority pyramid, except there were different types of mutual funds ranked according to their risk or volatility level. I groaned. "Elaine, you mean there are more than one type? This financial planning business is beginning to remind me of buying what used to be called running shoes. Now you have to know in advance exactly what you need them for, how often you're going to be using them, and if you'll be using them for something other than running. There are walking shoes, court shoes, trail running shoes, track shoes, racing shoes, killer aerobic shoes, high tops, low tops, women's, girls', men's, boys', infants', and cross-training shoes for those fools who want to do a bit of everything. Life used to be so much simpler."

"Quit your whining, my little protégé," Elaine responded. "As with anything worth having, a little work must be done before you reap any appreciable gain. Whether you wind up with a nest egg or a goose egg depends on the kind of chick you married."

"Six million comediennes in the world and look who I'm stuck with," I said.

Elaine grinned broadly. "Before we get into the nitty-gritty about investing, I need to take a minute to prepare you. The next part of the pyramid is dense. It's not that investing is hard to understand, it's just that there's a lot to understand. Also, with credit and estate planning, you've got credit card abuse and death and disability to keep things lively. The principles of investing and the anatomy of mutual funds are fascinating to be sure, but have you ever met someone who had a harrowing life and death experience with one? Persevere, Joanne. The information I'm about to impart will be the difference between Spam and pâté de foie gras in your future. The reality is that money can't buy love, happiness, or what it did last year. That's why mutual funds are your next step."

"Okay, I'm a willing pupil," I said. "But before we start, I need to get my tools to become prepared for all of this intense academic activity. These tools are the only way I got through university."

"Tools?"

"Food." I headed for the door. "It's that fuel thing. I'm going to grab some Vanilla Maple tea to wash down the boxcar full of nibblies that I intend to ingest." With that I walked out of Elaine's office to load up for my next lesson. When I returned I was heavily laden with all my favourite snacks, carrots and celery sticks noticeably absent. For this job, I had to ramp it up a few notches. As I settled into the biggest, most comfortable chair, I surrounded myself with enough chocolate to keep the shareholders of Laura Secord happy for several months.

Elaine glanced over at my chocolate stash. "Clearly your preferred food group," she quipped. She was revved up on her soapbox, ready to go. "Okay, are you focused Joanne?" I nodded contentedly as I began to pop the first of thousands of M&Ms into my mouth.

"Good. You know, once I got over my own initial fear of mutual funds through educating myself, I couldn't get into one fast enough. Mutual funds are a vital component of a solid, long-term financial plan. I believe every Canadian should be taking advantage of some form of mutual fund from the different families of funds. Mutual funds have been around in Canada since 1932. To give you an indication of the explosive growth in this industry, in December 1992 there was $67 billion under management. By December 31, 1994, it had grown to over $130 billion. As of December 2003, it's in the $438 billion range. As the pyramid shows, there are many types of mutual funds to fit the many reasons people have for investing in them.

"Simply put, mutual funds take advantage of the principle of shared resources and risk. For example, if you went into a bank with $50 to put in a term deposit, you'd likely get a paltry rate of return. If you had $50,000, your interest rate would improve immeasurably. Now imagine having $500,000 or $5 million and what you could get as an interest rate."

"I can imagine that just about as well as I can imagine myself looking like Gwyneth Paltrow," I replied.

"You're right. Not even in my wildest dreams. But what I can envision is putting my $50 in a pot with a large group of people and giving it to a company to invest as part of a much bigger sum. By pooling your money with other investors, you can take advantage of investments you otherwise couldn't afford. Not only do you get an expanded variety of investment choices, you do so more safely. If the money goes into term deposits and other guaranteed investments, it's called a money market mutual fund. If it goes into stocks, it's called an equity mutual fund; mortgages, a mortgage fund, and so on. This is the principle of mutual funds. You give your money, along with a zillion other investors, to a company that invests your $50 a month in whatever type of investment you choose. You may choose from risk-free term deposits to the more adventurous stocks and bonds, precious metals, or specialty investments. Or, if you like, a combination of the lot. The wonderful part of these invest-ments is that you may cash them in at any time."

"Possibly at a loss, of course," I added.

"Yes, depending on market prices. In other words, it comes down to what price a buyer is willing to pay for something and how much the seller is willing to charge. So they're essentially liquid. Depending on the type of fund you choose, they may even get preferred tax treatment."

And Elaine was off. Here's the general gist of her imparted wisdom.

There's no shortage of media stories about job losses, wage freezes, and doubts about the future of government and company pension plans. This changed economy has made bill collectors out of just about everybody. Today, Canadians look more closely at getting the best bang for our buck. This search has led us, rightly or wrongly, to mutual funds. Rightly, because many mutual funds do offer excellent opportunities for as little as $25 a month. Wrongly, because many people have unrealistic expectations or unknowingly invest in poor performers. As the expression goes, it's not the bulls and bears you need to avoid, it's the bum steers. But for investors who take the time to do a little homework, mutual funds offer the following benefits.

First, looking at an equity fund as an example, your mutual fund may hold stocks in anywhere from 50 to over 100 companies and in many different industries such as automobiles, pharmaceuticals, and banking. Spreading your money among many different companies and industries in this way reduces the possibility that you'll lose money over a period of time. Second, the amount of money and knowledge you'd need to do it yourself would be mind-boggling. A mutual fund is known as an "institutional trader," meaning it buys securities in large volumes, essentially getting wholesale prices—like bulk shopping, investment style. Third, mutual funds are run by money managers—people experienced in analyzing data, choosing securities to meet the fund's objectives, and deciding when to buy and sell. They, in most cases, actually go out and meet the key people in the organizations. Fourth, mutual funds tend to do better over the long term when compared to guaranteed investments. (However, not all. Of the 4,800 investment funds that PALtrak, an investment tracking service, counts, about half give above-average returns. About 130 beat their benchmark on a consistent basis.)

Buying a mutual fund isn't complicated and can be done in person, by telephone, over the Internet, or by mail. All mutual fund companies provide you with regular statements that tell you everything from the total value of all funds held to the tax status of all earnings from the fund. Record keeping is a breeze.

Growth, income, and balanced funds

Since there are a mere 4,800 different funds available, it's important to have a clear idea of your investment goals before choosing. Don't panic about having a few thousand to choose from. Many of these funds are simply clones of each other or different classes of the same fund carrying different commission structures. Some funds are more suited for certain ends and types of investors than others. If you want to buy a business in six months, putting your cash resources into an equity fund wouldn't be wise. If you want to retire 30 years from now in the lap of luxury in your country chalet, having your entire portfolio in a money market fund will not get you there.

There are two broad categories of mutual funds. The first offers long-term growth potential and invests in things like common stocks. When you see an investment described as a "growth" investment, it means volatility. It'll go up and down, sort of like a roller coaster. Stocks are particularly prone to this kind of movement. Common stocks are shares of ownership in a company. We're able to buy stocks because a company sells shares to raise the money it needs to expand. If the stocks you buy are from blue chip companies like the big banks and huge corporations, volatility tends to be less of a factor. These stocks, or shares (the two terms are used interchangeably), are more stable and don't fluctuate nearly as much as shares in newer, just-emerging companies. Although not the case over the last few years, blue chip stocks have historically been slower-moving investments that are conservative in nature. If, on the other hand, the company is newer and just beginning to grow, there's likely to be much greater volatility. However, you've got a better chance to be on hand for a wild ride to the top if the company flourishes.

This volatility isn't a bad thing. It can actually be a very good thing. There's a new emerging economy that's considered "leading edge," and it includes medical technology, telecommunications, the Internet, and environmentally concerned companies. By way of contrast, companies that are heavily involved in coal mining and beef cattle, for example, are undoubtedly on the decline, no matter how massive they may be. The smaller, leaner, more progressive companies have more opportunity, provided they're managed well and stay ahead of their competition. There may be lots of growing pains, but over the long term they might be a good bet. In investing jargon, these companies are referred to as "small cap" (capitalization) companies. They're definitely much riskier, but the growth potential can be very good. "Big cap" companies, like the top five chartered banks and Bell Canada, don't offer the same growth potential, but make up for it with slow, stable, secure growth.

Mutual funds are available now that take advantage of the growth potential of these small cap companies. And, of course, there are and always will be the blue chip variety. There are also funds that offer a combination of the two so that you can have both growth and stability.

Returns from mutual funds include interest and dividends earned on the funds' investments. They also come from the profits of the sale of stocks inside the mutual fund portfolio. This type of return is called capital gains. Returns are also earned when stocks increase in value (otherwise known as capital appreciation). This happens when the companies do well and the demand for their shares increases. When the demand increases, the share value increases. There's absolutely no way of knowing for sure how a growth-oriented fund will perform. It depends partly on how well the stock market as a whole performs and partly on the stocks that the fund manager selects. You could enjoy a banner year and get 35 percent as a rate of return, then lick your wounds because of a minus 5 percent return the next year. Because of their diversified nature, mutual funds tend not to fluctuate wildly day by day unless there's some sort of hugely upsetting event. They tend to fluctuate less than individual stocks do, with the exception of specialty funds.

At this point, I woke from my academic reverie and asked Elaine, "So mutual funds are better than investing in individual stocks?"

"Not necessarily," she replied. "Like investing in stocks and bonds, growth-oriented mutual funds are long-term investments. After all, as the old proverb says, 'You can't fatten the pig on market day.' I can't emphasize strongly enough that you need to think of seven years as an absolute minimum, with 10 years being far more preferable. Investment guru Warren Buffett says his favourite holding period is forever."

I nodded as I slipped back into academic catatonia.

"The second category of mutual funds is more income oriented and provides not only income that you can use today, but stable, low to moderate growth for the future. These are income mutual funds. These funds invest in debt instruments like bonds and mortgages. Let's say the federal government (or a corporation) needs to raise money for something like modernizing a plant. It will issue a piece of paper called a bond or debenture. You give them your money and they promise to pay it back at the maturity date, with a predetermined amount of interest. In other words, you're loaning money to the government or corporation with the expectation of making a profit from the interest they pay you in return. That's why bonds are called debt instruments or securities. The income you receive from these kinds of mutual funds comes from the interest that's been generated. The exception is dividend funds. You get income from this type of fund from, you guessed it, dividends. Dividends are your share of a company's profit in a given year.

"Balanced funds are a combination of growth-oriented and income-producing investments, but are still considered to be in the growth category. Give these types of funds at least five years to grow while they roll with the ups and downs. Historically speaking, growth funds have provided a better return over the long run than the more moderate income funds.

"These, then," Elaine finished, "are the two broad categories of mutual funds. Mutual funds are also grouped into other categories, depending on what they invest in and what they're designed to do. There are three major considerations when buying mutual funds: safety, capital growth, and income-producing ability. Each type of fund offers one, two, or all three of these benefits in varying degrees. The most common types of funds are balanced funds, common stock or growth funds, specialty or sector funds, and fixed-income funds. In the '70s, a number of new funds evolved whose function is to take advantage of the new needs and developments in the securities industry. Examples include money market funds, mortgage funds, dividend funds, and real estate funds. The '90s also saw new evolutions—index funds, index-linked GICs, ethical investing, as well as an explosion of interest in segregated funds."

(Author's note: After two negative years in equity markets to start the new century, two new types of funds emerged: income funds bought not only bonds and dividend stocks, but also the growing number of "income trust" issues; the other type of high-growth-rate funds in the early years of this century have been hedge funds, or "fund of fund" packages that include several hedging strategies and can be tied to a bank note that offers protection of the principal.)

Income-generating funds

Money market funds

Elaine grinned. "Saving money these days is harder than playing a trumpet at the wrong end."

I levelled at her my best "You've got to be kidding" stare. "Keep your day job, Elaine. You'd starve as a comedienne."

She blushed but carried on. "But if by some queer quirk of fate you actually find yourself with extra cash and you're looking for a short-term parking place, you actually have a couple of choices. The first thing you don't do is dump it into a savings account. You could do better with money market mutual funds. But you need to have realistic expectations. We live in a low-interest-rate world, so regardless of what you choose, the returns won't be huge. But they'll be a darned sight better than stuffing the cash in a mattress. Money market funds are the safest of funds."

"Why?" I asked.

"Because they invest in cash. These funds invest in high-quality short-term investments like term deposits, treasury bills, and high-quality corporate bonds that have a term of anything under a year. Term deposits, for example, guarantee a fixed rate of return no matter what happens, and this return is generally higher than premium savings accounts. You deposit a fixed amount for a fixed period of time, anything from 30 days to one year.

"As for T-bills, think of these as government IOUs. You buy them at a discount and receive full value when they mature. However, most financial institutions won't sell anything less than $25,000 in T-bills. That's why we have money market funds. They do the same as T-bills only in smaller amounts. There are no penalties to get in or out quickly, nor are there any penalties for marrying into the same fund family."

"Not like the same penalty one gets from marrying their cousin," I joked.

Elaine ignored me. "A money market fund is a great place for an emergency fund because it's completely liquid, yet will give you a higher rate of return than a savings account. This is why they're a very suitable parking lot for short periods before deciding where to go for the long haul. They're also quite suitable as the cash component of an overall asset allocation strategy."

"What's asset allocation? I asked, purely to let Elaine know that I was still awake.

"Later," she replied. "Get this stuff down first.

"Investors who believe that interest rates are going to rise will take advantage of this type of fund. The differences between money market funds are minimal, but be sure to find one that has no load—in other words, that there's no charge to buy or sell it. Also, Canadian money market funds are RRSP-eligible.

"There are also U.S. money market funds that invest in short-term U.S. securities like treasury bills. These are good for those who travel to the United States and require frequent access to American funds. International money market funds invest in international commercial paper and short-term securities."

Mortgage funds

Elaine pressed on. "Mortgage funds are another low-risk form of mutual fund, though slightly riskier than a savings account or money market fund. On the other hand, they've been known to offer a somewhat higher rate of return than a money market fund. However, that hasn't been the case over the last few years because of the general decline in the real estate market. As with all low-risk investments, however, you enjoy stability and security at the cost of a high rate of return. These funds invest primarily in residential first mortgages, but some will invest in commercial and industrial mortgages. Mortgages are loans secured by property, so the house itself becomes the collateral. For most bank-offered mortgage funds, the bank will guarantee the mortgage in the event of default. In commercial or industrial loans, the factory or office building secures the loan. Since these funds invest in first mortgages, which are safer than second and third mortgages, you don't have to worry about losing your shirt."

"You mean blouse."

"Blouse. They don't tend to be volatile; however, their value is affected by changes in interest rates. Mortgage funds are increasingly investing in mortgage-backed securities, which tend to be safer because they're government guaranteed. Mortgage funds are ideal for a novice eager to learn about the investing world. Investors who rate security, stability, and moderate returns high in their investment priorities will also like these types of funds. They're also RRSP-eligible."

Bond funds

"These funds invest mainly in medium- to long-term bonds of federal, provincial, and municipal governments. Depending on the fund mandate, some bonds are short-, medium-, or long-term. Quality corporate bonds might also be included. You may experience major swings in bond prices depending on how interest rates fare. In general, bond funds can be more stable than equity funds except when interest rates move sharply up or down. There've been times when bond funds have outperformed equity funds. When interest rates drop, bonds will do well. When interest rates start to rise, bonds typically decline in value, which isn't good if you own the fund, but great if you're looking to buy. If you're conservative and want a steady monthly or annual income from your investment, bond funds are a good choice. They offer better than average returns and flexibility. They aren't like GICs that lock in your money for a set period of time. Bond funds are especially popular with people approaching retirement who want to move their investments from the more volatile equity funds to something possibly more stable and secure.

"Now, if you combine bond funds with mortgage funds you get what's called an income fund or fixed-income fund. There are also high-yield bond funds that offer higher returns but with higher credit risk. This means that the company borrowing the money is willing to pay a higher interest rate because there may be less certainty that they'll pay it back. A good example of this is any level of government. They can guarantee payback, whereas perhaps a company will not. Bond funds and income funds are RRSP-eligible. You can also invest in international bond funds, which invest in bonds from different countries.

"There are also funds that invest in stocks as well as bonds. These are called balanced funds. Typically, balanced funds will hold at least 25 percent of their assets in stocks and are a convenient and simple way for investors to diversify. If you can stay with me, I'll explain more about these funds later."

Dividend funds

"Okay Joanne, here's one for you. When is $1.00 worth $1.30?"

"When it's in my mother's hands," I responded, referring to her remarkable ability to make a dollar stretch.

"Try when it's a dividend. A dividend is how a company pays the people who own its stock. It qualifies for what's called a dividend tax credit, which is how you end up with a buck being worth $1.30. No matter how much money you make, a dollar's worth of dividends from taxable Canadian corporations will leave more money in your pocket than a dollar in interest or a dollar in capital gains. You see, dividends are the lowest-taxed form of income.

"They offer good tax breaks for the well-heeled investor through the dividend tax credit, and because only 50 percent of the capital gains in these funds is taxable. Here's an example. You've just made $5,000. Assuming a 40 percent marginal tax rate, this is what you'll really end up with: if you put it in a GIC, what's left after tax is $3,000. If you invested it in stocks that generated a capital gain, you'd actually have $4,000. If you put it in Canadian stocks that generated dividends, you'd have $3,750 in your pocket. Considering you started with the same $5,000 investment in each case, it's easy to see that type of income generated by an investment is a big factor in determining how much of its return you are going to keep on an after-tax basis. Of the three types of investment returns, you pay the least tax on capital gains and the most tax on interest. Dividends fall in the middle.

"The government likes it when you invest in Canadian companies. In order to encourage you to do so, they give investors a tax break in the form of the dividend tax credit, which reduces the tax you have to pay. You'll end up in a better tax position with these funds than you would with interest-bearing investments like GICs and Canada Savings Bonds (CSBs). On these investments, you have to pay the full tax. With dividend funds, you have the dividend tax credit at your disposal to relieve some of your tax burden.

"These funds invest in high-quality common shares, for example from blue chip companies like Bell, and preferred shares. Preferred shares have a guaranteed value attached to them, unlike common shares which fluctuate according to a number of factors, including supply and demand. Common shares, though offering no guarantees, will most often provide a higher rate of return than preferred shares. Shareholders owning preferred shares are paid by the corporation before the owners of common shares. These kinds of funds are designed specifically to give you maximum dividend opportunity."

As Elaine's voice took on a droning quality, my eyes glazed over and I slipped back into that conscious but zombie-like state. Here's what I picked up from what she said next.

There are three main types of dividend funds: the first is dividend growth funds, which invest in dividend-paying common stocks. If you want growth but don't want to stay awake at night worrying about it, this might be for you. Research has shown that over the long term, stocks that have a high dividend yield tend to outperform the market and with less risk and volatility. Then there are dividend income shares, which hold mostly preferred shares and some bonds. Not a lot to choose from here because there's a lack of preferred shares on the market.

The last one is a relatively new category—the income trust—that invests in royalty trusts, business trusts, and real estate investments (REITS). These investments are typically too risky or too expensive to own as stand-alone investments. Owning one of these funds actually makes you a co-owner of an oil field or a mega-hotel. Income trusts such as REITS have become increasingly popular and, as of 2003, have done well in the market.

Dividend funds are RRSP-eligible, but because of the tax breaks you get through the dividend tax credit it's usually recommended that you hold these funds outside your RRSP. However, because of today's low interest rates, people are putting them into their RRSPs to capitalize on the growth potential.

Real estate funds

Income-producing real estate properties are the order of the day here. These funds allow Canadians to participate in another market from which they might normally be excluded—real estate. They invest in things like office buildings, shopping centres, medical facilities, and apartment buildings. Unlike other mutual funds, these funds offer deferred taxation through what's called a capital cost allowance. This allowance tax shelters portions of the rental income that's distributed within the fund. These funds are designed for long-term growth, through the increase in the value of the property in the fund and through having the rental income reinvested in the fund. They aren't very liquid, since they're generally valued quarterly and can only be redeemed on certain days, with 30 days' notice often being required. Real estate funds are quite new in Canada and the recession in the early '90s hurt their performance, especially those heavily invested in shopping centres. These funds are more risky than mortgage and bond funds and, because of the current commercial real estate climate, have become more volatile than dividend funds.

Because REITs are more liquid than the actual properties, it's much easier to buy and sell them as required within a mutual fund. If the fund only owns actual real estate, there can be problems if the market softens and investors wish to get their money out. If the fund owns a blend of actual real estate and publicly traded shares of real estate companies, then these shares can be more easily redeemed or purchased in periods of market volatility.

These funds are RRSP-eligible, but because of the tax-preferred treatment of the capital cost allowance, putting REITs into an RRSP is not generally recommended. The benefit of holding income trusts is optimized in a taxable account, as opposed to an RRSP, where you don't pay tax on the income earned anyway.

High-income funds incorporate REITs and other income trusts, high-yield corporate bonds, and real return bonds, as well as government paper. A good example is the Guardian Group of Funds (GGOF) Monthly High Income Fund (commonly know as MOHI, its acronym). This fund provides exposure to a cross-section of all the various types of income trusts and is managed by John Priestman, considered by many to be the "grand-daddy" of income trusts. The GGOF MOHI did so well it was capped, and a second fund, "MOHI 2," opened. The market cap of the income trust asset class has shot up from only around $5 billion in 1995 to over $45 billion today. It is expected that income trusts will soon be recognized in the TSX 60 Index.

Bev Evans, an investment advisor with RBC Dominion Securities who has more letters after her name than the entire alphabet, offers this advice: "High-yield bonds have also been getting attention over the past year or two, particularly as falling interest rates have made it very challenging to get 'acceptable/attractive' returns from bonds as an asset class. High-yield bonds are those of less than 'investment grade' quality, namely, rated as BB or lower by a bond rating agency. Because you are buying corporate debt when you buy these more speculative bonds, you need to know a lot about the status of the issuer, so considerable research and expertise is required. As a result, it is best to buy high-yield bonds through a specialized mutual fund, as opposed to trying to buy them on your own. The Trimark Advantage Bond fund is a good example of a high-yield bond fund that has done very well—again, it was closed to new investors in 2003 once it reached a certain asset level. Many new 'income-oriented' balanced funds, for example, are now including a high-yield bond component in order to try to 'juice up' their yields. It is a risky asset class and it is not to be treated lightly … as always, proper diversification is the key—it should only be one component of an overall diversified portfolio."

Growth-oriented funds

Canadian equity funds

Canadian equity funds specialize in stocks in Canadian companies. These funds are ideal for people wanting to invest in the Canadian economy.

However, they can be volatile. The Toronto Stock Exchange annual rate of return varies widely. Over the 10-year period ending December 2003, the annual return of the TSX Composite Index was 6.46 percent. Individual returns ranged from −13.97 percent to 29.72 percent.

This fluctuation is why equity funds are a long-term investment. Equity funds offer the best long-term growth potential and are your best bet to compensate for the eroding power of inflation and taxation. That's again why these funds are an essential part of financial planning. Moreover, equity funds ensure your money will outlive you if you plan carefully. Equity funds are designed for long-term investing, which makes them ideal for retirement planning. These funds are popular for RRSPs. People who hold these funds outside their RRSPs will enjoy the tax advantages of the dividend tax credit and the fact that most of the tax on these investments won't be paid until you actually sell them. Even when they are cashed in, only 50 percent of the gain is taxed, unlike investments like GICs and Canada Savings Bonds whose interest is 100 percent taxable, every year, whether you receive it or not. Equity funds can include cash and bonds, but are primarily stocks. They can therefore provide the three forms of income—interest, capital gains, and dividends—in varying degrees. That's why they're a good bet.

World Market Capitalization

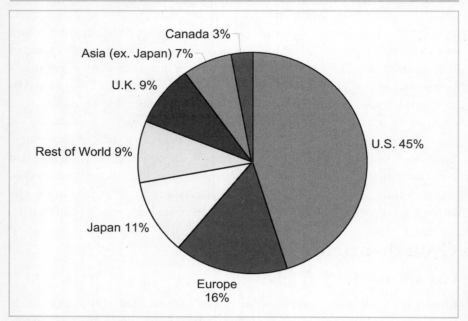

SOURCE: RBC DOMINION SECURITIES. REPRODUCED WITH PERMISSION.

Canadian equity funds are very popular. But remember the importance of diversification. Mutual funds are by their very nature diversified, but you can take it one step further. Although an important market, Canada is considered small by world standards (see the chart opposite), representing only 3 percent of the world market. The Canadian stock market is also primarily based on natural resources, which makes it more susceptible to market swings. Smart investors will expand their holdings to outside of the country to take advantage of opportunities internationally.

U.S. equity funds

As the name suggests, these funds specialize in American stocks. The U.S. market is one of the world's largest and has more to choose from, including some of the biggest companies in the world. There are, however, certain considerations to be aware of when choosing a U.S. equity fund. The vast majority of American funds aren't RRSP-eligible, unless they fall under the 30 percent allowable foreign content rule, and they can't take advantage of any of the Canadian dividend tax breaks, although they are eligible for the tax benefits of capital gains. They've performed better than Canadian funds over the long term and play an important role in a diversified portfolio.

International equity funds

These funds take advantage of the entire world as a potential marketplace. The fund managers try to invest in parts of the world that have the best growth potential, purchasing the common stocks of growth-oriented companies located in different countries. Some funds invest only in a certain country or region of the world, like Japan or the Pacific Rim. These funds are for the well-established investor who's in the "accumulation" phase of his or her financial plan. They're also great for people who understand and want to capitalize on world market trends. International funds are a very aggressive part of your portfolio. They're riskier than Canadian or U.S. funds because you're also playing against the fluctuations of currencies in the different countries. The same tax and RRSP restrictions apply with international funds as with U.S. funds. Like those available in the U.S. equity category, RRSP-eligible international equity funds are also widely available from a growing number of fund companies.

Specialty or sector funds

Specialty funds concentrate on common shares of a group of companies in one industry or geographic location. For those people who are sure that a particular industry is going to do well, a specialty or sector fund is an option. Some examples of specialty funds are Asian funds, natural resource funds, gold

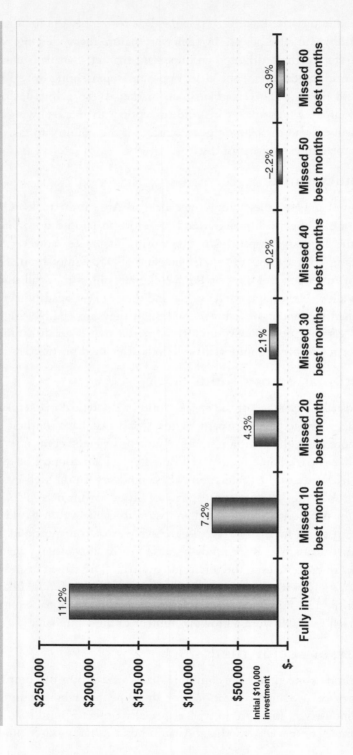

Value of $10,000 Invested in the S&P/TSX Composite Index — From January 1975 to January 2004

Fully invested	11.2%
Missed 10 best months	7.2%
Missed 20 best months	4.3%
Missed 30 best months	2.1%
Missed 40 best months	-0.2%
Missed 50 best months	-2.2%
Missed 60 best months	-3.9%

$250,000
$200,000
$150,000
$100,000
$50,000
Initial $10,000 investment
$-

SOURCE: FIDELITY INVESTMENTS CANADA LIMITED. REPRODUCED WITH PERMISSION. FROM DATASTREAM, S&P/TSX COMPOSITE INDEX PRICE RETURNS FROM JANUARY 31, 1975 TO DECEMBER 31, 2003. EFFECTIVE MAY 1, 2002, THE TSE 300 COMPOSITE INDEX WAS RETIRED AND REPLACED WITH THE S&P/TSX COMPOSITE INDEX. FOR MORE INFORMATION ON THE CHANGES TO THIS INDEX, PLEASE VISIT WWW.TSE.COM. PAST PERFORMANCE IS NO GUARANTEE OF FUTURE RESULTS. IT IS NOT POSSIBLE TO INVEST DIRECTLY IN AN INDEX.

or energy funds, and technology funds. Specialty funds also include ethical funds, whose investment decisions are based on moral criteria. These criteria might include not investing in companies that produce arms, tobacco, or alcohol. A variation of this theme is a new fund started in the United States that invests only in "women-friendly" corporations. These companies must have a certain percentage of women in top management and must offer programs like job sharing and daycare.

Because they don't have the benefit of diversification, sector funds tend to be quite volatile. They can provide stupendous rates of return, but the reverse is also a real possibility. They're a very "boom or bust" form of investing, highly speculative and not for the faint of heart. Ethical funds don't tend to be as volatile as the other funds in this category since they may still be diversified across many sectors.

With the exception of foreign specialty funds (which can be used only up to the allowed foreign content), these are RRSP-eligible. However, because of the tax-preferred treatment of the capital cost allowance, putting sector funds into an RRSP is not generally recommended. (If you're interested in learning more about how capital cost allowance works—although I can't imagine why—talk with your accountant.)

Elaine stopped long enough to help herself to some of my chocolate stash. Munching away, she continued. "Now here's a surprise, Joanne. There's a lot more to an equity fund than meets the eye. Surprisingly, it's cash. Equity funds always have a lesser component of other investments, like cash and bonds, to balance the risk. The ratio will entirely depend on the state of the market and the investment philosophy of the fund manager. Sometimes money managers gaze into their crystal balls and see that all hell is going to break loose. Many will seriously up the cash component of their funds in order to protect investors from the onslaught. Sometimes the average cash level among Canadian equity mutual funds during turbulent times can be double the level a typical fund might hold in a fast-rising market."

"But don't most people who invest in equity funds do so because they want the growth potential they can't get with cash? I don't think people want their equity funds to be large cash cows," I said.

"Ah yes," Elaine agreed. "But what happens when the market crashes? Being in a fund heavy in cash almost guarantees that you'll fare better than someone who isn't.

"But," Elaine continued, "beware of the downside of having a high cash component. What happens when the market picks up again?"

(Author's note: There was a dramatic drop just after September 11, 2001, due to the terrorist attacks in the United States, but markets recovered quickly and had made up their ground by December 2001, with a very strong rally in the last quarter of the year. Then came January 2002 with the Enron debacle, so the investor confidence crisis just came back with a vengeance, and the three-year bear market that had started earlier in 2001 continued. However, if an investor had panicked after 9/11 and cashed out, he or she would have lost any exposure to the rally immediately afterward. Ultimately, the bear market that started after the tech bubble burst [in March 2000] and that lasted through 2001 and 2002 finally ended in 2003. This period was very trying for investors, as the losses in equity markets were prolonged. The markets came back strongly over 2003, however, with 20 percent rallies in both Canada and the United States. Investors would have had to stick with it in order to benefit from this.)

"Which is going to fare better, the fund that's still predominantly invested in equities or the one carrying a wad of cash?"

I sighed. "I suspect this is exactly why we pay what we pay in management fees. I'd rather have the money managers make the decision as to how much of what and when, though even they find it tough to time the market."

Elaine added, "It never hurts to remember the immortal words of investing guru Warren Buffett: 'I never attempt to make money on the stock market. I buy on the assumption that they could close the market the next day and not reopen it for five years.'"

Elaine decided to stop and take a sanity check. "Are your eyes crossing yet?"

I was too dazed to answer.

"Why don't you get up and shake the numbness out from your brain and your bottom? Judging from the knee-high mound of wrappers, you'll need a refill. When you come back, I'll give you the scoop on balanced funds."

Balanced funds

Different balanced funds have different objectives, but generally they try to provide some combination of income and growth. The mix of stocks and bonds also helps to reduce the risks of losing money. These funds include a little bit of everything—stocks, bonds, cash, and mortgages. They're also RRSP-eligible. The idea behind them is to maximize the growth potential of your investments while preserving the capital. This can be achieved by anticipating market conditions. The fund manager will adjust the asset mix or percentage of each asset according to the pulse of the economy. If the stock market isn't performing to expectations, then the manager may increase the cash portion of the portfolio. If interest rates are rising, the manager may minimize the bond portion of the fund and add equities. You'll rarely see an even

50/50 split of aggressive and conservative investments. A higher percentage of fixed-income securities, like bonds and preferred shares, tends to provide higher immediate income and reduces the price fluctuations of the fund. Although balanced funds are considered reasonably safe, a combination of poor market performance and rising interest rates will wreak havoc with them. For example, the average balanced fund dropped by about 13 percent during the summer '98 meltdown from May to August, while the average Canadian equity fund dropped by almost twice that amount—24 percent. (The TSX as a whole dropped 27.5 percent.)

According to Bev Evans, "Balanced funds only go down when they have a 'double whammy,' i.e., rising rates and a dropping market. This was the case starting in March 1994, when rates spiked by 2 percent in a three-month period. This hurt balanced funds because of the rate increase at the same time the markets were falling. In the early 2000s, rates were falling, which is good for fixed income investments. This nicely offset the bear market of dropping equities. Balanced funds did their job in this scenario—reducing risk and providing a diversification offset for the poor returns in equities. This is why they're typically an effective 'one-stop' investment from a diversification/risk control point of view."

Balanced funds are a relatively safe way to introduce yourself to investing. They're also recommended for older investors who want to start switching their equity investments over to less volatile or risky funds. They can help you have your cake and eat it too. They'll provide long-term growth possibilities with stability. Elaine told me that she used to think balanced funds couldn't keep pace with equity funds over the long term, but that the 10-year average for Canadian balanced funds ending December 31, 2003, was 6.7 percent and the median for Canadian equity mutual funds was 7.6 percent.

There are really two types of balanced or, as they're also called, asset allocation funds. Those that practise what's called strategic asset allocation (SAA) set a long-term target asset mix, such as 60 percent stock, 40 percent bonds. The fund won't typically deviate much from this target. Tactical asset allocation (TAA) funds, on the other hand, anticipate what's going to happen in the economy and more actively manage the stock/bond/cash mix based on the manager's near-term economic outlook and return expectations. Even though balanced funds may be expensive because of the management fee structure, they still remain an ideal solution for investors who don't want to manage their own asset mix and don't have an advisor to do it for them. It's the price one pays for simplicity, convenience, and accessibility.

There are a couple of options for thrifty investors looking for a relatively stable mix of stocks and bonds. First, most fund families offering balanced funds also offer a pure equity fund and a pure bond fund. Let's assume you want a 60/40 mix in favour of stocks. By taking 60 percent of your balanced fund and placing it directly into the pure stock fund and putting the other 40 percent into a pure bond fund, you can save an average of 0.35 percent *annually* on your balanced fund holdings. With some fund families (e.g., AIM Trimark) you can save as much as 0.60 percent per year by using this same strategy. The other option is to simply take the 40 percent bond portion and invest directly into a government bond. Since bonds have no annual expenses, you can reduce your expenses by an average of 0.90 percent per year. Anything you can save in annual expenses goes straight to your bottom line in the form of increased returns. If you really want to get into it, you can buy the actual bonds themselves. There's no annual management fee and the different maturity dates give you the diversification that you need.

My mind was overflowing with all the possibilities. "Short answer, Elaine. What fund should I invest in?"

"It depends entirely on what you want it to do," she replied. "Look at the numbers but be acutely aware that the numbers by no means tell you that Japanese equity funds are better than Canadian. What the numbers do tell you is that at the moment they are. Next year's numbers could look markedly different."

"Tell me, oh great guru. This, I trust, is the end of the lesson?" I asked hopefully.

"Not even close." Elaine was a tough taskmaster.

Other stuff to look at
Index-linked GICs

These GICs are being sold as "mutual funds on training wheels" or "GICs with guts." Index-linked GICs come in different flavours. Typically they offer a guaranteed return of your principal, a minimum compounded annual interest rate—say, 3 percent—and some of the upside potential from the stock market. But watch out—some may have a ceiling of 8 percent. They can offer an advantage for those who spend sleepless nights worrying about their money in the market. They're also a great idea for those with a short time horizon, say, those in their mid-50s or those who are saving for a house or a car.

But this type of GIC is not without risk. If you buy one of these GICs outside of your RRSP, you pay tax as though the gain were interest income. This is a bad thing. Not like the tax-advantaged status of dividends or capital gains, which is a good thing. And, just like a regular GIC, you can't cash it in until it matures. If you have a three-year GIC and the index goes up 40 percent and you want to take the money out before the market falls, you can't. Some institutions are offering a feature where you can lock in your gains once during the term, and although being able to do so is helpful, you may end up giving up any future gains. Some of these GICs have caps (e.g., 20 percent total return over two years). The lock-in feature would be helpful with these GICs if the market appreciates 20 percent or more in a relatively short period of time.

Index-linked GICs are seeing hybrids evolve. For example, Royal Bank has a "market-linked GIC." It has a three-year term and the principal is guaranteed at that time. It's linked to the performance of the TSX 60. According to Evans, "There are very complicated calculations involved, but the investor ends up participating in 45 percent of 'upside,' the degree to which market goes up over their holding period. The bottom line is, they have the principal guarantee of a traditional GIC, and, *if* the market increases over the three-year holding period, they can also benefit from that to an extent as well. Linked GICs have lost some of their appeal, as in most cases over the past several years investors wanted to avoid anything to do with the market. They primarily were looking for income and security, and were satisfied with a simple 2 percent to 3 percent GIC because at least they knew they wouldn't lose the principal. Most financial institutions offer some variation on the index-linked GIC theme. They use hedging techniques to guarantee the principal and tie the return to the performance of market indices. They can also use other benchmarks of their own creation."

Then there's Citizen's Bank "ethical" GIC. The return from this product is linked to 22 companies that have strong environmental and social records. There are many GICs linked to other market indices, such as the S&P 500. Others offer global opportunities. Scotiabank links its products to indices from countries that are members of the G7. The upside to index-linked GICs is the guarantee of principal. The downside is that the return on investment is not guaranteed.

However, the appeal of "linking" to anything to do with equities dimmed during the bear market of 2001 to 2003. Interestingly enough, there was even a "bear"-linked note designed to take advantage of the falling market.

No two index-linked GICs are alike, so that makes comparison shopping difficult. Here's what you need to consider: What's the minimum investment required and the length of term? Is the return capped at a maximum? What's the formula for calculating the return and to what markets is the return linked? All this affects performance. But the real key to successful investing is knowledge. It's the only commodity on earth that doesn't deteriorate with use and time.

Bottom line? If you do buy these index-linked GICs, do so in your RRSP where they get a tax break. If you have a long-term horizon and can ride the bumps in the market, you may be better off with a balanced portfolio: cash, stocks, and bonds.

Segregated funds

Just as we finally begin to get a handle on the world of mutual funds, enter segregated funds. Now seg funds have been around for about 30 years, but until recently they were only sold by life insurance companies and accounted for 3 percent of the Canadian market. Now some mutual fund companies have teamed up with insurance carriers to offer seg funds to the public. They look, taste, and feel like a mutual fund, but seg funds are actually an insurance product. And because they're an insurance product, they offer things not available with a traditional mutual fund.

Seg funds seem to attract investors who are nervous and don't like a lot of volatility but need the earning power of equities over time. Investors are guaranteed up to 75 percent to 100 percent of their investment if they keep the money in for a minimum period, such as 10 years. There are now also guaranteed funds, similar to seg funds, that offer guarantees over terms as short as five years. And if you've named a beneficiary, they'll receive the guaranteed amount without incurring probate fees, before the rest of the estate is settled, just like an insurance policy. As well, under certain circumstances, seg fund assets are protected from creditors should you find yourself in financial hot water. There's another benefit called the reset option. This allows you the opportunity to lock in investment appreciation to increase their guaranteed amounts without triggering capital gains, but the 10-year period starts all over again.

Maturity and death benefits are insured within certain limits by the insurance industry's consumer protection organization, Comcorp. But be aware that the fees for seg funds are higher than for regular mutual funds. If guarantees and credit protection mean something to you, it might be worth the cost. For example, the additional cost of a bond fund might add 0.2 percent or 0.3 percent while an equity fund might cost an extra 40 to 70 basis points for the principal guarantee.

Joe Chisholm, partner at Queensbury Insurance Brokers, warns, "Another difference between seg funds and mutual funds is how they report capital gains and losses. This is significant for non-registered investors only. Mutual funds report a net of capital gains and losses for each fund. Seg funds report gains and losses separately. As capital losses can be carried forward or brought back for three years, a seg fund owner may have more flexibility in preparing his or her income taxes. Also, mutual funds issue a T3 (capital gain or loss) for everyone who owns units at the end of each year. You could buy a mutual fund in December and have a gain or loss to report that you never realized. Seg funds will prorate gains and losses based on the number of days you owned the funds."

RRSP-eligible mutual funds

The foreign content rule allows 30 percent of your RRSP to be made up from investments outside of Canada. (To remember why this is so important, go back and take another look at the World Market Capitalization chart on page 190.) No such limit exists on segregated funds, although this loophole is under Canada Revenue Agency's microscope and could change at any moment to come in line with mutual funds. Every year investment firms find more creative ways to enhance the foreign content portion of RRSP-eligible funds, many of which have RRSP limits of well over 40 percent. Some firms, with the use of sophisticated strategies including derivatives (we won't go there ...), can actually get the foreign limit on RRSP funds to 100 percent.

Today there's a batch of specific RRSP-eligible foreign equity funds. These funds provide investors with exposure to foreign stocks but are considered Canadian content because they don't invest directly in foreign markets. There's now a decent selection of funds that cover the U.S. stock market but count as Canadian content (and usually have the word "RRSP" in the name). They're able to keep their Canadian content status, and thus remain 100 percent RRSP-eligible, by buying even more complex financial instruments called index futures. Buying index futures essentially buys you "exposure" to stock indexes without actually having to invest directly in the stocks.

Index mutual funds

There's another growing trend in Canada marked by the launch of a number of index mutual funds. These funds are designed to mirror the performance of specific stock indexes in a variety of benchmark indices, including Canada (the TSX) and the United States (Standard & Poor's 500), as well as Europe and Japan. (A benchmark index is a micro version within a stock market index; for example, there's a technology index within the S&P 500.)

I had to stop Elaine once more. "And an index is, uh, what again?" I asked wearily.

"Okay, Joanne, I'll bring it down a level. Let's use the S&P and TSX 60 as an example. S&P stands for Standard & Poor's, the firm that created this basket of stocks, tracks the performance of the index, and does the record keeping of the units. The TSX is a grouping of the 60 most significant

Canadian companies traded on the Toronto Stock Exchange. They represent the main 14 industry groups that Statistics Canada uses to describe our economy. This index is a benchmark that reflects the daily price activity of these stocks, and it's one of the leading barometers of the health of our economy. The index acts as an indicator as to how much money is being invested in and how much is being taken out of the market. It basically provides a snapshot of both Canadian stock market activity and the performance of the different groups within it."

Until 2002, the exchange measured Canada's largest 300 companies and the index was called TSE 300. Because in Canada the bottom 100 companies in this index were so small in capitalization, they could have significant swings without having any bearing on the index as a whole and thus served no useful purpose in measuring the Canadian economy as a whole. At the market closing on January 1, 1977, the aggregate performance of these 300 stocks was pegged at 1,000. This is the very base against which daily price performance is measured today.

With index-linked mutual funds, portfolio managers don't research or analyze in order to select stocks that they believe will outperform the benchmark. This enables the fund to save money and pass those returns on to investors in the form of lower fees. Remember, with an index fund you won't significantly underperform the benchmark index, nor will you outperform it. If the market declines, your investment will decline, and if the market rises, your portfolio grows.

A new trend is emerging—exchange traded funds. These are securities that trade like stocks (they're listed on an exchange, and can be bought and sold in real time) and represent a "basket" of exposure, which could be an index (like the S&P 500) or even a specific sector such as Canadian financial services companies. Barclay's is the biggest player here; they do the tracking and record keeping for a very low management expense ratio (MER—that is, the cost of maintaining the fund), say 10 to 20 basis points, so it's cheaper than a fund MER. *But* the investor has to know what exposure she or he wants and how and when to reallocate from a portfolio strategy point of view.

Always do your research. Be sure to ask whether index-linked products reflect the whole TSX or only certain portions of it. And follow the wisdom of Will Rogers: "Buy some good stocks and hold it till it goes up, then sell it. If it don't go up, don't buy it."

What kind of fund should I get?

"Well, well," I announced to Elaine with my usual enthusiasm. "I'm getting the general drift of things, but how on earth am I supposed to know what I want or, worse yet, need? Remember me? The one who throws hissy-fits in sporting goods stores because they turned buying running shoes into a bloody science experiment?"

"That's what I'm here for, Joanne," Elaine replied. "That, and to listen to your bad jokes."

I brushed off her comment regarding my rapier wit and said, "Give it to me quick then. How do I know what to do?"

"Again, what do you want to do?" she inquired. "Secure your retirement 30 years away or finance a trip to France six months from now? Do you want your fund to give you a regular income now or when you're in your prime at 65? The question to ask yourself is 'When am I going to need the money?' If it's within a year, your options are considerably narrowed. Forget about anything in the stock market. But for the 10 percent you've reserved for long-term savings—say over 10 years—the stock market is perfect, provided the ups and downs don't keep you awake at night. You have to figure out your comfort zone."

My head was reeling from all these questions. "You'll forgive me, Elaine, if I don't answer all hundred questions at once. I've heard that I should never invest my money in anything that eats or needs repairing. I also know for sure that inflation and taxes are most proficient at sucking up my hard-earned money. If I understand what you've been saying, my GICs and Canada Savings Bonds are only a moderate hedge, if any, against inflation. If history repeats itself, the stock market will beat inflation by a much wider margin but I may have to sacrifice a few sleepless nights. Correct?"

"Yes ma'am. You need to tell me if you want safety and security, which means more modest returns, or if you want to devote your money to higher returns, which means no guarantees. Or maybe something in the middle might be more to your liking. I'm afraid mutual funds are much like the rest of life; the more fun it is, the greater the chance you'll feel some pain. In other words, the greater the potential for a substantial return, the higher the risk. Similarly for the tax benefits of mutual funds. Are you willing to accept some risk to reduce the amount of tax you have to pay on your investments? That's an important factor if you own mutual funds outside your RRSP. If it's your retirement you're saving for, you must have a portion of your investments in equity funds. It's the best way to stay ahead of inflation. The number of years you have before retirement will have an impact on which fund you purchase."

"Okay," I said, braced for the next step. "How do I know whose fund to buy? What do I need to know?"

How do I choose a fund?

Start with your own personal risk profile. Some people like skydiving. Some people find that a Sunday afternoon stroll down Main Street gets their adrenaline pumping. You need to keep this in mind when you're trying to decide what investments make sense for you. How much risk you're willing to take is a function of your personality. If the thought of losing any of your savings makes you anxious, even if it was fairly certain your investment would recover and reward you with a profit, then you're risk averse. Financial writer Tony Martin has an interesting take on those who can stomach risk. He says you're way at the end of the spectrum if you can wad up a chunk of bills, throw them in the garbage can, and bet your buddy that she won't be able to hit them with a lit match.

But deciding how much risk you can, and should, take with your investments involves more than personality. You should consider your goals, time horizons, what you're currently investing in, taxes, and so on. For example, if you're saving to buy a house, safety is likely a vital concern. You don't want to find yourself without a down payment because the stock market has dropped when it's time to buy. On the other hand, if you're relatively young and are saving for retirement, you have time on your side. You can afford to ride out the ups and downs of riskier investments such as stocks or equity mutual funds. Age is an important consideration in risk tolerance because the younger you are, the more time you have to recover from market setbacks. At the other end of the spectrum, retirees generally can afford less risk, especially if they depend on investments to provide most of their retirement income. Single people can take greater risks than their married or cohabiting friends because they don't have to worry about affecting others should an investment turn sour. Regardless of where you are in the spectrum, remember the wise words of Erica Jong: "The greatest risk of all is not taking any."

Buy on the way up, not on the way down

When I began my search for the right mutual fund, I discovered that if my neighbour starts talking about the hot new fund she's picked up, it probably means it's too late and I've missed the bandwagon. You need to catch the fund on its way up, not when it's already at the top. It's important to find a fund that has steadily achieved good results over a long period. This can be a problem given the myriad of new funds popping up almost on a daily basis. In considering these funds, you have to rely on other criteria, such as the fund manager and her or his economic philosophy. A good gauge might be to find a fund that's a consistently solid performer; around 8 percent to 10 percent over 10 years is quite realistic and respectable.

The reason you don't want to buy a big-time best seller is pure and simple—cost. As the fund does better, the cost of the shares you purchase increases. In mutual fund lingo, the shares you purchase are called units and what they're worth is referred to as net asset value per share, or NAVPS. Remember, the fundamental principle of successful investing is to buy low and sell high.

Watch out for the one-hit wonders. Anyone can have one stellar year. It's much more difficult to produce consistent results in bad times as well as good. When examining the performance of a particular fund, you need to look at a sufficient length of time that allows you to see a fund and/or manager go through various market conditions—good, bad, neutral, and ugly. Five years is good, 10 years is better, if the fund has been around that long. The hard part about buying a mutual find is that the decision is based on what the fund has done in the past. No one can predict how it will do in the future. A certain amount of faith and a belief that "history will repeat itself" is necessary. If you look at 10 individual years and the fund is in the top half seven times, it can be considered one of your best choices. Being in the top half still gives it room to grow. The reasons for not buying a fund consistently positioned in the bottom half are pretty self-evident.

Diversify, diversify, diversify

Elaine was on a roll. Nothing short of insurrection was going to slow her down. She launched into another topic. "To paraphrase a well-known saying, stuff happens. We just don't know when. So until a reliable crystal ball is in mass production, one of the handiest tools of protecting your hard-earned assets from loss is diversification. There are three ways or levels to consider."

Diversify by asset type "Here's the asset allocation part that you asked about earlier, Joanne. It's nothing more than 'Don't put all your eggs in one basket.'"

"Profound," I replied, the sarcasm hard to miss.

"You can choose between different classes of investments: cash or cash equivalents, equities, the stock market, and fixed-income investments like bonds. Now, you may think equities or stocks are riskier than others, but that may not be so. If you put your money under your mattress or only invest in things like GICs and Canada Savings Bonds, you could end up in the poor-house at retirement. These investments don't tend to keep pace with inflation. There's also a belief that bonds are less risky as well, but rising interest rates should set that straight."

"So what does this have to do with asset allocation?" I asked.

"In investing, the idea is to limit risk while you make money. Asset allocation is simply a fancy way of saying pick the right mix and the right amounts of types of investments in cash, stocks, and bonds. The percentage of each asset class depends on your age and tolerance of risk, as well as market conditions like inflation and where interest rates are.

"Studies have shown that as much as 85 percent of a portfolio's return stems from the asset mix decision, and only 5 to 10 percent from market timing. And that's an important point to remember: never attempt to second-guess the behaviour of the market. That's hard enough for the professionals."

"Mind you, Elaine, these days the world changes so fast you couldn't stay wrong all the time if you tried," I said.

Laughing, she continued. "The actual securities you choose affect the returns as little as 5 to 10 percent. Asset mix is more important in the long term than timing. People are generally poor at knowing when to buy and when to sell. This is a very good reason to be sure you review your portfolio on an annual basis. Your asset mix will change as you get older and as your life circumstances change."

"In investing, I gather progress has little to do with speed but much to do with direction," I surmised.

"That's it exactly. At the very least, however, I always recommend an equity fund for long-term growth and a money market fund for more immediate needs."

Diversify by geography "Investing globally is an important part of an overall investment strategy," Elaine continued.

"My grandmother used to say that the best way to make your money go far was to mail it overseas," I joked.

"She was right. Diversifying your investments exposes you to growth opportunities outside of Canada and allows you to spread your risk with geographic diversity. Different countries or regions may experience different economic cycles or may be affected differently by the global economy. While some countries may be flourishing, others may be underperforming. No one geographic market continuously outperforms all others. There are studies that show that exposure to equity markets in different countries will help to diversify risk and boost your returns."

Diversify by management style Elaine moved on to the management style of the fund. "I take it this doesn't mean how well a fund manager dresses?" I asked.

"Management style breaks down the asset classes and geographic locations one step further, and examines not just what's in a mutual fund portfolio but also how the manager is managing it," Elaine explained. "I'm delighted to see people getting savvy to this. I now hear people asking, 'What's the manager's philosophy about investing?' and 'How do they figure out what stocks or bonds are appropriate for their portfolios?'

"There's usually a team of people involved in managing a mutual fund, but in most cases the final decision rests with one individual—the fund manager. Who this person is should be an important consideration in your purchase of a mutual fund. You know that mutual fund that was in the headlines a while back, the one that was performing extremely well?" Elaine asked. "People were literally calling and placing orders over the phone. The manager of this fund was highly regarded and had an astounding acumen for picking winners."

"I couldn't pick up a newspaper without seeing her in the headlines," I said. "Didn't many people invest in this fund specifically because of her?"

"They did indeed. Then one day, she up and left and went to the competition. The mutual fund's performance since her departure has been lacklustre. Now, there could be other variables contributing to this, but you can't ignore the importance of the person running the fund. You can't, on the other hand, use the manager as the sole reason for investing in a fund. Long-term performance will always be an important part of the equation. When you're considering buying a fund, ask the salesperson how long the manager has been there. You want a successful long-term track record not only for the fund but for the person managing it.

"But even though the managers are the experts, don't leave your financial future entirely in their hands. Don't assume that they'll guarantee your country villa at retirement. You still need to keep an eye on the fund's performance, bearing in mind the long-term nature of the investment. It's also worth finding out the management firm's policy on personal trades. Does the lead manager invest his/her own money in the fund? If so, the manager's own best interests are more clearly aligned with those of the fund's unitholders."

Elaine offered this advice: a quick way to determine an investment manager's style is to find out how the manager looks at the stock. The two most recognized investment styles are "growth" and "value." Growth managers search for stocks with solid future growth potential. They look for companies with a history of high growth in earnings and share price and with a reasonable expectation that this trend will continue. Growth stocks tend to be in the "new economy" sectors such as biotechnology, but even bank and resource stocks can show growth characteristics.

Value managers, on the other hand, focus on price and generally aren't concerned about the growth prospects of a company. For a stock to conform to a value investor's discipline, it must be perceived as being "cheap" relative to similar companies. Value managers assume that a cheap stock is out of favour due to false assumptions in the market and, most likely, will return to typical industry standards. This can result in solid returns for the manager. What's hilarious to watch is when two reputable managers maintain conflicting opinions on the same stock. A stock that's enjoying high growth and is trading at a premium to its sector is obviously appealing to the growth manager. The value manager would see the same stock as being too expensive and would sell or not buy it until its price is below that of its peer group. It can make your head spin. The good news? Most managers will claim that they have a blend of both value and growth styles.

Management style can explain the vast difference in performance between the hundreds of mutual funds that invest in essentially the same 300 stocks of the TSE Index. And style is hard to define, because there really are no hard and fast definitive categories. Think of style as more of a continuum, and have a variation of styles within your portfolio. Especially over recent years, we've seen how different management styles make a difference in performance, since they perform differently in different market environments. By blending the styles, the ride will become much smoother over a long period of time. A number of investment firms now offer multi-style, multi-manager portfolio designs to improve consistency of returns.

Volatility

"Another important question to ponder is how volatile is the fund," Elaine said philosophically.

"Isn't volatility a polite way of saying you could lose your money?" I asked.

"It's a term that's synonymous with risk," Elaine replied. "Money market funds have the lowest volatility factor and specialty or sector funds have the highest. This is another way of saying stocks are more volatile than cash, like T-bills, for example. Really volatile funds tend to do exceptionally well when there's a bull—good—market and choke when there's a bear—bad—market."

"What exactly *is* the difference between a bear market and a market correction? I hear these terms all the time and I'm not sure of the difference," I asked.

"The main difference between the two is this: amount and duration. A stock market correction is typically a decline of about 10 percent or more. A nasty old bear market is a decline that's twice that. And while a correction rebounds in days or weeks, it could take several months for a bear market to come back.

"Stock markets go up, stock markets go down. And sometimes they go down and down and down. Don't panic. Before you've fully recovered from your nervous breakdown, they'll be up again. Now, if you're a new investor, you may feel frightened and unable to cope as markets slide. Fight that urge to bolt. Buying when the market is high and selling when it's low is a common but expensive mistake newcomers sometimes make.

"As an investor, though, you shouldn't be too concerned about fluctuations. You have to look at what's going on around you. If it's just a general stock market decline, we know from a historical perspective that the market will rise again."

"When you think about it, you have to put your money somewhere," I offered. "And there are really only three places: cash, bonds, and stocks. Your money should go where it's treated best. And over the long term, the stock market appears to still be the answer. Assuming of course, that interest rates remain this low." I was begining to feel rather pleased with myself.

Elaine nodded and continued. "Oh, and one minor point, you only lose money when you pull out of the market. In the meantime, look on the bright side. If the market is sliding, it's an excellent opportunity to buy good-quality stocks at bargain basement prices. Here's an example of why not to sell high-quality stocks because of market dips. Say you held shares of Coca-Cola in 1987. After the crash, the shares cost US$3.81. Over the next nine years, those shares rose to over US$50 a share. Keep a long-term perspective."

"I picture it this way, Elaine. A child walks upstairs with a yo-yo. The yo-yo is going up and down, but the child still eventually gets to the top of the stairs."

"You really do think in pictures, don't you?" Elaine laughed. "It's essential that you develop enough investment savvy not to move cash from your mutual fund to your mattress. Rather than trying to time the market, it's better to stay invested and keep your money working. The best thing to do is to develop a long-term plan that you're comfortable with and stick to it. Tailor your plan to suit your tolerance for risk so you won't be tempted to get out at the worst possible time. Do this by finding a good balance between safe, fixed-income investments such as bonds and higher-risk stocks. When the market's in a state of flux, use it as a time to make sure you're comfortable with your mix of investments. As I explained earlier, make sure your investments are diversified by geographic region, management style, and types of assets. And as for the bolder investors, the lows in the market give them the chance to scoop up some good, affordable stocks."

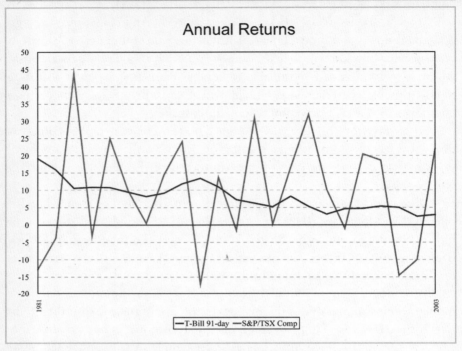

Annual Returns

SOURCE: INTEGRA PRIVATE INVESTMENT MANAGEMENT. REPRODUCED WITH PERMISSION.

"These people realize that running away from the market when it's going down is like running away from a store when there's a sale on," I said. "So when would I sell a fund?"

Three reasons to sell

"Let's imagine this scenario, Joanne. After careful deliberation, you decide to follow your advisor's advice and you sink a bundle into her recommended mutual fund. The first year, the fund enjoys stratospheric returns. However, 12 months later you scan the stock pages for the year-end results, only to discover that this pistol-hot fund has dived so hard it got the bends. What should you do?"

"Any financial advisor worth their dust will tell you it's important to keep a long-term view when investing in mutual funds," I intoned.

"Yes, but it's equally important to understand why the fund has underperformed. One bad year does not a dog make. In fact, it's pretty normal to have a bad year. So when do you know it's time to sell? There are several reasons to sell, and here are just three.

"One—sell if the fund has been a consistent dog in its class. You can't fault a U.S. equity manager just because the whole sector, or country, in this case, is underperforming. The bear market was particularly brutal in the United States and consequently underperformed in general globally. Look at what other funds in the neighbourhood have been doing over the long term, say 10 years. And look at individual years, not just the 10-year-end number. One banner year over 9 bad ones can skew the results. It's tough to take a loss and you may be inclined to sit and hold until the fund comes back. But you may be missing other, better opportunities.

"Two—sell if the MER is higher than that of other funds in its class. Investors are becoming savvier and are recognizing how deeply MERs cut into returns. This is important for balanced and fixed-income funds, and for any funds charging extremely high fees.

"Three—sell when your asset allocation is out of whack. If you're 100 percent in income trust funds, you've goofed. Don't have too much of a good thing. Remember, the key to a properly managed portfolio is to be diversified. You need to re-balance your portfolio to a more appropriate asset mix containing a variety of asset classes, and reduce your risk. Always give yourself a brief cooling-off period and talk to your advisor. Ask hard questions. Then you can make an educated decision."

(Author's note: People got seriously burnt by Nortel. Evans says that, in her experience, people didn't listen to the advice to "take profits and sell." It was easy and thrilling to watch the stock go up daily. She said greed was a major motivator in the Nortel situation.)

Elaine decided it was time for another sanity break. "Wake up!" she yelled, startling me out of my trance. I must have jumped six feet. "Stick your head out a window and breathe some fresh air," she ordered.

"Are you trying to kill me? I asked. "We're in Toronto, remember? Doing such a thing could land one in a hospital." I groaned as I lifted myself out of my chair. "It's time for a food break. I need replenishing. Oh!" I started. "I just remembered I have something in the office freezer." I returned gleefully, brandishing a bowl full of frozen green grapes.

"Didn't you say you had something in the freezer?" Elaine asked, looking at the grapes.

"This would be that."

"Grapes?" she asked incredulously.

"True story. Don't ask me how, but somehow freezing them makes them even sweeter. They rank pretty close to chocolate."

"Rather high praise, indeed," Elaine noted. "Now let's figure out what we have to pay for the privilege of owning a mutual fund."

Know what you're paying for

"I suspect mutual funds were not created as a generous gesture by the investment community to give us poor, struggling novices a break," I offered, throwing grapes into the air and catching them smartly in my mouth.

"Yes, companies are in it to make a profit. There are different types of fees associated with owning a mutual fund. They'll vary widely from fund to fund, so you need to develop your comparison-shopping instincts. Fees come in two categories: sales charges called loads, and administration and management fees. These fees can have a significant effect on your net rate of return. There are front-end load, back-end load, no load ..."

"You'd think we were talking about farming instead of mutual funds," I interrupted.

Elaine went on. "Loads are how you pay the salespeople who sell the funds; there are typically three ways to pay sales fees. Pay particular attention here. I'm going to cover management fees as well. These are areas that are becoming of great concern to investors."

And she was off.

Sales fees on mutual funds

Back-end load Also known as deferred sales charges, these funds charge a redemption fee when you sell the fund. There's a declining back-end load that enables you to pay a lower fee the longer you keep the money in the fund. Let's say you inherited $10,000 and you decided to invest it in a mutual fund. The company you bought it from will pay the fund dealer $350 to $500, of which the advisor gets a certain percentage. That way, your whole $10,000 is invested and the whole amount works for you. The fund company recovers that $500, amortizing it over several years out of the management fees it collects from the fund. However, if you cash out the fund, you'll have to pay a redemption fee. The longer you've had the fund, the more the redemption fee declines. These funds are popular with advisors because they receive an upfront commission and an annual trailer fee that's paid as long as you remain in the fund. Investors are beginning to turn away from these funds, however. In the first year, the sales charge can be as high as 6 percent but can decline to 0 percent after seven years. Some fund companies charge this fee based on market value, while others base it on original cost. Ten percent of your money can be taken back in cash each year without triggering any deferred sales charges (the penalty investors pay if they withdraw funds from the fund family within a specified holding period, typically six or seven years). These funds are a great idea if you're in it for the long haul, but forget it if you plan to move the money around.

One further point: if their recommendations will incur a redemption fee on your behalf, many advisors are able to reimburse you through a practice known as "commission rebating." Most investors don't know about this program, but it's worth asking about if your advisor recommends selling some holdings that may incur a back-end charge.

Front-end load You pay the commission up front. Depending on how much you're investing, expect to pay anywhere from 2 percent to 5 percent commission. The disadvantage to front-end loads is that a fraction of your money never sees the market. If you invest $1,000 in a fund that charges 5 percent commission, you'll be purchasing only $950 worth of fund units. The other $50 goes to pay the commission. The advantage is that once you've paid the admission, the rest of the ride is free (except for management fees), so those big profits stay in your pocket.

In cases where mutual fund companies offer a lower MER to buy front-end rather than back-end, it's usually worth paying a front-end fee as high as 2 percent to 3 percent for the privilege of paying less every year.

Advisors charge 0 percent for front-end load because the trailer fees paid to the advisor are higher, so a more conservative, "fee-based" advisor would be happy with this. Note, though, that advisors who work on a "fee-for-service" basis will use F-class funds. F stands for "fee-based," meaning that the account is being charged a management charge calculated as a percentage of assets. You don't want to double charge the investor by buying mutual funds that charge the full MER, including trailer fees. When you buy F-class funds in a fee-based account, the advisor *does not* receive any trailer fee—his or her compensation comes from the management fee charged directly to the client.

These funds have a lower MER because the advisor will bill the client directly. In the case of non-registered funds, this makes the commission tax deductible to the unit holder. So, the brand X Canadian balanced fund might have a 2.5 percent MER. The F-class version might be 1.5 percent, and then the advisor bills the unit holder 1 percent. The client pays the same but gets to deduct the 1 percent from her or his income as an investment consulting fee.

You can buy the F-class version of most mutual funds, depending on whether you are going to hold it in an account where you are already paying a management fee to the advisor. The investments do not change. You are still buying the same fund or portfolio; just the fee structure or MER is affected.

Low load This is a hybrid option. The investor is locked in for two years or faces a 3 percent charge for early redemption. The advisory firm gets 1 percent up front and gets a slightly higher trailer fee than deferred service charge would pay. AIM Trimark is one of the few fund families that offers this option as a compromise between front-end load and the lengthy holding period of deferred service charge funds.

No load For this sort of fund, no commission is charged going in or coming out. You buy the fund directly from the "manufacturer." No-load funds allow all your money to go to work for you, and you can redeem the fund at any time with no penalty. There are many excellent no-load funds in the money market and fixed-income categories. No-load funds are primarily offered by the banks, though a few other companies such as Altamira and Phillips, Hager & North (PH&N) sell them. Historically, the bank's equity funds have been somewhat more conservative than those of load companies. They tended to underperform in rising markets and outperform in down markets. The frenzy around "no load" has died down considerably from the heyday of the late '90s.

Evans says there has, in fact, been a shift from the no-load fund craze during the late '90s when it was very easy to make money in mutual funds, particularly tech funds. As the bear market continued from 2000 to 2003, investors realized that they did, in fact, need advice and from advisors. Evans says, "Investors needed to re-learn the basics of investing like asset allocation, diversification, and having a disciplined approach. As such, there was a return to advice, as investors admitted they were their own worst enemy, with many having 'blown themselves up' in the tech wreck. The no-load players were all consolidated—the banks and Altamira still remain the dominant no-load providers. PH&N is also no load, but they are really an investment counsellor and cater to high net worth clients with big money. The no-load option is designed, for example, for 'sub' accounts of their counsellor clients who have 'small amounts' such as the accounts of their kids. However, a minimum of $25,000 is required for PH&N funds, so they're not really for the average investor."

Load versus no load There's no correlation between a fund's performance and whether or not you had to pay a load to buy it. A general rule is that if you're a savvy investor with no need for advice or have a solid awareness of what you want, look at the no-load funds. There are many excellent no-load funds, especially in the money market and fixed-income categories. Consider the following when choosing a fund: its ability to meet your objectives, its performance record, and, considering the difficult market conditions we've been through, whether its managers provide advice. These are all serious considerations for any investor and should be your primary focus, regardless of the fee structure.

Evans adds, "Today, the trend has gone away from the 'no-load' funds of the late '90s, back to the 'load' funds because of the advice component you get with load funds. Investors thought investing was easy in the late '90s because of the raging bull market and tech bubble—hence, they didn't think they need[ed] advisors anymore, and shifted to no-load funds, … abandoning advice givers. So many [investors] were 'blown up' by the lack of proper portfolio diversification—(e.g., having five different tech funds would have commonly and mistakenly [been] considered to be proper portfolio diversification by the year 2000 do it yourselfer). Since the 'tech wreck,' investors again realize they need professional guidance in order to have proper portfolio strategy, and there is a value to receiving advice. As such, the no-load funds, many since consolidated anyway, are no longer popular or they require higher than average minimums and are not available to the typical investor."

Management expense ratios If you're a mutual fund holder, you may be unaware that you're paying an annual fee that can take a significant chunk out of each year's performance. Many new investors bring their experience with CSBs or GICs into the world of mutual funds. But these two worlds are as different as chalk and cheese. You don't pay any fees for these kind of guaranteed investments. But pay you do when you buy a mutual fund. It's called a management expense ratio, or MER, and it's what the mutual fund company takes out each year to pay the salespeople and to cover a variety of the fund's operating expenses, like the legal costs and the costs of the trustee, the keeper of the money.

And you can't forget Canada Revenue Agency's and your broker's or sales rep's share.

Remember, the idea behind mutual funds is to pool resources, and this principle also applies to paying for the management of the fund. The costs of managing a fund are generally very high, but since the costs are shared among all the investors, you pay only a small portion of the total in proportion to the size of your own investment in the fund. These fees tend to be lower among bond and money market funds—around 1 percent of your fund value. MERs are higher on funds that are tough to sell and run, for example labour-sponsored funds, where they can be as high as 8 percent. The average in Canada for equity funds is around 2.35 percent. This means that 2.35 percent of the fund's profits go directly to the managers and expenses. The remainder is what gets distributed to the investors.

The MER expresses the costs of running the fund as a percentage of the total assets. At the low end, money market funds will have an expense ratio of 1 percent of the asset value. Some international funds will charge up to 3 percent.

The MER matters because it has an impact on how much money you get to keep. This seems to matter less when we enjoy 20 percent as a rate of return. (Ah ... what's a half a percent?!) But remember the roller coaster principle of the market: what goes up must come down, and that's when you will feel the squeeze. MERs of even a few percentage points add up over time and can reduce the actual growth of funds and cut the rate of compounding.

Looking at the top 10 performers over a 15-year period, 5 of the funds have an MER at 2 percent or more. However, 5 out of the 10 have a higher minimum requirement than regular mutual funds. That may mean the average Canadian would not be able to invest in these funds.

Bev Evans says, "It would not be correct to say that the better funds have lower than 2 percent MERs any longer. There have been increased costs across the board that have affected MERs: increased regulatory requirements and disclosure costs, for example. Also GST is now included in MERs, so they are generally higher overall. We also need to factor in that everything in Canada has to be published in both English and French. The bottom line? As an investor, you simply don't want to pay higher MERS than is *necessary*."

While the pursuit of lower fees shouldn't obscure the hunt for perform-ance, you should always take the low-fee alternative when there's a choice. Whatever fund you choose, remember that in life you never get something for nothing. But try to get it for as little as possible.

That's why you need to devour your prospectus.

The prospectus

The goal of reading your mutual fund prospectus is not only to stay awake, but to find out the following information. The most important is what the fund is actually trying to do—in other words, the goals of the fund and what plans are in place to achieve them. The prospectus should also tell you how volatile or risky the fund is. Now, some funds, like ethical funds, invest only in certain companies. The prospectus will outline policy on what's deemed to be ethical corporate behaviour. (This varies from company to company. And what you deem to be ethical may not be the same as what the fund deems.) You can learn about how you get paid or the types of distributions you may receive, for example interest, dividends, and/or capital gains. You'll also want to know how often those distributions are made. The prospectus will tell you how and from whom you can buy the fund. The minimum you'll need to invest will be detailed, as well as what commissions you'll have to pay to buy or sell the fund. If there are costs for redeeming your units, you can find that out from the prospectus. The actual administrative process is spelled out: whether you can sell your units over the phone or by fax, or whether you need to fill out a form in person. You can also find in the prospectus how the fund arrives at the price you'll get for your units.

Now, many people like investing with large fund families because they can easily move their money between different types of funds, often at no cost. However, to limit the administrative work involved, and to deter people from trading their funds frequently, fund companies often have specific rules, which the prospectus states. It outlines management fees and MERs. Pay particular attention to this section. As well, many funds pay an annual commission to salespeople, often referred to as a "trailer fee." This is usually a percentage of the total dollars the salesperson's clients have invested in the fund. You'll want to know how much that is. As for performance figures, these often aren't included in a simplified prospectus. But you can find them either in the fund's full prospectus or its annual or quarterly reports, or by visiting the fund company's website. Between the prospectus and your advisor, you should be able to glean what you need to know in order to make an informed choice.

Elaine decided to stop at that point to see if her student was still earth-bound. I was slumped in my chair, my ears resting on my shoulders. My jaw was slack. Astutely, she saw that as a sign.

"Get outta here. Go read the comics in the newspaper and don't come back until you've smiled twice and laughed out loud once. Stop in Andrea's office on the way. She has a ton of her kid's Halloween candy in her cupboard left over from last year. When you come back we'll be moving into the riveting area of taxation."

"Taxation?" I exclaimed as I bolted for the door. Over my shoulder, I shot back, "I can easily find out more than I need to know—all I have to do is look at my paycheque."

An hour later I returned, renewed and energized. Year-old candy kisses can do that to you.

How will my investments be taxed when they grow up?

"Now we're at the fun part," Elaine said. "You need to learn how different investments are taxed."

"Why?" I pouted.

"Because, today's dime is really a dollar with all the taxes deducted. You'd better know what you're doing. There are three ways you can earn income on your investments and they're all taxed differently."

Interest income

"The first is interest income from Canadian sources, such as interest earned on a GIC or Canada Savings Bond. Canadians love their CSBs and GICs. They're right up there with our love for maple syrup and hockey, but the problem is that the interest from these investments is taxed at our marginal, or top, tax rate.

"Let's imagine, for simplicity's sake, that you're in a 50 percent tax bracket. You earn $100 in interest on a GIC. Canada Revenue Agency will squirrel away its share of $50 out of that $100 interest in its pocket. This happens for anything on which you earn a guaranteed interest, things like daily interest savings accounts, CSBs, term deposits, and GICs. So if you stay in the base of our beloved pyramid, you'll get chewed up in taxes (the exceptions being your principal residence and RRSPs). The higher you travel up the pyramid, the better the tax picture looks. For example, stocks, bonds, and certain types of mutual funds aren't subject to this high form of taxation. It's the government's way of creating a little incentive for Canadians to invest in themselves and the Canadian economy."

The dividend tax credit

"Remember we spoke earlier about how dividends from Canadian corporations are eligible for the dividend tax credit?" Elaine asked.

"Vaguely," I said. "Something about the credit reducing the rate of tax paid."

"Exactly. Dividend income, whether paid directly to you or through a mutual fund, certainly gets better tax treatment than does plain old interest income. If you own shares in BCE Inc. (Bell Canada) and receive $500 in dividends, you'll pay less tax than if you receive the same amount in interest from Canada Savings Bonds. The way in which the dividend tax credit is calculated is complex, to say the least."

Elaine passed me the formula to look at. I laughed out loud from pure disbelief that they could make something so complicated and cumbersome.

"The main reason for the complex calculation is to avoid what's called 'double taxation,'" Elaine explained. "Let me read you this quote from *The Money Companion* by Elaine Wyatt. It's as simple as I've seen it explained anywhere." Elaine began to read: "'Because the corporation in which you've invested has already paid taxes on the dividends it has paid to you, there is a dividend tax credit you can use to reduce your taxes. To claim this complicated credit, you must "gross-up"—a peculiar phrase meaning "increase"—the dividend you've received by 25 percent and then calculate your federal tax on this increased amount. You then subtract the dividend tax credit of 13.33 percent of the dividend you actually received. Finally, you add your provincial tax.'"[1]

"Ah, yes," I said, eyes rolling. "You are so right. That's incredibly simple. Thank you for sharing." I didn't have a clue what she'd just said.

"Your accountant can explain this to you in more detail. But as a starting point, it's important to be aware that this credit can be of benefit to your overall after-tax picture. Let's move on to the third way investments get taxed."

Capital gains and losses

"If you bought something for $15 and sold it for $20, you've made a $5 capital gain. If, however, you bought something for $15 and sold it for $5, you've experienced a capital loss of $10. It's not a whole lot more complicated than that.

"Capital gains are a better bargain because they're taxed at a lower rate than interest. In fact, only 50 percent of the gain is taxable. This includes real estate, stocks, mutual funds, and precious metals. Gains on the sale of your principal residence are tax free, but not so for the sale of a second property, such as a cottage."

"Now this I get," I said. "Let's see. If I hit the jackpot and made $50,000 on the sale of my currently non-existent cottage, I'd have to pay tax on only $25,000 or 50 percent of the total gain. And yes, that $25,000 would be taxable at my marginal rate."

"You see how you can keep a lot more money in your pocket if you develop a little tax savvy?" Elaine asked.

"Yes ma'am," I replied. "You know, most of us should feel honoured to pay taxes in this great country. But the problem is we could feel just as honoured for half the price."

Dollar cost averaging

"I gotta headache," I complained, rubbing my temples. I was attempting to digest all the choices I had.

Elaine shot back, "It wouldn't have anything to do with the forklift truck full of chocolate you've eaten?"

She had a point. I had consumed more sugar than a small country does in a year.

I was comfortable with the fact that I needed equity funds to save for my retirement. I thought a money market fund to save for the down payment on a house seemed like a good idea. I'd figured out what I was going to use for what, but I didn't have a clue how to go about getting those funds.

"Elaine," I began, "I guess I'm like most people who think they need to save a chunk of money before they can get into mutual funds. I have visions of needing hundreds or even thousands of dollars before I can play in this league."

Elaine smiled patiently. "Got 25 bucks?" she inquired.

"You got me on a good day. I have $27."

"Can you come up with $25 every month?" she asked.

"With the 'Iron Lady' as my financial advisor, that had better be the least I do," I replied.

"Then you've started your mutual fund." It was as simple as that.

You can get started in any type of mutual fund with 15 minutes of your time and as little as $25 a month at a bank or $50 monthly with a fund company. That's after you've decided what you'll buy, of course. Not only will you see your investment program take shape, you'll start to take advantage of a concept called dollar cost averaging. Let's say you've saved $1,200 to invest in a Canadian equity fund. You go to your institution of choice and make the deposit. If your luck is anything like mine, that will be the very day the stock market peaks and breaks all records. This also means the cost of the individual units of the fund will have gone up, so your $1,200 doesn't buy as much as if the units were valued at a lower amount.

The better approach is to take that $100 a month you were saving and put it directly into an equity fund on a monthly basis. We already know the stock market goes up and down. So one month the value of the units might be lower than the following month. Or higher. The point is, if you put in the same amount of money every month, you're likely to end up owning more units at the end of a year than if you'd made a lump sum deposit at the mercy of whatever the market looked like on that particular day. One month your $100 may buy seven units, the following month it might buy eight. The month after that your $100 gets you six units, and so on. On average, you'll be further ahead than if you'd made a single deposit. Hence the name "dollar cost averaging."

In a nutshell, the real reason dollar cost averaging works so well is that it forces the "buy low" part of the "buy low, sell high" equation upon you. It's only human nature to avoid investing in something that's going down in value. But that's not the way you should look at buying stocks or equity mutual funds. When they're lower in value, that's exactly when you should buy. Think of it this way: they're on sale.

To put dollar cost averaging into effect, all you need to do is set up a preauthorized chequing (PAC) program whereby your financial institution will take the $100 a month directly from your bank account. You simply fill out a form and give the company a "void" cheque. Usually there's a minimum required. No muss, no fuss. Several objectives are met this way. You don't have to rely on your own initiative and discipline to make monthly payments. Since the money comes out of your account automatically, you're forced to save.

Dollar Cost Averaging

As illustrated in the table below, $600 invested over six months is worth $662.91—a gain of 10.5 percent.

Month	Unit Price	Units Bought	Amount Invested	Total Value
1	$13	7.692	$100	$100.00
2	$12	8.333	$100	$192.30
3	$15	6.667	$100	$340.38
4	$13	7.692	$100	$394.99
5	$14	7.143	$100	$525.38
6	$15	6.667	$100	$662.91
	Average Price	Total Units	Average Cost Per Unit	
	$13.66	44.19	$13.58	

This is exactly how I set up my 10 percent "pay myself first" long-term savings program. Dollar cost averaging through PAC is also how I make my RRSP contribution to a Canadian equity fund. I divide my annual contribution by 12 and set up PAC to take that amount out each month. Not only is my RRSP contribution easily taken care of, I've also taken advantage of dollar cost averaging and started to earn a profit sooner than if I'd waited until the last minute.

Now, there's another school of thought which holds that the best way to invest for the long term is to buy all at once. Since markets tend to go up over time you're better off just to simply get in the market rather than trying to time the market—even if it is random timing, as it is with dollar cost averaging. The jury is still out on this. Regardless, the true benefit of dollar cost averaging is that it creates a disciplined approach to saving. The other point in the dollar cost averaging camp is this: "Put your hand up, how many of us have big lump sums to invest?" Ah. I thought so.

Whom should I buy from and how?

"Whom should people buy their funds from, Elaine? I mean, everyone is selling mutual funds these days."

"People now have lots of choices. They can buy them through appropriately licensed people at their bank, trust company, and insurance company. And of course there's always their investment advisor and mutual fund specialist. People who work for a bank or insurance company, or companies like Investors Group, for example, will sell only their own family of funds. Investment advisors and independent dealers offer a variety of choices. But although these people have access to a wider range of funds, some of the funds that are sold through a captive sales force have done quite well. No one company has a top performer in all the categories, so it's important to be sure that people choose the company that offers them the best fund for their particular needs."

"Excuse me Elaine," I interrupted. "My back teeth are wearing life jackets. I need a nature break."

I returned to my "keener student" sitting position, leaning forward in my chair, elbows on knees and eyes wide open.

"So, how about investing in stocks and bonds directly on my own?" I asked Elaine.

"In a word: sure. But not before your financial base is solidly established. Remember that mutual funds are a method of buying stocks, bonds, treasury bills, and real estate. You may not need to go at it directly yourself. If you do, make sure the following are in place before tackling the wilds of the market on your own.

- Have all your non-deductible debt paid off.
- Be sure your will, power of attorney, and living will are set up.
- Look after your life and disability insurance needs.
- Have a proper accessible emergency fund.
- Make your maximum RRSP contribution every year.

"Once you've finally established a solid ground in mutual funds, particularly equity funds, you'll have learned the general principles of how the market works. That's when it's a good time to take the plunge into the market on your own.

"Investing directly in the stock market can be a very rewarding and exhilarating experience," Elaine continued. "You can realize more profit if you pick a stock that's a winner than you can from a mutual fund that's a winner. Because funds are diversified, you enjoy relative safety at the expense of really dramatic rates of return. But for many, including myself, the risk of losing money is too high. I'd never put into the stock market any money that I wasn't prepared to lose. If you've 'found' money, or consider yourself a well-rounded investor, go for it, it can be a lot of fun."

"I personally know of tons of women who are jumping into the market through investment clubs," I commented. "I know two women in particular who had dramatically different experiences." Elaine listened intently as I told her the story.

Investment clubs

These are the tales, one woeful, one cheerful, of two friends. Denise Araiche (our friend the banker) and Sabine Steinbrecher had identical goals: they both wanted to *learn* about making money, but ranking even higher up the priority scale was actually *making* money. So, in order to achieve that end, they became part of an exploding trend in this country—an investment club.

Their reasons were simple. An investment club is a place where they could learn, pay fewer brokerage fees and commissions, and very possibly get higher returns because of shared expertise, resources, and brain power. The best part was that the club also provided a fabulous reason to get out of the house once a month. Denise and Sabine could get started in investing for as little as $30 a month (or more if they wanted to) and be comfortable in an intimate and casual learning-based environment of 8 to 15 people. They could even pick the brains of investment specialists who'd come and speak to the club for free.

Alas, this is where their tales part company. Sabine's experience? In a word, fabulous. In 1994 Sabine decided, along with another woman, to start her own club called Financial Strategies for Women Investment Club (FSW). She and Peggy worked diligently at developing an investment philosophy that included the club's investment goals and types of stock they wanted to invest in. They created a club charter or constitution that set out the rules and bylaws of the club. Thankfully, there was no shortage of experts to help them. They used stockbrokers, the Canadian Shareowner Association, a whole variety of books on the subject, as well as the U.S.-based National Association of Investors Corporation (NAIC). Five years later, this group still meets monthly, each member investing $50 every month. FSW has 10 to 15 members at any given time.

Each member assumes different roles within the club. There's a recording partner, tracking partner, trading partner, senior partner, and so on. This gives members new skills that range from learning how to present technical material to charting and graphing stock movements. Sabine observes, "We stick with what we know." At the beginning, they started with high-growth stocks with at least a five-year track record. They moved on to include riskier stuff after the club had established a track record.

FSW also developed a standardized way of studying stocks so that everyone could understand the process and make informed decisions. They began by analyzing stocks monthly. For each meeting, members are required to do a research presentation on an assigned company. They've been known to call or even visit some of the companies' premises before deciding if they were worthy of investing in. The backbone of the club's analysis technique is the Canadian Shareowners Association's stock selection guide. They also use an online method that's a huge time-saver because it provides instant access to research during meetings. FSW even trades online, right from their meeting location.

FSW brings in guest speakers and has a portfolio manager who spends one meeting a year with them and reviews their portfolio. Sabine says, "He's been very impressed with our portfolio. Our performance has been quite remarkable; we've made 2 bad investments, 2 okay investments, and 10 really great investments." FSW takes pride in the fact that they soundly beat the monthly returns of the Toronto Stock Exchange just about all of the time. Their portfolio is valued at tens of thousands of dollars and right up to today boasts double-digit annual returns.

FSW has lost and replaced at least half the club members since its inception. All new members have been sponsored by a current member and are brought up to speed by that member. Sabine says, "This has been an incredible experience, but not without some challenges. Our success has been in the group's personality working. We don't bring anyone in who doesn't fit in some way, and only get involved with people we like and trust. This is a small group with important decisions to make."

Denise's experience? She describes it this way: "Brutal." Like Sabine, she started up a club with some like-minded friends. At the first meeting they developed their club goals: to create a learning environment, invest in ethical companies, and earn a solid rate of return. They wanted to make decisions as a group, diversify their portfolio, and reinvest the money they made back into more investments. Problems began almost immediately. Denise's group fell into the trap of establishing too many bylaws, which made everything really cumbersome. The language at the meetings was very technical (read: boring). Although the standard is once a month, Denise's group met more than that. Denise says, "Frankly there were way too many meetings and I was forced to miss a lot of them. Contrary to popular belief, I actually have a life."

The group dynamic around investing also began to change. Club members often vigorously debated the issue of what constituted an ethical investment. Some said companies that buy, sell, or invest in any way in tobacco were unethical. Others said that if the company president smoked, the company was unethical. Two of the members became very aggressive in their approach to buying stocks, yet there were people in the group who had never invested before. The club philosophy began to shift from "learn and earn" to "gnash and cash—fast." Inevitably, investing ideology and behaviour and group goals collided. And there was another problem—some people didn't pull their weight in researching companies. Denise says, "I've come to the conclusion that clubs have to find a way to make sure everybody pulls their weight. Free riders were the major cause of our club failing."

Denise's club was made up of 30-somethings. Denise exclaims, "People kept taking their money out of the club because they needed to buy things like homes and braces for their kids' teeth." Denise knew the writing was on the wall when she calculated how much money she was making. Zip, none, nada. When commissions were factored in, Denise wasn't even breaking even.

She quit.

If you're aware of the possible perils, joining an investment club can be a great experience. In fact, 15 percent of Canadian Shareowners Association members belong to a club. The Investment Institute of Canada estimates there are 5,000 clubs across the country, but their research shows that about half fail after two years. Lousy stock picks were cited as the biggest reason. But women are displaying natural aptitudes for investing. The U.S.-based NAIC says that 68 percent of its members are women. That's up from 61 percent in 1994. NAIC says that its women-only clubs reported an "average compounded life-time return" of 23.8 percent, compared with only 19.2 percent for men-only groups. Mixed gender did 21.4 percent. This was because of women's buy-and-hold pattern of investing.

Evans has some personal experience on this. "Women are less reactionary and tend to stick with a plan, once they have researched and established it. Therefore, they are more 'buy and hold' so have lower trading or transaction costs. I've seen women's portfolios typically outperform men's. I think it's because [women] make [fewer] stupid mistakes [than] men, who like to feel they are exercising control and tend to trade more!"

So, when you sit back and ponder the merits of joining a club, keep in mind that women are plain and simply good at this. It's an excellent way to get your feet wet in the world of investing.

Contact the Canadian Shareowners Association at 121 Richmond Street West, 7th Floor, Toronto, Ontario M5H 2K1. Phone 416-595-9600 or toll free 800-268-6881, or visit its website at www.shareowners.com. It provides its members with club startup packages that include sample constitutions and bylaws. The association also offers courses on the subject.

Another useful source is the Investor Learning Centre of Canada at 1-888-866-2601. Its website is www.investorlearning.ca. NAIC can help as well. And finally, you can contact different Canadian brokerage firms, which often have information on investment clubs.

Investing online

Colleen Moorehead, president of E★Trade Canada Securities Corp., has an interesting take on electronic trading. Colleen compares the traditional brokerage type of trading to an old-fashioned grocery store. You'd go in with a list, hand it over to someone who'd tell you what products are new and who'd measure out your ingredients, and so on. Electronic trading, however, is like a supermarket. You can go in and read the labels yourself. You choose what product you want, when, and at what cost. Electronic trading services allow you, the retail investor, to have direct access to the markets.

Internet trading is simply using a Web browser to place orders with a broker. Internet brokers often resell the order to a floor broker, earning a fee from this broker and delaying the transaction. In this way Internet trading is an extension of the discount brokerage industry. It was first introduced and accepted in the United States, then spread like wildfire around the world. The Canadian company E★Trade, an Internet broker, is a great example. It's now in Australia, New Zealand, UK, France, and Scandinavia. Unfortunately, less-developed countries are more at a disadvantage when it comes to embracing electronic trading due to their lack of funds, poor communications infrastructure, and lower savings rate.

Electronic trading has had an impressive impact on the market. It's improved market liquidity through electronic systems and the individual investor. Some critics say that the liquidity of only the most popular stocks has increased, and this is probably true; some critics have also said that electronic trading has destabilized markets.

The cost of executing trades will decrease as technology becomes faster, and these savings can be passed on to the consumer. Stock trades are cheap through the Internet. Yet as my good friend Pat McNeill—former corporate banker-cum-research analyst and an enthusiast of the market—rightly points out, "The cost of executing trades is already the lowest in the industry, as low as $8 in the United States. But it's still $29 in Canada. (Still pretty cheap.) The

Canadian financial services industry is an oligopoly and I doubt fees in Canada will fall. Canadians can and some should open accounts in the United States and offshore to beat the Canadian premium on transaction costs. U.S. brokerages can't advertise in Canada, but—ta da—there it all is on the Web!"

Electronic trading has increased the speed and lowered the cost of access to global markets. Since E★Trade, for example, is in other countries it allows us to invest in non–North American securities easily. To be sure, most Canadian brokerage houses are registered or have agents with all the major exchanges around the world. But online traders are less risk averse, or possibly more informed. E★Trade, for example, can process your order if you want to buy stocks, mutual funds, and other products online. It offers a live chat, called LiveContact, with a customer-service representative. Brief human contact can make all the difference when it comes to making those all-important investment decisions. E★Trade charges no fee for transactions in 700 mutual funds, provided that you hold the investment for at least 90 days. You can subscribe with a minimum $1,000 investment.

Unlimited access to information at any time of the day or night is what's appealing to many women, especially those who are out in the labour force during the day and who have children to be with at night. These women often do their financial management in the late evenings because it's the only time they have. Colleen Moorehead of E★Trade, for example, has two young sons. She orders everything online, from groceries to clothing, usually around 11:00 p.m. That's because the early evening is non-negotiable time she spends with her kids. Colleen says that, as a consumer of financial products, "I want my own needs met at a time that I dictate. I want questions answered in a fast and easy manner."

I asked Colleen how electronic trading would affect the traditional brokerage firm, and here's her response: "This whole information age has given the consumer the ability to access more and more information any time, and now there's a cost benefit to trading electronically. Brokers will have to change. Prices will have to come down for advice. You'll have to meet consumers at their time and that pretty much means communication through the Web. The 'broker' won't be extinct, but will no longer be able to charge for information. Information can't be sold as advice anymore, so they'll have to give more in-depth analysis, deductions, and conclusions. It's not good enough to get monthly statements anymore. People can get information up to the minute on the Internet."

Another interesting, albeit contrary view comes from Pat McNeill: "Discount brokerage and full-service brokerage are distinct market segments. In my view, both market segments will prosper. Full-service brokerages will continue to prosper because well-heeled investors don't have the time to absorb and analyze all that information. Often they don't have the confidence that comes from experience and a successful track record. The primary market for a full-service broker is someone with money who's well-informed about the nature of various investments, and isn't averse to taking risk in order to earn a return."

Most of the brokerage industry still struggles with how to deal with women. Our research shows that brokers are women's last choice for whom they'd go to for help. Studies have found that brokers spend less time with women prospects than they do with men and give women advice too conservative for their needs. Several studies conclude that gender has a dramatic influence on the type and quality of information that people receive from brokers. Stories abound of how brokers often talk down to women. Historically, brokers had control of the information and imparted what they thought investors needed. It was kind of an "information on a need-to-know basis" arrangement. With the Web, however, you learn as you go. And since women are education oriented, the Internet is perfect. Women can learn at their own pace, on their own time, and they gain control back. The Internet is an environment conducive to learning and has created a more level playing field for information accessed and cost reductions. Women don't have to feel uncomfortable about what they know and don't know. They can inform themselves and act accordingly.

So, how much are women using the Internet? Just as much as men are. Jim Carroll, author of numerous books about the Internet, says, "The Internet used to be a guy thing where only young, white males with big incomes were using it. Now it's 50/50 women and men." The Centre for Women's Business Research says that women entrepreneurs use the Internet more than men when it comes to research and e-commerce.[2] Another study says that women comprise half the Internet users, up from 18 percent in 1996.[3] Many people predict that more women will be using the Web than men. But everyone agrees that women use the Internet differently. Men surf; women have a destination. Women use the Internet primarily to get information. Men use it for entertainment, as well as to get information.

According to a report called *The On-line Gender Gap Is Closing,* done by Forrester Research Inc., women are closing in quickly on men when it comes to conducting their financial business online: 10 percent of women and 13 percent of men bank online, with 2 percent of women and 5 percent of men trading online.[4] The numbers are small but growing. Online investing is certainly not a serious threat to the community of full-service brokerages at the moment, but they had better be looking over their shoulder.

The differences between men and women online will diminish as the Net becomes more mainstream. Evidence of this can already be seen, as men and women who've been online less than one year are nearly identical in their online behaviour. According to the Forrester report, until recently the Internet was marketed to men and online content wasn't developed for female audiences. This situation has changed as websites such as iVillage develop more and more content for women. New marketing strategies focus on driving women online. Women prefer online content that can be used in their everyday lives. Providing useful information, as iVillage and Women's Wire do, will continue to attract women.

Jim Carroll also believes that electronic trading empowers the investor. In the past a lot of potential investors thought they weren't smart enough to invest, or were too embarrassed to go to a financial advisor. Now people are getting all kinds of information from the Internet and are doing their own trades. People can take their investments into their own hands; some (gasp!) are even turfing their financial advisors because they provide the same information that's right there on the Net. People have simply discovered that there are other financial services available that more closely meet their needs.

I'm not advocating dumping your advisor, not by a long shot. But I do believe in using the Internet to help you manage your personal financial life. Since most women prefer a relationship approach to doing business, the Internet can be a fabulous tool that works well in conjunction with an advisor. (Unless you have a warm, caring relationship with your computer and it's the kind that will take you out to lunch to calm your "après-market-crash" jitters, you will need an advisor.) You can get quick access to great information without having to listen to someone's voicemail message and wait forever for your call to be returned. You don't have to fight traffic to meet with your advisor. You can avoid the million-mile lineup during RRSP season and take care of business in the cozy confines of your office. Buying financial products from the Internet is mainstream now. E-commerce and investing online has matured and is quite safe. Technology can go a long way toward helping you make the best of your time. And time is like money—you can only spend it once.

Ethical investing

I'd been reduced to only two operational brain cells and Elaine and I had digressed from our riveting discussion of funds. Feeling somewhat philosophical, I asked her expansively, "What's our children's world going to be like? I worry about their future when I hear of oil tanker spills, clear-cut forests, and human rights violations. I worry about my twin nieces' future career prospects when I hear that almost half the Canadian companies that make up the TSX still list no women in senior management positions in their annual reports. What can one person do to help address problems so huge?"

Naturally, Elaine had an answer. And one I didn't expect. "You can find a way through ethical or social investing, a growing investment field. Ethical investors and their advisors look at a company's social record as well as its rates of return before deciding whether to invest. Ethical investors consider issues such as the environment, gender, labour relations, and human rights. They tend to avoid companies involved in military weapons, tobacco, and pornography. Be aware, however, that there's some controversy around the benchmarks some companies use. Research the mutual fund company's definition of "ethical" thoroughly. You may be surprised to find that your portfolio may actually hold a company that sells tobacco."

According to Eugene Ellmen, author of *The Canadian Ethical Money Guide,* ethical investments can perform as well as—and in some cases better than—conventional investments. Here's a case in point: from 1990 to the end of 1995, stock prices listed in the Domini 400, an index of socially responsible U.S. stocks, have grown 135.5 percent. By comparison, the leading U.S. stock measure, the Standard & Poor's 500, increased by 120.5 percent over the same period. One needs to also be aware, however, that ethical funds tend to have higher management fees than comparable funds.

"Ethical investing" styles vary. "Negative screen" managers will not buy companies in a certain industry or that do not follow a certain protocol—for example, companies that sell tobacco, are involved in defence contracting, or move their manufacturing to other countries where they can avoid having to abide by their home country's pollution laws. "Positive screen" managers do not care about the industry as long as they are making a positive difference. These managers might be in "dirty industries" such as oil and gas, but they are implementing a newer, more environmentally friendly process. Still other managers will use their position as shareholders to lobby businesses to act more responsibly.

"So how does an ethical investor make her choices?" I queried.

"If you have the time, money, and confidence to investigate and pick individual stocks, you can choose your investment according to your own mix of ethical concerns," Elaine said. "For those of us who are short on spare time and cash reserves, there are mutual funds with investments selected according to stated ethical criteria. Investors in many funds can start with contributions as low as $50 a month."

In either case, you'll want to do your ethical and investment homework. Start with the Social Investment Organization, a national nonprofit network of those who believe that corporate responsibility and business success go hand in hand. Contact them by phone at 416-461-6042 or by e-mail at info@socialinvestment.ca. Their website is www.socialinvestment.ca. If you're interested in picking your own stocks, Toronto-based Michael Jantzi Research Associates can help. They've developed Canada's first database that tracks the social and environmental performance of TSX companies plus 100 other publicly traded companies. They offer company profiles from their database for $25 and customized profiles of other companies for $200 to $400 each. Call them at 416-861-0403 or e-mail mjra@web.net.

"I really like this," I said. "Ethical investing won't single-handedly change the world that you or I leave for our children. But it will hit corporate culprits where it hurts—their bottom lines. And that's a start."

How can I track how well my fund is doing?

"How do I know how many millions I'm making, Elaine?" I groaned at the thought of having to make sense of all those small numbers on the financial pages of the newspaper. But as usual, it proved to be far more difficult in thought than in reality. Newspapers have responded to the growing popularity of mutual funds by making their reporting more accessible to the average Joe and Jane. I realized with chagrin that it took me approximately four

Jantzi Social Index Returns

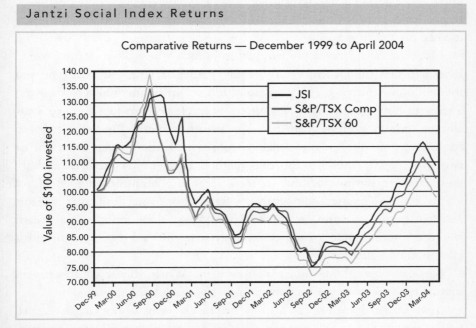

SOURCE: MICHAEL JANTZI RESEARCH ASSOCIATES INC. REPRODUCED WITH PERMISSION.

minutes to figure out how to read the mutual funds section. The major financial newspapers such as *The National/Financial Post* and *The Globe and Mail* have guidelines on how to read these pages. But watch how the results are reported.

I was shocked to learn how easy it is to be misled by mutual fund tables reported in the newspapers. It seems that most funds report their success or failures based on compound returns. But there's a major flaw with this: all it takes is one year to skew the real picture. For instance, take the AGF International Value Fund, which is a huge flagship fund for AGF. The fund manager didn't renew their contract with AGF in March 2002 in order to start up a fund family in Canada. The fund has $10 billion in it so the fund manager was considered to have a good following. During 2002, the fund suffered badly because of redemptions and bad markets and had dismal returns of −23 percent that year. In 2000, however, when this fund was a market darling, it had been up over 25 percent. The five-year return for AGF International Value Fund as of December 2003 was 5.1 percent, and the 10-year performance is 10.2 percent, ironically twice as good over the longer period. Averaging over time just highlights the smoothing of returns over time ("reversion to the mean" in investment terms). Investors should be aware of the volatility characteristics of a particular fund over shorter periods. For example, Morningstar (PALtrak) shows a three-year volatility rating of "medium high" on this fund, which certainly fits.

As our example clearly shows, with this method of reporting you don't know if the good rates of returns are because of consistent good performance or one lucky year. The more dramatic the variation is in fund returns from year to year, the riskier it is.

Now, the calendar-year returns method shows you what your fund would have returned on December 31 of any particular year, assuming you put money in on January 1. The purpose of this reporting method is to give you a sense of how a fund did over a variety of single years so that you can actually see the swings in performance. This reporting method makes it easier to see whether the fund is really making money or is the benefactor of one or two good years. Another reporting method is the rolling returns analysis, whose prime purpose is also to steer clear of the misleading effects of compounding. The method does this by figuring out your fund's best, average, and worst returns within certain time periods, say, three months or 10 years. Because it uses a wide variety of monthly start and end dates, you lose that compounding effect.

So, sometimes things aren't as they seem. When you scour the paper's mutual fund tables to see how much richer you are, be skeptical.

Your financial advisor can also be helpful in terms of tracking how well you're doing. She or he can show you different measurement parameters rather than just relying on historical performance numbers. These parameters can be quartile ranking; the ranking by Morningstar Rating System, which tracks "risk adjusted return" over various periods and ranks it using a number of stars; manager tenure; and volatility ranking. These parameters are commonly available and are used by advisors. There is a lot more to analyzing and assessing mutual funds than simply seeing how they've done lately.

If you're computer literate, you can tap into mutual fund tracking services provided by brokerage houses and independent software providers such as Globefund and Morningstar. Doing so allows you to use your computer to keep track of your portfolio's performance through a disk that's updated monthly. You can even plug in benchmarks to see how well it's performing relative to, say, the TSX 60.

The company from which you bought your fund will send you statements (monthly if you pay by PAC or quarterly) that will also tell you how the fund is faring. If you're investing for the long haul, however, don't be spooked by a bad month. There are likely to be many bad months over a 30- or 40-year span of investing. When my statement appears each month, I give it only a cursory glance to get a sense of whether it's up or down, then I mentally toss it. It's only if there's a general trend down, down, down over a long period that I might be inclined to get disturbed.

In summary

"Elaine, I'm going to blow up if you try to stuff one more fact into my head," I moaned.

"Let me net it out for you simply. Before leaping into the world of investing, think long and hard about the following.

"First, there's absolutely no guaranteed way to pick a winner. For most of us, experience is what we have left over after we've pulled a bonehead move. But we do have past performance to go on. Those interested in investing in a going concern should make sure they know which way it's headed. But keep in mind that the past doesn't necessarily determine the future. There are dozens of things you need to be looking for when determining the performance of a fund. It ain't just about numbers. Case in point: after the 10-year anniversary of the October crash in '87 passed, many fund performance numbers jumped up dramatically. It had nothing to do with brilliant management. It was because the unbelievably bad performance number in 1987 dropped off the 10-year average returns.

"There's an abundance of 'How to Pick the Right Mutual Fund' books in your local bookstore. In fact, there are so many now that it's beginning to rival the fiction section. Good bets are anything by Gordon Pape or Duff Young, but there are plenty of others. Go online and check out Morningstar and Globefund, to name only a few of the gazillion sources available on the Internet. Scour the business sections of your newspapers, most notably *The Globe and Mail* and *The National/Financial Post.*

"But remember, sometimes education allows us to make more intelligent mistakes. Rely on common sense. It's the sixth sense given to us to keep the other five from making fools of us."

"I need to get up and run around the room three times to get the feeling back in my legs. Okay, and head. Are we getting close to the end yet?" I asked. "Do I smell pizza?!?"

"Your unnatural attachment to food can only be eclipsed by your desire to learn," Elaine observed.

"Isn't that a woman thing?" I asked, stretching my arms over my head. "Women want information and lots of it."

Women as investors

According to American feminist critic Andrea Dworkin, "Money speaks, but it speaks with a male voice." On one level, Dworkin is so right. The industry is still loaded with men. Seventy-nine percent of the advisors in Canada are men.[5] That means only 21 percent of the financial advisors out there have a clue how much pantyhose cost. Buy a Canadian equity fund, and you're 14 times more likely to end up in the hands of a male portfolio manager.[6] However, on another, more telling level, Dworkin is also very wrong. Women's collective investing power is *huge*. And even more encouraging, women are getting into investing in unprecedented numbers. And here's my personal favourite: women are better investors than men.

Time and time again, women's learning style holds them in good stead in the world of investing. As investors and professional money managers, women have an advantage in the market because they research more diligently, listen to advice, and sit tight through price swings. Women are better at riding out losses. They're not too concerned that markets go up and down; they're more concerned with the end result. Terrance Odean, an economist at the University of California in Davis, near Sacramento, studied the trading habits of more than 35,000 households that used a discount broker from 1991 to 1997. His study, "Boys Will Be Boys,"[7] showed that men traded about 77 percent of their portfolio annually, 45 percent more than women. Single men were the biggest churners of all, changing their holdings 67 percent more than single women did. According to the study, the men ended up paying dearly: adjusting for the risks they took on, they earned 1.4 percentage points *less* than women a year, and 2.3 percentage points less than single women.

Then there's the experience of the National Association of Investors Corporation, which proved women's acumen for investing as shown in the statistics just cited. According to Jonathan Strong, manager of membership at NAIC, women's clubs do well because they often look at the broad picture of a growth company's prospects and the general trends in the stock market. Women's clubs tend not to drown in the many technical and financial details that may detract from a company's fundamental potential or long-term future growth prospects. Women's clubs often focus on the fundamentals of a company, such as management's performance, the characteristics of the industry the company operates within, and the company's markets, as well as important financial figures including sales, earnings per share, pre-tax profits, and the price earnings ratio of a stock. This broad-based, fundamental approach has proven to produce successful investors over the long term. Women also tend to be excellent students when approaching investing. Women's clubs pride themselves on not acting on the latest investment "hot tip" or market news. Instead they collect company information, data, and research and fully read and analyze all these resources as a group before making a buy or sell decision on a particular stock.

Strong says that women's clubs typically follow a buy-and-hold strategy when buying quality stocks for the long term. Women's clubs may not be too quick to act (buy or sell a stock) on the up or down price movement of a stock or current economic or stock market changes. Women's clubs tend to be more willing to ride out the rough times to realize a profit on an investment.[8] Women understand that the road to financial success often runs uphill, so they don't expect to break any speed records.

Also, Strong points out that women were traditionally the purchasers of many household goods and services. Today this may still be true in many households. As the "buyers," women tend to be keenly aware of fairly priced, quality goods and services, as well as of the companies that produce those goods and services. This valuable knowledge translates directly to stock investing—looking for competitive, growing, quality companies that are available at a good price. The best research for finding good companies to invest in is out in the marketplace—experiencing the company's products and services first-hand.

Another Canadian study was done by *Investment Executive,* a financial service industry newspaper that commissioned market research company Compas Inc. to conduct a poll of investors countrywide. Its findings? When it comes to personal financial management, the behaviour and attitudes of men and women are as different as night and day.[9]

Women are more likely to use the services of a financial advisor. (This is good news, because another study showed that people who use an advisor actually do better financially than those who don't.) On average, women say they've used a financial advisor for 8.0 years while men have used advisors for 6.8 years. Women also look for more counselling attention and prefer more contact with advisors than men. According to the poll, women are more likely to discuss money management with spouses or family members while men are twice as likely to claim that they wouldn't seek anyone's advice before investing.

The U.S. *Money Magazine* got Chicago-based fund rater Morningstar to analyze returns for 2,562 funds in 1997. Funds managed by a woman or a pair of women performed marginally better over three years than those run by one or two men in five broad categories, including U.S. diversified stocks and international stocks. Observers said that women do better partly because they're younger—42 for the average female manager, compared with 46 for men—and research shows that young fund managers typically outperform veterans.[10]

It's a good thing that women excel at investing. They need to. They live longer on less money and pay more than men do. Women *must* develop a sense of adventure with their money in order to be sure it lasts at least as long as they do. And the difference between making money and creating wealth can be captured in two words: buy stocks. Women must invest. And not just in GICs or Canada Savings Bonds.

The "women are risk-averse and conservative investors" debate

If I read one more book, industry brochure, or newspaper article espousing this sentiment, I just might have to go out and kill somebody. I've heard ludicrous statements that range from "As women, we can accept the fact that we are biologically less willing to take risk"[11] to "Women are more timid by nature."[12] Another two words: horse hockey. This I know to be true. Women are not nervous nellies, timidly biting their nails as they count their pennies into a sock. Women are calculated risk takers, not risk averse, and there is a huge difference between the two.

I have this ongoing friendly battle with my friend Pat McNeill (to whom you were introduced earlier in the electronic trading section). He's one of those deluded types that thinks Mother Nature plays a part in women's so-called aversion to risk. As much as it pains me to admit, Pat's not a stupid man. He has his years of experience as a corporate banker to draw from, as well as tons of book learning acquired through his MBA, CFA, and an engineering degree. So does that make him an expert on women? Not on your life. Like me, he couldn't get a date if his life depended on it. However, he has a fascinating theory on why many women trounce their male counterparts in the world of investing. This is what he says:

"As I'm sure you are aware, the metric used for portfolio performance is 'risk-adjusted return.' I would expect that on average women's portfolios earn the same risk-adjusted return as men's. [Author's note: This would be worthy of study.] However, women with little financial depth and low diversification will outperform men in the same circumstances. This is because women are, as you say, 'calculated risk-takers,' typically buying quality or value with a long-term, strategic, buy-and-hold plan. There are studies out there, which I read for my CFA, demonstrating that in the long term value investing has always been a strong performer. Just look at investment guru Warren Buffett's performance for an example of the success of the investment strategy that comes naturally to most women.

"No, women do not fear risk. But given the same circumstances, women accept less risk than men and this works to the advantage of women with fewer dollars and little diversification. And no, I don't have any studies to prove it, but the place to look is the profiles of people buying speculative instruments with their entire portfolio—uncovered options, penny stocks, futures. You don't have to be rich to be a speculator and I'm certain that most speculators are men. Men aren't educated this way, it's just that by their nature they like to drink whiskey and play with guns …

"Where men lose, and my friends and I are perfect examples, is by taking on excessive risk for the size of their portfolios. Most men don't have the financial depth for adequate diversification; they accept excessive risk and get shaken out at reversals. They're calculating, but are more short-term or tactically oriented. They tend to be traders rather than investors and are more inclined to act on tips, rumour, and emotion. This is a losing strategy for those who don't have the financial depth or patience to sit out reversals or when the trades they make are in instruments so risky that once the trend reverses the price might never come back. However, with enough dollars and diversification the traders should outperform the investors.

"So, let's persuade the women to take on more risk but only when they have the financial depth required for adequate diversification. Most of them will do fine without us. Let's persuade the men to take on less risk until they have the financial depth required for adequate diversification. Most of them are hurting.

"Coincidentally, this is a true story. On Monday night I went over to a friend's place (a woman) to show her how to use her Web browser. The first thing she wanted to do was learn how to trade stocks on the Web and escape her full-service broker. She wanted to invest based on her knowledge of the domestic pharmaceuticals industry and her broker wasn't very helpful (and charged $65 a side). She follows long-term buy-and-hold strategies in quality stocks and makes money. A few bucks, but not enough to diversify. Typical and smart.

"While up in cottage country on the weekend, the guys got to talking about their stock trades. Most of the talk was about the penny stocks purchased on tips that sewered. A few bucks but not enough to diversify. Typical and stupid. Strikes me that there might be a business case for a broker to handle all these risk-averse women and risk-happy men … and I stand by my statement that relative to men and by their nature, women are risk averse."

Much of what he says is true. Women are value investors and that serves them well in the long run. But his theory that women are averse to risk doesn't hold water. As evidenced by the following studies, research proves that when male and female investor samples are identical, women do better regardless of how diversified their portfolios are. Once educated, women are just as quick to invest in the higher-risk realm as men are.

A study by researchers at the Swiss Federal Institute of Technology titled "Financial Decision-Making: Are Women Really More Risk Averse?"[13] found that the answer is generally no. "Our findings suggest that gender-specific risk behaviour found in previous survey data may be due to differences in male and female opportunity sets rather than stereotype risk attitudes," the study concluded. "Our findings … suggest that preconceptions concerning the risk attitudes of female investors and managers may be more a prejudice than a solid fact." Another study the Swiss report cited was by Penelope Wang, who said, "Women are expected to be the more conservative investors and are consequently offered investments with lower risks and therefore lower expected returns than males."

Another expert readily agrees with the Swiss study. "Stereotypes are so strongly held, but [one's attitude toward] risk has nothing to do with being male or female," says Becky Reuber, a professor at the University of Toronto's Rotman School of Management.[14]

Women earning a salary may be just as willing as men to take risks when the playing field is levelled. Professors Scott and Harvey, who teach at Bishop's University in Lennoxville, Quebec, quizzed 303 workers enrolled in a large company's employee savings plan. The women in the study had put 37 percent of their assets in "high-risk" investments, only just short of the 38 percent for men.[15] "Previous studies that portrayed women as cautious may have been skewed because they used brokerage customers, many of whom were elderly widows. By comparison, we were using people in the workforce and I think there you get a more sophisticated type of investor."[16]

Still, the old views do linger. Risk aversion isn't an innate female characteristic as some had previously thought, but women's inexperience and their information-gathering process have made it appear that way. Risk aversion is not about gender, but about people's individual situation. Frankly, this timid, conservative thing insults most women. Women are just as likely as men to invest in equities once they're educated in that field.

Frankly, even if women tell you they're afraid of risk, they still probably aren't. Part of the reason some people assume that women are risk averse is that virtually everything they read tells them they are. Advisors read the same stuff. There's a big problem here. You can't underestimate the power of language. What people really mean when they say "risk averse" is often "calculated risk-taker." These two terms are by no means similar. Risk averse sounds like we're a bunch of fraidy cats. Calculated risk-taker makes us sound smart. The negative effect of using the term "risk averse" is very real. The Swiss Institute study, as well as another study done by *Working Women* magazine, concluded that women receive advice that's too conservative for their needs.[17]

One of the reasons research continually points out that women fear risk is because certain investment companies survey their women clients and find that a large percentage are investing primarily in guaranteed investments. But their samples are likely skewed, as the Bishop's University study revealed. Therefore the conservative profile fits the sample, but it isn't realistic. As for the women who aren't in that profile, the number one reason cited for seeking financial advice was *time*. (This, tied with the death of a woman's partner.) And time is another compelling reason why women may be investing in guaranteed stuff. Acquiring GICs and Canada Savings Bonds is simply a matter of filling out a form and watching them grow as they roll over each year with no interference or maintenance. I'd bet a dollar to a dozen doughnuts the real reason women do that GIC thing is because of time poverty.

Think about it. Canada boasts the largest percentage of women entrepreneurs and women managers in the industrialized world. Can a bunch of wimps make that claim? I think not.

Elaine stood up smiling. "Well now, I have some good news. You're done, for today, that is. You made it, congratulations. Although you may be five pounds heavier, you're likely much wiser about the difference between investing and saving. I sincerely hope that I've given you the incentive to continue to invest your money."

"Absolutely," I deadpanned. "You never know, someday it may be valuable again." With that, I left Elaine's office and headed straight for the gym.

seven

Your quantum of solace

Women constitute half the world's population, perform nearly two-thirds of its work hours, receive one-tenth of the world's income, and own less than one one-hundredth of the world's property.

UNITED NATIONS REPORT, 1980

According to Statistics Canada numbers, the number of Canadian women who live alone—without children, relatives, friends, or partners—in a home they own almost doubled to 612,640 from 314,610 during 1981 to 1996, 200,000 more than their male counterparts. That's a 136 percent increase.

STATISTICS CANADA

One day Elaine remarked, "Joanne, I think you're ready to consider buying your own home."

There was only one word to describe my feelings on home ownership: terror. I terminated further discussion with, "Thank you for your concern, Elaine. No."

She blinked with surprise. "Uh, no?"

"No, nada, no way José, nein, NOT!" I clarified for her.

In keeping with her usual style, she rolled right over my point of view. "That's ridiculous, Joanne. Give me one good reason why not."

"Because," I answered, trying to avoid the real reason, "experts say a house is not as great an investment as everyone thinks. I can do just as well by renting and investing the difference." I thought to myself what a remarkably quick recovery that was. Unfortunately, Elaine didn't buy it.

"You're afraid," she said quietly.

"Yeah, yeah, so what?" I replied, my pride just a little hurt at being found out.

Elaine was sympathetic. "Tell me what you fear. Twenty bucks says I felt the same thing."

I took a deep breath. "The whole idea is too big, too adult; there's too much debt, it's too locked in and it takes too long to save for; a house is too much trouble and I hate shovelling snow."

Elaine smiled. "Don't hold back, Joanne. Now, tell me how you really feel."

I made a face at her as I continued. "I never thought it was possible that I could own my own home. Unless of course I did it with a significant other. I guess I've always thought that my knight in shining armour was going to ride into my life and bring the castle with him. It never occurred to me to buy my own castle. Besides, I have a hectic lifestyle. I travel and I'm impulsive. I once drove a friend to the airport and on the spur of the moment ended up boarding the plane with her to go to Victoria, B.C., for the weekend. I like to move around a lot. I've lived in almost every major city in this country. I love the freedom of a nomadic lifestyle. And I'm not sure how intellectually stimulating I'd find fixing roofs and unplugging toilets."

"How long have you lived in Toronto, Joanne?" Elaine asked.

"Thirteen years now. Why?"

"How long ago was that stunt that took you 3,000 miles across the country for a weekend?" she asked.

"I don't know," I said, shifting uncomfortably. I didn't like where this was heading. "Maybe 11 years ago."

Elaine pressed on. "Have you ever heard of carpenters and plumbers? Maybe you even know high school kids who earn extra money shovelling snow and cutting grass? My dear, fear is the only reason you don't want to buy a house. And a darn fine one at that. There's not a person on the planet who hasn't experienced serious anxiety at the thought of buying their first home. And I must say that buying a house isn't for everyone. It's as much an emotional decision as a financial one. Never lose sight of that. A home is your quantum of solace, your safe haven from the world. A home should not be bought as an investment, although it can turn out to be a good one. Will Rogers said, 'Buy land. They aren't making any more of it.'"

"I guess that's why you own three?" I asked smugly.

"I happen to own three because in two cases the market turned against me as a seller," she countered. "This can be the downside to owning a house. The housing market took a serious dive and, had I sold the property, I would have taken a bath. I had to rent the house in Burlington to cover the monthly mortgage payments. The house in Toronto, well! This one really hurts. Like so many others bitten by the real estate bug, I bought when prices were exceedingly high in 1988. It astounds me how grossly inflated house prices were in the '80s. People weren't buying houses for shelter. Speculators would buy them and 10 minutes later put them back on the market and watch people kill each other trying to up the ante. People had an irrational fear that prices were going out of sight and they'd never be able to afford to buy a home. They rushed out to buy whatever they could, however they could. I saw the Toronto housing market drop 15 percent that year when mortgage rates spiked up and speculators dumped their houses and fled the market."

"I know this to be true, Elaine," I offered. "I have friends in the most precarious of financial positions today because they pushed their lines of credit and credit card limits to the maximum and borrowed well beyond their means to jump on this bandwagon. The pressure I got from so many people to buy a house during that period was unbearable. Most of my friends did. I don't glory in their misfortune, but look who's laughing now."

Elaine chuckled. "My house in Toronto was bought strategically at the top of the market. I watched in horror over the next two years as it dropped $60,000 in value. And when the housing market went down the drain, so did the rental market. There was such a glut of houses for rent that people were negotiating 25 percent off and first and last month free. People like me who had the choice to sell and take a huge loss or try to carry the monthly payments as best we could on the rental income were in a terrible bind. My choice was to try to hold on until the market turned around or the rental income increased enough to cover the expenses. That's why I find myself with such vast land holdings today; I have a strong belief that real estate is a wonderful investment, but I also have poor judgment in timing. It's a deadly combination if you're in only for the short term."

"Well, knowing my luck, I'd buy a house and a heavy metal band would buy the place next door. I don't know, Elaine. It sounds like a lot of trouble and risk," I said.

"That's a good point, Joanne," Elaine answered. "Many people believe that buying a house is risk free. As the '80s demonstrate, that's not true. Vancouver saw house prices climb 40 percent in 1980 and 48 percent in 1981 with the arrival of Hong Kong money. In 1982, the bottom fell out when the economy died and prices dropped almost 30 percent. But one thing's for sure, it's low risk if you're in for the long term and buy prudently. Historically real estate has had stable and secure growth and is a good hedge against inflation. The national average growth rate has been 10 percent a year. Some neighbourhoods have performed well above the average, with values rising as much as 20 to 25 percent. That isn't the reality in today's world, though. It is safe to say the growth rate will be much less for the foreseeable future.

"A good general guideline is to find a neighbourhood not often frequented by heavy metal bands. Here's the best reason why real estate is a great idea. Let's say you bought your house for $175,000, decided to sell it a few years later, and cleared $50,000 after the sale was completed. Canada Revenue Agency won't require you to give them a share. The beauty of this profit is that it's completely tax free, as long as the house is your principal residence. Since we Canadians are one of the highest-taxed people in the world, I'd suggest to you that it's in your best interest to take advantage of whatever tax breaks exist. And there isn't much to choose from."

"I see your point. But what if I wanted to take off for six months or move to Paris or buy a convertible? Or what if there's an emergency and I need cash and it's all tied up in the house? I can't sell the bath tub and buy it back later when I have the money again. As an investment, a house doesn't strike me as being very liquid." I lived for freedom of choice.

"You're right," Elaine said. "You don't take off for six months, you can't buy the convertible, and you sell the house when you move to Paris. You also never let yourself get so house poor that you can't take care of day-to-day emergencies. That's a big mistake many people make. However, you can take advantage of home equity lines of credit, which make it possible for you to tap into cash right under your own nose, the equity built up in your home. You don't have to sell it or worry about rigid repayment schedules. Mind you, you do have to own your house for an appreciable length of time to build up equity of any significance. Buying a house is a lifestyle choice. Unless you're one of the rich and famous, you give up certain things to gain others—things like pride in the home you own, and a forced savings program, since it's somewhat difficult to sell pieces of the house to raise cash. A house is an asset that will appreciate tax free over the long term. Owning your own home can also contribute to securing your retirement. Even if you don't sell your house when you stop working, there's much to be said for enjoying your last quarter in a paid-up home. Owning your own home can alleviate much of the uncertainty of old age.

"Joanne," Elaine continued, "I'm not suggesting you must do this. You can, in fact, rent and, if you consistently and wisely invest the difference, for example by maximizing your RRSPs, you'll do as well as and maybe even better than home owners. However, you also have to remember that we have the lowest fixed-term mortgage rates in 50 years. Because of this, buying may make more sense than renting in many situations.

"But don't let people tell you that by renting you're just throwing money out the window and paying someone else's mortgage. Most people realize that the monthly amount they put into their house is going toward building tax-free equity, and they assume that it's better to have their money going into something that's building capital. The mortgage payments for the house I live in are $2,100 a month. It's a dandy fine house and I believe worth the money. How much do you pay in rent, Joanne?"

"Nowhere near $2,100, I'll guarantee you that. And my place fits my needs perfectly," I replied. "Also I don't worry about utilities, property tax, insurance, upkeep, and hydro."

"There's my point," Elaine said. "You're paying less monthly than I am and as long as you continue to invest for the long term and in a vehicle that's tax sheltered, you'll be absolutely fine from an investment point of view. But this is where a house has the advantage. It forces you to save. You can't be tempted to forgo your savings program this month or year because of your cockamamie travel behaviour. The bottom line is that we all have to pay living costs one way or the other. That money can never be viewed as wasted."

"So I'm right after all?" I asked in disbelief.

"You could very well be and that's for you to decide. But the fact remains that the cost of borrowing for a home has never been lower. You know, Joanne, if home maintenance doesn't appeal to you, there's another option," Elaine said.

"I figured as much," I sighed.

"How about a condominium? Often the costs are similar to or only marginally higher than renting, especially if you settle in a comparable neighbourhood. No muss, no fuss," Elaine summed up.

"That means I use all my hard-earned savings for a down payment. I don't know why I don't like that, I just don't. I get a warmer, more secure feeling from having a variety of investments, not just one. I know the 'It's my own pad and it's tax free' argument. I agree that real estate can be a good investment, barring periods of political and economic havoc. But I'll have to mull the idea over. I'm not sure it suits me, not today anyway. I'll tell you, Elaine, I'll gladly put my investment portfolio on the line and in 10 or 20 years compare my net worth with that of a person who uses her home as her savings. We could very well be in the same place, or I could even be ahead. And I'll have flown to Bora Bora on 24 hours notice."

"You're hopeless," Elaine groaned.

My semi-serious house hunt, or how I learned about real estate

Well, I did take Elaine's advice and started to think about buying a house. I decided to "feel the fear, but do it anyway." The one thing that helped me move forward was being firm in my commitment to take all the time I needed. If I was going to spend my nest egg on a down payment and go into debt for hundreds of thousands of dollars, I was going to be very, very sure about my decision. Since I was in no hurry and content with my lifestyle as it was, I browsed on and off for four years. I looked in the country, in the suburbs, and downtown. I looked at houses, condominiums, and townhouses. I looked at all the price ranges to get a sense of what the different prices would buy. By far my favourite was a $750,000 job on a quiet tree-lined street. (That should come as no surprise.) Since I was attempting to find a place to live in for a long time, I needed to figure out what I'd be most comfortable with.

Location, lo ... you know the rest

I discovered a number of things about the housing market. It used to be the farther away from the city, the less expensive the house. But deurbanization has changed this somewhat. Although it still may generally be true, you need to check out the neighbourhood first. Recently there was a mini housing boom in the small town of Owen Sound that drove the housing prices up to Toronto levels. Go figure. I took a pass. Elaine and my new best friend, Peter the Real Estate Agent, stressed the three key points in buying real estate: location, location, location. I thought it meant plain and simply a good address. Peter was quick to point out it's more than that. It's the community at large, the street and neighbourhood, and lastly the actual siting of the dwelling on the property. If any of these "locations" are sub-optimal (Peter's word), it will affect the value and salability of the property.

Schools, public transportation, and shopping are important considerations, as long as they aren't parked immediately in your backyard. Since I had no children, drove my own car, and was averse to shopping of any sort, I didn't care about any of these things. But in her inimitable style, Elaine insisted I begin to care about them for two reasons. One, life can change in an instant— what if I actually went out on a date? What if I ended up marrying some poor bloke and having a family? Schools and shopping would then mean something. I needed to consider all the possibilities, short and long term, no matter how remote. The second reason was the resale value. Being near to these things makes a house more attractive to a wider range of potential buyers. I told Elaine that all I cared about was that my house have a fireplace, a big backyard with a stellar view, and three large bedrooms so I could set up an office and an exercise room. The kitchen was optional. Elaine reminded me that since these features are attractive for most people, having them could only increase the house's value. She did mention, however, that she'd never seen a house without a kitchen, so I might have to compromise.

As time went by, I got pretty good at sizing up almost instantly what I liked and what I didn't. Eventually I only went out to view specific houses in a certain price range, in the kind of neighbourhood I wanted, and with certain features. I actually began to enjoy the exercise. I mastered the art of walking casually through a house that made my heart pound with excitement and my head spin with anticipation. But my excitement would be known only to me. The real estate agent could no more guess that I liked this particular house than fly to the moon. The more non-committal I was, the more bargaining power I'd have.

Oh, those untold extra costs

As with everything else that I'd undertaken in financial planning, fear of the unknown was the worst part. Again, I demystified the process by becoming part of it. As I became more comfortable, I started to think about the financial end of buying a house. How much could I afford? How much would closing fees and insurance and taxes be? What should I put aside for hiring someone to move me, shovel snow, cut grass, clean out eavestroughs, garages, furnaces, and chimneys, repair roofs, caulk windows, and install the new shower? Rumour had it there was more to securing a mortgage than going to your bank manager and saying, "Please can I have one?" Typically, I was expected to cover 25 percent of the purchase price with my own money, though you can get away with as little as 5 percent. I also had to learn that money was needed not only to buy the house itself, but for a myriad of other costs as well.

Some of the possible extra costs are one-time costs, and others, such as condominium maintenance fees and property insurance, are ongoing monthly expenses. The good news is that not all of these costs may apply in your circumstances. Here's the laundry list: Property taxes are sky high in Toronto, for example, and can be more of a burden than expected. There's GST, appraisals, survey fees, property insurance, prepaid taxes or utility bills, land transfer tax, service charges, lawyer (notary) fees, mortgage loan insurance premium and application fee, mortgage broker's fee, moving costs, estoppel certificate, condominium fees, home inspection fee, renovation and repairs, and water quantity and quality certification. And don't forget the sales tax and application fee on mortgages insured by Canada Mortgage and Housing Corporation (CMHC, which is discussed later in this chapter). These vary from province to province.

How much can I afford?

RBC's latest affordability index shows it takes 38.4 percent of a typical household's pretax income to carry the costs of an average detached Toronto bungalow. Back in 1989, it took 66.2 percent. But we need perspective here. For the past 20 years, consumer debt has been rising faster than our incomes, while our savings rate has crashed to a dismal 2.4 percent.

CMHC's Affordability Guide can help you get an idea of the maximum home price you can afford and the maximum you can afford to pay in monthly housing costs.

It comes down to this: housing costs shouldn't be more than 32 percent of your gross monthly income. Housing costs include monthly mortgage principal and interest, taxes, and heating expenses (known as PITH for short). Lenders add up these costs to determine what percentage they are of your gross monthly income. This figure is your Gross Debt Service (GDS) ratio. Your entire monthly debt load shouldn't be more than 40 percent of your gross monthly income. This includes housing costs as well as other debts such as car loans and credit card payments.

Based on these ratios, lenders will advise you of the maximum home price they think you can afford. Keep in mind that most home buyers today keep their debt ratios comfortably below the maximums prescribed above. The lower your debt load, the more affordable your home and lifestyle will be.

When I saw the list of costs, my blood ran cold at the prospect of the financial hugeness of this endeavour. My thoughts turned to "How do I get enough money?" That's when the world of mortgages began to loom on my radar.

I turned my energy toward educating myself about mortgages, rates, terms, and—a word that sounded to me like some dreaded operation—amortization. First I had to find out exactly what all these words meant. I also had to figure out a way of getting this information without admitting my total ignorance to Elaine.

We were having lunch at our favourite crepe joint when, out of the blue, Elaine asked, "Are you able to handle a conventional mortgage or are you going with a high-ratio mortgage? You also need to think about whether you want a closed or open mortgage. Oh yes, I'm curious, what term are you interested in and over what amortization period? I guess that depends on what you think interest rates are going to do. Are you going fixed or variable?"

This was the moment of reckoning. Struggling not to look completely stupid, I said, "Elaine, when did you learn to speak Spanish?" My cover was blown. Elaine laughed all the way back to the office. My education in house-buying jargon began at that moment. And, as usual, it was all remarkably straightforward.

Income, Home Price, and Down Payment Guide

Household Income	5% Down Payment	Maximum Home Price	10% Down Payment	Maximum Home Price	25% Down Payment	Maximum Home Price
$ 25,000	$ 3,000	$ 60,000	$ 6,300	$ 63,000	$ 18,900	$ 75,600
$ 30,000	$ 3,900	$ 78,000	$ 8,200	$ 82,000	$ 24,700	$ 98,800
$ 35,000	$ 4,800	$ 96,000	$10,100	$101,000	$ 30,300	$121,300
$ 40,000	$ 5,700	$114,000	$12,000	$120,000	$ 36,000	$144,000
$ 45,000	$ 6,600	$132,000	$13,900	$139,000	$ 41,700	$166,800
$ 50,000	$ 7,500	$150,000	$15,800	$158,000	$ 47,400	$189,600
$ 60,000	$ 9,300	$186,000	$19,600	$196,000	$ 58,800	$235,200
$ 70,000	$11,050	$221,00	$23,400	$234,000	$ 70,100	$280,400
$ 80,000	$12,500	$250,000	$27,200	$272,000	$ 81,500	$326,000
$ 90,000	$12,500	$250,000	$31,000	$310,000	$ 92,800	$371,200
$100,000	$12,500	$250,000	$34,800	$348,000	$104,300	$417,200

FIGURES ARE ROUNDED TO THE NEAREST $100.

SOURCE: CANADIAN MORTGAGE AND HOUSING CORPORATION (CMHC). ALL RIGHTS RESERVED. REPRODUCED WITH THE CONSENT OF CMHC. ALL OTHER USES AND REPRODUCTIONS OF THIS MATERIAL ARE EXPRESSLY PROHIBITED.

Just what is a mortgage, anyway?

It was embarrassing how basic I needed to get. Like, beginning with what a mortgage actually was. When real estate, which is immovable property, is used to secure a loan, the borrower signs a contract called a mortgage. This is different from a chattel mortgage, discussed in chapter 2, which is generally used for movable goods. Although a mortgage is simply a large loan, the magnitude of the sum borrowed, how long it takes to pay it back, and the nature of the security make it somewhat complex.

Mortgage payments are set up as a combination of interest and principal so that by the end of, say, 25 years, the balance will be zero. The 25-year period you use to pay off the house is the amortization period. Simply put, it's the term during which the debt must be fully paid back. In the early years, you're paying off mostly interest. You don't actually begin to significantly wear away at the principal until several years later. At current rates of 6.5 percent with a 25-year amortization, 20 percent of the very first payment goes to principal. This is why it's a good policy to pay off as much of your mortgage as you can

Affordability Guide

Maximum monthly housing costs you can afford

Gross Debt Service Ratio (GDS)

Your gross monthly salary*	$
+ Your spouse's gross monthly salary	$
+ Other monthly income	$
Total	**A $**
	× 32%
= Maximum monthly housing costs you can afford	**B $**

This maximum monthly payment includes principal, interest, taxes, heating (P.I.T.H.), and if applicable, all of the annual site lease and 50% of the condominium fees.

* Gross salary is income before taxes.

Example:

Jane's gross monthly income is $2,500 and Deepak's is $2,000, for a total of $4,500 per month. They should pay no more than $1,440 ($4,500 × 32%) for their monthly housing expenses.

so you start to pay down the actual principal as soon as possible. This will dramatically lower your interest costs over the years. The shorter the amortization period, the less interest you have to pay. Remember the power of compounding. It works the same way with debt. By shaving off some of that debt in the early years with extra payments, you'll save significantly by cutting back on the compound interest on your debt. But don't cut off your nose to spite your face. I've seen many young couples who've given up any semblance of a normal life because they're so consumed with paying down their mortgage. Moderation is important. After all, we're only young once.

Paying your mortgage biweekly instead of monthly can make a sizeable difference. Let's assume you have a $200,000 mortgage amortized over 25 years with an 8 percent interest rate. If all you do is pay biweekly instead of monthly, you'll reduce the length of time you have to pay to 18.3 years instead of

Affordability Guide

Maximum monthly debt load you can afford

Total Debt Service Ratio (TDS)

Total monthly income	**A** $
	× 40%
= Maximum monthly debt service load you can afford	**C** $
– Monthly auto payment	$
– Monthly loan payment	$
– Monthly credit card/line of credit payment	$
– Other monthly payments	$
= Monthly income left for housing	**D** $

If the home you want costs more per month than you can afford right now (D), consider these strategies: lower your expectations and buy a cheaper home; lower your non-housing debt obligations; and/or raise a larger down payment.

Example:

Jane and Deepak have a gross monthly income of $4,500. Their total debt load should not exceed $1,800 ($4,500 × 40%). They have a monthly car payment of $400, a student loan of $200, and credit card payments of $150, for a total of $750 in non-housing debt payments each month. That means they would have no more than $1,050 available for monthly housing payments ($1,800 – $750). That's lower than the $1,440 suggested by their Gross Debt Service calculation (B).

25 years. And you'll reduce your interest charges from $257,926 to $195,430—a saving of almost $63,000. Remember though, there are two kinds of biweeklies: "accelerated," where each payment contributes a prepayment to principal of 1/26th; and "regular," where the bank saves up the prepayment and only applies it on the anniversary date. The accelerated biweekly versus a regular biweekly results in the equivalent of one month's payment more being deducted each year.

Maximum home price you can afford

It depends on how much your down payment is and how much you can carry in monthly debt service. And that depends on variables such as mortgage rates, your debts and monthly expenses, and personal preferences.

Example:

Jane and Deepak have a down payment of $30,000. They want a conventional mortgage with 25% down, so they estimate their maximum home price at $120,000.

That would leave them a mortgage of $90,000. At 8% interest, amortized over 25 years, that means monthly mortgage payments of $687.* Add monthly property tax installments of $200 and monthly heating costs of $120. Their total monthly housing costs will be $1,007. That's just below the maximum $1,050 allowed according to their Total Debt Service ratio calculations.

That's too close for comfort for Jane and Deepak. What if mortgage rates go up when it's time to renew? They decide to look for a home priced at a maximum of $100,000.

That would leave them with a $70,000 mortgage and monthly mortgage payments of $535,* plus lower taxes of $150 and heating costs of $100. Now their total monthly housing costs will be $785. That makes their Total Debt Service ratio 34% instead of the maximum 40%. And that gives Jane and Deepak a sense of financial comfort.

*FIGURES ARE ROUNDED TO THE NEAREST DOLLAR.

SOURCE: CANADIAN MORTGAGE AND HOUSING CORPORATION (CMHC). ALL RIGHTS RESERVED. REPRODUCED WITH THE CONSENT OF CMHC. ALL OTHER USES AND REPRODUCTIONS OF THIS MATERIAL ARE EXPRESSLY PROHIBITED.

The payment term you choose is often confused with the amortization period. They're two different things. The term you negotiate with the lender can be anywhere from 6 months to 10 years (with some lenders it's 6 months to 25 years). What you choose will depend on your view of which way interest rates are going. I'll explain this further when we get to variable-rate mortgages.

Types of mortgages

Financial institutions are becoming very competitive and remarkably innovative in the mortgage-lending world. It used to be pretty simple, like back in the days when running shoes were running shoes. (I think you've heard this story before.) We only shopped around to compare interest rates. But today's world of mortgages is mind-boggling. It's now become mandatory to shop around to see what new ideas financial institutions have come up with to lure us through their doors. They want your mortgage business very badly, and when I saw some of the numbers I began to understand why. In 1992, Canadians owed $289 billion to our financial institutions for our mortgages. A little over 10 years later, we owe about $600 billion in mortgage debt. It's big business, so it's a good time to negotiate. Even a 1 percent difference in the interest rate can make a huge difference because of the size of the principal.

Preapproved mortgages

I knew enough to know that I wanted a preapproved mortgage. As I'd later discover, lenders will give tentative approval for a mortgage amount based on an assessment, with final approval depending on an appraisal of the property you want to buy and credit approval by the lender. A preapproved mortgage would put me in a better bargaining position to make an offer, since I'd not only know that I could get the financing, but how much I could get. However, I was only guaranteed an interest rate for a short period of time, which varies from 60 to 90 days on home purchases to 90 days on homes being built. All kinds of financial institutions offer preapproved mortgages, so I had the freedom to shop around for the best financing terms and not feel obligated to deal with anyone in particular. I didn't stop at the first place that approved me, which tends to be human nature. People are generally so pleased they've been approved that they don't look any further. This works well for the lenders, but not necessarily for the borrowers.

Conventional and insured mortgages

The next step is to decide whether you qualify for a conventional or a high-ratio mortgage. According to Peter the Real Estate Agent, most first-time buyers go the high-ratio route. Why? To get a conventional mortgage, I needed at least 25 percent of the purchase price of the house as a down payment and my debt load had to be manageable and meet certain criteria. This is when I discovered what really frightened me about owning a home: the amount of money it's necessary to borrow. We're talking serious debt here. Even though it's investment debt and a wise debt, a necessary debt, or whatever else the lenders tell you, it's still a ton of money to owe to an institution. Don't minimize the feeling of apprehension you'll experience. Almost every home owner I've talked to feels exactly the same way.

At one time all mortgages were conventional, but in 1954 the federal government established a system to guarantee mortgage loans made by approved financial lenders as a way to increase the mortgage money available to home buyers and builders. This legislation is the National Housing Act and the crown corporation that looks after everything is known as the Canada Mortgage and Housing Corporation, or CMHC. A lender making a mortgage loan that's approved by CMHC can extend a mortgage that's more than 75 percent of the lower of the appraised value or the purchase price. In other words, these insured mortgages allow the buyer to obtain the mortgage with less than 25 percent of the value of the property as a down payment. If you default, the lender can go back to CMHC to attempt to recoup their losses.

To finance this mortgage insurance program, you, as a buyer, pay a fee—from 0.5 percent to 3.25 percent of the total mortgage loan—which is added to the principal at the outset. It's built right into the payment schedule. At first glance, it seems as though this insurance benefits only the lender. But without it, mortgages with low down payments wouldn't be available, or you'd have to resort to a more expensive second mortgage. These insured first mortgages are sometimes referred to as high-ratio loans.

For several years now, first-timers have been able to buy a house like some people buy home furnishings: a little money down, don't pay until the year 2010. But just like the so-called deals offered by their houseware-hawking cousins, Ottawa's hard sell on housing has some costly catches. The biggest is the cost of the insurance premium on a 95 percent mortgage at 3.25 percent. And while the difference doesn't sound like much, it can mean thousands in extra expense when carried over the life of a 25-year mortgage. For instance, a $170,000 house purchased with 5 percent down, or $8,500, translates into a high-ratio mortgage of $161,500. CMHC requires such mortgages to be insured. Until recently, that mortgage would have cost $4,000 in insurance premiums. Since most home owners build it into the mortgage, that means it will cost an additional $4,000 over 25 years, assuming a rate of 6.5 percent. Total cost: just over $8,000. Today, that insurance tab climbs to $6,000, with interest costs of more than $6,100. Total cost? Not $8,100, but over $12,000.

Borrowers are normally required to have a minimum 5 percent down payment from their own resources to purchase a home. However, CMHC has expanded eligible down payment sources to enable many Canadians to realize their homeownership dream sooner than would otherwise be possible.

Under this new product, effective March 1, 2003, the down payment can come from any source, such as lender incentives and borrowed funds. However, borrowers will still have to prove their ability to meet their debt requirements in order to qualify for mortgage insurance.

You are allowed to use bank loans, mortgage cash-back incentives, even credit cards or money borrowed from parents, friends, or relatives to make up a 5 percent down payment. The money people spend to help construct or upgrade their homes counts too. (But here's where it gets worrisome. Students with no credit history can jump in, as long as they have the income to qualify.)

Under the new product, lenders will be able to offer Canadians a variety of mortgage product offerings including mortgages with terms as low as six months and fixed, adjustable, and capped interest rate loans. But, you'll pay more to insure the mortgage. The fee is 3.4 percent, compared with 3.25 percent for a normal 5 percent down insured mortgage. Buyers who can come up with a 10 percent down payment pay a fee of only 2 percent. And people who manage to come up with a conventional 25 percent down payment don't pay a fee at all.

What's the solution? Take every possible step to get your hands on enough money to make a 10, 15, or even a 20 percent down payment. Go to the Bank of Mom and Dad if need be.

It used to be that you could buy a house with a basement suite that you could rent, but now it's pretty tough to operate a basement apartment. Too bad. Many first-time buyers relied on this extra income to help finance their mortgage and expenses. Of course, you can cut back on your own expenditures, socking away a little more cash before signing on the dotted line.

Closed and open mortgages

According to Peter the Real Estate Agent, people tend to strenuously avoid the terms "closed" and "open" because of the confusion they create. Here's a quick primer.

A "closed" mortgage is just that—not open to prepayment in part or in full at any time, penalty or not. Although usually they can't be paid off totally at any time without prohibitively costly penalties, most "closed" mortgages do have some kind of principal prepayment privilege. The strictest lenders allow prepayments of only up to 10 percent of the original principal exactly on the mortgage's anniversary date, while the most flexible permit extra payments, on any payment date, totalling as much as 20 percent of the original mortgage principal in a year. If you sold your house and had to get out of a typical mortgage, the early discharge penalties of getting out of your mortgage before the term is over are usually calculated to be the greater of either three months' interest or, if rates have fallen, the difference between the current rate and your mortgage rate all the way to the end of the term. For a new $100,000 mortgage at 7.5 percent, that could amount to about $2,500 or more.

Mortgages that can be paid off any time without any penalty, usually called "open" mortgages, do exist. They're only available for three-month to one-year terms and have somewhat higher interest rates (6-month closed— 7.15 percent; 6-month open—7.45 percent). Open mortgages are generally popular with home owners who know they'll be moving soon, anticipate paying off large amounts of principal, or hope that rates will go down and think they can lock in at the bottom.

Variable- versus fixed-rate mortgages (or, how long should you lock in?)

According to Elaine, I then needed to decide on a variable- versus fixed-rate mortgage. The former gives the lowest rate and the best prepayment privileges, and can be converted at any time to a fixed-rate term. These mortgages are very popular with veteran mortgagors who have higher equity in their homes and feel comfortable with a small amount of rate risk.

Variable-rate mortgages offer an interest rate that's immediately subject to fluctuations in the marketplace. A fixed payment schedule, based on a 20-year or 25-year amortization, is drawn up for a specific period, anywhere from one to five years, during which the borrower is committed to regular payments of a predictable amount. The interest rate on variable-rate mortgages may be half a percent lower than for other types, but, like I said, they're instantly subject to change.

While I contemplated what type of mortgage to get, it occurred to me that while the lenders get to sleep better at night, variable-rate mortgages could disrupt my blissful sleep patterns by making it harder for me to know what my future costs will be. If interest rates rise, I may find myself in the not-so-enviable position of my fixed monthly payment being composed entirely of interest with no reduction of the principal. It's conceivable that some of my payments might not cover all the interest due, and that the balance of the interest owing could be added to the outstanding principal. Then I'd end up increasing my liabilities instead of assets. I had to consider carefully what I believed interest rates would do over the next while in order to decide what type of financing to get.

One lender has taken some of the guessing out of the variable-rate mortgage solution. Scotiabank offers an Ultimate Variable Rate mortgage that combines the feature of floating rates, but adds a "cap." Here's how it works. The amount of your mortgage payment is based on the three-year term interest rate. But your interest rate floats relative to the prime rate. If rates drop, more of your payment will go toward paying principal. If rates rise, a Cap Rate Guarantee ensures that your interest rate during the five-year term will never be higher than the three-year mortgage rate at the time the mortgage was booked, so you're protected from sharp increases in interest rates.

Peter the Real Estate Agent says, "Variable- or adjustable-rate mortgages are great in relatively stable interest rate environments like we've enjoyed for the last several years. The benefits are that you get a rate at or below bank prime and that you can lock the rate to a fixed rate at any time. The prepayment privileges are usually much better on variable-rate mortgages than a fixed-rate mortgage. Studies have definitively shown that people who've had faith in the system and used a variable or adjustable mortgage that resets and compounds quarterly are way ahead of the game. The downside is that you have to keep a weather eye on rates, and take a very proactive role in the monthly management of your mortgage. There are chronic effects like inflation, and crisis effects like Quebec separating, that will affect rates. People should be concerned more about the former and less about the latter, which will readjust in time. With Canada's shrinking reliance on foreign money markets, our rates are considerably more stable and a variable mortgage may be a safer bet."

It's not unusual to see banks raise or lower mortgage rates several times in a year. There never seems to be an end to the mortgage shuffle. So what's a home owner to do? If you go short, you run the risk that there'll be more market volatility and rates will go up. But if you lock in for the long run, you run the risk of missing out on lower interest rates.

You know what? You'd go crazy if you tried to predict interest rates. Deciding what to do depends on how much risk you can live with. Plain and simple. There are two ways to go. Go short: a 1998 Bank of Montreal study showed that, historically, it almost always pays to go short term. Or go long: you can get a good night's sleep because you don't have to worry about waking up to discover that Russia is on the verge of another meltdown. The good news? You probably can't go too far wrong either way. The difference between a one- and a five-year mortgage may only be a few hundred dollars in costs. And rates are still extremely low, historically speaking. Remember, in the '80s people financed their homes with double-digit mortgages.

Where can I get mortgage information?

Today, homes are built with just about every convenience—except low payments. With fluctuating interest rates, it's become essential to become an astute shopper and spend some time figuring out where the best deals can be had.

Check the newspapers

Check the local newspaper listings of mortgage rates offered by different lenders. The bank rates are usually almost identical, but smaller institutions such as credit unions and trust companies can offer better deals. If you have a good relationship with your bank and hold other investments there, go in asking for at least a half to three-quarters of a percentage point off the posted rate.

There's always your bank

Talk to loan officers at local branches of trust companies, banks, and credit unions. They can explain the various mortgage types and features available. Even if you don't do business at that institution, ask for a deal. They may be willing to shave points off their advertised rates just to get you as a client. Remember, mortgages are a huge business. You're in the power seat.

Alberta Cefis and Roberta Hague have written a very friendly guide called *The Truth About Mortgages: How to Make the Most of Your Borrowing Power*. This book will equip you with more detail than I'm able to offer on the home buying process, mortgages, and borrowing. It offers guidance, helpful checklists, and commonsense advice on not only how to pay less for your borrowing, but also how to pay down that debt.

Use a mortgage broker

You can try a mortgage broker. Let's assume you've found your dream house. You're about to discover why: it's going to cost twice as much as you dreamed it would—not only the cost of maintaining it, but the cost of financing it. This is where a mortgage broker may come in handy. Today, people are turning to mortgage brokers to act on their behalf just as they rely on real estate agents to help them buy and sell property. A qualified mortgage broker is an intermediary who matches your needs as a borrower with the specialty of a lender. She or he can often negotiate more effectively than the average loan applicant can, especially a first-time home buyer. They deal with the standard lenders such as banks, trust companies, and insurance companies, but they often have access to other sources, such as pension funds, private lenders, foreign banks, and the like. Where mortgage brokers tend to be particularly helpful is in finding people willing to lend money for vacation properties.

But before you even consider this route, get the facts in writing. Find out what fees and deductions are associated with the loan. If you don't qualify for a conventional mortgage, a broker will charge you 1 or 2 percent of the mortgage, but only after finding an acceptable one. And as is the way in everything, there are the good, the bad, and the ugly—so use referrals.

If a broker saves you even a half a percentage point in your mortgage rate, it can be worth it. Such a saving can have a big impact on your monthly or weekly payment. And you know the old expression: There's no place like home, especially if you haven't any money to go out.

The Internet

Finally, surf the Net. Some sites offer one-stop mortgage shopping, including preapproval applications from lenders. Browse through the major lenders' own Web pages, which are an excellent source of information. Try www.scotia-bank.com or www.royalbank.com. Their mortgage websites offer helpful calculators and preapproval capabilities. Check out www.themortgage.com and www.imoney.com, which have interactive worksheets that let you compare the deals offered by different lenders. They'll help you figure out how much you can afford to pay for a house, how much your payments will be at different rates, and how long it will take you to pay down the mortgage.

Then there are websites like Royal LePage's, which has a virtual reality tour of selected homes feature that enables you to explore listings in full colour. A slowly rotating image of the neighbourhood will give you a sense of the area and surrounding homes. Rather than driving around with a sales agent, you can get an idea of what's out there from the website, a sort of 24-hour open house. The beauty of most real estate websites is that you can customize your search. You can pick the area, price range, and type of home, and quickly get an idea of what's available. Such sites also usually give you a sense of the local amenities and proximity to schools and synagogues or churches.

When my friend Rekka was looking for an apartment to rent, she discovered that they're usually open from 9 a.m. to 5 p.m. for viewing—just when she's busy making a living. So Rekka turned to the Net, and by typing in the keywords "apartment" and "Toronto," she found a listing of apartment buildings available in that area for rent. There's a growing number of renters and buyers turning to the World Wide Web to find accommodation.

There are websites specifically for renters, like www.rentcanada.com, which covers 21 cities in Canada. (If you're going to do this, get a high-speed modem, since many of the listings include photos that could be frustrating to download using a slower modem.) Another problem with Internet shopping is that not all websites list all buildings. Supplement your search with available newspapers and other media.

Using the Internet is obviously not a substitute for going out and seeing the real thing, but it can whittle down your search. As the old saying goes, technology will never replace human beings. Someone has to complain about the errors.

Deciding on a lender

They say that cyclists race faster against each other than they do against a clock. Banks are proving this adage to be true. Competition is stiff, especially for first-time home buyers.

Over the last few years, banks have been getting into more innovative solutions for borrowers. One example is the Scotia Total Equity Plan that uses your home equity to lower your overall cost of borrowing. You can put your mortgage account, line of credit, car loan, and even a credit card together under one borrowing plan with a one-time application. It's an interesting concept that offers credit for life, when you need it, how you need it, without ever having to ask again. So when you need a new roof and a new car in the same year that your oldest child is setting out for university, having access to borrowing options with the lowest interest rate available can offer peace of mind.

RBC Financial Group's Yes, You Can mortgage pays a cash startup bonus of 1 percent of your principal mortgage amount, up to a maximum of $1,500 after closing.

CIBC wants to help new buyers celebrate buying their home by getting away from it. Their AeroMortgage allows home buyers to collect Aeroplan miles for free flights just by paying regular mortgage interest. You get one Aeroplan mile for every dollar you pay. That's in addition to a sign-up bonus of 5,000 Aeroplan miles. In roughly one and a half years, the average home owner could earn enough for a short-haul flight, from, say, Toronto to New York. The bank also offers a similar program involving HBC Rewards points, which can be redeemed for merchandise at several stores, including Zellers. At the Bank of Montreal, home buyers can also earn up to 500 air miles when they take out a mortgage.

You need to take some time to think about the situation you're in and what product or promotion suits your needs. Be firm with your budget limit, because you can get carried away and end up in a bidding war. Shop around for the best rates, however, not the best bonuses. Remember, money is a wonderful thing, but it's possible to pay too high a price for it.

Then, once you've found your lender, don't be afraid to negotiate. The first step is to understand that posted mortgage rates are simply starting points for negotiations. If negotiating makes your heart race and palms sweat, think about this. If you negotiated 0.75 percent off your 7 percent rate with a 25-year amortization in November 1998, you'd have saved $50 a month and a cool $16,000 over the course of your mortgage term.

So how do you become a master negotiator? Just walking into a lender's office and asking for the best rate is often enough to get a discount over the advertised one. And if you bring other business with you to sweeten the pot, your chances improve even more dramatically. If money walks, money talks. This doesn't mean playing hardball necessarily. Just point out how valuable you are to the financial institution. Sell yourself by mentioning the savings accounts, loans, and RRSPs you have with the lender. If they're with someone else, say that you're willing to move them in exchange for a discounted rate. And be prepared to do so. Signing up for a new financial product and discussing your future requirements won't hurt either.

Play one vendor off the other to get the best deal. If you have a higher-than-market mortgage that expires soon, try to renew it before the term is actually up. Tell the lender you'll move your mortgage when it comes due if it won't let you renew early to take advantage of today's low rates. Most financial institutions will let you do so—and waive the fee, typically $100, if you ask. Don't be afraid to ask for the moon. The worst that could happen is "no."

RRSP Home Buyers Plan

Royal LePage Real Estate Services did a study that showed that first-time buyers are fuelling the residential market, accounting for almost half of sales in some cities. The RRSP Home Buyers Plan, low interest rates, and changes in rules about down payments are cited as the major reasons.

This plan allows first-time home buyers to withdraw up to $20,000 tax free from their RRSP and pay it back in installments over 15 years. If you default on the payments, the amount you borrowed becomes taxable as income that year. You're considered a first-time home buyer if neither you nor your spouse owned a home and lived in it as your principal place of residence in any of the five calendar years before the time of withdrawal. You can participate in this program only once. You're able to make a tax-deductible RRSP contribution up to 90 days before the money is withdrawn. Incidentally, there's also a break on the Land Transfer Tax for first-time buyers, which can save you up to $1,500.

My friends Irene and Dejan Ilic lived in a tiny two-bedroom apartment in downtown Toronto. One bedroom was used as an office for Irene, who was a self-employed voice teacher. When Irene announced to Dejan that she was pregnant, they felt a combination of joy and panic because they had no space for the baby. Had it not been for the RRSP Home Buyers Plan, they wouldn't have been able to buy the lovely townhouse they now happily share in Newmarket. This is the practical or human side of the plan. It sounds ideal, but it's far from it.

Let me throw up some red flags here. The plan can do some real damage to your retirement savings. From a purely technical point of view, it should be avoided. This is why:

• It can lure people into a market that, from an investment standpoint, has uncertain prospects.

- The repayments you make aren't tax deductible. If you skip one, the money is deemed an RRSP withdrawal and becomes taxable.
- The money isn't free. You give up the interest you would have earned in the RRSP as well as the future growth. If you take 15 years to pay it back, your withdrawal could be far more expensive than any conventional mortgage.
- If you can't make an RRSP contribution in a given year because of your repayment, the cost gets higher still. You not only lose a valued tax deduction, but years of compounded growth.

Like many financial advisors, I'm wary about this plan, if for no other reason than that it's hard enough for people to save for their retirement without an additional incentive to deviate from their RRSP's original intent. That is, of course, unless you plan on using your home as part of your retirement savings program. In fact, part of the rationale behind the federal government's decision to continue this plan was its recognition that owning a home is often a form of saving for retirement. However, a proper retirement portfolio should be diversified. It's also going to be difficult, if not impossible, for most people to make mortgage payments, maximize their RRSP contributions each year, and pay back the required annual installments from the RRSP loan.

The Bank of Montreal's Private Client Services did a study that concluded that RRSP withdrawal would be okay if your mortgage wouldn't be paid off by retirement anyway, or if your mortgage rate was higher than your RRSP growth rate. It wasn't worthwhile if your mortgage rate is similar to or lower than the RRSP growth rate and you planned to pay off your mortgage before you retire, since you wouldn't be able to access the investments that are earning high rates of return. Real estate isn't appreciating that fast these days.

The decision to use the RRSP Home Buyers Plan should be carefully weighed. In Irene and Dejan's case, there was no option. In the long term though, it can have a serious financial downside. But financial decisions aren't always about money. Lifestyle, philosophy, and personal contentment are of equal value. Whatever your decision, whether it be to have a fully-paid-for home, a bulging RRSP, or to use retirement savings to acquire your quantum of solace, if it's an informed decision and you sleep well at night, be happy with it.

To buy, or not to buy?

I always heard my mother's voice in my head every time I moved. "Put your money in bricks and mortar, Joanne, it's safe." But every time, I'd rent. (And like me, every renter has lived to tell a landlord story. I once went through hell when I inadvertently rented a house from "Hildegard the Horror." And now, for example, Ontario's new Tenant Protection Act actually swings the pendulum back toward the landlord's favour; among other things, it permits a landlord to sell a defaulting tenant's property.)

Nonetheless, my mom's advice, which can be sound given today's low interest rates, stills needs a balancing viewpoint. You can't ignore the sobering new reality that's beginning to infuse the minds of real estate hungry Canadians, who once believed that a home is one of the safest places to put your money. So what's been happening to create this monumental shift in attitude toward home buying? Let's look at yesterday's conventional wisdom (CW) and compare it to life today.

CW Then: Buying a home is an excellent investment with secure, long-term growth potential.

CW Now: For many reasons, the days of the standard 10 percent average long-term rate of return for most investments, even your home, are gone. The value of the investment can't be disputed when you actually own most or all of it. (It takes about 10 years before the cost of owning a home begins to compete with the cost of renting it. After 10 years you're earning principal on your home, and you've also paid off the initial costs, such as legal and moving fees.) But until you can actually burn your mortgage papers, there's risk involved. In today's world of 5 percent down, your home becomes a highly leveraged asset, and a drop of 10 percent in the market can have a serious impact. There's no shortage of home owners whose mortgage value is higher than their home value, especially in recessionary times. The correlation between inflation and the housing market is strong. In a good market, people have a measure of job security and feel confident that their wages will increase—as was the case in the thriving '80s. But inflation was also hitting double digits and, today, the worldwide effort to keep inflation low means that continued increases in wages are unlikely. And I needn't spend much time on the issue of job security. Housing markets vary from place to place as well, as Elaine and I talked about at the beginning of this chapter. So if you're looking at housing as a pure investment vehicle, it may make more sense to rent and put your money in the stock market. Choosing long-term financial investments such as the market instead of prepaying a mortgage may offer better returns than putting that same money into your house.

On the other hand, if you do buy, be sure to have an investor's eye. Many purchasers are now once again considering investment potential in their choice of what and where to buy. For example, in the late '80s, when one area appreciated the rest of the Greater Toronto Area went up as well. But now home buyers are being very selective about where they want to live, and they're willing to pay a premium for that choice. In Toronto's Beach, Forest Hill, and Riverdale areas prices have gone through the roof, whereas Scarborough and Vaughan haven't gone up at all.

Moreover, equity in your home can be tapped in the future through a variety of means, usually through a secured line of credit or equity takeout refinancing (e.g., home owners financing swimming pools, and older home owners obtaining reverse mortgages). Remember, one of the first questions you're asked when applying for new credit is "Do you own your own home?"

CW Then: It's the old supply and demand scenario. The peak of the boomers are people born around 1956 to 1958. Think of the proverbial pig moving through python analogy, which graphically describes the powerful consumer effect the boomers have on society. Scads of houses were built to accommodate this huge blip in population.

CW Now: Baby boomers are now becoming grey-be boomers (groan). Most already own homes, and as these people age they're becoming more interested in acquiring other kinds of assets. That population blip is now into the retirement planning phase of life. Moreover, boomers' kids (and there are fewer of them than their parents) still gotta grow up before they buy houses. Bottom line? Fewer houses are being bought, which negatively affects the market.

CW Then: Chances were good that we were born, went to school, worked, got married, quit, raised our families, doted on grandchildren, and were buried, all in the same town. We stayed in the same home or at least the same geographic location for much longer periods of time. We didn't run nearly as much risk of having to sell our home in a down market.

CW Now: I was born in Montreal, educated in Halifax, and worked in Ottawa, Toronto, and Vancouver. I don't even want to hazard a guess where I'll be spoiling my grandchildren. We've become a very transient bunch these days. The point is that if you move a lot, you're opening yourself to a potentially greater risk of hitting a downturn when you have to sell your home.

CW Then: Renting is throwing money away, since you're not building up any capital.

CW Now: Buying isn't an option for everyone. People have less money to spend, less job security, and fewer jobs, period. Not that long ago, it was often cheaper to rent, at least in the short run. In 1998, the average starter home cost $182,000. That house with 5 percent down would have cost about $1,500 to carry every month. You'd probably be able to rent that same home for about $1,300.

However, using today's lower interest rates and CMHC lower premiums, and considering higher rental averages, a mortgage today based on 95 percent of $182,000 multiplied by 3.25 percent would put payments at about $1,000 a month. You probably can't rent that same home for less than $1,500 a month, but obviously that depends on the market. And this may not always be the case.

Here's something else to think about as well: the difference in rent between a four-bedroom executive home and a three-bedroom townhouse could be only a couple of hundred dollars, while the difference in buying price could be $100,000 or more. (Mind you, there's some evidence that it's becoming increasingly difficult to find affordable, quality rental properties. So, you certainly have far less choice in the type of home you'll live in when you decide to rent rather than buy. You almost have to buy by default due to the lack of rental vacancy. As well, if you live farther away from the metropolitan area, you may even have to pay more in rent each month than you would in mortgage payments.)

It isn't always the case, but your monthly rent could be lower than your mortgage payment would be, and you don't have to pay homeowner-type expenses like taxes and major repairs. If you rent, you may find yourself with extra cash on hand. As Elaine and I discussed earlier in the chapter, if you invest this loot in a solidly producing mutual fund, for example, you might find yourself ahead of the home owner. Again, the key here is to develop the savvy and discipline to invest and not spend the difference. Try a preauthorized chequing plan that will automatically take the money out of your account (read: hands) each month.

CW Then: Your home is your only tax-free investment. If there's a gain in value, you don't have to pay tax on it.

CW Now: Thankfully, this is still true. But remember, you have to sell the house in order to capitalize on this. This is the upside to home ownership. Experts warn, however, never to let the tax tail wag the dog. Don't buy a house solely for the tax status. It's also likely the largest amount of money you'll ever borrow. You had better be sure all the other variables—like the ability to afford it and knowing exactly what you want, now and later—fall into place.

CW Then: It's the queen of forced savings vehicles.

CW Now: This still holds true, but don't make yourself completely cash poor in an effort to pay down your mortgage as quickly as possible. You can, however, borrow against the equity that has built up in the house, if there is any. And remember that renting can give you a certain flexibility to invest in a diverse range of products, not just your house.

William Shakespeare said that people are usually happiest at home. But he didn't say whether happiness depended on whether your home was rented or bought. Whether to rent or buy is such a personal decision that it's really up to the individual. Some people are very happy to rent because they don't need the hassle of repairing roofs. Others value pride of ownership.

If we all lived in crummy $300 basement apartments and invested the money we saved by doing so our whole life, we'd be rich when we retire. But what a lousy quality of life. So, buy if it's for the right reasons: for your quantum of solace, for a place where you can send down roots, raise bambinos, take personal and loving pride in ownership, and feel a permanent part of a community.

The best advice is to keep an open mind about both options. And if you still want to buy—after you've carefully weighed the pros and cons based on the reality of your lifestyle, not Uncle Gus's—then take the plunge. Remember, at the end of the day it's happiness and contentment inside the bricks and mortar that really count, not the rate of return.

Women and real estate

Let me repeat the Statistics Canada data cited at the beginning of this chapter: "the number of women who live alone—without children, relatives, friends, or partners—in a home they own almost doubled to 612,640 from 314,610 during 1981 to 1996, 200,000 more than their male counterparts." The number of single women aged 24 to 39 who own their own home increased 136 percent during the same time, the largest increase of any age group. Experts predict that number will continue to grow, especially if vacancies and mortgage rates remain low.

Traditionally, women have become home owners through inheritance or divorce settlements. According to StatsCan data, women above the age of 65 make up almost half of the total number of women across Canada living alone in a house they own. However, today women are no longer waiting for their knights in shining armour to come into their lives, bringing along a castle. Damned if they aren't going out and buying their own, especially condo lofts, town homes, and semi-detached houses.

And while more single women are buying homes than in the past, women who are single parents still have the lowest home ownership rates of all groups, primarily because of their low income levels. The overall trend, however, is heartening.

During my education in real estate jargon and the mortgage preapproval process, something happened that changed the course of my life. I was participating in a financial trade show in Toronto. As I stood in the booth kibbitzing with the other exhibitors, I was approached by an intense, yet good-humoured young man. He passed me his business card and asked if I'd join him for a coffee. As we walked toward the cafeteria, I looked at his card. He worked for a well-established Canadian publishing company. "What could he possibly want with me?" I wondered as we sat down. I was soon to find out. "Joanne," he began, "have you ever considered writing a book on personal finance for Canadian women?"

The rest, as they say, is history. I didn't end up buying a house after all. In fact, my down payment and the publisher's advance supported me during the year it took to write this book. My RRSP was still intact and I had the experience of publishing a book as a major accomplishment under my belt. One thing is for sure, though. Buying a house is a state of mind. As I got older, the desire to nest grew stronger and the urge to have my own quantum of solace was becoming quite pronounced. I'd have to play catch-up, but the goal of owning a home was firmly in place. Besides, who really needs to go to Bora Bora on 24 hours' notice?

eight

The gender tax

*David Liu, a Chinese-born Canadian, walks into a
downtown Toronto hair salon. The stylist is ringing
through the charge for Patrick White's haircut.
Mr. White is a Caucasian with straight, short hair,
which took about half an hour to cut and blow-dry. He
is charged $30. Mr. Liu steps into the stylist's chair. His
hair, straight and short, also takes about half an hour to
get cut and blow-dried. When the stylist finishes, he
tells Mr. Liu, "Let's see. You're of Southeast Asian
origin. I guess that'll be 45 dollars." Unimaginable?
Perhaps. But a huge number of salons charge another
group of people based solely on a similarly irrelevant
characteristic. That characteristic is gender. And pricing
policies based on gender are not limited to hair salons.*

AARON FREEMAN, "THE HUMAN RIGHTS LAW IMPLICATIONS OF
GENDER-BASED PRICING"

One day I was sitting hunched over my desk, completely immersed in some
mindless paperwork. All of a sudden the door to my office burst open. Red-
faced and actually huffing, Elaine threw herself in one of the empty chairs, her
purse narrowly missing another.

"I am so thoroughly pissed off," she announced.

Not saying anything, I looked at her with an amazed expression that
suggested, "Do tell!?"

Not needing any prodding to continue, she launched into a tirade. "As if it isn't hard enough to find the money to do all the things we're told to do in order to become financially independent. You wonder where all this money is supposed to come from that we're to be saving/investing. We constantly hear the drill about bringing our lunch, washing our own cars, ironing our own clothes, cleaning our own homes, quitting smoking/drinking/dancing the night hours away, and so on."

Still not having a clue where Elaine was heading, I was unable to resist. "Uh, Elaine, these ideas have merit, since it's hard to overspend in a convent."

Like a woman possessed, she railed on. "Very few women can realistically give up time-saving services. Women frequently depend on outside help because of their already heavy workloads. If I hear one more time how essential it is to cut out financial waste when I've discovered what I've just discovered, I'll have to kill someone."

"I always thought cutting out the 'unnecessities of life' was an admirable place to start," I ventured. "Of course, then there are those who don't have much wiggle room in their budgets. I suspect their choices are few." Sensing that Elaine was about to enlighten me, I added, "Or are they?"

With a heavy sigh, Elaine recounted her story. "I was Christmas shopping for my siblings. I found the most fabulous sweater for my brother in men's wear at a department store. I wandered over to ladies' wear to see what I could rustle up for my sister. Lo and behold, didn't I see the identical designer wool sweater. I picked it up to be sure and I had to shake my head because I figured I was seeing things. I took out my brother's sweater that I had just bought and put it side by side with this one. They were exactly the same, with one small exception. The price tag on my brother's sweater was $94.95. The same one in ladies' wear was $145. What the hell is that?!"

"That's the gender tax, Elaine," I said quietly.

"The what?" she barked.

"You may be interested to know that *The Washington Post* went undercover and exposed the exact same situation with women's and men's clothing that you just stumbled on. This is something that I've been fighting for years. Let me explain how this gender tax works. We all know that the price advertised is rarely the actual price we pay. Most things have the GST added, some just the PST, and the majority of goods and services have both. When you buy a book off the Internet or sports gear from a catalogue, count on shipping and handling fees. Then there are those beloved 'sin' taxes on gas, alcohol, and cigarettes. Import taxes are levied occasionally, and certain products may carry special fees. We as Canadians are simply resigned to this immutable law of pricing. We're used to the disparity between advertised prices and what we end up really forking over. But what most of us may not know is that another 'tax' has been added to the price, for no other reason than the purchaser is a woman. The gender tax is the extra amount women pay for certain products and services, including everything from deodorant and cars to dry cleaning. This pricing system is based on some pretty lame stereotypes about female intelligence and the female body."

Here are some of my personal favourites:

- Styling a woman's hair is more work than styling a man's.
- Women don't understand complicated mechanics or technology.
- Women come in different shapes and sizes but men are one-size-fits-all.
- Women are poor negotiators.
- Women's physical appearance is so essential to their well-being and station in life that they're prepared to pay far more money than men for anything that will make them look more attractive or appear thinner.

"Marketers milk that last one for all it's worth," Elaine muttered.

"While some of these stereotypes may have once had some basis in truth, like for instance, my grandmother's elaborate bouffant certainly took more time than my grandfather's crew cut, most of them are now profoundly outdated. Considering the extraordinary consumer power that women yield today, I'm always dumbfounded by how the purveyors of these goods and services can be so blatant and so cavalier when subscribing to gender-based pricing. It's as though they believe women have the collective intelligence of a shoelace.

"Even more disturbing is how few women, or men for that matter, are even aware that women pay more for a vast array of products and services. I, for one, refuse to pay more. I'll boycott the establishment and tell everyone I know about their discriminatory practices. I turn into their worst nightmare."

"We've got to radicalize, Joanne. We gotta do something," Elaine sputtered. Pausing for a moment she added, "Uh, what *can* we do?"

"At least take your coat off. Let me walk you through what I know about the problem so far." I put my pen down and stood up.

How odd. Elaine was the seminal teacher and now the roles were reversed. Don't think for a second I wasn't loving this. It was too bad, however, that the topic was so infuriating.

A sampling of gender-based pricing

The following is but a tiny sample of the thousands of Canadian and American stories and studies I've collected over the years on the various forms of gender-based pricing.

- Shaughnessy Cohen was Canada's much-loved Member of Parliament for Windsor/St. Clair in Ontario, vice-chair of the Federal Liberal Women's Caucus, and a criminal lawyer by trade. Before her untimely death, she shared this story with me. "I took on a dry cleaners a few years back when I discovered I was paying 'women's pricing' to have my court shirts cleaned. What made this so ironic was that court shirts only came in men's sizes. My male counterparts were charged 80 cents to have their court shirts cleaned and I was being charged $2.50. Even after I explained this to the cleaners, they still refused to lower the price. I rectified the situation by giving my shirts to a male colleague who took them in with his shirts. I looked high and low, and finally found a cleaner that didn't subscribe to gender-based pricing."

- I was witness to a "sting" done by CBC that sent a man and a woman into a Vancouver dry cleaners with the identical cotton shirt. Both were wearing a hidden microphone. The man was told it would cost $5.00 to have his shirt cleaned. Three minutes later the woman went in with the same shirt. She was told it would cost her $6.50.

- California's Assembly Office of Research found that 64 percent of laundries surveyed in that state charged more to clean a woman's white cotton shirt than a man's. Women can pay nearly 30 percent more than men for the identical service, which includes laundering and pressing a basic white cotton shirt. An average of 3 suits and 10 shirts cleaned per month results in an average increased cost of $77.52 or 17 percent over the course of a year. One establishment surveyed actually charged women double for the identical service offered to men.[1] Similar studies in New York, Boston, and Washington, D.C., turned up the exact same results.

- The New York City Department of Consumer Affairs found that two out of three hair stylists charge women 25 percent more than they charge men for a shampoo, cut, and blow-dry. In a survey of 80 haircutting establishments, two out of three charged women more than they did men.[2] Again, surveys in California and Washington found the same.

- City TV in Toronto did a story on the gender tax in hair salons. What struck me about this one was the complete lack of awareness exhibited by the person interviewed. The manager of one high-priced Yorkville establishment was asked how much it cost to cut men's hair. He replied, "$60." When asked about women's hair, without an ounce of hesitation he answered, "$120." When asked why it was twice as much, the manager shrugged his shoulders dismissively, smiled smugly at the reporter, and said in an unmistakably sarcastic tone, "Be damned if I know."

- Victoria, B.C.–based writer and researcher Marianne Scott realized that women can pay up to 50 percent more for deodorant. After noticing that her local drugstore offered 11 different scents of Lady Speed Stick at 50 grams and 15 different Mennen Speed Sticks for men at 75 grams, both priced at $2.99, she felt compelled to call Colgate-Palmolive Canada in Toronto to ask why women were getting one-third less than men. "The representative said the wholesale costs of women's deodorant are somewhat higher because the fragrances used are more expensive. (I do wonder, though, how much more 'Country Fresh' for women costs than 'Fresh Surf' for men.) I asked about the unscented version. That product, said the spokeswoman, is 'price-equalized' with the scented versions. She then stated that Colgate-Palmolive reduces the size of the 'ergonomically designed' Lady Speed Stick because women use less deodorant (men's armpits are larger and have more hair). She added that men and women thus use up the deodorant at roughly the same rate, so we get equal treatment!"

- According to Aaron Freeman, a former advisor to consumer advocate Ralph Nader, "Canadians spend more than $700 million on fragrances, a market dominated by women. Women are paying 32 percent more for these products, or, said another way, women are being taxed more than $100 million in this sector."[3]

- A survey of three major department stores, Nordstrom's, Macy's, and Weinstock's, found that all three hem men's pants for free but charge women $10 to $14 for the same alterations. At Nordstrom's, the alterations on men's suits are free, unless there's a jacket vent. Women will pay anywhere from $10 to $50 to have alterations on any suit. Two women sued Saks Fifth Avenue for their gender-based alteration policy and won.[4]

- A *Harvard Law Review* article told of researchers posing as car buyers at Chicago-area car dealers. This study was done by Chicago's Northwestern University in conjunction with the American Bar Association. In 165 visits, the dealers made as much as 37 percent more profit from women buyers. The Chicago study, which also examined how African-Americans were charged more than white people for new cars, found that white women paid a 40 percent higher markup than white men; African-American men paid twice as much markup as white men; and African-American women paid three times as much markup as white men. All buyers in the study were college educated, professionally dressed, followed the same script, and used the same bargaining techniques and body language. The women were quoted a higher price when bargaining began. One possible explanation is that the dealers, supporting the stereotype of women being ignorant about cars, set their initial, prebargaining prices higher than they would have for men, assuming women wouldn't know any better. The women, who did and often do know better, could only bargain the dealer down a certain amount from that initial price.[5] Studies in New York and Washington yielded the same results.

- The California Assembly Committee on Consumer Protection held an interim hearing on Gender Discrimination in the Pricing and Availability of Products and Services. Data collected in conjunction with the hearing documented that adult women effectively pay a gender tax of $1,351 annually, or about $15 billion for all women in California.[6]

Sadly, Canada seriously lags behind the United States when it comes to research and policy in the area of gender-based pricing. Most of the Canadian data is anecdotal, but real nevertheless.

In 1995 BCTV did a piece on gender-based pricing using one of my associates at The Thomas Yaccato Group in Vancouver. During the piece our representative announced that there was a petition available and gave out her home phone number on the air. Within three hours she'd been flooded with over 150 phone calls from people wanting copies of the petition. She called me in a total panic, claiming jokingly that her husband was threatening to leave her if the damned phone didn't stop ringing.

Research proves it. Women in North America pay anywhere from 30 percent to 50 percent more for goods and services like haircuts, alterations, cars, cosmetics, contracting services, and dry cleaning. According to Robert Kerton, an economist at the University of Waterloo, price discrimination exists in the marketplace "any time you can get more from one group than another, whether it's based on their wealth, or their degree of information, or their urgency. The question becomes, 'When you raise the price, does the person pay it or leave?' It depends on the priority the person places on the item, how important it is to them."[7] And according to one retail industry analyst, "We've been conditioned to the fact that that's the way the market has always operated [with men paying less for a haircut]. Until you have people asking the difficult questions, you won't see any change."[8]

The gender tax makes me see red and I am not alone. A few years ago I received a phone call from Aaron Freeman, one of "Nader's Raiders," as the employees of Ralph Nader's Center of Responsive Law in Washington, D.C., are sometimes called. He was Nader's associate editor of *The Multinational Monitor* and had worked on a book about the gender tax called *Why Women Pay More* by Frances Cerra Whittlesley. Aaron had heard about the work we were doing and wanted to know if he could help. So he and I collaborated on several initiatives. We did a survey of hair salons in four cities to see how prevalent gender-based pricing was in Canada (see the table on page 272).

Aaron used gender-based pricing as the basis of his study while attending law school at University of Ottawa. In his research paper "The Human Rights

Law Implications of Gender-Based Pricing," he writes, "Gender-based pricing certainly falls within the legal definition of discrimination, and the practice is completely inconsistent with contemporary attitudes regarding gender and equality. Compare gender-based pricing to more frequently complained of forms of sex discrimination, for instance, denials of job opportunities, or equal pay for equal work. For an individual woman, the denial of a job opportunity or a fair wage may have a greater economic and social impact than being nickelled and dimed by retailers. However, each nickel and dime, spread out across 52 percent of the population, has perhaps an even greater impact in the aggregate. Canadian women spend nearly $2.5 billion on hair services each year, and women comprise more than two-thirds of this market. If, as the evidence suggests, women are paying between 16 percent and 45 percent more than men for this service, gender-based pricing is costing women up to $750 million annually, and that's just for haircuts. And of course, women pay again in many other sectors where gender-based pricing has been shown to exist—new and used cars, dry cleaning, alterations, clothing, and others. When these sectors are considered, the overall tab for the gender tax in Canada is surely in the billions of dollars."

Getting scalped: hairstyling

The purported reasons for gender-based pricing are wide and varied. One of the worst culprits, the hairdressing industry, claims that women are fussier, take longer, and use more hair products. It's an odd claim, considering women aren't asked if they want these products used on their hair and a large contingent have very simple cuts that take no more than 20 to 30 minutes. As for being fussier, this definition is typically and conveniently the stylist's, not the client's. Men can be as fussy as some women. Women can be as "unfussy" as some men. Men can take 20 minutes or longer for a cut, have it done by the very same hairstylist, may even use the same hair products, and still pay up to 50 percent less. This industry has continued to perpetuate a standard that is nothing short of ancient, while continuing to allege that all women take longer and therefore must be charged more. Men also have the low-cost option of barbers, most of whom won't cut women's hair.

Aaron and I enlisted the support of friends and colleagues to help us with random surveys that were conducted in Toronto, Montreal, Saskatoon, and Vancouver. Lists of hair salons were taken from the Yellow Pages in each city, and each salon was either called (in Montreal, Saskatoon, and Vancouver surveys) or visited in person (Toronto survey). In each instance, the salon was asked how much the top stylist charges for a basic wash, cut, and style for someone with short hair. They were then asked for the price of a cut of identical specifications for someone of the opposite sex. Establishments advertised as "barber" were excluded, since such establishments tend to cater only to men. If a hair salon was closed, had moved, or had gone out of business, no attempt was made to track down or revisit the salon.

Gender-Based Pricing in Hair Salons

	Saskatoon	Vancouver	Toronto	Montreal
Number of Salons Surveyed	45	29	99	70
Percentage of Salons Charging GBP	76%	55%	84%	79%
Percentage More That GBP Salons Charged	35%	29%	54%	55%
Overall Average GBP	27%	16%	45%	43%

SOURCE: AARON FREEMAN. "THE HUMAN RIGHTS LAW IMPLICATIONS OF GENDER-BASED PRICING," 1998.

While the numbers vary from city to city, the results clearly indicate that gender-based pricing is widespread. Women are charged more by a clear majority of salons in each city, and by more than three-quarters in three of the four cities. At these establishments women pay an average of between 29 percent (Vancouver) and more than 50 percent (Toronto and Montreal) more than men.

Moreover, while you might think gender-based pricing would be more prevalent among more expensive salons, the raw data indicate only a slight rise at the higher end of the market. Of the 19 salons surveyed in Toronto's expensive Yorkville neighbourhood, 89 percent used gender-based pricing, with women being charged an overall average of 48 percent more (comparable to Toronto's overall averages of 84 percent and 45 percent, respectively).

Lorenzo Morra, current president of the Hairdressers' Guild, charges $40 for women and $20 to $25 for men, but said he'd make an exception for a woman who takes less time, or a man who takes longer. "Prices are based on gender because women take longer," he asserted. "In some situations it's not fair, but unfortunately, they generalize it."[9]

I recently went back to a hairdresser I used to go to years ago, Alan Davis, who has a shop (aptly named the Alan Davis Salon) in Toronto's thriving Greek community of Riverdale. As we were catching up, I let him know that I was the culprit behind the grief the hairdressing industry was getting of late. Fascinated, he started, with some trepidation, down the usual road of "women take longer, they're fussier" and so on. As he was talking, he broke into a big grin and said, "That is such bull! I've embarrassed myself with the drivel that just came out of my own mouth. The real reason women pay more is because men won't." He was almost talking to himself, saying that men had gone to barbers until the '60s, when beauty salons went unisex. In order to capture the men's market, unisex salons kept the price of men's cuts as close to barber levels as possible, and no one's bothered to equalize the prices since. I could have jumped out of my chair to hug him. Since the controversy had been raging, he'd been toying with the idea of eliminating gender-based pricing in his own salon. All of a sudden he felt greatly motivated. Since he owned the salon, he set the standard. He and I and a third hairdresser who worked there figured out a price schedule that was fair and equitable not only to the client, but to the hairdresser as well. One stylist's clientele was three-quarters male and she was charging them $15 less than she was her female customers. She split the difference between both genders: men paid $7.50 more, women $7.50 less. Alan was the senior stylist and had an established clientele composed primarily of women. He bumped men up to the women's level of pricing, easily justifying the move by pointing out that most of them took as much time as women did. Alan then put together copy for a sign to put in the front window of the store announcing the fairer system and the elimination of gender-based pricing. Besides knowing in his heart that it was the right thing to do, this business person saw dollar signs. Very smart man.

Perhaps the main reason why gender-based pricing is so prevalent in the hairstyling industry is the lack of consumer awareness. Even those who charge gender-based pricing implicitly recognize this. As Lorenzo Morra stated, "Our clientele is steady. They come because of our service. They don't ask questions. They're satisfied. They don't complain."[10]

Isn't it time this industry charged according to the time the service takes and eliminated the gender category entirely? If what they say is true, a time-based price structure will have no impact on their profits. Women who take longer to have their hair done will continue to pay more, but so will men. Men and women, like me, who zip in and out in 20 minutes, will pay the same. Though seemingly simple and fair, the problem with this approach is this: men won't pay the higher prices. The industry knows this, so gender-based pricing continues.

Getting taken to the cleaners: dry cleaning

Back to the day when Elaine had burst into my office. We'd moved onto the topic of the price of dry cleaning and found ourselves examining our suit jackets.

"Elaine, did you know the dry-cleaning industry is also a huge proponent of gender-based pricing? The arguments for it would be funny if they weren't so pathetic. For example, we're told that it costs more to dry-clean women's clothes because they come in widely varying shapes and sizes (and men's clothes don't?) and their buttons are on the opposite side from those of men (?!). Also, women's blouses are too small to fit the presses that are designed to accommodate only men's size clothing. Therefore, women's garments must be hand-pressed.

"My Aunt Margaret is bountifully blessed. There's lots of her to hug. One lunch with me equipped her with a new awareness that she drew upon when picking up her size 18 blouse at the cleaners. It was plain, boasting no frills or shoulder pads, yet she was charged 'women's pricing.' When she questioned this the dry cleaner gave her the typical argument that women's clothes are too small to fit on the 'buck' (the piece of equipment that clothes sit on in order to get cleaned and pressed) and therefore need to be hand-done. She was incensed. 'I'm larger than half the men I know,' she shot back. 'Some men's shirts are also too small, or occasionally even too big, to fit the machine, but men are rarely charged this extra fee. There's no way that my blouse doesn't easily fit on that silly buck.' She refused to pay women's pricing; the store finally relented and charged her the more reasonable men's pricing. Aunt Margaret's point to the cleaner: It's the detail and what the shirt's made of that should determine the price, not who wears it."

"So why hasn't an expandable press been designed to accommodate a mere 52 percent of the population?" Elaine asked. "It's even more odd when you consider that women make up 45 percent of middle management in corporate Canada. In fact, Canada boasts the highest number of women in management in the industrialized world. That's a lot of dry cleaning."

"You're dead-on right," I concurred. "Nobody's saying that women shouldn't pay extra for special dry-cleaning needs—delicate fabrics, ruffles and pleats, buttons and bows—but why should our plain, tailored garments cost more than men's? Many women are beginning to refuse to pay more just because the dry-cleaning industry hasn't seen fit to accommodate women's clothing in their press technology."

Dollars and scents: cosmetic fragrances

As part of Aaron's thesis he did a survey of the cosmetic fragrances industry. Products were chosen at random from the fragrance counter at major department stores, The Body Shop, Avon, and Mary Kay Cosmetics. Wherever possible, the survey compared the same type of fragrance (cologne, eau de toilette, etc.) for each of the men's and women's products. His conclusion?

Women pay an overall average of 32 percent more than men.

Aaron writes, "A majority of fragrances do not come in both a men's and women's version. Most carry separate men's and women's brand names. While this is less of a direct, 'apples to apples' comparison, it does show that, even when one looks at all the products of a particular brand name, gender-based pricing is still the rule. All brands surveyed showed some gender-based pricing, with the highest brand charging 140 percent more for its women's products.

"A spokesperson for Giorgio of Beverly Hills stated that the company's products are 'priced to the market.' The factors in pricing include research, technology, marketing, and ingredients. In addition, the packaging may be more expensive (for instance, women's fragrances tend to come in a crystal bottle, whereas the men's line comes in a regular glass bottle). In addition, she said, 'Women tend to look at the product differently.'

"This is undoubtedly true to some degree. When speaking of a men's brand and a women's brand of fragrance, one is dealing with two products of different composition, and the producer may always argue that they are pricing not based on gender, but on product. (And in this sense, the case against fragrance manufacturers is not as strong as the case against hairstylists.) But at the same time, one must ask to what extent gender-based pricing in the fragrance market is driven by consumer pressure and how much women are manipulated into paying the higher price. Women are not given the choice of paying for a less expensive product within each brand name, since all brands price their women's products higher than the men's."[11]

Legal challenges to gender-based pricing

In 1995, California passed a law banning gender-based pricing as part of the state's civil rights legislation. The act "provide[s] specifically that no business establishment may discriminate with respect to the price charged for services of similar or like kind, against a person because of the person's gender."[12] The Gender Tax Repeal Act, as it's called, is the first of its kind. The bill provides limited remedies for violations, which may be sought through the filing of a civil suit where actual damages and attorney fees may be awarded. Jacqueline Speier, the senator responsible for the bill, says, "All this bill does is say if you provide the same service, then you charge the same price ... Why are women forced to be assertive to get what should be available as an equitable position? Some colleagues say it's a marketplace issue and we should take our business elsewhere. But why should I be so inconvenienced?... It's a fundamental inequity that exists in the pricing of services and products for women as opposed to men when the products are the same likeness and kind."[13]

Senator Charles Calderon, also of California, introduced a bill to coincide with Speier's that would increase the fine from $250 to $1,000 plus reasonable attorney fees for any establishment caught subscribing to gender-based pricing. This statute also directs the Department of Consumer Affairs to send notices to licensed barbers and cosmetologists informing them of what constitutes illegal pricing practices.

The bill was passed, but not without opposition. Democrats favoured the bill and offered anecdotal evidence to back up Speier's points. Republicans objected to the measure as a needless intrusion into the marketplace. A well-documented argument in the U.S. press between Republican Assemblyman Bernie Richter and Democrat John Burton went as follows: Richter: "The most democratic system I know is the marketplace. You can vote with your dollar. You can vote with your feet." Burton: "You cannot vote with your feet or your pocketbook if you can't find a place to vote. The issue is economic rights for women."

In one exchange during the raucous, often humorous debate, Republican Assemblyman Stan Statham asked Assembly Speaker Willie Brown (Democrat), "How much do you pay for a haircut?" The Speaker, who was balding and had grey-flecked black hair on the sides, replied, "Whenever I'm in a position to get a haircut, it's a celebration. Clearly I pay more than it's worth."

Elizabeth Toledo of the California National Organization for Women says, "The basic premise of equal access is that you don't have to shop around town searching for equal rights. It goes against every law we have." Elise Thurau, a senior consultant at Speier's Sacramento office, says, "A dollar in the hands of a woman should purchase the same as a dollar in the hands of a man."[14]

Brian Doherty, editor of *Regulation* magazine (published by the Cato Institute, a right-wing Washington, D.C., think tank), argues that if there's no legitimate reason for charging women more, merchants who do so "are only hurting themselves and will perish in a free market." He believes the law "sounds like moral breast-beating on the part of lawmakers." However, *The Wall Street Journal* comments, "Consumer markets don't always punish irrational behaviour. Some retailers can get away with charging more based on convenience rather than price. And many consumers don't have time for comparison shopping." When you consider that most women have two full-time jobs (in the paid workforce and in the home), it's self-evident that time-consuming comparison shopping is a luxury few of them can afford.

The well-worn argument used by dry cleaners, haircutters, and department store tailors is that it costs more to provide services to women. But when such arguments have been challenged by regulators or in lawsuits, they usually haven't prevailed. In a June 30, 1989, settlement with the Washington, D.C., Office of Human Rights, the Metropolitan Drycleaners Association wrote that it's "inappropriate" for its members to "charge separate or different prices for the laundering or finishing of shirts and blouses based in any way on size, placement of buttons, whether it is a man's or woman's shirt or whether it is brought in for service by a man or a woman."

Most provincial human rights statutes contain provisions similar to that of Section 3 of the B.C. Human Rights Act, which states the following:

3. No person shall
   a) deny a person or class of persons any accommodation, service
      or facility customarily available to the public, or
   b) discriminate against a person or class of persons with respect to any
      accommodation, service or facility customarily available to the public,
      because of race, colour, ancestry, place of origin, religion, marital status,
      physical or mental disability or sex of that person or class of persons....

But the reality is that these practices have continued long after the reasons for them have ceased to exist. I hope we can find a way to implement legislation as they've done in California. But government legislation isn't the be all and end all. Market pressure is our best ammunition. Marketing 101 teaches there are two main elements in determining the cost of goods and services. One is the cost of bringing the product to market and the second is what the market will bear. It's the second part of this equation we're working against. No one objects to paying more if it costs more or the service takes longer. But if it's an arbitrary price set because that's what the market will bear, then it's up to the market to change that situation. Women have been paying these higher prices for years, complaining to each other but not doing anything collectively. This isn't surprising when you consider women's socialization: be nice, don't rock the boat, and accommodate others at all costs. It's time to claim our voices and economic strength (since women control 85 percent of the consumer dollars spent in North America) and place our concerns on the laps of those very people subscribing to gender-based pricing.

What to watch for

Once you discover gender-based pricing, the first step is to speak with someone at the company. I wouldn't have believed that people would take action had I not seen it with my own eyes, as I did with Alan Davis. Learn to speak up about price discrepancies. One woman attending a convention in Tucson, Arizona, was shopping for a swimsuit, and discovered that women's suits were priced from $48 to $90 while men's swim trunks in the same store were $25 to $35. Upon hearing the shopper's complaint, the salesperson gave her a 15 percent discount on a woman's suit. Many merchants are willing to lower their prices within reason to keep you as a customer. I always start with a minimum 15 percent off just to ease the tax burden. Start becoming aware of this kind of discrimination in your day-to-day activities; you could save yourself some money.

- "Boy"-cott. If the establishment doesn't resolve the issue to your liking, boogie on out of there, but not before management knows that you and everyone you know will be boycotting the product or business. Avoiding paying the gender tax in the first place is a great way for women to start saving money. Completely avoid places that provide free alterations for men but charge an arm and a leg for alterations for women.

- Watch out because some hairdressers can be wily. Few stylists outwardly admit to charging women more. When asked about the practice, Robin Barker, past president of the Guild of Hair Design (the hairdressers' industry association), quickly stated, "Not in our salon." Barker agreed that the price should be paid on time, not gender, but his own prices reveal an implicit gender-based pricing bias. Barker generally charges $75 for a client visiting every six weeks, and $65 for clients who visit every four weeks. However, men are charged $65, even if they visit every six weeks. In addition, women are charged a $100 first-time visit fee, because of a lengthy consultation. "For guys," he said, "consultation is less complicated. With women, I have to take into consideration make-up, hair colour, and other factors. If it's more complicated, sometimes I'll price it accordingly."[15] In other words, he charges according to the gender of the client.

- Anything automotive, from purchasing a car to having it serviced, is traditionally a danger area for women. Women are often charged more for cars because of their supposed gullibility. A friend of mine told me it was going to cost $1,500 to have her car repaired. The next day her son and husband took it out for three more quotes, all of which came in under $505. As appalling as this sounds, until you become knowledgeable enough about car repairs to know when you're getting ripped off, you may need to bring Dad, hubby, or baby brother along for the ride.

- Watch out when purchasing big-ticket items. The Montreal-based magazine *Elle Quebec* sent a male and a female reporter out to haggle price on a variety of items, from computers to landscaping. In the end, the woman reporter's total was 92 percent higher. When renovating, commissioning repairs, or shopping for pricey items like cars or appliances, get no fewer than three quotes. Let the salespeople know you're shopping around. Be sure to do your research—what did your male friends pay for the same service? If you have time and are really curious about gender differences in the marketplace, send a male colleague in to see what price he's quoted. If you're treated condescendingly or rudely, take your business elsewhere, but not before the offender and his or her manager know why.

- As Elaine discovered, be aware of clothing stores that sell unisex clothes for a lot less in the men's department than in the women's. I buy whatever I can in small men's sizes because these items are invariably cheaper than women's. This includes men's socks, shirts, jackets, sweaters, and running shoes. A man I knew quite well wanted me to help him update his closet. He was in his early 50s and had been married twice, the first time when he was a mere lad of 19, and had two grown children in their early 20s. He told me the story of his life as we went through his closet: "This was the suit I wore to my daughter's christening, this suit I wore to my wedding," and so on. Actually, he specified that that particular suit was the one he'd worn to his first wedding, not his second. He was still wearing it. In fact, he was still wearing all of them. Then it hit me. Why do women's fashions change every season of every year while men, on the other hand, are lucky if they see a fashion change every 50 years or so? Their ties get wide, then they get narrow. Big deal. This man wearing a suit for over 30 years might be a unique example, but I know many men who wear the same suits for 10 to 15 years, my own father being one of them. Societal pressure on women to be in fashion is tremendous, and very expensive. How come men aren't targeted the same way? It's time to send a different message to women's clothiers.

- Watch out when buying cosmetics and personal hygiene products. Marianne Scott also discovered that certain brands of women's shaving gel can be up to a dollar more expensive than men's shaving gel, probably because of the hair disbursement patterns on our legs! Take a look at any line of men's skin care products, particularly the cleanser and moisturizer, and compare the price to the women's equivalent. As Aaron Freeman found in his survey of fragrance prices, men's product lines are invariably cheaper, often by a substantial amount. Marianne says, "Next time you need deodorant, buy the men's size—you'll get 50 percent more. If we all do it, Colgate-Palmolive and Johnson & Johnson will get the message. Leave those 'equal,' 'ergonomic' sizes on the shelf. Show all those drug makers and drugstores that our little, delicate hands can somehow manage to hold those larger sizes."

- Finally, don't buy into the media's messages about having to be young, athletically thin without an ounce of fat on your tummy, perfectly made up and coiffed, toes and fingers perfectly manicured, all body hair regularly torn out by its roots with hot wax or other torture devices, delightfully fragrant and expensively clothed in the latest styles each year complete with three-inch heels for that extra "leggy" look before men will notice you. I used to be one of those women. Now I work out at home, and I lost weight by good old diet and exercise. I shave my own legs, I wear high heels only on special occasions, and I have come to like the hard-earned lines around my eyes. They're signs of maturity and wisdom. Okay, and worry. The money I save by having realistic expectations of myself physically and emotionally funds a good portion of my annual RRSP contribution. Rosalind Russell, famous Hollywood actor and renowned beauty, said: "Taking joy in life is a woman's best cosmetic." The health, diet, and beauty aids industry is fed billions of dollars by women who continue to subscribe to the pervasive social standard that women have to be thin and rich in order to be acceptable. As Ralph Nader, North America's consumer guru, is quoted in Frances Cerra Whittlesey's *Why Women Pay More:* "Time and time again sellers will exploit women's vulnerabilities, anxieties and passive self-images as long as they can profitably get away with such practices." I say it's time we begin to think more like men in this area. Women start to panic when they can't fit into the smallest-sized clothes in their closets. Men, on the other hand, start to flip when they can't fit into their cars. Whittlesey says the problem can be partially solved through laws, but women have to stop spending on items that are impractical and overpriced in their effort to please men. Perhaps times are slowly beginning to change. Louis Rukeyser reported on his PBS television show *Wall Street Week* that a *Women's Day* magazine survey of 50,000 American women asked whether they'd rather be rich, beautiful, famous, or younger. Fully 71 percent said they'd take the money and run.

The power of negotiating

Now back to Elaine's sweater-buying episode. She was feeling angry at herself for not having gone to the store manager about the higher price of the woman's sweater.

"How odd, it didn't even occur to me to complain. Could part of the problem be that women haven't been socialized to rock the boat, bargain, or negotiate price?" Elaine wondered aloud.

"Partly," I said. "Men negotiate with a win/lose scenario, in which one negotiator wins and the other loses, while women negotiate with a win/win scenario, in which a solution satisfactory to both negotiators is reached. As Dr. Weiss, a psychologist specializing in women's issues, noted, women are taught to please as many people as possible, an attitude that seems weak to male negotiators. Based on the language of the male business model, women's negotiating style isn't considered as effective as men's style. But I haven't paid list price for anything in years, even in major department stores. I negotiate for everything, and in 90 percent of the cases, I get what I ask for. Women have to learn to have the courage to ask."

In her study titled "Is It Her Voice or Her Place That Makes a Difference? A Consideration of Gender Issues in Negotiations,"[16] Harvard Law School professor Deborah M. Kolb notes, "Both men and women are taking more active roles in the traditional domains of each other, giving rise to gender questions. Can differences in style and approach be traced to gender? And how do they impact on the process of negotiation?" There's a tendency to reduce gender to a set of sex-linked behaviours and traits that are considered essential qualities of the individual. Being aware of Kolb's findings can help you better understand the process of negotiating, thereby becoming a more astute negotiator.

Here are the highlights:

- For men, the substantive issues under dispute are the primary matters to be dealt with in negotiation. For women, the quality of the relationship is more important than the issues. Women read the importance of relationships into negotiations and look for agreements that enhance relationships.
- Women see negotiation not as a separate and distinct activity but as part of an ongoing relationship with a past and a future.
- Women often learn through dialogue—a sharing of concerns and ideas—rather than through challenge and debate.
- Because a woman's status in negotiations isn't automatically assured, she often has to be tough and aggressive to establish her place.
- Stereotypes about the appropriate behaviour of women can affect negotiations. Women are generally expected to be passive, compliant, non-aggressive, noncompetitive, accommodating, and to attend to the social and emotional needs of those present. (When the VP of a big client of a major chartered bank in Toronto walked into its boardroom for a meeting, she overheard a bank VP quip to his cohorts: "Oh good. The women are here. That means the coffee has arrived.")
- Despite doing the same thing or speaking the same words, different meanings are attached to men's and women's behaviour. Whereas aggressiveness is an admired quality in men, an aggressive woman can still be thought of as a "ball breaker" or a "man in a skirt."

- Certain rituals of negotiation, such as extreme opening demands, grandstanding, and joke telling, may put women at a disadvantage. But to suggest that women learn to negotiate like men isn't an option. In order to level the playing field in negotiations we'll have to think about ways to find equality in the face of difference. If you want to train yourself to be a better negotiator, my recommended option is: practise, practise, practise. Give yourself permission to be uncomfortable and nervous the first few times you take on a car sales rep or hairdresser. Trust me, the more you do it, the better you get. I speak from personal experience. I was a wreck the first few times I attempted to negotiate or take someone to task for bad service. But once you begin to see improvement, you'll be inspired to carry on and expand your horizons. Read the many books available on the subject of haggling as well as those on gender differences in communications, such as Deborah Tannen's *You Just Don't Understand*. This book will open your eyes to the different ways women and men use language and will go a long way to helping you win the communication (i.e., negotiation) battle.

Knowledge is power

I removed a quote that I had thumb-tacked to my bulletin board. "Ralph Nader says it best, Elaine. 'Gender-based selling, where none is called for, keeps bouncing back on Main Street, notwithstanding what laws there are or what liberationist attitudes are nominally displayed. To expose and avoid this bias in the marketplace, nothing can surpass sharper shopping, questioning and acting. If more women, knowing their rights and equities, individually reject the notion that to have taste means you can be taken, then the practice of change would become widely emulated. Girls would learn these wiser ways from their mothers. Mothers could press for more education in the schools as part of existing courses to teach their daughters about this discrimination in the marketplace and how to end it. Billions of dollars of wasteful promotion, poor quality merchandise, and unnecessary surgery, drugs, and car/home repairs would be squeezed out of the economy. Greater health, safety, efficiency and peace of mind would be achieved.'[17]

"I believe the practice of gender-based pricing persists because the attitudes behind it persist. Until society undergoes a paradigm shift in its thinking about women, we'll be forced to rely on short-term solutions like buying as many men's products as we're comfortable with, including clothing, until we can get the retailers to wake up. It's a lousy and, quite frankly, offensive solution, and in a fair and equitable world we shouldn't have to do it. So, get bloody angry. Grassroots and direct consumer intervention like boycotts and letter writing campaigns really work. Write and talk to the managers of salons, dry cleaners, retail stores, and car dealerships. Write to your local Member of Parliament. It's time to stop being passive on this issue, and to start shaking the rafters to let these companies know we mean business."

"Education and awareness work wonders in inspiring people to take care of their own corner of the universe," Elaine agreed.

"After all," I added, "isn't this how women won the vote at the turn of the 20th century? Today there's a great deal of emphasis on pay and employment equity. How about market and consumer equity? As long as it exists, two-tiered gender-based pricing, also known as the gender tax, is going to stand in the way of women achieving true financial equality."

Elaine stood up and put her hand on my shoulder. "Well friend, you have certainly taught me a thing or two. Whoever said financial planning wasn't a gender issue was sadly mistaken. Women live longer on less money and pay more. Now, if you'll excuse me, I've got a hairdresser that needs my undivided attention."

The window shook when she shut the door.

Moving on

A couple of weeks later, I noticed the door to Elaine's office had been closed all morning. When it finally opened, Elaine and the top brass of the company emerged, joking and laughing. She stopped laughing when we made eye contact, and gestured to me to come into her office.

"Looks ominous, Elaine. What brings the upper echelon down to the slums?" I asked as I sat down in the chair that I'd occupied so many times before.

Elaine joked, "You still don't trust anyone over the age of 30! Which is odd, considering you're so firmly entrenched in that decade yourself."

"You're seriously misled if you think I trust myself," I said, grinning. "What's going on?"

Elaine braced herself and dropped the bombshell. "I've been offered a senior management position."

I blinked once as the implications of her announcement sunk in. Reeling from the shock of possibly losing my mentor, I asked, "Did they take it hard when you told them you weren't interested in the job?"

Elaine grimaced as she said, "I have to take it, the offer is too good to refuse. Besides, you're well on your way. You have a passion for your work that's clear to all who know you." Elaine smiled. "The student has outgrown the teacher."

"Nice try, Elaine. Flattery will get you everywhere," I answered despondently. "What will I do without you?"

"Joanne," Elaine asked, "who's taught you the most in the last year?"

I thought about this and answered honestly, "My clients."

"Bingo!" Elaine exclaimed. "Even though your technical education is ongoing, you reach a point where the really important learning comes from the experiences of the people you deal with every day, not from what you learn in books or from me. The financial planning you do for your clients is an exercise not only from your head, but from your heart and soul as well. You teach people how to balance their lives by giving them the financial tools to achieve their goals." Elaine smiled at me. "I'll still be helping you. I'll be doing my part from a different place, but I want you to continue carrying the message. Who knows, maybe someday you'll write a book on the subject and become a highly respected, world-renowned author."

"Of course," I responded smoothly. "And maybe Brad Pitt will dump Jennifer and we'll get married."

We sat in comfortable silence. I realized this was one of those moments in life called a crossroads. Saying goodbye to Elaine was going to be very hard, but much of her attitude and good sense were already instilled in me. "Elaine," I began, "at the risk of sounding maudlin, I believe that life is a series of attachments and losses. How good we are at living depends not only on how well we attach, but on how we accept loss. I'm going to miss you terribly, but perhaps we're both destined for greater things."

Elaine's eyes were misty as she said, "Joanne, you were one of my hardest cases. You taught me so much about tenacity and the courage of the human spirit. Once in a while I found myself wondering if you were going to be able to stay on track. When I talk to other women who express fear or reluctance about getting financially organized, I tell them the story of a woman I know. It's your story, Joanne, and it's one of your greatest strengths. Don't be afraid to tell it—many women will recognize themselves in your story. You may be surprised to see how it will inspire women to take action. Listen, my protégé, be sure you and Brad invite me to the wedding. With you, I've discovered, anything is possible."

nine

This thing called life

So you'll get mixed up, of course as you already know.
You'll get mixed up with many strange birds as you go.
So be sure when you step.
Step with care and great tact
And remember that Life's a Great Balancing Act
Just never forget to be dexterous and deft.
And never mix up your right foot with your left.
And will you succeed?
Yes! You will, indeed!
(98 and 3/4 percent guaranteed.)
Oh, The Places You'll Go!

(THE LAST BOOK WRITTEN BY DR. SEUSS BEFORE HE DIED)
© DR. SEUSS ENTERPRISES, L.P. QUOTED BY PERMISSION.

It's been a wondrous and hectic 10 years since *Balancing Act* was first released and 5 years since its last revision. My company, The Thomas Yaccato Group, has expanded and changed in focus. We educate women about money and companies about women. Today, we work with Home Depot, Toyota, Ikea, and Royal Bank, helping them to better meet the needs of women. My travel schedule precludes me from doing financial planning for individuals anymore, but Elaine and I still talk often. My now 15-year-old twin nieces are growing up healthy and happy, and I still spend time crisscrossing Canada speaking to women on taking financial control. Life has been a whirlwind of profound change since I became a published author and spokesperson for whatever is on my mind at the moment. To my amusement, the two most asked questions at my seminars are not "Should I maximize my RRSP or pay down my mortgage?" or "What type of life insurance should I buy?" In fact, the questions are (1) "Did you finally buy that house?" and (2) "Did you ever get a date?"

Well, I figured it's time to address that curiosity my readers seem to have. Not only did I get a date, I got a husband. Believe me, no one was more surprised than I to find my version of "Lance" smack in the midst of this maelstrom called my life. He wasn't Brad Pitt, as Elaine had so glibly predicted. His name is Michael and he's every bit as charming and brilliant as Brad. More so, in my totally unbiased opinion. Our story is so inspiring, or so I've been told—especially by those who are close to giving up hope of finding Mr. or Ms. Right—that I've decided to share it with you. It's a testament to the maxim that life is what happens when you're making other plans.

Frankly, folks, you'd be right in assuming that by the age of 38 I'd been around the block once or twice. I'd been perilously close to marriage but, thankfully, had always managed to narrowly escape unscathed. In retrospect, I'm sure these close encounters of the wrong kind would have ended up in divorce court. It had been eight years since I'd decided to become the man I wanted to marry. But the truth? I still quietly yearned for a partner to build a life with. Deep inside, I wanted to share my life's richness with someone special. I was firmly established in a successful career, living my dreams in a full and active life. I was also very single (read: profoundly lonely). There's nothing like a different hotel room every night for weeks on end to bring that point home.

Like so many of my peer group, I became solidly entrenched in the career track. I bought into the doctrine that women could "have it all." Interestingly, while I was going about the business of "getting it all," my biological clock began to tick insistently. The ticking was easy to ignore at first. Although persistent, it got easily buried under career distractions. My mother is fond of telling the story that, ever since the age of four, I've been planning for the time when I'd have babies. This has always been one of my primary goals. However, reality has a quiet way of shaping one's life without our really knowing it. I always thought I had time; I lived my life as though I did. Most of my decisions favoured the career side of the scale, not that I had much else to choose from. At the age of 35, I left a man I was supposed to marry in part because he changed his mind and decided he didn't want children. Even then I somehow had faith that the life I wanted, including partner and children, could still happen. But before I knew it, I was 38, Mr. Right was still vapourware, and the alarm on that infernal biological clock went off with a vengeance. Because of my age, I had some heavy decisions to make. I was giving serious thought to adopting a baby girl from China. The idea of becoming a single parent, though terrifying, seemed quite plausible when compared to the other option of remaining childless. For me at the time, that was untenable.

In November 1994, I was invited to go to my friend Sandy's Grey Cup party. I was amazed that Canadians still rallied around to eat chili and drink beer and watch—essentially ignore—this silly game on TV. I don't know what surprised me more: the fact that people still observed this annual tradition or that I actually agreed to participate. In my opinion, football has the same socially redeeming value as picking your teeth in public. For a lark, I decided to go. As I was sitting there watching grown men attempt to kill each other to get possession of a small pigskin ball, my gaze wandered over to a distinguished, athletic, quiet gentleman across the room. I found out that he bore my favourite moniker in all the world: Michael. I took that as a sign. I found myself praying that none of the many women present was his girlfriend or wife. There was something compelling about this man. He didn't fall into the category of "my normal type." In fact, he seemed quite the opposite—casual, uncomplicated, very quick to smile, quietly yet undeniably confident. My "type" had always been uptight, complicated, brooding, and overconfident. I'd often said that with my track record, if I found myself attracted to someone I should immediately hightail it out of the room. While it's true that there are many things I do well, choosing appropriate men doesn't top the list. They either don't want children, live in Tuktoyaktuk, like scotch with their morning orange juice, or like to burn down empty buildings as a favourite pastime. It's true that each of these people improved my quality of living, if in no other way than through the wisdom I gained on our brief journeys together. (All but the pyromaniac. Last I heard, he was seen skulking about the scores of empty high-rises in downtown Toronto.) For some unknown reason, I also seemed to gravitate to the suave, business-suited, corporate executive type. Michael, however, was an aerospace engineer and triathlete and lived in T-shirts and jeans. Luckily for me, he didn't belong to anyone in that room. Anyone in any room for that matter. I promptly fell head over heels in love.

From the beginning, our relationship was characterized by its complete absence of fear. And by speed. On our second date, we started talking about our respective desires to settle down and start a family. On our third, we started talking about settling down and starting a family with each other. Even though he owned the home where he lived with two other bachelor engineer types, Michael almost immediately adopted my home as his. I often tease him by saying he came for dinner and never left. Every weekend, more and more "boy's stuff" stayed behind, invading my female space. Shaving cream, razor, a suit, some shirts and underwear, running gear, and a bicycle. I knew it was getting serious when, after one prolonged visit, he left his electric drill behind. Weekend visits were initially from Friday to Monday morning, but quickly extended to Tuesday, Wednesday—soon he was here more than there. Many other signs indicated that he was destined to be my life partner. We wanted the same things in life: family, friends, travel, and balance. He was very healthy and fitness-conscious, as I tried to be, chocolate habit notwithstanding. When two people come together later in life, the experience can often be quite jarring. People get used to their own ways of doing things. Mine and Michael's life fell in together with absolutely no effort or disruption. This was another good omen.

In early February 1995, a mere three months after we had met, Michael and I took a ski trip to Whistler, B.C. I'll always remember this trip because it was the point in our relationship when I started to get seriously honest with myself and Michael about the path we were on. We'd already agreed we were going to get married. Michael wanted a family and a good-sized one at that. He thought three kids would be ideal, which had my 38-year-old ovaries nervously twitching. He came from a family of five boys, all of whom became engineers. (Ironically, neither of his parents could even use a screwdriver.) It was Michael's birthday, and we were cozying up in our hotel room admiring the breathtaking skyline of Vancouver. We'd just finished an elaborate birthday breakfast feast. I'm ashamed to admit it, but I instinctively decided to exploit that wonderful intimate moment. As I was worried about my ability to have children, I began to probe how deeply committed he was to having his own children. I told him I had concerns because of my age and because of a possible tipped womb. I asked him how he felt about reproductive technology or adoption if we ran into trouble conceiving. It turned out to be a non-issue for him. "We'll do what we can, and if it's meant to be, it will happen," he responded. Talk about the right answer. I remember mentally looking skyward and nodding as I accepted this as another sign that he was to be Mr. Thomas Yaccato.

Two weeks later, I found myself back in lotus-land, in the lovely community of White Rock, to do a keynote speech for a well-known brokerage firm. I was in the hotel where I was to speak, attempting to pull myself together and get ready for the evening's event after a long, gruelling flight. This would be a big one. The sponsors had had to shut down the marketing machine soon after they'd started to advertise the seminar, since the response had been overwhelming. They'd reached the hotel's capacity of 800 people in a mere two weeks.

It was two hours to curtain time when I discovered I'd forgotten my lipstick. I took a cab to a nearby drugstore to buy a new one. As I wandered up and down the aisles, I found myself staring at a colourful array of home pregnancy tests. To this day, I have no idea what compelled me to buy one. Without any forethought whatsoever, I reached out and grabbed it. Till that very moment, I hadn't consciously thought I might be pregnant. True, my period was a week late, but with my travel schedule, that happened quite often.

I'll never forget how I felt preparing for the test—a combination of nervous anticipation and "Oh, what's the big deal. You know it's going to be negative anyway." A blue line meant no go, a single red line meant a good chance you're pregnant, and a double red line meant "Congratulations, you're having triplets!" As the little stick rested comfortably in the sample, I proceeded to get ready for my rendezvous with the sponsors less than an hour away. I was a bit nervous, so I actually put the test out of my mind for close to 15 minutes. As I was slipping into my pantyhose, I remembered with a start to check the little wand. I hopped across the bathroom, struggling to balance while shoving my remaining foot into the hosiery. With a nonchalant motion, I removed the wand from the sample and found myself face to face with two of the brightest red lines I'd ever seen. I caught my reflection in the mirror and started to giggle as I saw my eyes and mouth gaping wide open. I reminded myself of a big, old, ugly sea bass. I promptly fell backwards on the toilet seat which was fortunately closed, blinking with complete disbelief.

There's no way to describe the onslaught of feelings that hit me in the next five minutes. I had no idea a human being was capable of such a wide variety of emotions with that much intensity in such a short time. My mind kept repeating, "Impossible, impossible, impossible." The thought of Michael flashed through my mind. "Oh Lord!" I groaned. "He wants this, but he did say at the right time." I could only presume that meant after we were married. We hadn't even set a date. As reality began to penetrate my consciousness, I started to think this was the supreme sign that he was to be the one. Let's hope he agreed with my conclusion. A raging battle ensued in my brain: do I call him right away, or wait and tell him face to face the next day? I did what any mature, independent thinker would do. I called my mother.

Moms are hilarious. The first thing she wanted to know was why I had to wait until I was alone in a hotel room 3,000 miles from home and one hour from a major presentation before deciding to do the test. She had a point. Then she started to gush. The advent of another grandchild sent her straight into a tizzy. I've always said grandchildren are parents' rewards for not killing their children. We thought the look on Michael's face would be too good to miss, so I decided to wait a day before dropping the bomb.

Incidentally, the seminar went well. As I proceeded through the slide presentation, thoughts blasted randomly to the front of my mind: "I'm bloody well pregnant!" I was momentarily thrown off guard, but managed to get back in stride each time. The sponsors were none the wiser, until two months later when I called and told them what had happened. They howled with laughter and delight.

Michael's reaction was as I had expected. After engaging him in a heart-to-heart discussion about how wonderful our relationship was and how we in such a short time had built a solid foundation—all of which he enthusiastically agreed with—I hit him with "I'm so glad we're in synch. We're pregnant." Stunned silence followed my announcement. It seemed to me to last 20 minutes; 20 seconds is probably more accurate. Slowly, a boyish grin spread across his face as he looked into what felt like my soul and said, "Neat!" I was crying as I hugged the stuffing out of him. The rest, as they say, is history.

We began to plan a wedding in earnest. Those of you who've been in my shoes, remember the first trimester exhaustion? It was all I could do to keep up with work demands in between the urgent and incessant need for sleep. Then there was the matter of what I've come to call affectionately "pregnancy Alzheimer's." I've also heard it called "baby brain." With every pound I gained, I lost the corresponding weight of brain cells. Clumsiness and forgetfulness became my two new best friends. The experts say you'd better develop a sense of humour about it in a hurry; it gets worse as you progress. Planning a wedding, running a company, and adjusting emotionally to my new life in that mental and physical state was all proving to be much too challenging. It was the first time in my life I had to throw in the towel and admit I couldn't do it all. I was feeling completely overwhelmed by the changes and had to start making some choices. Michael and I were also surprised at how quickly the expenses began to add up. We wanted a small, private affair with immediate family and a handful of close friends. Even so, we were looking at bills totalling $10,000 to $15,000. For a one-day event. Yes, I've heard it all a million times. It's supposed to be the most special day of your life, money should be no object. Women in particular have had this message drilled into their heads since they were little girls playing with Bridal Barbie. I say enough already. Weddings are as much for the bride and groom as they are for family and friends. In fact, more so. Michael and I began to wonder: if we could choose a perfect day, what would it look like? It didn't look overly traditional. We decided to break with convention and change our plans mid-stream. We up and eloped.

It was a Sunday; we were due to visit my sister and her fiancé for the long weekend the following Friday. They live just outside Manitoulin Island in a small town in northern Ontario called Espanola. I called Lori and asked if she and John had anything special planned for that weekend. She was excited about our visit and was bubbling over with ideas of things for us to do. I mentioned quietly that Michael and I had only one thing we really wanted to do. "Oh?" Lori asked. "What do you have in mind?"

"What about a wedding?" I asked.

"Jeez," Lori shot back. "And I thought I was a demanding houseguest!" She then went on in good Irish-Italian fashion to have an absolute fit on the telephone. She couldn't imagine anything more perfect. She and John would stand for us. To this day I'm astounded at what she pulled off. My dear sister put together an entire wedding in four days. She found a non-denominational minister, a plan A and plan B location for the ceremony (plan A was outdoors), arranged the flowers, hired a photographer/videographer, and booked the most romantic room for our wedding night. There was nothing for Michael and me to do but get the marriage certificate and the wedding rings.

We woke up on our wedding day to one of the most beautiful days God could have ordered. The cloudless sky was a brilliant blue broken occasionally by the dramatic horizon of northern Ontario. The air was so fresh and clean, it actually smelled foreign. Everything seemed more vivid blue and deeper green. Our approach to the day was remarkably casual. We wanted this to be a celebration that Michael and I would enjoy. We didn't want to be exhausted and stressed out. In fact, our approach to our wedding day was so casual my beloved husband-to-be had overlooked bringing anything to wear that day. A half hour before we were to leave, Lori and I found Michael and John rummaging through John's closet trying to find something appropriate for Michael to wear. If I hadn't been feeling so downright calm, I'd have brained him. The wedding party consisted of the four of us, the minister, and Cleaver, John's best friend and fellow physician. Cleaver was a delightful addition to our group. His business card could have read "surgeon/coroner/photographer/videographer/pianist/all-round nice guy." He not only took our pictures and videographed the ceremony, he played the piano so Michael and I could have the traditional "first dance" on our wedding night. After getting ready we proceeded to Manitoulin Island which, in the Native culture, is a very spiritual place. Manitou means "great spirit." As the wedding party approached our plan A destination, a breathlessly beautiful point overlooking a massive valley, the sky literally opened up and the heavens poured down on us. We were clearly not meant to have an outdoor wedding. Undaunted, we jumped back into our cars and immediately shifted to plan B. In retrospect, it was perfect enough to have been plan A. It was a Native chapel sequestered in a wilderness setting beside a remote, crystal-clear lake. Michael and I thought it was the most beautiful place to get married in. And get married we did.

As we took our leave of the chapel after the ceremony, I turned to take a last look at nature's bounty. I saw a sight that made me gasp and brought tears to my eyes. Across the full expanse of the lake, in full dazzling splendour, stretched a double rainbow—not one, but two, positioned one on top of the other to create a magnificent colour display. We stood there awestruck. Michael and I looked at each other and slowly smiled. It was a sign. This one was divinely sent especially for us.

It was the most romantic and fulfilling experience Michael and I had ever had. Our wedding day was filled with lots of laughter; a sense of calm and peace pervaded the day. These are not the emotions I normally associate with a wedding. Here's the kicker: our picture-perfect wedding day, including the wedding night at a gorgeous lodge on an island that one could reach only by boat, cost $1,006. It's true what they say: There are lots of things money can't buy. I learned that lesson in spades on May 20, 1995.

The shock of the new

Michael and I settled very quickly into our new lives as a married couple. I shake my head when I think of how often I said naively of marriage, "It's only a piece of paper." Don't you believe it. Something very fundamental changes when you take part in a ceremony that symbolizes lifelong commitment.

One of the other changes I experienced was my perception of financial planning. Of course, even as a single person, I'd thought financial planning was an essential part of life. But now that I was married with a baby on the way, certain parts of the planning process took on a whole new dimension. Everything had to be revisited. The most compelling revelation was how difficult all the advice I'd given as a single financial advisor had become to maintain. Six months' salary as an emergency fund? Yeah, right. We needed cribs, car seats, and clothes. Maximize RRSPs? Uh, more like possibly having to cash in RRSPs. Since Kate was a bit of a surprise and I was self-employed, I didn't have any maternity benefits and no time to put a contingency plan in place. There was the very real possibility that I was going to have to live off my RRSPs. Ten percent savings? There was Kate's education to think about. Frankly, sending Kate off to engineering school to follow in Michael's family tradition of five brothers, five engineers will have a serious price tag.

My head was reeling with questions: What's the best way to save for her education? How different is our tax situation now that we're married? Do we need a marriage contract? Where do we want to live now that my nesting instinct has kicked into full swing? A rented house started not to feel right for the first time in my life. And how the heck do we even organize our finances? All of a sudden, our financial responsibilities had grown exponentially and we had to figure out who was doing what and how. We each had had decades of doing our own financial planning, thinking only of our own needs and wants. This was not going to work in our "new economy."

Know what you're getting into

Nothing has made me feel more "married" (read: "grown up") than sitting down with Michael and reviewing each other's financial health to determine our respective fiscal responsibilities. We went through this exercise before it was even official that we were living together. All too often I've seen couples put their relationship through unnecessary strain because they discovered after they moved in together that he was $52,000 in debt or that she had $15,000 owing on her credit card. "Whaddya mean you only earn $21,000 a year? You drive an $18,000 car!" This is not a revelation that should come after you've filled the bookcase with your books. This is not to suggest for a second that someone's earning $21,000 should preclude you from moving in with or marrying that person. It's not necessarily what someone makes that counts but how he or she manages it. This will speak volumes about the character of your partner. What I am suggesting is, don't wait until after the fact to find out the financial condition of your partner. It's just as important as his or her emotional, spiritual, and physical condition. All these elements contribute to why you love the person. As Michael says, "It's important to know what you're getting into, all of it."

The fact that women now have earning power is giving them a great deal more clout in the decision-making process—as well as in the executing process, for everything from buying cars to investing in mutual funds. Although the pattern of money management in the household is undergoing a dramatic shift as a result of women's increased economic power, there's a downside to this new world order. As American writer Anita Jones-Lee writes in her book *Women and Money,* "Studies show that men and women fight more about money than any other topic. Part of the reason, it seems, is that women are acquiring more economic resources within the marriage. Heightened by the emergence of women as capable breadwinners, the battle over money rages across the dinner table, the bedroom, appearing at some period and in some guise in almost all marriages. Sometimes the battle is a subtle shift of roles and expectations: Who should pay the taxes, who should control the chequebook? For most couples, the money issue emerges during first dating—who should pay or appear to pay at dinner—and, if not addressed, it can begin a slow silent erosion of the relationship. Many couples sweep the issue of how they relate to money under the rug, postponing it for consideration after they have tackled what they view as more pressing issues.

But, sooner or later, certainly after marriage, the rug gets rather lumpy, and those pesky unanswered money issues can resurface, only this time in fights and hurt feelings that seem to build over nothing."

Jones-Lee suggests you ask the following four questions to identify whether you and your partner are relating poorly about money:

1. Do you ever feel embarrassed if you have to pay for items while in public with your mate?
2. Does your mate ever feel embarrassed if you have to pay for items while he is in public with you?
3. Do you feel a need to keep up appearances by hiding your mate's inability to earn more or his inability to handle finances in any way, such as budgeting or paying for taxes?
4. Do you resent (a) consulting your mate about how to spend money you earn, or (b) your mate's failure to consult you about how he spends money he earns?

If you answered yes to any of these questions, there's a chance that you're experiencing some difficulty, consciously or unconsciously, around the issue of money and the alignment of power in your relationship. You should get help, maybe in the form of financial therapy, which most good therapists can provide.

Women who delegate the financial responsibility to their partner do so for primarily two reasons: lack of interest or fear, or pronounced time constraints. Financial planning becomes an additional task that's deferred or passed over because there's no time to do it. I get nervous when I see women let their partners take over money matters completely, because the amount of money you control in a relationship will in large part determine your independence. Financial control can increase women's influence in decision-making, which can give them a greater sense of competence and more power within the marriage. This is easier for women who work in the paid labour force and bring in their own money. But what about women who work full-time unpaid at home raising families? Issues of power and independence can become very tricky. It becomes even more important for these women to understand their partner's mindset around money. For women who choose not to get directly involved, I always recommend, at the very least, having a complete understanding of the state of the family finances in the event disaster strikes.

For the most part, however, today's women are involved in deciding where the money goes. Whatever method you choose to organize the family finances, remember to be sure you and your partner both have money that doesn't need to be accounted for. When entering into a common-law relationship or marriage, the following four points should be followed at all times. For many women, this is simply standard procedure. But for those who haven't given their financial lives much thought, take heed:

1. Always maintain an independent credit history. Don't co-sign or guarantee loans unless there's a financial benefit to you or you share control over the source of income being used to repay the loan. A while back I read about a judge who had severely reprimanded a bank for going aggressively after a client's wife who had guaranteed a business loan. She was a homemaker earning no income and had no input into or knowledge of her husband's business. Yet when he defaulted on the loan, the bank went after her for close to half a million dollars. The judge ruled that not only was the woman in no position to pay back the loan, but that she hadn't fully grasped what she was signing. The woman had to go through the nightmare of court proceedings and having her name dragged through the media. Granted, this is an extreme example, but the basic premise holds true: don't put your money where your brain isn't welcome.

2. Always maintain a separate bank account, even if you hold joint accounts. As discussed in chapter 2, many people find themselves wiped out because their partners were fast off the mark in getting to the joint accounts. Aspire to keep three to six months' salary accessible in case of disaster.

3. For those women who depend on their partners to keep them safe and dry in their retirement—don't. Plan your pension, taking into account death or divorce. That's where marriage contracts, family law, proper estate planning, and good solid savings principles come into play.

4. Speaking of estate planning, it's essential that you and your partner get a will. As we discussed in chapter 5, 8 out of 10 people left behind after the death of a partner are women. Don't let the government step in and make decisions for you because you didn't look after this vital detail.

Since Michael and I started living together, and especially since our dear little Kate became a reality (we named her in utero), we have come to realize that financial planning isn't a static or rigid exercise. It has to be fluid and flexible to encompass the myriad changes one undergoes during one's time on earth. I brought this home dramatically to Michael one morning shortly after we got married. Intending to illustrate a point, over breakfast I killed him.

I took him through what would happen to Kate and me should he leave this world too soon. No quicker way to jolt someone out of newlywed bliss than to run them over with a bus. But Michael has remarkable common sense (he married me, didn't he?) and he saw the need to address these less than cheerful financial issues. This meant redoing our wills and power of attorney, since the moment we'd signed the marriage certificate, our previous wills became null and void. Then there was life insurance to consider, now that Kate was on the way. We looked at Michael's company benefits (being self-employed, I have none) only to discover that his group plan wasn't nearly enough to cover what Kate would need in the event that anything happened to him. He needed to buy his own coverage anyway. There are no guarantees in the workplace today and we both felt it would be better for him to have control of his own plan. I already had my own insurance, but I needed to do some serious upgrading because of my new family responsibilities. I was reminded of this every time I looked down and couldn't see my feet. Michael got his first taste of reality about his impending family one day when, as he casually rested his hand on my protruding tummy, Kate walloped him with such force that he moved his hand away as though he had been electrocuted. The look on his face was priceless. "She kicked me!" he exclaimed with awe. Meanwhile, I was gasping for breath, laughing hysterically. She actually scared the daylights out of him. After that he'd try to reproduce the experience every chance he got. He took to shaking my tummy to wake her up and make her mad so that she'd kick. Men can be so weird.

We spent time with Elaine to top up our life and disability insurance requirements. After being in the industry for many years, I wasn't shocked to learn how much we'd need to cover our family needs. Michael, however, was stunned. It was becoming a permanent state of mind.

Should I pay down my mortgage or invest in RRSPs?

Well it happened, just as I predicted. I was a homeowner by 40. Nothing like raging maternal hormones to kick-start that old nesting feeling. With Kate on her way, homeownership scrambled up the priority list. Michael had brought his own house into our marriage, but the location was too far off the beaten path and way too small for this burgeoning family. We sold it and commenced our search for a suitable quantum of solace in which to set down roots. Our search ended in Aurora, Ontario.

Now here was a perfect example of how my new life was affecting my standard financial advice of old. I was and continue to be a strong advocate of maximizing RRSPs. Except that now I had a mortgage to get rid of.

I have to laugh. Now that it's become common knowledge that I actually found a date, the number one question asked of me at my seminars has moved from my despondent love life to: "Should I contribute to an RRSP or pay down my mortgage?" I really hate this question. It's one of the more difficult ones to answer because, as with all aspects of financial planning, the answer can vary depending on your financial situation and your personal philosophy.

This is an attempt to give you, dear readers, some loose guidelines to follow when making this decision. The fast answer is clearly to do both. In a perfect world (the Cleaver family variety), you should maximize your RRSP contribution every year. You should also rapidly pay down your mortgage by diligently making weekly payments and socking all that extra cash you have hanging around from huge company bonuses and generous tax refunds into your mortgage. In the real world however, the lifestyle of June and Ward is no more.

Ward worked for the same company for 45 years and shared 60 years of pure marital bliss with his perfectly coiffed, pearl-adorned bride June. (Even when I was a youngster watching *Leave It to Beaver* I couldn't figure out why she dressed as though she was going out to dinner to do housework.) Ward built up a hefty company pension, paid off the mortgage by the time he was 40, sold their home at retirement, and moved to a condo in Florida where he and June lived out the rest of their long lives attempting to recover from Beaver's inane antics.

As for today? People rarely stay at the same company for more than five years, there's a high divorce rate, and women have entered the workforce in unprecedented numbers, with a huge percentage becoming self-employed. Homeownership is not the guaranteed financial ace-in-the-hole it once was. With people being so transient, you can't count on company pensions (the self-employed don't have pension plans at all), CPP is in peril, and for those women who work full-time raising Canada's next generation, CPP isn't an option at all.

Let's look at my new neighbours, Jeanette and Eric Greenwood. Jeanette, 46, has been very busy at home raising three delightful children for the last 17 years. Eric, 51, is the family breadwinner. They own their own home and, like most Canadians, merrily went about living their busy lives with a typical "live for today" mentality. Eric received annual bonuses, which they freely and guiltlessly spent, mostly on stuff for the house and kids. That is, until Eric hit 40. It was then, with a big gulp, Eric and Jeanette began to contemplate the daunting realities of funding their retirement. After taking a financial snapshot, they realized they'd better make a decision. They had no RRSPs, and Eric's company pension wouldn't take them too far, since he'd had four jobs in 15 years. Jeanette had been out of the paid workforce for 12 years, and when she does return, she'll be doing what many women are doing today: starting her own business, which of course means no pension plan.

In their view, they had two possibilities for Eric's annual bonus: maximize the prepayment options on their mortgage to pay it off as quickly as possible, or contribute to their RRSPs. And the RRSP won. Even if they had to borrow to do it.

This is why: Eric is in the highest tax bracket—46.4 percent. The amount he had to pay Canada Revenue Agency every year made his blood pressure rise. For every $1,000 he contributed to his RRSP he'd get back $464 in a tax refund. This didn't include the gain in the investment itself, which one could comfortably forecast at around 6 percent each year. The tax refund would then go toward paying off the mortgage. Interestingly enough, this isn't a tax strategy solely for the wealthy. You don't have to make a gazillion dollars to be in a high tax bracket. People earning $30,000 to $35,000 a year are in the stratospheric marginal tax bracket of 34 percent and will get back $400 for every $1,000 contributed to an RRSP.

They also liked the flexibility that RRSPs offered in terms of investment choices and spousal options. If they could get 8 percent to 10 percent in an equity-based mutual fund, as well as a cheap mortgage (today they run around 5 percent to 7 percent), it made more sense for them to diversify. Eric also started to contribute to a spousal RRSP, which means Jeanette indirectly gets paid for the work she does at home. Eric gets the deduction part of the RRSP but Jeanette owns the cash. This spousal RRSP would be taxed back to Eric if Jeanette took it out before three years had passed since the last contribution plus the year of withdrawal. If Jeanette takes it out after this period, it's taxed at her rate. For example, if Eric makes a spousal contribution in September 2001 and withdrawals anytime in 2004, he's okay. (The YOW—the year of withdrawal—is 2004, and 2003 and 2002 are in the attribution period.) *But,* if the deposit was made in 2002 and was withdrawn in 2004, the withdrawal would be attributed back to Eric.

On the other hand, RRSPs tend not to benefit people who are in a low tax bracket nearly as much as those in the higher ones. If you earn between $6,700 and $29,500, your tax bracket is in the range of 25 percent, so you won't likely see as great a tax benefit as did Eric and Jeanette. Paying down your mortgage in this case is likely to be a better bet. Having a fully-paid-for home, no matter how you cut it, has got to be the best feeling on the planet. Considering that the gain in value on your principal residence is fully tax free, it can still be a relatively enticing investment.

Then there's the burgeoning ranks of the self-employed. Women are filling these ranks at a fast and furious rate. This is an easy call. I proclaim: "We the self-employed have no pension plans and most of us never get tax refunds, so maximizing RRSPs is mandatory. "

It comes down to what marginal tax rate you're at and how you view debt. The research bears out that many women tend to really hate debt, even investment debt like a mortgage, and want to get rid of it at all costs. As we've seen, sometimes carrying the debt and investing elsewhere will get you farther. The key to a successful financial plan is to get your fingers in a lot of pies. The more variety, the better served you'll be as long as you don't make a pig of yourself.

Getting through the financial services maze

As a financial advisor I knew the ropes, but I also knew that you can be too close to your own financial situation to see the forest for the trees. With this new "couple" thing, and the major new asset of a house, we decided it was a good idea to get an independent third party to help us assess our financial picture. And, I might add, don't wait until you're in a serious relationship to do this. Financial advice doesn't give a hoot about your marital status. Here's what you need to know.

Just about anyone can hang out a "financial planner" shingle. The reality is that only 1 in 10 people who call themselves financial planners is actually a "certified financial planner." This is an international designation that shows the individual is appropriately licensed. However, the Canadian Securities Administrators (CSA, which describes itself on its website, www.csa-acvm.ca/home.html, as "a forum for the 13 securities regulators of Canada's provinces and territories to coordinate and harmonize regulation of the Canadian capital markets") are working on a plan that will require financial planners, as the CSA will define them, to pass some prerequisite licensing test. The nature and complexity of this test is still unknown, and it won't apply to fee-for-service planners. The good planners, though, will identify where you are today, help you set your goals and objectives, and point out any obstacles or opportunities along the way. They'll provide written recommendations and will either implement them for you, if they're licensed to do so, or coordinate making your plan happen. They'll review your plan each year and update you every so often on what's new.

Financial advisors and planners do just that—advise and plan. They're not in the business to make unfounded or unreasonable guarantees. If they do, step lively to the front door and beat a hasty retreat. You must be crystal clear on what service your advisor provides. How often do they intend to be in contact with you? What resources can they draw upon? Is the firm they work for stable? Who's their typical client? Do they specialize in a certain clientele or product? What's their investment philosophy and approach? Is it consistent with yours? Do they have not only the designation, but also the experience that you need?

Let's assume you've figured out that you need help and, based on your understanding of what a planner or advisor is supposed to do, you've decided to take the plunge. Chances are you're standing in the middle of your kitchen, kind of blinking blankly at the phone. You're thinking, "Exactly where are they hiding? And when I find out where they nest, how do I choose one?" At this point in your journey, anyone who knows how to pronounce "equity" will sound good. There are a few things to keep front and centre before charging off. One is the level of complexity of your portfolio, finances, and lifestyle. If you're just starting out, choosing an investment counsellor who specializes in portfolios of $250,000 or over may be a slight case of overkill. If you want a partnership agreement with a split dollar buy-sell arrangement, a rookie in the insurance business is obviously not a wise choice. Let's begin to narrow down the field by looking at the different categories of financial experts.

These are your choices

If you think this part is simple, it isn't. The people in the following categories all call themselves financial advisors or planners, though each group still has a defined area of expertise. You may want to choose one advisor or a team, depending on what your needs are and what you're comfortable with.

Certified financial planners These people can streamline operations by drawing on the resources of other types of financial advisors and coordinating the information for you. No one knows everything, so what expertise they lack, certified financial planners will get from other experts like accountants, lawyers, and insurance specialists. In fact, insurance agents, stockbrokers, and mutual fund sales representatives can have this designation or an equivalent. People with a certified financial planner (CFP) designation are bound by a code of ethics called the Code of Professional Ethics of the Financial Planners Standards Council of Canada. Effective in the spring of 2005, all CFPs will have to abide by mandatory practice standards. You can check out the details on their website, www.cfp-ca.org.

Investment advisors (formerly known as stockbrokers) It used to be that stockbrokers sold only stocks and bonds. Not anymore. In fact, that's why they now want to be called investment advisors (IAs). They offer a full range of financial products: stocks, bonds, mutual funds, treasury bills, mortgage-backed securities, GICs, RRSPs, RESPs, Canada Savings Bonds, options, and futures. Many offer insurance advice, and some firms make it mandatory that they have their insurance licence before they can even join them. IAs aren't supposed to be allied with any particular company.

Life insurance agents Life insurance agents are specialists in many of the areas that you'll find in the bottom half of the priority pyramid. That's where the products they're generally licensed to sell fall. They sell term deposits, GICs, annuities, segregated funds, RRSPs, RRIFs, children's education plans, employee benefit plans, pensions, and all types of insurance including life, disability, travel, critical illness, and long-term care insurance.

If you need insurance because you're starting a family, expanding a business, or starting a new business with a partner, need estate planning, or just want to learn the basics of financial planning, a stop at your life insurance agent's office is a serious consideration. They also tend to be specialists in retirement income planning because of the type of products they sell. What you should look for is a chartered life underwriter (CLU) and chartered financial consultant (ChFC). At the very least, your agent should be working toward obtaining these designations.

Mutual fund sales representatives Many companies, such as AIM Trimark and Fidelity, don't sell directly to investors. Some, like Altamira, mostly sell directly to investors. How you buy your fund often depends on whether or not you want a financial advisor. There are four sources from which you can buy mutual funds:

1. Brokers and dealers: These are investment advisors, mutual fund dealers, or financial advisors or planners who sell funds, among other types of securities.
2. Direct sellers: These are companies that sell directly to the investors, such as Altamira Management Limited, Phillips, Hager & North Limited of Vancouver, and MD Management (which caters directly to doctors and their families). They offer no-load funds because the companies don't use a sales force that can offer financial advice.
3. Tied sales force: The most well known in this category and certainly the largest is Investors Group of Winnipeg. The sales representatives working for Investors Group sell only the house brand, but have a ton of products to choose from. Since they sell only their own company's product, definitely look for a sales representative with a professional designation.
4. Financial institutions: Banks, trust companies, insurance companies—all those having extensive branch networks—are a major force in selling mutual funds. Financial institutions offer a good variety of funds to choose from. Some banks have "financial planner" roles and are now able to sell individual third-party funds, such as Fidelity, for example, albeit usually from a short or restricted list.

Bankers Because banks have effectively bought up most of the country's largest brokerages and trust companies, they have access to all kinds of expertise.

They're now in the investment business in a big way. Banks license their employees to sell mutual funds. The designation of choice for bankers is that of "personal financial planner" offered by the Institute of Canadian Bankers, the industry's education arm. They're called account managers, investment specialists, or financial advisors.

Accountants This is where you go for tax advice. Many people depend on their accountants for all their financial advice, including investing, but unless the accountant has taken specific courses or is a registered financial planner (see the "Designations" discussion below), getting advice from this person may not be wise. Accountants can, however, help you evaluate the performance of your portfolio. Use your accountant if you're setting up or expanding a business or are self-employed, have rental property, are filing tax returns, or are establishing a proper tax and estate plan. If you have a relatively simple tax return, you don't need to pay the fees of an accountant. Often bookkeepers are less expensive and can do a perfectly adequate job. If you're currently using your accountant for investment advice, ask what credentials she or he has in this area.

Investment counsellors These folks are big league. Investment counsellors don't handle portfolios of less than $500,000.

Although this sounds like a lot of money, you'll likely end up using their services for your retirement portfolio after it's been accumulating for several years, or if you've inherited a lot of money or get a big severance package. They're usually paid by taking a percentage (1 percent to 3 percent) of the total of your portfolio or a set fee. Most of these counsellors work in a discretionary manner, meaning the investor plays a more passive role in the day-to-day management of the portfolio.

Financial planning computer software The market is now beginning to offer financial planning software for people who are technologically inclined. This software can be a wonderful tool for getting the basics and developing a sense of what you need to know before going to an advisor. It will let you develop or customize your own scenarios, depending on your own views of the economy, interest rates, and your projected potential investment returns. Two examples of popular yet basic software are Quicken and Microsoft Money.

Another great idea is to get access to this stuff for nothing. Look at mutual fund companies, brokerage firms, and bank websites. They often provide calculators that you can use to figure out things like how much money you need to retire comfortably or to send your children to school.

People in the financial planning business should have achieved or be working toward certain designations.

Designations Only people who have earned the designation registered financial planner (RFP) or certified financial planner (CFP) are legitimately entitled to call themselves a financial planner, though many people who have not earned those designations do so anyway. There are very few RFPs around, but they are probably the group most qualified to provide financial planning advice. The RFP designation is awarded to members of the Institute of Advanced Financial Planners (IAFP) who have been engaged in the practice of financial planning for a minimum of two years, have fulfilled certain educational requirements, and carry errors and omissions insurance. All IAFP members are bound by the institute's Code of Professional Ethics.

Many people in the profession have other designations, such as chartered accountant (CA), certified general accountant (CGA), certified management accountant (CMA), the securities industry's certified investment manager (CIM), master of business administration (MBA), and bachelor of laws (LLB). In the insurance industry, the equivalent designations are chartered life underwriter and chartered financial consultant. As well, other people with no designation have been providing valuable financial advice for many years.

How do you choose a financial planner?

You have to shop around for the best person for the job. Anything worth having requires a little work. As with looking for a doctor, lawyer, or mechanic, the best place to start when looking for a financial planner is referrals. Try asking your accountant for a good life insurance agent or your lawyer for her IA. Naturally, your close friends and family members may be able to recommend a financial planner. Go to the many seminars and luncheons sponsored by financial planning professionals. You can also begin to narrow the field by contacting Advocis, which is the leading organization for financial planners. Check out the organization's website, www.advocis.ca. Advocis came about when the CAFP merged with the Canadian Association of Insurance and Financial Advisors (CAIFA). You can also look at the IAFP website, www.iafp.ca. IAFP certifies registered financial planners. You can search for qualified planners through the institute's website. IAFP will only give you the names of the planners who are geographically close to you and do not make recommendations.

Now, before actually choosing a financial planner, it's good to meet at least three of them. Before you even set foot in their office or let them in your front door, do your homework. Get them to send you some reading material on their company that you can peruse in advance of meeting them. This advanced research will give you a decided edge in the planner comparison process. And here's the big one: never leave a planner/advisor's office without being crystal clear on how they're paid.

Sales commission or fee for service?

There are three ways your financial advisor or planner gets paid. The first is fee-for-service. Fee-for-service people don't usually sell financial products. These people sell their financial planning services and then send you to a salesperson to implement their recommendations. The fee is based on the value of the client's assets and/or income, or on an hourly rate. The hourly rate will vary from about $100 to a whole lot more than that. The minimum fee is in the $150 range for a computer-generated plan which doesn't include any continuing service. For a custom-developed plan, expect to pay anywhere from $500 to $5,000, depending on its complexity. Fee-for-service planners are typically used by people with larger portfolios. This type of planner is in the minority, but their presence is growing.

Another way advisors or planners are paid is exclusively through commission on the sale of financial products. Straight sales-commissioned advisors generally offer free financial consultations. Upon determining your particular needs, they're then paid commission on any product they subsequently sell to you. The challenge is to be sure you aren't being sold something you don't need. This should be easy enough if you listen to that inner voice, or if you do some research (for example, reading this book and others like it) before going to see an advisor. This kind of advisor offers a wealth of information that can be gathered at no cost, provided you become adept at weeding out the sales pitches from the concrete facts. Most salespeople are responsible in their claims because the ramifications are too great if they're not. There are the few bad apples who ruin it for everyone, however. To avoid problems, your advisor is obligated to declare any conflicts of interest. You may also ask for an engagement letter explaining the terms and conditions and how the fees are charged.

The third way an advisor is paid is through a combination of commission and a fee for services. Some fee-based planners will charge for certain services and also make a commission when they sell certain products, like mutual funds, insurance, or securities. The fee is determined by the amount of work involved in designing the client's plan and the need for ongoing updating.

There's no doubt that good advice is available from all types of advisors or planners. Ultimately you make the decision as to what's best for you, not your advisor. If the financial products the advisor recommends meet your needs, then the fact that the advisor earns a living from selling them shouldn't be a major factor in your decision. Simply make it your business to know how your advisor or planner is paid, whether that payment can be negotiated, and whether it fits within your budget. If you sense that a particular product or company is being pushed too hard, try someone else. If you're convinced that commissioned advisors will not offer you objective advice, then a fee-for-services advisor is your answer. Remember, however, that whatever type of financial advisor you choose, you'll end up dealing with a commissioned sales-person at some point to purchase your mutual fund, RRSP, or insurance.

I've actually seen books written on this topic, but it all comes down to one thing and one thing only: *trust your gut.* Women are blessed with a wonderful intuition, so use it. And if for some reason you begin to get uncomfortable after the relationship has started, dump the planner. I've seen too many women hang on to bad planners for no other reason than loyalty or fear of confrontation. So, I can summarize an entire book's worth of information on this topic with this: trust your gut and if it doesn't work out … next!!

Now that Michael and I agreed to get an independent assessment, we then had to move into one of the least romantic areas of building our family's financial foundation—domestic contracts.

Domestic contracts

Oh, yippee. The terms "marriage contract" or "cohabitation agreement" are an anathema to newlyweds or engaged people. Try as I might to impart the wisdom of this to women, very few wanted to go down that road. Even citing the sobering divorce rate in this country wasn't enough. "It won't happen to us." I heard that more times than I care to count. Judging by the statistics, it sure as hell was happening to somebody.

Michael and I were of the same mind on this issue. It was a no-brainer. Historically, these agreements helped to protect men because they owned all the assets. Michael and I were pretty evenly matched asset-wise, but I was bringing a growing business into the partnership. Family law in Ontario dictated that the value of my business would be included in the net family property calculation. And who knows how I'd feel about that if we ever became part of the divorce statistics? Marriage contracts and cohabitation agreements can benefit everyone by an early mastering of the "who gets what" dance. Marriage contracts, in a nutshell, allow you to opt out of family law legislation and the Divorce Act and determine your own destiny as a couple. They can be entered into at any time, before or after the marriage, except that there's less incentive to sign a marriage contract post-nuptials, since you're giving up rights you automatically acquired by simply getting married. The same goes for cohabitation agreements, except they can be converted into a marriage contract should the couple choose that route. In either of these agreements you can "opt out" of support payments, essentially modifying or creating your own regime. The possibilities are endless. However, you can't deal with custody or access to children issues, and although technically you can deal with child support, it's not necessarily enforceable.

The bottom line is that a marriage contract or prenuptial agreement doesn't have to set a negative tone for your marriage. It certainly didn't for Michael and me. You're free to do whatever you want, whether that be split everything down the middle or give it all away. But should your marriage break down, you're not obligated to do anything other than what's stipulated in the agreement. I brought a company into the marriage; Michael brought a house. Now, I may choose to give Michael half the company and he may give me half the house, but we don't have to. (Whatever you do, seek legal counsel when it comes to determining what would happen with a house.) But had we not had a marriage contract, we would have been required to do so by law. We both have excellent earning capabilities, so we waived support obligations no matter how dramatically our financial circumstances changed.

The agreement doesn't have to be drafted by a lawyer, but it does have to be signed and witnessed. Whether a lawyer drafts the agreement or not, getting independent legal advice is essential. Furthermore, it's important to review this document whenever major life changes occur. A case in point: since I waived the right to any financial support in the event of marriage breakdown, what would happen to me if we decided a couple of years from now that I'd stay at home to look after our family? I would have put myself in a very precarious position. Significant changes in circumstances should automatically trigger a trip to the basement filing cabinet to review all your documents, from your will to the marriage contract.

Because common-law spouses have no statutory property rights in Canada, it's especially important that people who live together have an agreement. Like a marriage contract, a cohabitation agreement predetermines what happens to assets in the event one of you dies or you separate. I strongly recommend getting good legal advice before you go down the aisle or decide to share someone's address.

It was a remarkably freeing experience, having all these details—new wills and powers of attorneys, additional life and disability insurance—looked after. I gained a stronger sense of well-being knowing that Kate was going to be properly looked after should anything dire happen. All that was left to do was meet her.

Kate, on her way

It was Saturday and I was now only days away from my due date. My girth had expanded so much in the last month that my only chance of finding something comfortable to wear would have been from Joe's Tent and Awning. The day began as it usually did: breakfast, shopping at St. Lawrence Market, and home by lunch—except that I'd technically gone into labour earlier that morning, but didn't know it. We went to the hospital that afternoon because hours earlier my water had broken, but I felt not an ounce of pain. We were remarkably calm as we headed off just to be sure everything was where it should be. The nurse at the hospital hooked me up to a machine to see if I was really in labour. According to the monitor, I was indeed. The nurse announced, "Looks like your contractions are five minutes apart." Every ounce of calmness fled.

"How is that possible?" I asked incredulously. "I don't feel anything! Is it possible that I *won't* feel anything?"

The nurse smiled. "No," she said simply, and left it at that.

"Why don't you guys go home or go out for dinner?" she suggested casually. "This could take hours."

So, as mind-boggling as it seemed, we went home with the knowledge that our little girl was on her way. Michael and I couldn't stop grinning. This incessant little thought was niggling at the back of my mind that I was going to breeze through this with little pain. I couldn't shake the fact that my contractions were five minutes apart and I wasn't feeling anything worse than the dull ache similar to a period.

Around 7:00 that evening Michael decided to take a nap in preparation for the very long night ahead. My intellectual side agreed that was a good idea. My emotional side wanted to drive a steamroller over him. He went to sleep and I was left alone feeling bereft, abandoned, and completely neglected. I paced for two hours solid planning ways that I could make him pay.

At 9:00 p.m. the nurse's smile when I'd asked if I might not feel pain flashed briefly through my mind as an intense contraction ripped through my body, taking my breath away and doubling me over in a split second. A wave of fear and incredible excitement passed through me simultaneously.

So imagine this. The woman who dared entertain the thought that her labour was going to be painless is now on the way to the hospital, screaming like she was being murdered. At one point, my beloved husband was forced to make a U-turn in the middle of a major street, driving over the sidewalk in the process, because the police had blocked off the main road to the hospital. Apparently there was a shoot-out of some sort going on. Welcome to Toronto.

When we finally did get to the hospital, Michael and I took the time to have a fight about whether he should park in public parking (since he had no idea when he'd get back to the car) or, my preference, drive the car right into the damned lobby. Thankfully, calmer heads prevailed and he parked in the lot that was only a few feet away from the entrance.

Which turned out to be locked.

A sign said to use the south entrance after midnight. It was now close to 1:00 a.m. Michael remarked innocently that we needed to use another door. I launched straight into the stratosphere. In between contractions, which were coming fast and furious, I yelled to no one in particular that I had no idea where north let alone south was and as far as I knew all women had their babies in the wee hours of the morning and this had to be some kind of plot from some bonehead, probably a man, who didn't realize this small, minor detail and if someone didn't let us in immediately, I was going to have this baby on the front lawn of this esteemed establishment and I'd sue the pants off whomever was the closest.

Someone from the cleaning staff happened to walk by. I started to pound on the door. This whole thing began to seem very unreal. I'm having a baby, for God's sake, and Michael and I were pounding on the front door of the hospital to let us in. The woman shook her head and pointed to the sign that had sent me into a fit the first time around. I pounded even harder, threatening to burn the entire building down with her in it if she didn't open the door. She opened the door a tiny crack with the intention of telling us to go to another entrance. It was all we needed. Her eyes flew wide open as I pushed the door open and marched right past her. She began gesticulating wildly as Michael and I hurried over to the elevators. By the time we got to the labour room, my contractions were less than two minutes apart. Kate was making her way—fast.

A scant four hours later, at 5:00 a.m., my darling husband, with a little help from the nurse, delivered a stunningly beautiful seven-pound eight-ounce ball of perfection. Thirty-eight years had I waited for such a moment. The circle was completed.

By now I had completely forgiven Michael for his earlier transgression of falling asleep. It seemed so minor compared to the miracle we had created.

The new world order

Ten toes, 10 fingers, and very healthy lungs. It was clear there was a new boss in town. We now had to deal with the economics of childcare. After gazing into those baby blues, I knew no one but me and her dad were going to look after her in her first nine months. However, I now understand what they mean when they say "It takes a village to raise a child." That, and a truckload of money. Herein lay my dilemma. Being self-employed, I had no maternity benefits. Not only that, I sure as heck didn't have the money to hire a replacement, not that anyone really could replace me at work. My alleged maternity leave did last nine months, but I had to stay connected to the office every day or all would be lost. A recent StatsCan study showed that one in five Canadian women are forced back to work one month after their babies are born because of money. Two-thirds of that group are self-employed women. I sure understand why.

Rosa (my general manager at The Thomas Yaccato Group), Michael, and I worked out a fabulous arrangement. Rosa is one of those classic Italian moms brimming with love for children. To this day, Auntie Rosa ranks in Kate's top five favourite people. Using Rosa was ideal from another view-point: if I had a question about work, I just asked my nanny. Michael took one day a week and Rosa and I handled the rest. Essentially, Rosa filled in on the days when I was absolutely needed at work. Since I was breastfeed-ing, I couldn't go far. So, Kate came with me. For example, I was asked to speak at an important conference when Kate was five weeks old. I couldn't say no because of the business opportunities. So I brought Kate and Rosa. Royal Bank needed me to do some training for them in Winnipeg for two days when Kate was only four months old. Kate and Rosa came with me on the bank's dime. I did a documentary in Vancouver and Kate was there. In fact, this child clocked more air miles in her first year than most adults I know. If I had to attend an important meeting, which was rare, I brought Kate right into the boardroom with me. One or two eyebrows were raised, but generally people were flat-out delighted. I sat on the board of directors of Lester B. Pearson Airport in Toronto for four years. When I had to attend a board meeting, the president of the airport almost gleefully abdicated his office so that Kate and Rosa would have a quiet place to be. (The meetings were several hours long, and I brought Kate so that I could breastfeed and tickle during breaks.) We had a blast.

The cost of raising a child

As the nine-month anniversary drew closer, we had to start thinking about care on a full-time basis. We chose the nanny route. Although both Michael and I had downtown offices, we were fortunate enough to be able to work from home most of the time. It was very cozy. We all had breakfast and lunch together, and with both of us being home, we had ample time for tons of baby breaks.

The Cost of Raising a Girl to Age 18

Age	Food	Clothes	Health care	Personal care	Recreation and school	Transport	Child-care	Shelter	Total
Infant	$1,452	$1,669	$162	$ 0	$ 0	$ 0	$4,568	$2,079	$9,961
1	755	508	162	103	563	0	6,200	2,142	10,434
2	805	507	162	103	563	0	5,200	2,101	9,441
3	805	507	244	103	563	0	5,200	2,059	9,482
4	1,077	542	244	103	563	0	5,200	2,059	9,790
5	1,077	542	244	103	662	73	5,200	2,059	9,961
6	1,077	678	244	100	778	73	3,805	2,059	8,813
7	1,259	678	244	100	1,065	73	3,805	2,059	9,282
8	1,259	678	244	100	1,065	73	3,805	2,059	9,282
9	1,259	709	244	100	1,065	73	3,805	2,059	9,314
10	1,472	709	244	100	1,065	73	3,805	2,059	9,526
11	1,472	709	244	100	1,065	73	3,805	2,059	9,526
12	1,472	1,106	278	296	1,021	485	0	2,059	6,717
13	1,588	1,106	278	296	1,021	485	0	2,059	6,883
14	1,588	1,106	278	296	1,021	485	0	2,059	6,883
15	1,588	1,138	278	372	1,175	485	0	2,059	7,095
16	1,526	1,138	278	372	1,175	485	0	2,059	7,033
17	1,526	1,138	278	372	1,175	485	0	2,059	7,033
18	1,526	1,138	278	372	1,249	485	0	2,059	7,108
TOTAL	24,584	16,336	4,620	3,492	16,855	3,907	54,397	39,274	163,464

SOURCE: THIS CHART IS TAKEN FROM "BUDGET GUIDES," A DATABASE PRODUCED BY MANITOBA AGRICULTURE, FOOD, AND RURAL INITIATIVES AND CAN BE USED AS A GUIDELINE FOR FAMILY LIVING COSTS IN MANITOBA. REPRODUCED WITH PERMISSION.

Now, I agree wholeheartedly with descriptions like bundles of joy, one of life's greatest gifts, and so on. That still doesn't remove the fact that raising kids is damned expensive. It costs more to amuse kids than it did once to educate their parents. Take a gander at these charts showing the cost of raising a child.[1]

The Cost of Raising a Boy to Age 18*

Age	Food	Clothes	Health care	Personal care	Recreation and school	Transport	Child-care	Shelter	Total
Infant	$1,452	$1,699	$162	$ 0	$ 0	$ 0	$4,568	$2,079	$9,961
1	755	423	162	103	563	0	6,200	2,142	10,349
2	805	434	162	103	563	0	5,200	2,101	9,368
3	805	434	244	103	563	0	5,200	2,059	9,409
4	1,077	458	244	103	563	0	5,200	2,059	9,705
5	1,077	458	244	103	662	73	5,200	2,059	9,876
6	1,077	553	244	103	778	73	3,805	2,059	8,693
7	1,315	553	244	100	1,605	73	3,805	2,059	9,214
8	1,315	553	244	100	1,605	73	3,805	2,059	9,214
9	1,315	595	244	100	1,605	73	3,805	2,059	9,256
10	1,613	595	244	100	1,605	73	3,805	2,059	9,554
11	1,613	595	244	100	1,605	73	3,805	2,059	9,554
12	1,613	1,064	278	178	1,021	485	0	2,059	6,698
13	1,891	1,064	278	178	1,021	485	0	2,059	6,976
14	1,891	1,064	278	178	1,021	485	0	2,059	6,976
15	1,891	1,020	278	178	1,175	485	0	2,059	7,164
16	2,208	1,020	278	256	1,175	485	0	2,059	7,481
17	2,208	1,020	278	256	1,175	485	0	2,059	7,481
18	2,208	1,020	278	256	1,249	485	0	2,059	7,55
TOTAL	28,132	14,622	4,620	2,676	16,855	3,907	54,397	39,274	164,483

SOURCE: THIS CHART IS TAKEN FROM "BUDGET GUIDES," A DATABASE PRODUCED BY MANITOBA AGRICULTURE, FOOD, AND RURAL INITIATIVES AND CAN BE USED AS A GUIDELINE FOR FAMILY LIVING COSTS IN MANITOBA. REPRODUCED WITH PERMISSION.

Although the information in them is for Winnipeg, they still reflect good general guidelines. You can count on paying more if you live in Vancouver or Toronto. These charts don't include the costs of expensive stuff like hockey or equestrian equipment.

Whether it be nanny or daycare, the costs of childcare represent one big "Gulp!" And after two years of having a nanny, I began to realize that I was losing valuable Kate-time. While I was at work I constantly felt guilty about time missed with Kate; and when I was with Kate I felt guilty about not being at work. I decided it was much easier to live with the guilt about work than the guilt about Kate. We dusted the full-time nanny and I chose to stay home with Kate part-time until she went to school full-time. (She, believe it or not, is in grade three this year.)

The financial price of staying home for nine months took many years for me to pay. Then the decision to work part-time added to the financial challenges. This is what's meant by the costs of jumping in and out of the labour force during childbearing years. For me it meant many a lost business opportunity, although I wouldn't have it any other way. For women who work for corporate Canada, it can mean being bypassed for promotions. It can also mean lost retirement planning opportunities, since pension and RRSP calculations are based on earned income. Needless to say, my earned income was considerably less in the year I had Kate than in other years. I was lucky, however. I didn't end up having to access my RRSPs, although technically it would have been a good time to. Since my income was lower, my marginal tax rate was lower; therefore the tax hit from early RRSP withdrawal would have been lower. Many women are forced to use RRSPs as maternity benefits, either as a sole means of money or to top up Employment Insurance.

Many accountants believe that making RRSPs accessible for things like maternity leave, buying a home for the first time, or going back to school to better your lot in life is a good thing. I'm so torn here. The financial advisor part of me says "Don't do it—saving for your retirement is hard enough." The mother part of me says, "If it's all you've got and it makes your life better, go for it."

The one good thing about RRSPs and family planning is that the ability to carry forward unused RRSP contribution room can be helpful. Carry forward also enables those with little discretionary income to save their earned credits until such time as they have the money to contribute, or until their income is higher. This can be a great tax planning and tax deferral tool. I also had to remember that caregiving is often short-term (though it can feel otherwise) and that most women at some point re-enter the workforce.

The following are some of the tax planning tools and strategies that Michael and I could use now that we were parents.

Deducting childcare expenses

Childcare expenses are only deductible by the lower-income spouse, which would be me, of course, since I was the one who was off work as the primary caregiver. The deduction limit is $7,000 for each child under 7 and $4,000 for children 7 to 16. A child of any age with prolonged and severe mental or physical impairment receives up to a maximum of $10,000. I had to ensure that all my childcare payments for the year were made by December 31. Naturally, we needed to keep all receipts and keep track of the name and, when applicable, the social insurance number of the person we were paying. Childcare expenses can now be claimed for anyone under 16 at any time in the year, should you ever find yourself short of cash. All my single-parent friends attending school may now be able to claim a childcare expense deduction as well.

Canada Child Tax Benefit

The Canada Child Tax Benefit (CCTB) is a tax-free monthly payment made to eligible families to help them with the cost of raising children under age 18. Included with the CCTB is the National Child Benefit Supplement (NCBS), a monthly benefit for low-income families with children. The NCBS is the Government of Canada's contribution to the National Child Benefit (NCB), a joint initiative of federal, provincial, and territorial governments. As part of the NCB, certain provinces and territories also provide complementary benefits and services for children in low-income families, such as child benefits, earned income supplements, childcare, supplementary health benefits, and early prevention programs for children at risk.

To qualify, you have to be the person who's primarily responsible for the care and upbringing of the child. This means you're responsible for such things as supervising the child's daily activities and needs, ensuring the child's medical needs are met, and arranging for childcare when necessary. This person is usually the mother; however it can be the father, a grandparent, or a guardian.

When a marital breakdown has occurred, you may also have a court order or separation agreement that includes details concerning the care and upbringing of your child. There is a Children's Special Allowance for a child under age 18 who's under the care of a government department, agency, or institution. But you're not entitled to receive the CCTB for that child for any month in which the Children's Special Allowance is payable.

If you're the person who can receive the CCTB, you should apply as soon as possible, either after your child is born, a child starts to live with you, or you or your spouse meets the conditions outlined in the previous section. You shouldn't delay in applying because the government can generally only make retroactive payments for up to 11 months from the month it receives your application. However, if circumstances beyond your control prevented you from sending in your application on time, you can attach a note to your application or write to your tax centre to ask for an extension. In addition, if you apply for the benefit after the child is one year old, you have to attach proof of birth.

You should apply for the benefit even if you don't think you'll be entitled to receive it based on your current family net income. The government automatically recalculates your entitlement every July after receiving your tax information. If your family net income changes and you've already applied for the benefit, you won't need to remember to apply at that time. I've never been able to qualify, since my income (such as it was) was too high. No recriminations, however. This benefit should go to those who need it most.

For many low-income earners, the money from the tax credit is a good source of savings for their kids' education. Remember in the old days when our mothers put our baby bonus into a savings account for us? You can do the same with the Child Tax Benefit. And today there's even more help for saving for our children's education, in the form of RRSPs.

Income splitting

It's getting so that children have to be educated to realize that "damn" and "taxes" are two separate words. It's clear that we need to lower our household tax bill whatever way we can, and income-splitting is one of the few ways left. Spousal RRSPs allow you to split your income with your partner and accumulate tax-sheltered money in the hands of a lower-income spouse. The person with the higher income gets to write off the RRSP contribution, but, at retirement, the lower-income spouse will pay tax on the income. There is no immediate income splitting—it is long-term tax planning. Also, the higher-income earner putting money into the RRSP can only use his or her deduction limit to do this.

For example, Mom, who's in a 48 percent tax bracket, can split some of her income either with Dad, who's in a 26 percent tax bracket, or with her daughter, Sally, who's in the lowest possible tax bracket because she's still in school. Once Sally starts to work and earns an income, her tax liability will go up. This family is saving money on every dollar of taxable income transferred over. This is because the investment will be taxed in Dad's or Sally's hands, at their lower tax rate, when they cash it in. What's a little tax among family, right?

While there are some rules you'll need to keep in mind, income splitting is incredibly simple. Here are some ideas.

Get the family on the payroll

If you're self-employed, enlist the help of your family. Pay your kids or spouse a reasonable fee for the service they perform, while keeping it below the personal deduction threshold. Paying reasonable wages to family members for actual services rendered has four advantages: (1) the salaries will be deductible to the corporation or sole proprietorship; (2) the salaries will be taxed in the hands of those who get it, and, depending on the circumstances, probably at rates lower than the top marginal rate; (3) the salaries will enable family members to contribute to their own RRSPs; and (4) the tuition fee and education tax credits may mean that salaries paid to family members attending university may attract little or no tax at all.

When I was a teenager my dad had me work in his office doing odd jobs. At the time I thought he was just doing the dad thing, but as it turns out, he was actually income splitting. In other words, he was trying to slim down his tax bill. This is how it works: say Dad made $60,000. His marginal tax bracket would be around 33 percent. Since he owned his own business, he hired me to do some filing and telemarketing for him. I got paid about $5,000 over the year for my work. So he ended up with an expense of $5,000, which would reduce his income by the same amount. That means he saved 33 percent of that, or $1,650 in taxes. Since I didn't have any other income, I pocketed the money tax free. The results? The family was ahead by $1,650.

Get the lower-income spouse investing

Another idea is to try to maximize the amount of money the lower-income spouse can invest. Why? Because the lower your marginal tax bracket, the lower the tax rate you'll pay on any earnings from your investments. If the higher-income spouse buys a GIC, for instance, he or she will pay 50 percent tax on the interest. If the lower-income spouse bought the same GIC, depending on his or her income he or she could pay anything from 0 percent to 41 percent on the interest. That means the higher-income spouse should try to pay for as much of the ongoing, non-tax-deductible living expenses as possible. This is so the lower-income spouse can free up money to invest at their lower tax rate. Another way to income split is if you're an entrepreneur. As my dad did, you can hire your spouse and children. The money you pay them becomes a deductible cost of business. But this has to be legit. They must do what you hire them to do and be paid market rates. This reduces your income, which is taxable at a high rate, and increases the income of your family, who are taxed at a lower rate.

Spousal RRSPs

This was dealt with in some detail in chapter 5. But from an income-splitting point of view, it essentially shifts retirement income to the spouse with the lower tax rate in retirement. Let's look at Sherez and Miguel, a retired couple. Miguel earned their $80,000 retirement income, while Sherez raised the family. Sherez saw that they'd pay top tax rate if Miguel contributed only to a regular RRSP, and that the more preferred option was if they each earned $40,000. The net income is the same, but it's taxed at a lower rate. But this isn't the key point with spousal RRSPs. The primary purpose is to build spousal RRSPs so that at retirement both partners' incomes would be as equal as possible. Another option at retirement in this type of situation is to split CPP benefits between spouses.

Remember that you can put any amount into a spousal RRSP up to your limit. If your RRSP contribution goes into a spousal plan, it's taxed differently. The contributing partner gets the deduction, but it's taxed in the lower-income partner's hands when it's taken out.

Here are some ideal scenarios for using spousal RRSPs for income splitting:

- The classic one is you work unpaid in the home.
- Both partners work at the moment, but one is planning to take time away from the workforce to have and raise the kids. This could also apply if one partner wants to go back to school. There is a way to use spousal RRSPs to help plan for baby. You can "bank" your RRSP savings and withdraw them later with little or no tax. However, you need to plan way in advance for this to work. You have to wait two years after the contributions into the spousal plan were made to withdraw. Otherwise, they're taxed back to the contributor's hands, which kind of defeats the whole purpose. This can be avoided by having one RRSP purely for spousal money and another for personal contributions that can be withdrawn any time. Where the two-year rule doesn't apply is if the partners break up, one of them dies, or one becomes a non-resident. In the event of a relationship breakdown, spousal RRSPs are subject to asset-splitting rules under provincial family law, though those of common-law couples may not be. Exercise care.
- One has a good pension plan and the other one doesn't.
- Both you and your partner work in the paid labour force, neither of you has access to pension plans, and one earns far more than the other. At retirement, if your spouse has C/QPP benefits that are significantly lower and he or she is in a lower tax bracket, you can transfer up to half of your benefits into his or her hands and lower your tax bill. At retirement, you can apply to have the benefit equalized.

If you receive Child Tax Benefit payments, put them into a bank or trust account in your child's name so that they aren't subject to the attribution rules. Since your child won't be earning significant income for many years, the tax hit will be negligible. What a terrific way to save up for medical school. Today's dime is really a dollar with all the taxes deducted. That's why income splitting makes sense.

It really comes down to levelling out the amount of money the different members in your family make. For example, my dad made a good deal of money and Mom made none, being a stay-at-home mother, and as a result they may have paid much more to Canada Revenue Agency than a household where both people have modest incomes. So Dad's goal in income splitting was to simply move some income out of the hands of the person in the higher tax bracket and into the hands of the person in the lower tax bracket.

As already mentioned, a small business owner may have more opportunities for income splitting than salaried employees.

You must be very careful to follow these rules or Canada Revenue Agency will tax income back to the higher earner. Canada Revenue Agency will not allow one spouse to give sizeable amounts of investment assets (except spousal RRSPs) to the other without the income from those assets being attributed back to the spouse who gave them. There are ways around this—for example, loaning money at interest. Your accountant will help you explore legal ways to split income.

Saving for your child's education
RESPs and the CESG

After making the mortgage and minivan payments and forking out a small fortune on Kate's miniature wardrobe, financing her university education seems daunting. The latest number-crunching suggests a four-year degree could hit $75,000 by the time Kate is ready for university.

A Registered Education Savings Plan (RESP) is one answer to saving for your kids' education while saving you some money in the tax department. Distinct improvements have been made to loosen the pronounced restrictions that applied to RESPs in the past. Most notably, Ottawa will match up to 20 percent of the first $2,000 contributed to an RESP, to a maximum of $400 a year. This is the Canada Savings Education Grant (CESG). Parents, grandparents, or other family members can contribute up to $4,000 per beneficiary annually, for up to 21 years. This is up to a lifetime maximum of $42,000. Like an RRSP, you have a choice of investment options, mutual funds likely being the best.

Saving in such a plan offers several advantages: income earned within the plan is sheltered from taxes; students cashing in an RESP will likely be in such a low income bracket they won't be hit hard by the tax collector; and the 20 percent federal education savings grant could, over the 18 years of a child's growth, add more than $7,000 to the RESP. However, unlike an RRSP, contributions aren't deductible.

Other good news is that regulations around getting your money out should your offspring reject academic life have been relaxed, though restrictions still apply. The importance of this was brought home one day while I was watching Kate, then two, try to fit one of her father's hiking boots on her head. Not the actions of a budding brain surgeon. As I watched her goofy antics, I started to think about her wide-open future, which, as far as her parents are concerned, includes university. Michael and I decided to contribute jointly to an RESP for her, but what if she decided not to go? What happens if Kate decides she'd rather become an entrepreneur like her mom, instead of a student? What would happen to all that money we stashed away for her?

If Kate doesn't attend a qualifying educational program at a postsecondary educational institution, she doesn't get to use the money in the RESP. We can pull out the amount we contributed with no tax consequences. But the income earned inside the RESP is a different story. We can withdraw it, but the plan must have been in existence for 10 years and none of the beneficiaries can be in school, with the youngest being at least 21. The subscriber must be a resident at the time of withdrawal, as well. We can defer tax on the RESP withdrawal if we transfer up to the lifetime limit of $50,000 into our own or a spousal RRSP and if we have the RRSP contribution room. If we do not have the RRSP room, we will have to pay regular income tax on the withdrawal, plus a 20 percent penalty tax. Those are pretty big "ifs" with very big consequences, so it is important to do the tax math before we make a decision.

Naturally, the government's CESG must be repaid. We, as her parents, can name another beneficiary, but the money still must be used within the original 25-year time frame. This is a giant pain. One way around this is to open a new RESP every five years since there's no restriction on how many plans you can hold. With staggered maturity dates, Kate has a bit more flexibility should she decide to "do Europe" for a year or two after high school. For those who haven't been in a plan for 10 years, contributions would be returned, but without any interest or other income generated. Or the RESP money can be donated to a postsecondary institution, which would be generous to say the least, but not the wisest move from a personal finance point of view. Finally, we could simply withdraw her contributions and pay a 20 percent penalty on top of regular income taxes. This was a lot to think about. Life is always a gamble, but after witnessing Kate finally getting that boot on her head, I figured it was worth a try. I just pray that her stick-to-it-iveness is an indication of more worldly academic pursuits.

Talk to an advisor to get the full scope of the different options concerning RESPs and the CESG. The advice about RESPs used to be simple: don't invest in them. That isn't the case anymore.

In-trust accounts

Among the few things that are more expensive than an education these days is the lack of it. So with the money we received from Kate's grandparents when she was born Michael and I have decided to also take advantage of an in-trust account. This we started shortly after Kate and I were wheeled out of the delivery suite. We set up the account because a minor can't enter into a binding contract. Most in-trust accounts are informal. Creating one that keeps Canada Revenue Agency happy requires the following steps.

First, clearly spell out who's giving the money, who's receiving the money, and who's controlling the money. Under the Income Tax Act, the trustee—the person who controls it—can't be the person giving it. Make sure the account is set up as "parents' name in trust for the child" as opposed to just the child's name. And finally, make sure you state that the property is irrevocable, meaning the person who gives the money can't get it back and has no control over how it's invested or used. Remember, though the trustee has legal ownership of the assets, the child is the beneficiary of the owner of the trust assets. You can't go dipping into it every time you're short of cash, no matter how informal the trust is. Once Kate has reached the age of majority and assumes control of the trust, it's hers. (This can be a major downside if Kate turns out to be less than responsible on the financial side of life.) Interest and dividends will be taxed in my and Michael's hands and Kate gets the capital gains.

Michael and I really deliberated on the best way to save for Kate's education. Many people have the same dilemma: RESP or in-trust account? The generally accepted wisdom that I follow is this: first, contribute $2,000 to the RESP, which will maximize the 20 percent grant; and second, contribute any leftover cash flow (a pretty major if …) to an informal trust account. An RESP qualifies for almost any kind of education program. Looking forward, I can't imagine how a young adult wouldn't take some postsecondary education that wouldn't qualify.

Bev Evans suggests that if the parents had the cash, she would advise them to put the additional funds into the RESP also. Though they won't get any more grant money (it only applies to the first $2,000), the additional funds will be tax sheltered as well.

Life insurance savings plans

Life insurance companies have life insurance plans that they sell specifically for children's education. The tax-sheltered cash value of the policy is used to fund the cost of education. This cash value has no restrictions of any kind; it can be used for education for your children or to buy yourself a boat. If used for the children, the money is taxed back to the student at the rate applicable to his or her low tax bracket when the policy is cashed in. But remember, the cash value in the plan is based on projections. Make sure the interest rate being projected is reasonable. Withdrawals and cancellation fees can be onerous. You're also buying insurance with these plans, so be sure you're comfortable with this. Review the whole life and universal life sections of chapter 6. These are precisely what insurance company education plans are. Make sure that as a savings tool for your child's education the plan you choose suits your needs specifically.

Paying off your mortgage early

Well, why not? The idea here is to eliminate your largest debt in order to free up cash later that can then be put aside to fund your child's education. There are several ways to pay down your mortgage quickly, as outlined in chapter 7. You can make prepayments, increase your payments, and pay weekly. The thing to consider here is that each mortgage payment contributes to a possibly healthy tax-free return. Once the mortgage is paid off, ideally a few years before your child will need the money, continue putting the same amount aside into an education fund. Since you don't have time on your side, be careful about investing in higher-risk investments. If you use the mortgage pay-down method and still find yourself short of cash for school, you can always borrow on the built-up equity in your house.

Mutual funds

If you start early enough, a stock market–based or equity mutual fund outside of an RESP can be a great way to save for your children's education. You're not limited to any specific contribution amount, nor to how the money is spent. And since you could have 15 to 18 years to let the money accumulate, you'll get the maximum benefit of compound growth. If market swings bother you, invest in a balanced fund, which generally fluctuates less although the chances for superior growth are fewer.

By way of comparison, if you use a Canada Savings Bond, for example, to save for your child's education, all the interest it earns is attributed back to the parent until the child reaches the age of majority. This isn't the case with the capital gain you receive with equity mutual funds. Mutual funds can act as a significant tax deferral, since you don't pay any tax until you actually cash them in. It's important to choose equity mutual funds that emphasize capital gain over income because the parents will have to pay tax on dividends or distributions from their children's equity investments. However, keep in mind that even though the attribution rules will tax you on dividends or interest, the amount is usually pretty small.

In our discussion of mutual funds in chapter 6, we talked about small and large cap funds. Though riskier, choose mutual funds that concentrate on smaller companies that don't pay dividends rather than blue chip banks and phone companies that do. Make sure you have a good cross-section of industries and countries represented in the fund so that you can benefit from the superior returns one gets from diversification. The same standard applies: maintain that long-term view of a minimum of 10 years and you'll generally come out in good shape. Funding your child's education through equity funds involves the same principles as does your retirement planning. When your child gets closer to the age when the money will be needed, start to protect your gains by shifting into more guaranteed investments. When your child is 11 or 12, 10 percent a year should start going into money market funds, GICs, and the like. Others advise starting to shift as your child moves through high school. Your financial advisor will help you pick a fund that's appropriate for your specific goals.

Your children's earnings

I learned early in life that anything worth having requires a little pain and sacrifice. I saved for my own university tuition. I worked part-time from the age of 15, full-time in the summer, and I put money aside into a separate account earmarked for school. My dad had his own business and he paid me to do odd jobs. My savings, plus a student loan, got me through school. Michael did the same. He got through engineering school with money earned through summer jobs and student loans. The wonderful lessons your children learn by becoming part of the process of putting themselves through school are invaluable. Michael and I plan on making sure Kate learns some of these life skills. Because the costs of education are escalating dramatically, we'll be sure to give her a significant head start, but not a free ride. The enormous costs mean that it's important to make your kid's education a financial priority, for them and you. It's not about us footing Kate's entire education bill. Like me, kids who work their way to and through university are a pretty good bet to be able to work their way through life.

Money management for your children

Educating children in money matters should be a matter of course, just like teaching them the facts of life or how to drive. Kids who don't learn to manage money have a way of showing up later on their parents' doorstep. You need only ask my parents. Done in the right way, teaching your children about money can be a wonderful experience for both of you. Many young people will reach adulthood in an unforgiving economy and brutal job market, along with the burden of providing social programs for the baby boomers. Teaching them money management skills is the kindest thing you can do.

One approach is to have your children manage their own bank account and their allowance. Allowance shouldn't be tied to doing chores; it should be used strictly as a tool to teach children about saving and budgeting. Also, with this approach they don't learn that the only reason to do things around the house is for the money. Making beds and doing dishes are a fundamental part of family life. But if they want to earn extra money, doing extra chores is an ideal way.

You could give your teenager a larger allowance, say an amount monthly instead of weekly, and a freer rein on spending. And a monthly clothing allowance above their regular allowance will save you the headache of doing their shopping, and will teach your teenagers good shopping habits, say, the value of one good piece over several cheaper pieces. They'll also learn the fine art of budgeting in a real hurry. This method will only succeed if you can abide the inevitable whining that will come the first few times it doesn't work. Patience and ear plugs will be essential. It's vital that kids understand the consequences of their actions. They need to learn the art of setting goals and be allowed to feel the elation of success and the depths of defeat.

Teach them the principles of comparison shopping when you go to buy groceries and involve them in your next car purchase. As they get older, try to educate them as well as you can about the world of marketing and advertising. Use the Saturday morning cartoon advertising blitz as an example of how companies target young children. Then show them how advertising changes on weekday afternoons to get to the women's market, and how Saturday afternoon sports go right after dad's money, and so on. This way you can instill in your child both a good understanding of and a healthy dose of cynicism toward the ads they're bombarded with on TV.

As for investing, my favourite technique is to catch their interest in the stock market by giving them a stock in something they can identify with, like McDonald's, Sony, or Microsoft. These stocks make great birthday or "welcome to the world" gifts. Get the children involved in the decision-making process and explain the inner workings of the market in a way that's applicable to their lives. I had a friend who did this with some McDonald's stock that I'd given to her daughter. A stock split gave my friend an opportunity to teach her child even more about how things worked. They'll learn about dividends and dividend re-investment. Don't for a second think this stuff is over the child's head. Remember, they're the ones teaching you the difference between RAM and ROM. (For the technological Luddites, these are computer terms.) Remember, your children learn much about life through what you do. Role modelling is a powerful influence on your kids. Make sure your own house is clean. You never know what messages are being sent to your children.

A case in point. I spent a week with my twin nieces when they were five years old. These kids, incidentally, have been getting a financial education from me since they were three. We were sitting around the dining room table after lunch one day gravely discussing why green trucks drive faster than blue ones. One of my nieces claimed she was going to "pay cash" for a green truck just like Auntie Jo's when she grew up. (I drive a green jeep.)

I became curious. Heaven knows where she had picked up the term "pay cash." I didn't imagine she even knew what it meant. My brother, the father of these bright and talented children, was roaming about doing whatever. He overheard our chatter and came into the dining room to listen in. I decided to test the children's financial literacy. "Okay girls," I began, "if Auntie Jo gave you a loonie right now, what would you do with it?"

Leaning against the china cabinet with his arms folded across his chest, my brother looked on with decided interest. If the twins are anything like we used to be, his expression suggested, we're about to hear a litany of the freezies, licorice, sour candies, and chocolate bars they'd buy. My nieces didn't miss a beat. Not even a slight hesitation. "We'd put it in our piggy bank until we grew up."

My brother and I looked at each other. A knowing and relieved smile spread across our faces. All was well with the world.

Tax planning for kids

If you want the definition of poverty, ask parents with two or three teenagers in the family. It makes a certain amount of sense to take what appears to be a financial liability—your kids—and turn them into a tax planning tool. The first step is to get them educated that liquid assets aren't a case of beer. Then you need to find a way to get them interested in the family tax planning process. When you think about it, our most expensive dependant these days is the government.

One way is to get your kids into the habit of filing a tax return, even if there are no taxes owing. This will start them down the road to RRSPs, the best tax-sheltered savings tool available. I read about a kid who had been filing tax returns since she was 13. By the time she graduated from university, she had accumulated $6,000 in RRSP contribution room. She made her first contribution of $6,000 the first year after school and saved over $2,500 in taxes.

Here's another great idea. As soon as Kate's old enough to start earning an income, I'll have her start contributing to an RRSP. My dad was quick to point out that she doesn't need the deduction. But Kate can save the deduction indefinitely and claim it in the future when she needs it. That also means the money is compounding tax free for a much longer period of time. And when you consider that your money doubles every seven years with an interest rate of 10 percent it's pretty motivating.

Since I run my own business, when Kate's old enough I'll pay her a reasonable salary or wages for lending a hand. Then I can deduct what I pay her. So when doing your tax return, take the family approach. These days, doing your tax return is like a do-it-yourself mugging. We need all the help we can get.

Banks and kids

Financial institutions see today's small change as tomorrow's fortune. To tap into this pool of adolescent cash, there's a huge array of kid-friendly programs, services, and savings vehicles. When I opened Kate's first bank account, she got a higher interest rate than I would have on a comparable account. She's now learning about the value of earning interest.

Some banks offer rewards for opening an account. Scotiabank has a Getting There account that reduces service charges until the account holder reaches age 18.

Royal Bank deposits $5 into every new account. CIBC gives its new customers a kid's pack that includes a wallet, pencil, ruler, and stickers. Royal Bank has a Building Block GIC for youngsters 12 and under. The minimum GIC is $250, but kids can contribute as little as $5 a week and take up to one year to accumulate the principal. RBC is also increasing financial literacy by developing curriculum-based seminars on such topics as money and banking, saving, spending, and sharing, and is making the cost of postsecondary education real to students.

Add CD-ROMs and websites to the list, and you can see there's no excuse for kids growing up financially illiterate. But, the marketing premise aside, these excellent programs create incentive and can make learning profitable and a lot of fun.

These are but a few of the strategies and ideas Michael and I have and will use for family financial planning. But I needed to pay attention to something else. Not only had my life dramatically changed as a result of becoming a mom, I was a self-employed mom.

Being a woman entrepreneur

Most women I know, including those who don't have children, often refer to their business as "my baby." It was during my second year of running my own business that I had Kate, and I was profoundly struck by the similarities in conceiving, giving birth to, and raising both of my babies—Kate and my business. Whether they relate to a child or a business, conception and the prenatal phase, birth, the first year, and the toddler years are very different stages. You conceive the business idea and grow it to the point that it can be born strong and healthy. You take the first year to nurture the business, tenderly guiding it, looking after all of its most basic needs. Once your business reaches the toddler stage, you let it venture out cautiously to explore and expand in the world.

The personal finance life of a woman entrepreneur can be quite involved, and is beyond the scope of this book. So allow me to pause for a brief commercial break. Recognizing and having lived through the supreme financial and emotional challenges of running a business and having a family, I decided to write about the experience. *Raising Your Business: A Canadian Woman's Guide to Entrepreneurship* chronicles the life cycle of a business. With my story as the glue, each chapter deals with a different part of the process, from conception of the business idea, the planning that goes into the birth of a business, the screaming meemies of the first year, and finally the toddler years, up to and including age five, when you deal with growth issues. Each chapter addresses the requirements and issues around human resources, accounting, financial management, technology, and sales and marketing, but as they pertain to that particular phase of the business and to women as entrepreneurs. The book is filled with painfully honest details of the many mistakes I made as a struggling entrepreneur. My mother laughs and says my role in life is to fall down, bump my chin, scrape my knee, get up, and write about it.

Relationship breakdown

I'm often asked what, from a financial perspective, women who find themselves in this heartbreaking position need to do. From a financial point of view, a woman going through a relationship breakdown needs to do the exact same thing as someone single or still married. The major difference between women going through, say, a divorce, and those who aren't may be that they haven't managed money before. They either didn't do it as a couple or their partner did the financial planning. Women may also find themselves being forced to make important financial decisions when they're the least capable of doing so. Women living the trauma of a relationship breakdown need to know the questions to ask, or at least someone who does.

Sharon Cohen is a family lawyer and mediator in Toronto. She is a partner at a 10-lawyer all-woman law firm, Dickson MacGregor Appell LLP. They practise in the area of family law, adoption, and estates. Sharon stresses that separation or divorce needn't be acrimonious or adversarial. Mediation or Collaborative Family Law can ensure that the family plans for the future in the most supportive manner possible; just because you do not wish to remain spouses doesn't mean you can't continue to work together as a family. The financial and emotional savings in a non-adversarial process help to control the damage of separation for you and, most importantly, for your children.

Collaborative Family Law is an interest-based negotiation process whereby both clients and their lawyers sign a contract not to go to court. The clients, their lawyers, and other jointly retained professionals work as a team to resolve all issues. For more information, visit the Collaborative Family Law Association of Ontario website, www.collaborativefamilylawassociation.com.

Slow and easy are the watchwords here. Women in this position need to build their own financial foundation based on the power of one instead of a unit of two. That means getting debt under control, establishing an emergency fund, and getting wills and powers of attorney in place or adjusted. You need to change the beneficiaries on your RRSPs, survivor benefits on pensions, existing life insurance policies, or plain and simply just get life insurance. You've got to learn how to manage the family's budget and make investment and retirement planning decisions that will ensure your money will last at least as long as you do. You basically need to do everything outlined in this book.

The most common mistakes

Toby Condliffe is an investment counsellor who deals with many women living through a divorce. In his experience, the following are the most common mistakes made by women going through relationship breakdown.

- Making too many concessions on financial issues in the hope that their ex will make concessions on the more important issue of custody. Toby says, "At the end of the day, the two issues are separate; one has nothing to do with the other. When going through a breakdown, don't be your own negotiator. Involve a lawyer or mediator quickly, at least as quickly as your partner does." In fact, if you're the party doing the leaving, consult a matrimonial lawyer before you leave so that you can be aware of all the issues that ignite from relationship breakdown. In other words, get your house in order before you walk out the door.

- Here are a couple of good tips. Bad-mouthing your spouse during legal proceedings can make the situation worse. Try finding a therapist who's an objective observer and to whom you can bad-mouth your spouse all you want. This may help you remain calm during tense negotiations where calm is essential. Secondly, evaluate what's really important and don't get too distracted to keep those items in the forefront. For example, if keeping the children happy is a major priority (as one would assume), then evaluate needs and demands between the spouses with that priority in mind. It will help to keep you focused.

- Not knowing what they don't know. Many women aren't aware of the value of such things as their husband's pension plan or deferred profit sharing plan, which may not be obvious assets in the way a bank balance is. It might not occur to them to probe into such things. So it comes down to getting educated and knowing what to ask. The emotional backlash that results from a situation like this isn't often conducive to learning, which is all the more reason to be financially literate at as young an age as possible. Waiting until catastrophe strikes to learn something as important as managing your money won't serve people's best interest. If this is you, get a lawyer who does a lot of divorce work. They'll know the answers to questions like "What happens to his pension plan upon divorce?"

- Not knowing how to find a good expert to help, whether that be a lawyer, financial advisor, or therapist. As stated earlier, you want to go to a lawyer who does a lot of divorces. Ask the question, "How many divorces have you done in the last year?" (If she or he answers "Ten," know that that isn't a lot and that her or his inexperience could mean that you can quickly run up the costs.) Shop around to find a lawyer who's compatible with you. Get a good understanding of the basic process and principles involved. Then, if it's at all possible thereafter, do the stuff yourself where lawyers aren't needed, such as arranging child visits, etc. This can save you a small fortune.

  As for financial advice, I'm of the mind that you can get good advice from all forms of financial planners or advisors as long as you know how they're paid. However, in this situation, I suggest you find someone who's paid by you directly for their services, in other words, a fee-for-service planner as opposed to commission-based sales people. You've got enough to worry about right now. Whether or not you're being sold something you don't need should not be on your list.

- Not knowing how to determine if the advisor to whom they've been referred is truly good and expert. It comes down to this: if the person comes to you well referred by someone who lived through a similar situation, it's as good a place to start as any. Check with the provincial law society, which can make referrals.

Also, be aware of gender bias. It is still rampant in the business world, as Chester the credit risk manager will attest. Believe me, the legal and financial planning professions are by no means exceptions. Ask the lawyer or planner how many women he or she works with. Ask the lawyer if he or she represents more women than men in divorces. Most will likely say both. Figure out a way to flush out gender bias. Remember Lynn's lawyer, who upon finding out Stan had stashed assets commented, "If I were him I'd do the same thing"? Don't let comments like that fly by unheeded. They're a warning sign of huge proportions.

- Not knowing enough about the family budget. It's difficult to agree to a financial settlement and child support without hands-on experience and detailed knowledge of at least a year's worth of expenses and how these will change as the children grow older. And even if you do have this knowledge, there are a lot of expenses you can forget to include when you're negotiating a settlement. Buy yourself a copy of Quicken or Microsoft Money, get out the family chequebook, and enter the transactions from the last year. Or get a bookkeeper to do it. That way, you'll be in a better position to know what to ask for.

- Not being aware of the implications of a second marriage or relationship. Statistically, a second marriage is more likely than a first marriage to break up. Since there may be unequal assets going into a second relationship, a domestic contract, albeit unromantic, is desirable.

This is a classic divorce story with a twist. Michelle's story is compelling because it's from the perspective of "the other woman." Michelle, a close friend of mine, married a man who'd gone through a messy divorce. This was before she even arrived on the scene. What's worse, he had an atrocious lawyer. Gerard, her husband, came from a place of fear because he wanted to protect the right to see his children. He gave away almost everything in order to do just that. (See the first point above.) Understandably, marriage or more children was not a reality for him at that time.

Enter Michelle. Today, the two of them barely have enough money to survive. They're forced to live in a high-rise apartment with two young kids because he pays his ex $1,100 a month. Gerard is self-employed and has all the challenges that entails. He doesn't make a lot of money. His kids are now 17 and 20 and show up at Michelle and Gerard's home wearing $150 running shoes. Michelle can barely afford shoes for her own children. Her children are suffering and she's suffering. Their car just blew up and she can't figure out a way to get her daughter to school.

The financial picture aside, the emotional toll has been dramatic. Although Michelle and Gerard are still very tight, this divorce has affected the quality of their marriage and has taken an emotional toll on the children. Michelle has this advice for anyone considering getting into a second serious relationship: "Unless he's a millionaire, you'll likely be financially responsible for your children. He'll be busy having to financially look after the children from the first marriage. My God, sit down and talk intimately about money before you even consider going down that aisle. Educate yourself to the possibility that the first wife can and will come back if you're doing well, especially if you have additional kids. It doesn't matter if you have 1 child or 20, you still have to pay the child support. When we got married, we were sued for more support. When we got our condo and had our first child, we were sued again. We lost the condo. I didn't know what I didn't know and I should have been more prepared for what happened. In retrospect I should have said, I'm not marrying you until I'm convinced your ex-wife isn't an emotional issue for you anymore. Get therapy. I should have got myself educated on family law and money matters. Bottom line? Just know the guy you're going to marry, especially financially."

About the child support initiative

According to StatsCan, only 56 percent of single-parent, female heads of households with children under 18 receive support from their departed partner.

On May 1, 1997, the new federal Child Support Guidelines became law, changing the manner in which child support amounts are determined under the Divorce Act. The provinces also have legislation in place that pretty much mirrors the federal legislation. The guidelines consist of a set of rules and tables for calculating the amount of support that a paying parent should contribute toward his or her children. This legislation was essential in order to improve and modernize Canada's child support system. There was so much controversy around the old way—men could deduct the amount paid to their spouses but women were required to pay tax on what they received.

The federal Child Support Guidelines make the calculation of child support fair, predictable, and more consistent. The guidelines take into account the average costs of raising a child and include rules for calculating child support payments. The calculation is based on the support-paying parent's income, the number of children, and the province or territory where the support-paying parent lives. The guidelines recognize that the custodial parent contributes a similar percentage of his or her income to the needs of the child or children because the standards of living of the custodial parent and child are inseparable.

Under the guidelines, child support payments can be adjusted to recognize a child's special expenses or to prevent financial hardship for a parent or child in extraordinary circumstances.

The new child support system also includes new tax rules for child support payments. Child support paid under a written agreement or court order made on or after May 1, 1997 will no longer be deductible to the payer, or included in the income of the recipient for tax purposes. The new tax treatment will apply to all new child support orders made on or after May 1, 1997. However, if either spouse with an existing child support order wishes to change their order, they have a right to do so and the new tax laws will apply to their new child support order.

Although not part of the legislation, it's important to note that enforcement procedures have been strengthened to help provincial and territorial enforcement agencies ensure that family support obligations are respected. The changes include:

- the suspension of certain federal licences, including passports and various licences issued by Transport Canada, in cases of persistent default
- the addition of Canada Revenue Agency to the list of departments whose databanks can be searched to locate defaulters
- expanding access to federal pension benefits to satisfy support arrears, and improvements to computer systems to permit online computer access between federal, provincial, and territorial enforcement services

Same-sex couples

The Family Law Act in Ontario has been amended to include same-sex partners with respect to claims for spousal support and states that "same-sex partner" means either two persons of the same sex who have cohabited (a) continuously for a period of not less than three years or (b) in a relationship of some permanence, if they are the natural or adoptive parents of a child.

The Family Law Act has no definition, however, that includes same-sex partners with respect to claims for a division of property or the "matrimonial" home. The Supreme Court of Canada recently decided that it was not a breach of the Charter of Rights and Freedoms to exclude common-law heterosexual spouses from claims to division of property and the matrimonial home. However, in Ontario, British Columbia, and Quebec, same-sex partners now have the right to marry. Therefore, while same-sex married partners may be able to claim property division, the Family Law Act has not been amended to include them as defined "spouses" in the property sections of the act. In addition, the Divorce Act does not include same-sex partners in its definition of spouses for claims under that statute.

In the meantime, this doesn't mean there aren't legal ways to protect a partner's interest in property that's in the other person's name alone. One method is to put real estate, bank accounts, and investments in joint names and to maintain the other partner as a beneficiary on life insurance policies and RRSPs. Doing so will protect that person in "estate" situations where other family members may attempt to exert a "blood" priority over assets. Including a partner in a will will also help to ensure that the person is protected in an estate division.

In death, a claim under the Dependent's Relief Act might be enough to provide the dependent partner with support, though the criteria and term of support may be decided differently by a court than would a spousal support award.

Same-sex partners may now enter into a domestic contract to opt in or out of any of the rights and responsibilities dictated by legislation. Quebec, Nova Scotia, and shortly Manitoba have put into place Registered Domestic Partnerships that provide certain rights to both same-sex and heterosexual cohabiting partners who do not wish to marry.

Exerting rights against a partner directly in a separation is somewhat harder when the relationship isn't recognized by statute directly. One possibility is for a person to claim either a "resulting trust" or a "constructive trust" in the assets. A resulting trust occurs when both people intended that there be an interest in the asset, even if the asset isn't in the name of both parties.

A constructive trust is when a person has put time, effort, and/or finances into an asset and therefore is entitled to an equitable interest. The argument can extend to a division in the equity in a pension and investments. Since spousal support isn't a possibility (but will likely be very soon), a claim under the Dependent's Relief Act might be sufficient to provide the dependent partner with support, though the criteria and term of support may be decided differently by a court than would a spousal support award in a heterosexual relationship. Also, consider a contract between the partners. It needn't be a domestic contract, since same-sex couples aren't currently covered, but a regular contract.

According to Hamilton-based lawyer Gabe Araiche, "Employment benefits still cause a great deal of problems as the internal policies of most companies still do not recognize same-sex relationships as forming a marital or common-law relationship. Therefore benefits are often denied a same-sex partner. Same-sex partners are often denied other benefits as well, such as the ability to share RRSP contribution through a spousal rollover."

It looks like the federal government has leapt into the 21st century. In 2000, it passed legislation including the Income Tax Act, changing the definition of spouse to include same-sex partners. The definition is two persons cohabiting in a conjugal relationship for at least one year. Same-sex partners can now share certain benefits, such as the ability to share RRSP contribution through a spousal rollover. The federal government is currently debating changes to the definition of marriage to expand it to include same-sex partners.

Elder care

A close friend of mine recently had a huge fight with her older brother about the whereabouts of their mother's $80,000 estate. Lisa was her mother's primary caregiver and power of attorney during her mother's 18-month illness. Her brother demanded to know where all the money went, since it had been earmarked as an inheritance. Lisa had to tell him she spent every dime of it. Her brother naturally flipped out, yelling at her, "What could you possibly have spent that amount of money on?" Lisa said she watched her brother's face redden with shame as she replied, "A full-time nurse, a palliative care course, a hospital bed, a wheelchair, an IV stand, medication, bed pans ..." and the list goes on.

Lisa and countless others like her are part of the sandwich generation, a term coined by Dorothy Miller in 1981.[2] This is a person around the age of 52 who has aging parents who require help and who at the same time has at least one adult child who's returned to live at home. The numbers are staggering.

A recent survey by Angus Reid showed that 40 percent of Canadians expect to be financially responsible for their elderly parents at some time in the future. Sandy Morris, a family law lawyer, makes a compelling point. She says, "Family law legislation says every child who is not a minor has an obligation to provide support, in accordance with need, for his or her parent who has cared for or provided support for the child, to the extent that the child is capable of doing so. People should also know there is a glitch in the Income Tax Act that means all payments by these children are not tax deductible nor includable as income by the parent."

Over 75 percent of these caregivers will be women, with daughters and daughters-in-law making up the largest group of sandwiched souciaires, or caregivers. Nearly 9 out of 10 women will be souciaires of parents, or children, or both, at some time in their lives. More than 8 out of 10 will care for children; nearly 4 out of 10[3] will care for a disabled adult.

In North America research shows that the help men give tends to divide along gender lines. Women provide more emotional and nurturing help than do men, perhaps because of their past experience caring for children.[4] Another study[5] showed men to be less empathic than women to the needs of elders, and saw men's excuses for not taking on the primary caregiving role as more reasonable than women's, however ill-founded this might be. Women face a tremendous amount of guilt over parents' well-being, and that leads to stress as they try to give their parents everything they need and want. Women have greater difficulty distancing themselves from the emotion involved, whereas men can easily distance themselves emotionally and hire the care needed instead of giving it themselves.

The likelihood that senior women live alone rises with age. Statistics show that almost 75 percent of our elders live independent lives until well into their 80s, and remain at home until they can no longer cope. Well over half (58 percent) of women aged 85 and over and almost half (49 percent) of those aged 75 to 84 lived alone. This compares with around 30 percent or less of senior men of all ages. More than 80 percent of those folks over 65 described their health as pretty good or very good.[6]

It used to be we worried about outliving our capital. Now we worry about our parents outliving their capital and needing ours. Couple longer life spans with government cutbacks, and you've got one hell of a situation brewing. People have to take unpaid time off, reduce their work hours, turn down promotions, and change jobs.

So how can we meet these incredible challenges? Remember Laura of Hans and Laura fame in the wills section? Listen to her story.

I've known Laura's parents for years, sharing many a Thanksgiving dinner with them. You couldn't meet sweeter, more gentle people. Evan and Shirley have an active life that comes with five children and rapidly expanding numbers of grandkids. Evan is a lawyer, as are Laura's sister and husband. Laura's mom stayed home raising the family. Five years ago, Laura's mom was diagnosed with Alzheimer's. Now, I know how I felt watching this once vibrant and bright woman deteriorate, and I can only imagine the trauma for the family. With some part-time help, Evan looked after Shirley as they continued living in their home. Then the worst happened. Laura's dad was also diagnosed with Alzheimer's. It shouldn't have been a surprise, considering four of his six siblings died from the same disease. That's when Laura's nightmare began.

The part-time caregivers in the home became very concerned. They informed the family that Evan and Shirley needed 24-hour care. There was constant worry about them wandering off at night. Everything finally culminated when the severity of Evan's illness forced him to lose his driver's licence. The family was rocked to the core by his reaction to losing his last form of independence. This once easy-going, gentle man turned into a man filled with anger, disbelief, and despair. In short, he was completely devastated. Laura believes losing his licence was what pushed her dad over the edge. One day, Evan up and walked to Hull, Quebec. Yes, Quebec. Though he lived in Ottawa, it was still a considerable distance. He was eventually brought home by the Quebec Provincial Police. The family whole-heartedly believes Evan was heading for the bridge with the intention to jump, but thankfully he forgot or got distracted.

Laura and her family were thrown into shock at the amount of time required to look after their parents. When Evan went missing, the Ontario Provincial Police called them to notify them. They had to leave work to go look for him. Laura's sister Janice has had to take time from work to make and provide transportation for doctor's appointments, coordinate caregivers, and drive around looking for her parents when they were missing. In fact, the amount of time taken up with their care is so severe that Janice's nine-year-old son is beginning to resent his grandparents because they take so much of his mother's time. As is often the case, though all the siblings were involved, the majority of the work fell to the three who lived in the same city.

While all of this was going on, Janice was investigating homes with assisted care and any other options she could find. The siblings called a family meeting with the intention to tell their dad it was time to go into a home. Evan had no advance warning. The family couldn't believe what they witnessed. Evan's legal skills training came out and he argued against it brilliantly. They were all very impressed, but knew that his acuity came and went, as is the case with Alzheimer's, so there was still no choice.

Suzanne Kingsmill, author of *The Family Squeeze: Surviving the Sandwich Generation,*[7] strongly suggests that you have a very frank discussion with your parents long before their situation reaches critical proportions. I often wonder if Laura and her family could have avoided much of the heartache if they'd addressed many of these issues before calamity struck. I've had this discussion with my own parents while they're both of sound mind and body. I asked the really hard questions, but we all feel better off knowing that we're all on the same page should disaster strike.

Find out now if there's a danger that your parents may last longer than their money. What do they have by way of money, pensions, and RRSPs? If they're relying on their pension and don't have an RRSP, suggest they get started. Kingsmill recommends that if you have funds after you've maximized your RRSP and paid off your mortgage, then how about setting up a monthly RRSP plan for your parents? Find out what other things their company provides—health care benefits, and pensions that can be rolled over to spouses. Review their private health care coverage, insurance policies, estate planning, and funeral arrangements. Hopefully this will allow you time to plan for future needs and apply for additional coverage if your parents are still eligible.

The bottom line is to give attention to your parents' situation as early as you can. This can be tough when you consider that our parents' generation believed that money was private and shouldn't be talked about. Kingsmill warns that it's even harder to talk between generations because of the belief that your parents are supposed to know more than you. As well, you need to make sure that your mother knows as much about their financial affairs as you do, since she may have left the financial planning to your dad. You taking over the reins to care for them can be quite difficult. Equally as important but often neglected: discuss your own financial situation. If you aren't in good shape, your parents need to know that getting money from you isn't an option for them.

One question I asked my folks was, "What do you want to have happen if you become too sick to look after yourself?" My parents are independent old cusses and they both insisted they won't be sponging off their kids if they can't look after themselves in old age. When I reminded them that private nursing homes can cost up to $6,000 a month, they asked me about the closet space in our spare room.

I also asked them what should happen if they get mildly ill or get to a point where they need their meals prepared. Would they like to stay in their home with a caregiver, or look at retirement homes? In Canada, retirement homes are a "nightmare" to get into and have waiting lists of one to two years. Kingsmill says not to wait until you need one before you explore this option, since by then it could be too late. Her advice is to visit the retirement homes with your parents when they're able-bodied so that you can explore different places. Try to find one that's pleasing to your parents and also close by so that they're not moved away from their support network. Good retirement homes are expensive, and those that aren't expensive tend to be drab and dreary. So when you find a good place, put your name on the waiting list immediately. Every time an opening comes up, the facility will call you. The key is to get on the list as soon as possible so that the place is there when needed.

Now, a nursing home is a different situation. Should your parents need 24-hour care, the government will step in and find a place. It could be in a nursing home or in a chronic ward of a hospital, depending on the space. My mother works with many of these places. I've been to many myself with my mother, visiting some of her patients. It's a grave understatement to say these places aren't very uplifting.

Laura said it was a complete fluke that they found one so quickly for Evan and Shirley. Although her parents were unwilling participants, the family took Evan and Shirley to see a few places. Shirley was fine throughout all of this since, unlike Evan, her disease symptoms hadn't involved anger. She was content to be wherever she was at the time. The family chose a home in the same neighbourhood that the family home had been in for almost 40 years. Laura shudders as she recalls what happened next. "Mom and Dad moved in on a Monday and we made sure that members of the family were with them at every meal. But it was the nighttime that finally got to them. At night, Dad went crazy and became like a caged animal. I got a call from the home on Friday night asking us to come immediately and get them. We couldn't respond that fast so they gave us until 8:30 a.m. the next morning to get them out. Permanently."

There was no choice but to bring them back to Evan and Shirley's home. The family arranged daily care from 8 a.m. to 8 p.m., and so it remains for the moment. Evan and Shirley are on a waiting list now for a place that keeps Alzheimer's sufferers separate from the physically disabled. However, had they done this earlier, Evan and Shirley's chances could have been much better that when they needed it, it would have been a viable option. If an opening had come up when they did not yet need it, their name would have gone back on the list.

Laura says, "The whole family is sitting on pins and needles, waiting for the other shoe to drop. I'm so frustrated that there aren't more options available—and we have money. What do people do who don't have much money? I remember this tremor of fear that went through the entire family. If we're having this much trouble now, what's the situation going to be like when we reach old age? Hans and I are starting to think about setting up our own Alzheimer's fund. We're scared to death. The situation could be dire by the time we hit our 60s."

Laura briefly thought of bringing her parents home, but they have three young noisy children. Not only would it have been hard on the children, but her parents' difficulty with being removed from all they know would have been pronounced. As it is, her parents can only tolerate the noise of three rambunctious kids for—best case?—an hour. It's important to think of this aspect of bringing parents to live with you. As well, if parents have to move into your home, sometimes the home needs to be renovated with handles in the stairwells and bathrooms or renovated to give both the (grand)parents and the children privacy. Parents moving in can be either a tremendous blessing or a very intrusive change for all involved. My husband Michael's grandfather lived with his family since before Michael was even born and was a wonderful addition to the family. Whatever your family situation, you need to think ahead about what is best for everyone concerned and how to pay for it.

When you take a parent or parents into your home, it becomes paramount that everyone be involved. The stress and guilt levels rise dramatically and everyone should be contributing equal time and money to providing elder care. Incidentally, there's help for kids who find themselves in the role of care-giver. It's called respite care—temporary care provided to enable a caregiver to leave his or her parents for a week, or two, or three. Respite care can give the usual caregiver a rest or a holiday so that he or she can rejuvenate. Another idea is to get a "granny sitter," someone to sit with the elderly parents in the evenings to allow their caregiver to have a night out.

Thankfully, Laura's parents had money, which made caring for them easier, but not easy. Laura and her family still needed to provide intense moral support to her parents and give them the strength to help them through this change in their life and also the huge task of managing her parents' financial life. For those people who don't envision being in a financial position to help with their parents, if appropriate, they can suggest that their parents look at the seniors-oriented insurance plans like long-term care insurance. This pays for expenses not covered under provincial plans, such as nursing service, private hospitalization, or a nursing home. Critical illness insurance pays a benefit when a parent suffers a stroke or heart attack.

Long-term care insurance

I know a woman who experienced what she called a 10-year marathon of paying 100 percent of the costs for nursing home care for both parents. She found out first-hand that such care can cost as much as $40,000 in her home province of Nova Scotia. Government nursing homes are cheaper but often have a waiting list. Even with government subsidies, ward coverage in, say, Ontario can cost $1,225 a month. And then you can be stuck paying for things like toenail clipping, hair washing, and so on. Should I ever convince my folks to come and live with us, I'm still looking at big bucks—up to $50 an hour for a private registered nurse and $95 an hour for an occupational therapist or physiotherapist who comes to the house. And this at a time when I, as a self-employed person, need to be making RRSP contributions, paying down a mortgage, and saving for Kate's education.

So, how do we plan to deal with this potential financial albatross? Well, one option is to begin today by taking $50 or $100 a month and putting it aside in a balanced fund where we can get some controlled growth. Another option might be long-term care insurance, which can help defray some of the astro-nomical costs associated with a long-term medical problem.

That's how long-term care insurance is defined—the kind of care a person needs if they're unable to care for themselves due to a lengthy illness or disability. It covers everything from skilled nursing care to help with daily life at home. It's kind of like life insurance for the living.

Although it sounds like an ideal way to take some of the financial pressure off, if you're only getting it when you need it the most, it ain't cheap. Let's assume you're a very proactive 40-year-old. The premium for a $100-a-day benefit that you start receiving 90 days after you become sick or are injured costs around $480 a year. The maximum amount payable to you is 750 times the daily benefit, in this case, $75,000. If you decide to wait until your bones are doing some serious creaking, like at age 80, for a $100-a-day benefit with no waiting period (certainly advisable at this age) be prepared to fork out a heart-stopping $19,730 a year. It used to be that death and taxes were life's two constants. One would be wise to add old-age medical treatment to that list. According to studies done with people in their 50s and older, an overwhelming number of people want to stay in their own homes as long as possible and only want to move in with their kids as a last resort. Studies also show that people would rather go to a retirement home than live with their kids. Think of long-term care insurance as a parachute. Handy in an emergency, but pray like hell you'll never need it.

Now let's be real. Discussions about death, disability, and nursing homes aren't easy ones to have with your parents, but frankly, your future and theirs depend on having such talks. Money is a very touchy subject in many families, so if you find yourself totally uncomfortable with this notion, enlist the help of an impartial third person like a qualified financial advisor. Once this difficult part is behind you, you can get on with enjoying what hopefully will be the best years of your parents' lives.

Janet Freedman has a not surprisingly strong point of view on long-term care insurance. "If you have an existing life insurance policy or are approaching age 65 when most disability insurance stops, consider *reallocating* the premium dollars to long-term care insurance when life or disability insurance is no longer needed. Unless there are tax reasons, generally you don't necessarily need life or disability insurance once your children are grown, you have no debts, and you have reached age 65. This strategy also works well when there is permanent life insurance (such as *whole life*), which may not really be needed. The life insurance premiums can be redirected to long-term care insurance and any accumulated value in the life insurance policy can be used to pay premiums or for other purposes.

"A client of mine who is single and has no family was very concerned about long-term care issues. She had an existing whole life policy which she cashed in and used to pay off her mortgage. She then took out [long-term care coverage] to age 100 with the same premium dollars she [had] been paying before. Me? I've told my kids I'll do my best to never be dependent but, if I live too long there's no guarantee that help won't be needed. Of course, my daughter says she's done her bit while I was in hospital. It's her brother's turn now."

EI Compassionate Care Benefit

Canadians can access Employment Insurance (EI) to take care of relatives with disabilities. This is a start. But it is only available for six weeks and only when the person with the disability is terminally ill. "But what about the Canadians who have been performing the role for many years already?" Freedman points out. "What about their Canada Pension Plan contributions that have been forfeited to take care of a relative? What about all the people who aren't eligible because they were self-employed and not covered by EI? There are too many inconsistencies that make the current system unfair and inequitable."

In conclusion

I laugh now when I think of what my life was like when I first chose *Balancing Act* as a title for this book. I didn't have a clue, but believe me, the title is very relevant now. I'm trying to balance family with running a business, I'm attempting to stay fit so that I can keep up with Kate, and I'm preparing for the added time pressure that will come when I'll be responsible for my parents' welfare. As she always is, my mother was so right—life is a balancing act. Because of our ability to juggle it all, women are the true leaders in the world. I often think of the words of my mentor, Gloria Steinem, who says, "The majority of the country now agrees that women can do what men can do. But it remains for the next century to show that men can do what women can do."

Michael and I have been together for eight years now. Kate has been around for most of that time. I'm amazed at the changes in our lives. Michael jokes that he's become the kind of man who goes to Canadian Tire on Saturday mornings even if he has nothing to buy. Kate (who's decked out in her own little overalls) passes him his tools as he works under the car or helps him spread black goo around with her kid-sized broom as he resurfaces the driveway. With Michael's steadfast, well-balanced male influence and my highly developed feminine perspective, this little girl is blessed with well-rounded role modelling.

I've discovered first-hand the supreme challenges of trying to do it all—career, family, personal time, and sanity. I struggle with it every single day. Part of what keeps me sane is knowing that I've done everything I could, by whatever means I had at the time, to ensure that our family is and remains financially secure. Trust me, this doesn't mean a staggering investment portfolio. I, like everyone else on the planet, struggle to make ends meet. I often joke that the quickest way to make money disappear is to own your own business. For the first three years after Kate was born, I had to borrow to make my RRSP contribution. But at least I knew I'd be far better off borrowing than doing nothing at all. Because a new business takes inordinate amounts of cash to run, I had to borrow a small amount from my RRSP through the Home Buyers Plan in order to be able to come up with the full 25 percent we wanted for the down payment on our house. (Remember? My first home at 40 ...) But I knew enough to be assured that it was the right financial move for us. Today, our mortgage is almost paid off. I knew that if we were going to have a decent shot at helping Kate with her education, it would be a darned sight cheaper for us to start saving while I was still breastfeeding her rather than waiting till she pierced her nose. I even knew the best investment to put into the education fund, even if we could only afford small amounts each month. I knew the importance of having a proper will so that guardian issues would be looked after. I've had the tough talks with my parents, so I'm somewhat prepared for their old age. And so it goes.

As you can see, it's not about having a million bucks. It's about knowing what to do with what you've got. This is what I teach Kate: You've gotta give a little, spend a little, and save a little. Most importantly, you've gotta know a lot. That's what sets you free.

Notes

Chapter one

1 Joanne Thomas Yaccato with Judy Jaeger, *The 80% Minority: Reaching the Real World of Women Consumers* (Toronto: Viking Canada), 2003.

2 John Stackhouse, "Women Everywhere Still Trail in Wages, Power, UN Reports," *The Globe and Mail,* August 1995.

3 1995 *UN Development Report* (Gender and Human Development) or 2002 OECD Employment Outlook (Women at Work).

4 John Stackhouse, "Women Everywhere Still Trail in Wages, Power, UN Reports," *The Globe and Mail,* August 1995.

5 1999 *UN Development Report* (Globalization with a Human Face).

6 1995 *UN Development Report* (Gender and Human Development).

7 Statistics Canada, Income Statistics Division, 1997.

Chapter two

1 Anthony Kirby, "Check Credit Rating to Save Embarrassment," *The Globe and Mail,* November 15, 1991.

2 Interac Association, "More Canadian Retailers Than Ever Adopt Interac Direct Payment," press release June 10, 1999, table "Annual Dollar Values of IDP Use per Retail Sector."

Chapter four

1 The Trust Companies Association of Canada National Survey, Angus Reid Group and Consumer Line Omnibus, 1992.

2 1996 Census, The Nation Series (Statistics provided for this table called Population by Marital Status—Widowed—for Canada, 1996 Census).

3 D. Molloy, M.D., "The Living Will—A Physician's Perspective," The Canadian Bar Association, 1991.

4 Donald Flynn, *The Truth About Funerals: How to Beat the High Cost of Dying (An Insider's Perspective)* (Burlington, ON: Funeral Consultants International Inc.), 1993.

5 "Disabilsurance: Where Will the Money Come from If You're Disabled?" Canadian Life and Health Association, 1992.

6 DAWN speech, 1991.

Chapter five

1 Statistics Canada, Tax Statistics on Individuals, 1998 Edition (1996 taxation year), Table 12 "All Returns with RRSP Contributions and/or Pension Adjustment Amount by Age, Total Income Class, and Sex."

2 *Canadian Retirement Income Social Security Programs,* Report of the Task Force on Social Security Financing, Canadian Institute of Actuaries, November 1993.

3 Ibid.

4 Hubert Frenken and Karen Maser, "RRSPs—New Rules, New Growth," *Perspectives on Labour and Income* (Ottawa: Statistics Canada) Winter 1993, Vol. 5, No. 4.

Chapter six

1 Elaine Wyatt, *The Money Companion* (Scarborough, ON: ITP Nelson Canada), 1999.

2 "Embracing the Information Age: A Comparison of Women and Men Business Owners," National Foundation for Women Business Owners (NFWBO), September 30, 1997.

3 "Changing Face of the Net," *Media Matrix,* March 22, 1999.

4 Nicki Maraganore with Shelley Morrisette, *The Forrester Brief: The On-line Gender Gap Is Closing* (Cambridge, MA: Forrester Research, Inc.), 1998.

5 Ibid.

6 Andrew Bell, "I Am Woman, Watch My Stocks Soar," *The Globe and Mail,* April 17, 1999.

7 Brad M. Barber and Terrance Odean, "Boys Will Be Boys: Gender, Overconfidence, and Common Stock Investment," Graduate School of Management, University of California, May 1999.

8 Jonathan H. Strong, Manager, Membership, National Association of Investors Corporation (NAIC).

9 Grant McIntyre, "Getting Good Advice," *Investment Executive,* Fall 1998.

10 Andrew Bell, "I Am Woman, Watch My Stocks Soar," *The Globe and Mail,* April 17, 1999.

11 Gail Vaz-Oxlade, *A Woman of Independent Means: A Woman's Guide to Full Financial Security* (Don Mills, ON: Stoddart Publishing Co. Ltd.), 1999.

12 Ibid.

13 "Financial Decision-Making: Are Women Really More Risk Averse?" Swiss Federal Institute of Technology.

14 Natalie Southworth, "Women Debunk Risk-Taking Myth," *The Globe and Mail,* June 7, 1999.

15 Andrew Bell, "I Am Woman, Watch My Stocks Soar," *The Globe and Mail,* April 17, 1999, quoted from study by Julia Scott and Steve Harvey of Bishop's University in Lennoxville, Quebec, "Men's and Women's Investment Practices" for an article that appeared in *The Canadian Investment Review,* Summer 1997.

16 Ibid.

17 "Is Financial Advice Sexist?" *Working Women Magazine,* 1995.

Chapter eight

1 Aaron Freeman, "The Human Rights Law Implications of Gender-Based Pricing," 1998.

2 "Gypped by Gender," The New York City Department of Consumer Affairs, 1992.

3 Aaron Freeman, "The Human Rights Law Implications of Gender-Based Pricing," 1998.

4 Frances Cerra Whittelsey and Marcia Carroll, *Women Pay More (and How to Put a Stop to It),* (New York: New Press), 1995 (originally published by Center for Study of Responsive Law, 1993 and 1995).

5 Aaron Freeman, "The Human Rights Law Implications of Gender-Based Pricing," 1998.

6 California Assembly Committee on Consumer Protection, 1994.

7 Interview with Robert Kerton, June 1999.

8 "Why Do Female Consumers Pay More Than Men Do?" *The Toronto Star,* January 3, 1992.

9 Aaron Freeman, "The Human Rights Law Implications of Gender-Based Pricing," 1998.

10 Ibid.

11 Ibid.

12 Assembly Bill No. 1100, *An act to add Section 51.6 to the Civil Code, relating to civil rights* [Approved by Governor, 13 Oct. 1995].

13 Jackie Speier, Democratic member of the California Assembly.

14 Elise Thurau, senior consultant for Jackie Speier, Democratic member of the California Assembly.

15 Aaron Freeman, "The Human Rights Law Implications of Gender-Based Pricing," 1998.

16 Deborah Kolb, "Is It Her Voice or Her Place That Makes a Difference? A Consideration of Gender Issues in Negotiations," Industrial Relations Centre, Queen's University, 1992.

17 Frances Cerra Whittelsey and Marcia Carroll, *Women Pay More (and How to Put a Stop to It)* (New York: New Press), 1995 (originally published by Center for Study of Responsive Law, 1993 and 1995).

Chapter nine

1 Bruce Cohen with Alyssa Diamond, *The Money Advisor* (Don Mills, ON: Stoddart Publishing Co. Ltd.), 1998. Source from Manitoba Agriculture, 1998, pp. 279–280.

2 D. Miller, "The Sandwich Generation: Adult Children of the Aging," *Social Work* 26, (1981), pp. 419–423.

3 Suzanne Kingsmill and Benjamin Schlesinger, *The Family Squeeze: Surviving the Sandwich Generation* (Toronto: University of Toronto Press), 1998.

4 L. Kaye and J. Applegate, "Men as Elder Caregivers: A Response to Changing Families," *American Journal of Orthopsychiatry 60* (1990), pp. 86–95.

5 Suzanne Kingsmill and Benjamin Schlesinger, *The Family Squeeze: Surviving the Sandwich Generation* (Toronto: University of Toronto Press), 1998.

6 Ibid.

7 Ibid.

Index